P9-CJV-493

STANFORD UNIVERSITY LIBRARIES

WITHDRAWN

Dictionary of literary
PSEUDONYMS

a selection of popular modern writers in English
third edition

FRANK ATKINSON

CLIVE BINGLEY LONDON

Other books by Frank Atkinson

The public library
Yesterday's money (with John Fines)
Librarianship
Illustrated teach yourself coins (with J Matthews)
The best of Robert Shallow
Fiction librarianship

FIRST EDITION PUBLISHED 1975
SECOND EDITION PUBLISHED 1977
THIS THIRD, ENLARGED EDITION FIRST PUBLISHED 1982 BY
CLIVE BINGLEY LTD, 16 PEMBRIDGE ROAD, LONDON W11 3HL
SET IN 10 ON 12 POINT PRESS ROMAN BY ALLSET
PRINTED AND BOUND IN THE UK BY
REDWOOD BURN LTD, TROWBRIDGE, WILTS
© FRANK ATKINSON 1982
ALL RIGHTS RESERVED
ISBN: 0-85157-323-1

In Memory of Charles Bogle

British Library Cataloguing in Publication Data

Atkinson, Frank
    Dictionary of literary pseudonyms.—3rd ed.
    1. Anonyms and pseudonyms—Dictionaries
    I. Title
    808   Z1041

ISBN 0-85157-323-1

CONTENTS

INTRODUCTION TO THE FIRST EDITION

We had a bottle of port for dinner, and drank dear Willie's health. He said, 'Oh, by the by, did I tell you I've cut my first name William, and taken the second name Lupin? In fact, I'm only known at Oldham as Lupin Pooter. If you were to 'Willie' me there, they wouldn't know what you meant.'

The names wished on us by our parents don't always please, and lots of people fiddle about varying the order of the components to suit themselves better; or they manage to get themselves nicknamed. The Grossmiths, in the piece quoted above from *The diary of a nobody*, satirised this harmless foible—but quite gently. And they did allow young W L Pooter, who could not come to terms with life as a Willie, to prosper as Lupin. His champagne flows at the end of the book.

Choosing a pen-name

Authors are great name-fiddlers, and many have performed quite drastic nomenectomies in order to achieve a satisfactory pseudonym. Arthur Elliott Elliott-Cannon lopped off Arthur and the spare Elliott; Reginald David Stanley Courtney-Browne excised his three forenames, and most understandably, Richard Nathaniel Twisleton-Wykeham-Fiennes writes as Richard Fiennes.

Many people would like to adopt an entirely new name, but most of them are inhibited by family and friends, business and other encumbrances. In the separate world of books, however, writers please themselves. They choose the name, it is solemnised on the title-page and perpetuated in lists, catalogues and the less-probing bibliographies.

Generally speaking, there is no deep thought, and little ingenuity, in the devising of pseudonyms. Obvious punning and word association provide one popular method: for example, Cecil John Street became John Rhode; Morris West about-faced to Michael East and Owen Seaman thought up Nauticus. Very basic anagrams or part anagrams, such as

7

Melusa Moolson for Samuel Solomon, John Gannold for John Langdon and Walter De la Mare's Walter Ramal, come a close second.

Producing a more profound pseudonym takes a little longer. *Life* magazine carried a letter from Edward Stratemeyer, author of the Rover Boys stories in the 1920s, explaining how he got his pseudonym of Arthur M Winfield:

One evening when writing, with my mother sitting near sewing, I remarked that I wanted an unusual name—that I wasn't going to use my own name on the manuscript. She thought a moment and suggested Winfield. 'For then', she said, 'you may win in that field.' I thought that good. She then supplied the first name saying, 'You are going to be an author, so why not make it Arthur?'

Stratemeyer added the M himself, reasoning that as M stood for thousand, it might help to sell thousands of books.

Corey Ford, in his *Time of laughter*, quotes this Stratemeyer letter, and also gives a highly dubious version of how he selected a pseudonym for himself. 'Unfortunately', he writes, 'I did not have Mr Stratemeyer's mother to help me out. So I shut my eyes, opened the New York telephone directory at random and put my finger on a name. The name turned out to be Runkelschmelz, so I threw the phone book away and thought up John Riddell.'

Part of a package

It is not always personal preference alone that motivates an author's name change. Often it is done to match a particular type of book, on the grounds that any product sells better under a familiar label. Westerns, for example, should appear to be the work of lean and saddle-sore cow-pokes, a six-shooter in either hand—with which, presumably, after bacon and beans round the ole campfire, they whack their typewriter keys.

So, when offering their readers *Rustlers and powder-smoke, Hopa-long Cassidy, The big corral*, or similar horsesweat, the respective authors Charles Horace Snow, Louis L'Amour and Archibald Lynn Joscelyn, become Charles Ballew, Tex Burns and Al Cody.

Romantic fiction, on the other hand, is not expected to be penned by the Bucks and Hanks of this world. That *genre* requires authors' names suggestive of crisp, clean blouses and commonsense, yet with a hint of madcap moments; names like Elaine Carr, Phyllis Marlow and Caroline Holmes—all three of which are pseudonyms of one Charles Mason.

8

Tandem names

When two writers work together and decide to share a pseudonym, they rarely come up with an Ellery Queen. (And even Dannay and Lee took some time to drop Barnaby Ross in favour of the peerless Ellery.) Usually, like married couples naming their house Marjalf or Gladern, they make one name from bits of the two. Kelley Roos is made up from two surnames (Audrey Kelley and William Roos), as is Manning Coles (Adelaide Manning and Cyril Coles).

The two first names of Constance and Gwenyth Little, lopped fore and aft, form this couple's pseudonym of Conyth Little; while David Eliades and Robert Forrest Webb decided on David Forrest for their joint works.

Hilary Aidan St George Saunders and John Leslie Palmer, on the other hand, settled firstly for Francis Beeding as a joint pseudonym and later for David Pilgrim, simply because they liked these names.

The game of the name

All this suggests that the pseudonym business is a bit of a lark. For the most part, as far as British and American writers are concerned, it is. Although some of them are compelled (or find it politic) for professional or contractual reasons not to publish under their real names, very few can be in fear of serious prosecution or persecution.

It is often said that some writers adopt pseudonyms in order to deceive the taxman. At best, this could be only playing for time. Death and taxes are still the two certainties of life.

So it really is a game—a mixture of fantasising, crossword puzzling and riddle-me-ree. When the game gets a good grip on a writer he may soon, like John Creasey, Michael Angelo Avallone Jr, or a number of others, clock up a double-figure pseudonym total. Some real fanatics for false names have acquired bumper collections. François Marie Arouet is usually cited as the top man in this field. In addition to the pseudonym Voltaire, he is credited with some 136 others; but most of them he used only for signing letters. Within the scope of this work, however, Lauran Paine leads the field with sixty-five discovered pen-names.

What a tangled web

The real name-pseudonym area of research is more full of snags than most. In the first place there is the writers' intention to deceive. This may be an ephemeral and relatively light-hearted intention—as witnessed by the number of authors who freely declare their pen-names in the various biographical reference works. Or it may be a serious and long-standing determination such as that of the former librarian Eric Leyland, of whom Lofts and Adley, in their *Men behind boys' fiction*, say: 'Written nearly 150 books for young people . . . and another 100 books under various pen-names which are strictly private.'

Shifts do occur, from the second group to the first, as circumstances change—usually for business reasons. The commercial success of a writer often leads to her, or his, pseudonyms being blazoned on dust jackets and in advertisements.

Secondly, there are the publishers. With few exceptions, those contacted in the course of compiling this work may be divided into two groups. One group considers authors' pseudonyms to be such close and vital secrets that any enquiry after them is treated, at best, as an impertinence but, more often, as attempted subversion. The other group consists of firms carrying on business in cheerful ignorance of the true identity of many of those whose work they publish. Enquiries there cause amused surprise that anybody should be interested. As to practical help, well that's not possible because no-one really knows and then, you see, royalties are mostly paid to authors' agents and no-one, apparently, cares.

Call me Sappho, call me Chloris

Of the writers who kindly replied to our enquiries, a number were vague about the various names under which they had written. Of those who were certain, two gave spellings of their pseudonyms which differed from those on the title-pages of their books. It is not surprising then, that the great catalogues of the British Museum and the Library of Congress, and the *British national bibliography* and the *Cumulative book index*, are sometimes at odds with one another as to whether a name is real or assumed. For the period 1900-1950, volume eight of Halkett and Laing's *Dictionary of anonymous and pseudonymous English literature* is a further contender except, of course, when it quotes the British Museum catalogue as its authority. Since 1968, the cumulations and indexes of the *British national bibliography* have not distinguished between real names and pseudonyms.

A few threads teased out

This dictionary is limited to writers in English and the selection has been made from those writing in the years 1900 to date. It is hoped

10

that it will help librarians and booksellers to answer some of the many questions which are asked about authors—particularly contemporary authors—who write under more than one name. It may also assist in solving some of the queries about pseudonymous contributors to newspapers and magazines during the early decades of this century.

On a less practical, but equally justifiable level, there is the intention to satisfy people's curiosity. W P Courtney called his book on British anonymous and pseudonymous writings, which was published in 1908, *The secrets of our national literature.* In the first paragraph he wrote: 'The pleasure of finding out the secrets of our neighbours appeals to most minds.'

Many readers are even more curious about their favourite authors than they are about their neighbours. This book may give them some small pleasure.

F A

April 1975

INTRODUCTION TO THE SECOND EDITION

There are now over 8,000 names and pseudonyms in this dictionary—an increase of more than one-third over the first edition total.

A number of names have been included or varied as a result of comments received from correspondents in many countries, to whom I am very grateful. Most of the additional names are of North American authors, which makes this a more representative selection of modern writers in English.

Once again many authors, and colleagues in libraries and the book trade, have given me information about authors' names and I am grateful to them all.

I am especially grateful to Eric Leyland for giving me a list of his pseudonyms, previously kept strictly private; and to W Howard Baker for patiently explaining the circumstances under which he and Wilfred McNeilly have used, and continue to use, the pseudonym W A Ballinger jointly and separately.

The exigencies of the publishing business have imposed a very tight schedule on the preparation of this edition. I acknowledge, with gratitude, the fact that it would not have been completed on time without the help of kind friends and the invaluable assistance of my wife who shelved her own work during the final weeks.

Frank Atkinson

Broad Oak
Heathfield Sussex
March 1977

INTRODUCTION TO THE THIRD EDITION

In the introduction to the first edition of this book I discussed some of the many, and often devious, reasons why authors adopt pseudonyms. Writing in 1978 in the *Telegraph Sunday magazine*, David Pryce-Jones had one simple explanation for the whole matter: 'It is the librarians who encourage pseudonyms', he stated, 'because they are unwilling to buy more than two or three books a year by the same author'.

Well, whatever the reasons, there is no decline in pseudonymous writings—nor in the number of men writing under women's names, thus making a nonsense of the statement from Cassell's *Encyclopaedia of literature* quoted in the pseudonym section of this book.

Among the newcomers in this edition are 'Charlotte Massey' (former boxer Vincent Capriani) and 'Laura Black' (Roger Longrigg, author of *The history of foxhunting* and *The English squire and his sport*, who also writes as 'Rosalind Erskine').

This edition has some 1,500 additional names and pseudonyms. Again, most of these are of North American authors and many of them were supplied by American and Canadian correspondents. I must thank, among others, Max Gruber, of New York; Paul Delaney, of Washington; and Robert K Grahame, of the National Library of Canada. My thanks also to Charles W Mann, who not only reviewed the second edition most kindly in *American reference books annual 1978*, but also offered a dozen useful pseudonyms.

I am particularly indebted to my friend and ex-colleague Michael Richardson, of Toronto. During the past six years he has been supplying me with frequent and generous lists of North American writers and their pseudonyms. I am very grateful to him.

Horsham   Frank Atkinson
West Sussex
July 1981

Real names

§ §

Who gave you this name?
My godfathers and godmothers.
—Church of England Catechism

§ §

AARONS, Edward Sidney
  Ayres, Paul
  Ronns, Edward
ABBOTT, Harold Daniel
  Deborah, Leonard
ABRAHALL, Clare Hoskyns
  Drury, C M
  Drury, Clare
ABRAHAM, James Johnston
  Harpole, James
ABRAHAM, Peter L
  Graham, Peter
ABRAHAMS, Doris Caroline
  Brahms, Caryl
ABRAHAMS, Henry B
  Henry, B A
ABRAHAMSON, Maurice Noel
  Chub, Sergeant
ACWORTH, Marion W
  Neon
ADAM, C G M
  Stewart, C R

ADAM, Robin
  MacTyre, Paul
ADAM, Ronald
  Blake
ADAM SMITH, Janet Buchanan
  Carleton, Janet
ADAMS, Agnes
  Logan, Agnes
ADAMS, Charles William Dunlop
  Montrose
ADAMS, Cleve Franklin
  Charles, Franklin
  Spain, John
ADAMS, Clifton
  Randall, Clay
ADAMS, Franklin Pierce
  F P A
ADAMS, Harriet S
  Keene, Carolyn (*after*
  Edward Stratemeyer)
ADAMS, Henry
  Compton, Frances Snow
ADAMS, Herbert
  Gray, Jonathan
ADAMS, Samuel Hopkins
  Fabian, Warner
ADCOCK, A St John
  Cobber, *Lance Corporal*
ADDIS, E E
  Drax, Peter

15

ADDIS, Hazel Iris
  Adair, Hazel
  Heritage, A J
  Mao
ADDLESHAW, Percy
  Hemingway, Percy
ADLER, Bill
  David, Jay
ADLER, Irving
  Irving, Robert
AGATE, James
  Prentis, Richard
  Sir Topaz
  Warrington, George
AGELASTO, Charlotte Priestley
  Watson, C P
AIKEN, John
  Paget, John
AINSWORTH, Mary Dinsmore
  Salter, Mary D
  Salter Ainsworth, Mary D
AITKEN, Andrew
  Arnold, Wilcox
AITKEN, E H
  E H A
AKERMAN, Anthony Charles
  Anthony, Charles
AKERS, Elizabeth
  Percy, Florence
ALBANESI, Effie Maria
  Rowlands, Effie Adelaide
ALBERT, Harold A
  Priestly, Mark
ALBERT, Marvin H
  Quarry, Nick
  Rome, Anthony
  Rome, Tony

ALDRED, Margaret
  Saunders, Anne
ALDRICH, Rhoda Truax
  Truax, Rhoda
ALEXANDER, Colin James
  Jay, Simon
ALEXANDER, Janet
  McNeill, Janet
ALEXANDER, Joan
  Pepper, Joan
ALEXANDER, John McKnight
  Linter, Lavender
ALEXANDER, Robert William
  Butler, Joan
  Temple, Ruth
ALGER, Leclaire Gowans
  Leodhas, Sorche Nic
  Macleodhas, Sorche
ALGIE, James
  Lloyd, Wallace
ALINGTON, Argentine Francis
  Talbot, Hugh
ALINGTON, Cyril Argentine
  Westerham, S C
ALLAN, Frederick William
  Leo, Alan
ALLAN, Mabel Esther
  Estoril, Jean
  Hagon, Priscilla
  Pilgrim, Anne
ALLAN, Philip Bertram Murray
  Cabochon, Francis
  Phillip, Alban M
ALLBEURY, Theo Edward le
  Bouthillier
  Butler, Richard
ALLDRIDGE, John Stratten
  Stratton, John

ALLEGRO, John Marco
  McGill, Ian
ALLEN, Grant
  Power, Cecil
  Rayner, Olive Pratt
ALLEN, Henry
  Fisher, Clay
  Henry, Will
ALLEN, John E
  Danforth, Paul M
ALLEN, Stephen Valentine
  Allen, Steve
  Stevens, William Christopher
ALLEN-BALLARD, Eric
  Allen, Eric
ALLFREE, P S
  Blackburn, Martin
ALLISON, William
  Blinkhoalie
ALMOND, Brian
  Vaughan, Julian
ALPERS, Mary Rose
  Campion, Sarah
AMBLER, Eric *and* RODDA,
  Charles
  Reed, Eliot
AMES, Francis
  Watson, Frank
AMES, Jennifer
  Greig, Maysie
AMES, R F
  Black, Jack
AMIS, Kingsley
  Markham, Robert
AMY, William Lacey
  Allan, Luke
ANDERS, Edith Mary
  England, Edith M

ANDERSON, Alexander
  Surfaceman
ANDERSON, Betty
  Canyon, Claudia
ANDERSON, *Lady* Flavia
  Portobello, Petronella
ANDERSON, Martin
  Cynicus
ANDERSON, Poul
  Craig, A A
  Karageorge, Michael
  Sanders, Winston P
ANDREWS, Claire *and*
 ANDREWS, Keith
  Claire, Keith
ANDREWS, John Arthur
  Bach, Sebastian
ANDREWS, Naomi Cornelia
  Madgett, Naomi Long
ANSELL, Edward Clarence
  Trelawney
  Crad, Joseph
ANSLE, Dorothy Phoebe
  Conway, Laura
  Elsna, Hebe
  Lancaster, Vicky
  Snow, Lyndon
ANTHONY, Barbara
  Barber, Antonia
ANTHONY, E
  Parr, *Dr* John Anthony
ANTHONY, Edward
  Cleo et Anthony
  Gate, A G
APPLEBY, Carol McAfee
  Morgan, Carol McAfee

APPLEMAN, John Alan
  Daley, Bill
  Montrose, James St David
APPLIN, Arthur
  Swift, Julian
APPS, Edwin *and*
 DEVANEY, Pauline
  Wraith, John
ARCHIBALD, Edith Jessie
  Eye Witness
ARD, William
  Kerr, Ben
  Wills, Thomas
ARDEN, Adrian
  Ariel
ARMITAGE, John
  Hin Me Geong
ARMSTRONG, Charlotte
  Valentine, Jo
ARMSTRONG, Douglas
  Douglas, Albert
  Windsor, Rex
ARMSTRONG, Paul
  Right Cross
ARMSTRONG, Richard
  Renton, Cam
ARMSTRONG, T I F *see*
 FYTTON ARMSTRONG, T I
ARSHAVSKY, Abraham Isaac
  Shaw, Artie
ARTER, Wallace E
  Kay, Wallace
ARTHUR, Chester Alan
  Arthur, Gavin
ARTHUR, Frances Browne
  Cunningham, Ray
ARTHUR, Herbert
  Arthur, Burt

ARTHUR, Ruth M
  Huggins, Ruth Mabel
ASHBROOK, Hariette Cora
  Shane, Susannah
ASHBY, Rubie Constance
  Freugon, Ruby
ASHFORD, F C
  Charles, Frederick
ASHLEY, Arthur Ernest
  Vivian, Francis
ASHMORE, Basil
  Marlin, Roy
ASHTON, *Lady*
  Garland, Madge
ASHTON, Winifred
  Dane, Clemence
ASHTON-WARNER, Sylvia
  Henderson, Sylvia
  Sylvia
ASHWORTH, Edward Montague
  Abbott, Johnston
ASIMOV, Isaac
  Dr A
  French, Paul
ASTON, *Sir* George
  Amphibian
  Southcote, George
ATKEY, Philip
  Perowne, Barry
ATKINS, Frank A
  Ash, Fenton
  Ashley, Fred
  Aubrey, Frank
  St Mars, F
ATKINSON, Frank
  Curnow, Frank
  Shallow, Robert

ATKINSON, John
  Aye, John
ATTENBOROUGH, Bernard
  George
  Rand, James S
AUBREY-FLETCHER, *Sir*
  Henry Lancelot
  Wade, Henry
AUCHINCLOSS, Louis
  Lee, Andrew
AUSTIN, Benjamin Fish
  Nitsua, Benjamin
AUSTIN, John *and*
  AUSTIN, Richard
  Gun Buster
AVALLONE, Michael Angelo Jr
  Blaine, James
  Carter, Nick
  Conway, Troy
  Dalton, Priscilla
  Dane, Mark
  De Pre, Jean-Anne
  Michaels, Steve
  Nile, Dorothea
  Noone, Edwina
  Patrick, John
  Stanton, Vance
  Stuart, Sidney
AVENELL, Donne
  King, Charles
AVERY, Harold
  Westridge, Harold
AVEY, Ruby D
  Page, Vicky
AYCKBOURNE, Alan
  Allen, Ronald

BABCOCK, Frederick
  Mark, Matthew
BABCOCK, Maurice P
  Bea, Empy
BABER, Douglas
  Ritson, John
BACK, Karl John
  Australianus
BACKUS, Jean L
  Montross, David
BACON, Elizabeth
  Morrow, Betty
BACON, Josephine Dodge
  Lovell, Ingraham
BAILEY, Francis Evans
  Wilson, Ann
BAILEY, Gordon
  Gordon, Keith
BAIN, Kenneth Bruce Findlater
  Findlater, Richard
BAIR, Patrick
  Gurney, David
BAKER, Anne
  Cross, Nancy
BAKER, Betty
  Renier, Elizabeth
BAKER, Kate
  K B
BAKER, Laura
  Minier, Nelson
BAKER, Louise Alice
  Alien
BAKER, Marcell Genée
  Miller, Marc
BAKER, Marjorie
  McMaster, Alison
BAKER, Mary Gladys Steel
  Stuart, Sheila

19

BAKER, Ray Stannard
  Grayson, David
BAKER, William Howard
  Arthur, William
  Ballinger, W A
  Reid, Desmond
  Saxon, Peter
BAKER, William Howard *and*
  MCNEILLY, Wilfred
  Ballinger, W A
BALCHIN, Nigel
  Spade, Mark
BALDWIN, Dorothy
  Jones, Clara
BALDWIN, Gordon C
  Gordon, Lew
BALDWIN, Oliver
  Hussingtree, Martin
BALFOUR, Eve *and* HERNDEN,
  Beryl
  Hearnden, Balfour
BALFOUR, William
  Russell, Raymond
BALL, Brian N
  Kinsey-Jones, Brian
BALL, Doris Bell Collier
  Bell, Josephine
BALLARD, Willis Todhunter
  Ballard, P D
  Ballard, Todhunter
  Bonner, Parker
  Bowie, Sam
  Hunt, Harrison
  Hunter, George
  Hunter, John
  MacNeil, Neil
  Shepherd, John

BALLINGER, William Sanborn
  Freyer, Frederic
  Sanborn, B X
BALOGH, Penelope
  Fox, Petronella
BAMBERGER, Helen R
  Berger, Helen
BAMBERGER, Helen R *and*
  BAMBERGER, Raymond S
  Aresbys, The
BAMFIELD, Veronica
  Wood, Mary
BANBURY, Olive Lethbridge
  Lethbridge, Olive
BANDY, Eugene Franklin Jr
  Franklin, Eugene
BAR-ZOHAR, Michael
  Barak, Michael
BARACH, Alvan Leroy
  Coignard, John
BARBER, Dulan Friar
  Fletcher, David
BARBER, Margaret Fairless
  Fairless, Michael
BARBER-STARKEY, Roger
  Shropshire Lad
BARCLAY, George
  Kinnoch, R G B
BARCLAY, Oliver Rainsford
  Triton, A N
BARCLAY, Vera C
  Beech, Margaret
BARCZA, Alicja
  Orme, Alexandra
BARDIN, John Franklin
  Tree, Gregory
BARFIELD, Arthur Owen
  Burgeon, G A L

BARFORD, John Leslie
 Philebus
BARKER, Albert H
 King, Reefe
 Macrae, Hawk
BARKER, Clarence Hedley
 Hedley, Frank
 Seafarer
BARKER, Dudley
 Black, Lionel
 Matthews, Anthony
BARKER, E M
 Jordan, Neill
BARKER, Ilse Eva L
 Talbot, Kathrine
BARKER, Leonard Noel
 Noel, L
BARKER, Michael
 Barker, Jack
BARKER, Ronald Ernest
 Ronald, E B
BARKER, Ronnie
 Wiley, Gerald
BARKER, S Omar
 Canusi, Jose
 Squires, Phil
BARKER, Will
 Demarest, Doug
BARLING, Muriel Vere
 Barling, Charles
 Barrington, P V
 Barrington, Pamela
BARLOW, James
 Forden, James
BARLTROP, Mabel
 Octavia

BARNARD, Marjorie Faith *and*
 ELDERSHAW, Flora Sydney
 Eldershaw, M Barnard
BARNES, Arthur *and*
 KUTTNER, Henry
 Kent, Kelvin
BARNES, Julian
 Kavanagh, Dan
 Seal, Basil
BARNES, Patricia
 Abercrombie, Patricia Barnes
BARNITT, Nedda Lemmon
 Lamont, N B
BARNSLEY, Alan G
 Fielding, Gabriel
BARONAS, Aloyzas
 Aliunas, S
BARR, Patricia
 Hazard, Laurence
BARR, Robert
 Sharp, Luke
BARRADELL-SMITH, Walter
 Bird, Lilian
 Bird, Richard
BARRAUD, E M
 Johns, Hilary
BARRE, Jean
 Lindsay, Lee
BARRETT, Alfred Walter
 Andom, R
BARRETT, Geoffrey John
 Anders, Rex
 Blaine, Jeff
 Cole, Richard
 Kilbourn, Matt
 Macey, Carn
 Rickard, Cole
 Royal, Dan

21

BARRETT, G J (cont'd)
  Sanders, Brett
  Summers, D B
  Wade, Bill
BARRETT, Hugh Gilchrist
  Bellman, Walter
BARRETT, Romana
  Lane, Carla
BARRINGTON, Howard
  Stone, Simon
BARROW, Albert Stewart
  Sabretache
BARROWS, Marjorie
  Alden, Jack
  Dixon, Ruth
BARRY, John Arthur
  L L
BARTHOLOMEW, John Eric
  Morecambe, Eric
BARTLETT, Marie
  Lee, Rowena
  Rift, Valerie
BARTLETT, Stephen
  Slade, Gurney
BARTLETT, Vernon
  Oldfield, Peter
BARTON, Emily Mary
  E M B
BARTON, Eustace Robert
  Eustace, Robert
BARTROP, Edgar James
  Portrab
BASCH, Ernst
  Ashton, A B
  Ashton, E B
  Ashton, E E
BASHAM, Daisy
  Aunt Daisy

BASHFORD, *Sir* Henry Howarth
  Carp, Augustus
BASS, Clara May
  Overy, Claire May
BASSETT, Ronald
  Clive, William
BASTIN, John
  Sturgus, J B
BATEMAN, Robert Moyes
  Moyes, Robin
BATES, Herbert Ernest
  Flying Officer X
BATT, Malcolm John
  Malcolm, John
BATTYE, Gladys
  Lynn, Margaret
BAUM, Lyman Frank
  Akens, Floyd
  Bartlett, Laura
  Cook, John Estes
  Fitzgerald, *Captain* Hugh
  Metcalf, Suzanne
  Stanton, Schuyler
  Van Dyne, Edith
BAUMANN, Arthur A
  A A B
BAUMANN, Margaret
  Lees, Marguerite
BAX, *Sir* Arnold
  O'Byrne, Dermot
BAXTER, Elizabeth
  Holland, Elizabeth
BAYBARS, Taner
  Bayliss, Timothy
BAYER, Eleanor *and*
 BAYER, Leo
  Bayer, Oliver Weld

BAYLISS, John Clifford
  Clifford, John
BAYLY, Ada Ellen
  Lyall, Edna
BAYNES, Dorothy Julia
  Creston, Dormer
BAYS, J W
  Roadster
BEADLE, Gwyneth Gordon
  Gordon, Glenda
BEAR, Joan E
  Mayhew, Elizabeth
BEARDMORE, George
  Stokes, Cedric
  Wolfenden, George
BEATY, David
  Stanton, Paul
BEAUCHAMP, Kathleen Mansfield
  Berry, Matilda
  Mansfield, Katherine
BEAUMONT, Dr Edgar
  Halifax, Clifford
BECHOFFER ROBERTS, C E
  Ephesian
BECK, Lily Adams
  Barrington, E
  Moresby, Louis
BECK, Roland Stanley
  St Anbeck, Roland
BECKER, Peter
  Vul' Indlela
BECKER, Stephen David
  Dodge, Steve
BECKET, Ronald Brymer
  Anthony, John
BEDFORD-JONES, Henry
  Keyes, Gordon
  Wycliffe, John

BEDFORD-JONES, Henry;
  FRIEDE, Donald *and*
  FEARING, Kenneth
  Bedford, Donald F
BEEBE, Elswyth Thane
  Thane, Elswyth
BEESTON, L J
  Camden, Richard
  Davies, Lucian
BEETON, D R
  Barratt, Robert
BEHAN, Brendan
  Street, Emmett
BEHANNA, Gertrude Florence
  Burns, Elizabeth
BEILES, Sinclair
  Wu Wu Meng
BEITH, John Hay
  Hay, Ian
  Junior Sub
BELANEY, Archie
  Grey Owl
BELL, Alexander
  Young, Filson
BELL, Alison Clare Harvey
  Bell, Leigh
BELL, Eric Temple
  Taine, John
BELL, Gerard
  Landis, John
BELL, John Keble
  Howard, Keble
  Methuen, John
BELL, Martin
  Oates, Titus
BELLASIS, Margaret Rosa
  Marton, Francesca

BENARY, Margot
  Benary-Isbert, Margot
BENCHLEY, Robert
  Fawkes, Guy
BENDER, Arnold
  Philippi, Mark
BENDIT, Gladys
  Presland, John
BENJAMIN, Lewis S
  Melville, Lewis
BENNETT, Arnold
  King, Sampson
  Tonson, Jacob
BENNETT, Dorothy
  Kingsley, Laura
BENNETT, Geoffrey Martin
  Sea-Lion
BENNETT, J J
  Jackstaff
BENNETT, William E
  Armstrong, Warren
BENSON, Arthur Christopher
  Carr, Christopher
BENSON, Michael
  Thomas, Michael
BENTLEY, Edmund Clerihew
  Clerihew, E
BENTLEY, Frederick Horace
  Wilson, D M
BENTLEY, James W B
  Claughton-James, James
  Nostalgia
BENTLEY, Phyllis
  Bachelor of Arts, A
BENTLEY, Verna Bessie
  Harden, Verna Loveday
BENTON, Peggie
  Burke, Shifty

BERESFORD, Claude R De La
Poer
  Seebee
BERESFORD, Leslie
  Pan
BERGER, Josef
  Digges, Jeremiah
BERMANGE, Maurine J L
  Ross, Maggie
BEST, Allena
  Berry, Erick
  Maxton, Anne
BEST, Carol Anne
  Ashe, Susan
  Darlington, Con
  Martin, Ann
  Wayne, Marcia
BEST, Rayleigh Breton Amis
  Amis, Breton
  Bentinck, Ray
  Haddow, Leigh
  Hughes, Terence
  Roberts, Desmond
  Wilde, Leslie
BETHELL, Leonard Arthur
  Cailloux, Pousse
  Severn, Forepoint
BETHELL, Mary
  Hayes, Evelyn
BETTANY, F G
  N O B
BETTERIDGE, Anne
  Newman, Margaret
  Potter, Margaret
BEUTTLER, Edward I O
  Butler, Ivan
BEVAN, Aneurin
  Celticus

24

BEVAN, Tom
  Bamfylde, Walter
BEVANS, Florence Edith
  Remington, Jemima
BEYNON, Jane
  Lewis, Lange
BHATIA, June
  Edwards, June
  Rana, J
BHATTACHARYA, Basudeb
  Acharya, Pundit
  Basudeb, Sree
BICKHAM, Jack Miles
  Clinton, Jeff
  Miles, John
BICKLE, Judith
  Tweedale, J
BIDWELL, Marjory Elizabeth
  Sarah
  Gibbs, Mary Ann
BIERCE, Ambrose
  Bowers, *Mrs* J Milton
  Grile, Dod
  Herman, William
  Sloluck, J Milton
BIERMANN, June *and*
  TOOHEY, Barbara
  Bennett, Margaret
BIGG, Patricia Nina
  Ainsworth, Patricia
BILSKY, Eva
  Aunt Eva
BINGHAM, E A *and*
  LA COSTE, Guy R
  Berton, Guy
BINGLEY, David Ernest
  Adams, Bart
  Benson, Adam

BINGLEY, D E (cont'd)
  Bridger, Adam
  Canuck, Abe
  Carver, Dave
  Chatham, Larry
  Chesham, Henry
  Coltman, Will
  Coniston, Ed
  Dorman, Luke
  Fallon, George
  Horsley, David
  Jefford, Bat
  Kingston, Syd
  Lynch, Eric
  Martell, James
  North, Colin
  Plummer, Ben
  Prescott, Caleb
  Remington, Mark
  Roberts, John
  Romney, Steve
  Silvester, Frank
  Starr, Henry
  Tucker, Link
  Wigan, Christopher
  Yorke, Roger
BINNS, Ottwell
  Bolt, Ben
BIOY-CASARES, Adolfo *and*
  BORGES, Jorge Luis
  Bustos Domecq, Honorio
  Suárez Lynch, B
BIRCH, Jack Ernest Lionel *and*
  MURRAY, Venetia Pauline
  Flight, Francies
BIRD, Cyril Kenneth
  Fougasse

25

BIRD, Dennis Leslie
 Noel, John
BIRD, William Henry Fleming
 Fleming, Harry
BIRKENHEAD, Elijah
 Birkenhead, Edward
BIRKIN, Charles
 Lloyd, Charles
BIRNEY, Hoffman
 Kent, David
BIRT, Francis Bradley
 Bradley, Shelland
BISHOP, Curtis Kent
 Brandon, Curt
BISHOP, Morris Gilbert
 Johnson, W Bolingbroke
BISHOP, Stanley
 Edgar, Icarus Walter
BISSET-SMITH, G T
 Bizet, George
BLACK, Dorothy
 Black, Kitty
BLACK, Hazleton
 Graham, Scott
BLACK, Ladbroke Lionel Day
 Day, Lionel
 Urquhart, Paul
BLACK, Maureen
 Black, Veronica
 Darby, Catherine
 Peters, Maureen
 Rothmann, Judith
 Whitby, Sharon
BLACK, Oliver
 Black, Jett
BLACKBURN, Barbara
 Grant, Jane

BLACKBURN, James Garford
 Garford, James
BLACKBURN, Victoria Grace
 Fan-Fan
BLACKETT, Veronica
 Heath, Veronica
BLACKMORE, Anauta
 Anauta
BLAGBROUGH, Harriet
 Eastertide
BLAIKLOCK, Edward
 Grammaticus
BLAIR, Dorothy
 Bolitho, Ray D
BLAIR, Dorothy *and*
 PAGE, Evelyn
 Scarlett, Roger
BLAIR, Eric
 Orwell, George
BLAIR, Kathryn
 Brett, Rosalind
 Conway, Celine
BLAIR, Norma Hunter
 Hunter, Alison
BLAIR, Pauline Hunter
 Clare, Helen
 Clarke, Pauline
BLAIR-FISH, Wallace Wilfred
 Blair
BLAKE, George
 Vagabond
BLAKE, Leslie James
 Tabard, Peter
BLAKE, Sally Mirliss
 Sara
BLAKE, Wilfrid Theodore
 Wing Adjutant

BLAKESTON, Oswell *and*
 BURFORD, Roger d'Este
 Simon
BLAND, *Mrs* Edith (Nesbit)
 Bland, E
 Bland, *Mrs* Hubert
 Nesbit, E
BLAND, *Mrs* Edith (Nesbit) *and*
 BLAND, Hubert
 Bland, Fabian
BLAND, Hubert
 Hubert
BLATCHFORD, Robert
 Nunquam
BLAUSTEIN, Albert P
 De Graeff, Allen
BLAUTH-MUSZKOWSKI, Peter
 Blauth, Christopher
BLECH, William James
 Blake, William
 Blake, William James
BLEWITT, Dorothy
 Praize, Ann
BLISH, James
 Atheling, William *Jr*
BLIXEN-FINECKE, Karen
 Christence, *Baroness*
 Andrézel, Pierre
 Blixen, Karen
 Dinesen, Isak
BLOCH, Robert
 Fiske, Tarleton
 Folke, Will
 Hindin, Nathan
 Kane, Wilson
 Sheldon, John
BLOFELD, John
 Chu Feng

BLOOD, Marje
 McKenzie, Paige
BLOOM, Jack Don
 Donne, Jack
BLOOM, Ursula
 Burns, Sheila
 Essex, Mary
 Harvey, Rachel
 Mann, Deborah
 Prole, Lozania
 Sloane, Sara
BLOOMER, Arnold
 More, Euston
BLOOMFIELD, Anthony John
 Westgate
 Westgate, John
BLOOR, W A
 Scott, A
BLOSSOM, D Bradford
 Bradford, De Witt
BLOXAM, John Francis
 Lawrence, Bertram
 X
BLUNDELL, Harold
 Bellairs, George
BLUNDELL, V R
 Nixon, Kathleen
BLYTH, Harry
 Meredith, Hal
BLYTON, Enid
 Pollock, Mary
BOATFIELD, Jeffrey
 Jeffries, Jeff
BOBIN, John W
 Ascott, Adelie
 Greenhalgh, Katherine
 Nelson, Gertrude

BODENHAM, Hilda
  Boden, Hilda
BODINGTON, Nancy Hermione
  Smith, Shelley
BOEHM, David Alfred
  Masters, Robert V
BOGGIS, David
  Vaughan, Gary
BOGGS, Helen
  Gwynne, Nell
  Bernard
BOGGS, Winifred
  Burke, Edmund
BOHANNAN, Laura M Smith
  Bowen, Elenore Sith
BOLSTER, *Sister* M Angela
  Bolster, Evelyn
BOLTON, Miriam
  Davis, Stratford
  Sharman, Miriam
BOND, Florence D F
  Demarest, Anne
BOND, Gladys Baker
  Mendel, Jo
  Walker, Holly Beth
BOND, Grace
  Todhunter, Philippa
BOON, Violet Mary
  Williams, Violet M
BOOTH, John Bennion
  Costs
BOOTH, Philip Arthur
  Werner, Peter
BORBOLLA, Barbara
  Martyn, Don
BORDEN, Deal
  Borden, Leo

BOREMAN, Linda
  Lovelace, Linda
BORG, Philip Anthony John
  Bexar, Phil
  Borg, Jack
  Pickard, John Q
BORGES, Jorge Luis *and*
  BIOY-CASARES, Adolfo
  Bustos Domecq, Honorio
  Suárez Lynch, B
BORLAND, Harold Glen
  Borland, Hal
  West, Ward
BORLAND, Kathryn K *and*
  SPEICHER, Helen Ross
  Abbott, Alice
  Land, Jane and Ross
BORNEMAN, Ernest
  McCabe, Cameron
BORNEMANN, Eva
  Geisel, Eva
BOSHELL, Gordon
  Bee
BOSWORTH, Willan George
  Borth, Willan G
  Leonid
  Worth, Maurice
BOTTOMLEY, Kate Madeline
  Vera
BOULTON, A Harding
  Harding, Richard
BOUNDS, Sydney J
  Marshall, James
  Saunders, Wes
BOURQUIN, Paul
  Amberley, Richard
BOWDEN, Jean
  Barry, Jocelyn

Bland, Jennifer
Curry, Avon
Dell, Belinda
BOWEN, Reuben
  Kajar
BOWEN-JUDD, Sara Hutton
  Woods, Sara
BOWER, John Graham
  Klaxon
BOWMAN, Gerald
  Magnus, Gerald
BOYD, Elizabeth Orr
  MacCall, Isabel
BOYD, Martin à Beckett
  Mills, Martin
BOYES, W Watson
  Oyster, An
BOYLE, John Howard Jackson
  Dawson, Michael
BRADBURY, Parnell
  Dermott, Stephen
  Lynn, Stephen
BRADBY, Rachel
  Anderson, Rachel
BRADLEY, Ian *and*
 HOLLOWS, Norman F
  Duplex
BRADLEY, Katherine H *and*
 COOPER, Edith E
  Field, Michael
BRADLEY, Marion Z *and*
 COULSON, Juanita
  Wells, John J
BRADSHAW-JONES, Malcolm
 Henry
  Jones, Bradshaw
BRADY, Jane Frances
  White, Jane

BRAEME, Charlotte Monica
  Clay, Bertha M
BRAHAM, Hal
  Colton, Mel
  Trask, Merrill
BRAINERD, Edith *and*
  BRAINERD, J Chauncey
  Rath, E J
BRAITHWAITE, Althea
  Althea
BRAMBLEBY, Ailsa
  Craig, Jennifer
BRAMWELL, James Guy
  Byrom, James
BRAND, Charles Neville
  Lorne, Charles
BRANDENBERG, Alyce
  Christina
  Aliki
BRAUN, Wilbur
  Albert, Ned
  Brandon, Bruce
  Fernway, Peggy
  Ring, Basil
  Warren, Wayne
BRAYBROOKE, Patrick
  P B
BRECKENFELD, Vivian Gurney
  Breck, Vivian
BRENAN, Edward Fitzgerald
  Beaton, George
  Brenan, Gerald
BRENNAN, John
  Welcome, John
BRENT, Peter Ludwig
  Peters, Ludovic
BRERETON, John Le Gay
  Garstang, Basil

29

BRESLIN, Howard
  Niall, Michael
BRETHERTON, C H
  Algol
BRETON-SMITH, Clare
  Boon, August
  Caldwell, Elinor
  Vernon, Claire
  Wilde, Hilary
BRETT, Leslie Frederick
  Brett, Michael
BRIDGES, Thomas Charles
  Beck, Christopher
  Bridges, Tom
BRIGGS, Phyllis
  Briggs, Philip
BRIGHOUSE, Harold *and*
  WALTON, John
  Conway, Olive
BRIGHT, Mary C
  Egerton, George
BRINSMEAD, Hesba
  Brinsmead, H F
  Hurgerford, Pixie
BRINTON, Henry
  Fraser, Alex
BROCK, Alan St Hill
  Dewdney, Peter
BROCKIES, Enid Florence
  Magriska, Hélène, *Countess*
BRODEY, Jim
  Femora
  Taylor, Ann
BRODIE, John
  Guthrie, John
BRODIE, Julian Paul *and*
  GREEN, Alan Baer
  Denbie, Roger

BROGAN, Colm
  Candidus
BROGAN, Denis
  Barrington, Maurice
BROOKE, Peter
  Carson, Anthony
BROOKER, Bertram
  Herne, Huxley
BROOKES, Ewart Stanley
  Tyler, Clarke
BROOKMAN, Laura L
  Wilson, Edwina H
BROOKS, Anne
  Carter, Ann
  Carter, Anne
  Milburn, Cynthia
  Millburn, Cynthia
BROOKS, Collin
  Brook, Barnaby
BROOKS, Edwy Searles
  Comrade, Robert W
  Gray, Berkeley
  Gunn, Victor
BROOKS, Ern
  Orion
BROOKS, Jeremy
  Meikle, Clive
BROOKS, Vivian Collin
  Mills, Osmington
BROSIA, D M
  D'Ambrosio, Raymond
BROSSARD, Chandler
  Harper, Daniel
BROWN, E
  Cavendish
BROWN, George Douglas
  Douglas, George
  King, Kennedy

BROWN, Ivor
  I B
BROWN, John
  Browning, John
BROWN, John Ridley
  Castle, Douglas
BROWN, Kay
  Back-Back
BROWN, L Rowland
  Grey, Rowland
BROWN, Laurence Oliver
  Oliver, Laurence
BROWN, Margaret Elizabeth Snow
  Brown, Marel
BROWN, May
  Blake, Vanessa
  Brown, Mandy
BROWN, Morna D
  Ferrars, E X
  Ferrars, Elizabeth
BROWN, Rosalie
  Moore, Rosalie
BROWN, Zenith
  Conrad, Brenda
  Ford, Leslie
  Frome, David
BROWNE, Charles Farrar
  Ward, Artemus
BROWNE, Harry T
  John o' the North
BROWNE, Howard
  Evans, John
BROWNE, Thomas Alexander
  Boldrewood, Rolf
BROWNJOHN, Alan
  Berrington, John
BROWNLEE, Frances
  Dickinson, Frankie

BRUFF, Nancy
  Gardner, Nancy Bruff
BRUNDLE, John
  John, A Suffolk Herd Boy
BRUNNER, John
  Loxmith, John
  Staines, Trevor
  Woodcott, Keith
BRUSTLEIN, Daniel
  Alain
BRUSTLEIN, Janice
  Janice
BRYANT, Baird
  Baron, Willie
BRYANT, Denny
  Drake, Winifred
BRYSON, Charles
  Barry, Charles
BUCHAN, Anna
  Douglas, O
BUCHAN, John Stuart
  Erskine, Douglas
BUCHANAN, B J
  Shepherd, Joan
BUCKBY, Samuel
  Blair, Frank
BUCKHAM, Bernard
  B B B
BUCKLAND-WRIGHT, Mary
  Hume, Frances
BUCKLEY, Fergus Reid
  Crumpet, Peter
BUDD, John
  Prescot, Julian
BUDD, William John
  Budd, Jackson
  Jackson, Wallace

BUDDEE, Paul
  Richards, Paul
BUGAEV, Boris Nikolaevich
  Biely, Andrey
BUGGIE, Olive M
  Bugy, Oly
BUITENKANT, Nathan
  Mark, David
BULLEID, H A V
  Collins, D
BULLETT, Gerald
  Fox, Sebastian
BULMER, Kenneth
  Zetford, Tully
BUMPUS, Doris Marjorie
  Alan, Marjorie
BUNCE, Oliver Bell
  Censor
BUNCH, David R
  Groupe, Darryl R
BUNDEY, Ellen Milne
  Dunne, Lyell
BUNTING, D G
  George, Daniel
BURBRIDGE, Edith Joan
  Cockin, Joan
BURDEN, Jean
  Ames, Felicia
BURFORD, Roger d'Este
  East, Roger
BURFORD, Roger d'Este *and*
  BLAKESTON, Oswell
  Simon
BURG, David
  Dolberg, Alexander
BURGE, Milward Rodon Kennedy
  Kennedy, Milward

BURGESS, Thornton W
  Thornton, W B
BURGIN, G B
  Smee, Wentworth
BURKE, John Frederick
  Burke, Jonathan
  Esmond, Harriet
  George, Jonathan
  Jones, Joanna
  Miall, Robert
  Morris, Sara
  Sands, Martin
BURKHARDT, Eve *and*
BURKHARDT, Robert
Ferdinand
  Bliss, Adam
  Eden, Rob
  Jardin, Rex
BURKS, Arthur J
  Critchie, Estil
  Whitney, Spencer
BURNE, Clendennin Talbot
  Hawkes, John
BURNETT, Hallie
  Hutchinson, Anne
BURNETT, Hugh
  Phelix
BURNETT-SMITH, Annie S
  Swan, Annie S
BURNS, Bernard
  Auld, Philip
BURNS, Vincent
  Burns, Bobby
BURRAGE, Alfred M
  Ex-Private X
BURROUGHS, William
  Lee, William

BURROWS, Hermann
  Rag Man
BURTON, Alice Elizabeth
  Kerby, Susan Alice
BUSCHLEN, John Preston
  Preston, Jack
BUSH, Christopher
  Home, Michael
BUSH-FEKETE, Marie Ilona
  Fagyas, Maria
BUSSY, Dorothy
  Olivia
BUTLER, Arthur Ronald
  Butler, Richard
BUTLER, Bill
  Sabbah, Hassan i
BUTLER, Gwendolyn
  Melville, Jennie
BUTLER, Samuel
  Owen, John Pickard
BUTLER, Teresa Mary
  Hooley, Teresa
BUTLER, William Vivian
  ('writing as')
  Marric, J J
BUTTERS, Dorothy Gilman
  Gilman, Dorothy
BUTTERS, Paul
  Williamson, Paul
BUTTERWORTH, Frank Nestle
  Blundell, Peter
BUTTON, Margaret
  Leona
BUXTON, Anne
  Maybury, Anne
  Troy, Katherine
BYERS, Amy
  Barry, Ann

BYFORD-JONES, Wilfred
  Quaestor

§ §

Oh Amos Cottle!—
Phoebus what a name
To fill the speaking trump
of future fame.
—Lord Byron. English bards and
Scotch reviewers

§ §

CADELL, Elizabeth
  Ainsworth, Harriet
CAESAR, Gene
  Laredo, Johnny
CAESAR, Richard Dynely *and*
  MAYNE, William J C
  James, Dynely
CAFFYN, Kathleen M
  Iota
CAIN, Arthur Homer
  King, Arthur
CAIN, Paul
  Ruric, Peter
CALDWELL, Janet Taylor *and*
  REBACK, Marcus
  Caldwell, Taylor
  Reiner, Max
CALLAHAN, Claire Wallis
  Hartwell, Nancy
CALLARD, Thomas H
  Ross, Sutherland
CAMERON, Elizabeth Jane
  Duncan, Jane
CAMERON, William Ernest
  Allerton, Mark

33

CAMM, Frederick James
 N I
 Waysider
CAMPBELL, Alice Ormond
 Ingram, Martin
CAMPBELL, Barbara Mary
 Cam
CAMPBELL, Gabrielle Margaret
 Vere
 Bowen, Marjorie
 Paye, Robert
 Preedy, George
 Preedy, George R
 Shearing, Joseph
 Winch, John
CAMPBELL, John Lorne
 Chanaidh, Fear
CAMPBELL, John Wood Jr
 Stuart, Don A
CAMPBELL, Margaret *and*
JANSEN, Johanna
 Bayard, Fred
CAMPBELL, R O
 Staveley, Robert
CAMPBELL, Ramsay
 Comfort, Montgomery
 Undercliffe, Errol
CAMPBELL, Sydney George
 Campbell, Stuart
CAMPBELL, Walter Stanley
 Vestal, Stanley
CAMPBELL, William Edward
 March
 March, William
CAMPION, Sidney
 Swayne, Geoffrey
CANADAY, John
 Head, Matthew

CANAWAY, W H
 Canaway, Bill
 Hamilton, William
 Hermes
CANNING, Victor
 Gould, Alan
CAPLIN, Alfred Gerald
 Capp, Al
CAPRIANI, Vincent
 Massey, Charlotte
CAPSTICK, Elizabeth
 Scott, Elizabeth
CARAS, Roger
 Sarac, Roger
CARDENA, Clement
 De Laube
CARDIF, Maurice
 Lincoln, John
CARDUS, Sir Neville
 Cricketer
CAREW, John Mohun
 Carew, Tim
CAREW-SLATER, Harold James
 Carey, James
CAREY, Joyce
 Mallory, Jay
CARLE, C E *and* DORN, Dean M
 Morgan, Michael
CARLISLE, R H
 Hawkeye
CARLTON, Grace
 Garth, Cecil
CARMAN, Bliss
 Norman, Louis
CARNEGIE, Raymond Alexander
 Carnegie, Sacha
CARNEY, Jack
 Eff, B

CARR, Barbara Irene Veronica
 Comyns
  Comyns, Barbara
CARR, John Dickson
 Dickson, Carr
 Dickson, Carter
CARR, Margaret
 Carroll, Martin
 Kerr, Carole
CARRIER, Robert *and*
 DICK, Oliver Lawson
 Oliver, Robert
CARRINGTON, Charles
 Edmonds, Charles
CARRINGTON, Hereward
 Lavington, Hubert
CARTER, Bryan
 Carter, Nick
CARTER, Compton Irving
 Carter, John L
CARTER, Ernest
 Giffin, Frank
CARTER, Felicity Winifred
 Bonett, Emery
CARTER, John Franklin
 Diplomat
 Franklin, J
 Unofficial Observer
CARTER, Thomas
 Wood, J Claverdon
CARTWRIGHT, Justin
 Crispin, Suzy
 Sutton, Penny
CARUSO, Joseph
 Barnwell, J O
CARY, Joyce
 Cary, Arthur
 Joyce, Thomas

CASEMENT, Christina
 Maclean, Christina
CASEY, Michael T *and*
 CASEY, Rosemary
 Casey, Mart
CASMAN, Frances White
 Keene, Frances W
CASSELEYR, Camille
 Danvers, Jack
CASSIDY, Robert John
 Gilrooney
CASSITY, June
 Mo, Manager
CASSON, Frederick
 Beatty, Baden
CASTLE, Brenda
 Ferrand, Georgina
CASTLE, Frances Mundy
 Whitehouse, Peggy
CASTLE, Frank
 Thurman, Steve
CASTLE SMITH, *Mrs* G
 Brenda
CASWELL, Anne
 Orr, Mary
CATALANI, Victoria
 Haas, Carola
CATHER, Willa
 Micklemann, Henry
CATHERALL, Arthur
 Channel, A R
 Corby, Dan
 Hallard, Peter
CATTO, Maxwell Jeffrey
 Catto, Max
 Finkell, Max
 Kent, Simon

35

CAULFIELD, Max
  McCoy, Malachy
CAUTE, David
  Salisbury, John
CAVE, Hugh Barnett
  Beck, Allen
  Case, Justin
  Vace, Geoffrey
CAVE, Peter
  Maxwell, Peter
CAVERHILL, William Melville
  Melville, Alan
CHADWICK, Joseph
  Barton, Jack
  Callahan, John
  Conroy, Jim
CHADWICK, Paul
  House, Brant
CHALKE, Herbert
  Blacker, Hereth
CHALLANS, Mary
  Renault, Mary
CHALMERS, Patrick
  P C
CHALONER, John Seymour
  Chalon, Jon
CHAMBERS, Aidan
  Blacklin, Malcolm
CHANCE, John Newton
  Chance, Jonathan
  Drummond, John
  Lymington, John
  Newton, David C
CHANDLER, Arthur
  Whitley, George

CHAPMAN, Mary I *and*
  CHAPMAN, John Stanton
  Chapman, Mariston
  Selkirk, Jane
CHAPMAN, Raymond
  Nash, Simon
CHAPPELL, George S
  Traprock, Walter E
CHARLES, Richard
  Awdry, R C
CHARLTON, Joan *and others*
  Heptagon
CHARNOCK, Joan
  Thomson, Joan
CHAUNDLER, Christine
  Martin, Peter
CHEETHAM, James
  Cheetham, Hal
CHESHIRE, Gifford Paul
  Cheshire, Giff
  Merriman, Chad
  Pendleton, Ford
CHESTER, Charlie
  Noone, Carl
CHESTERTON, G K
  Arion
  G K C
CHETHAM-STRODE, Warren
  Douglas, Noel
  Hamilton, Michael
CHEVALIER, Paul Eugene
  George
  George, Eugene
CHEYNE, *Sir* Joseph
  Munroe, R
CHILD, Philip A G
  Wentworth, John

CHIPPERFIELD, Joseph E
  Craig, John Eland
CHISHOLM, Lilian
  Alan, Jane
  Lorraine, Anne
CHITTY, Margaret Hazel
  Whitton, Barbara
CHITTY, *Sir* Thomas Willes
  Hinde, Thomas
CHOSACK, Cyril
  Maclean, Barry
CHOVIL, Alfred Harold
  Brook, Peter
CHRISTIE, *Dame* Agatha
  Mallowen, Agatha Christie
  Westmacott, Mary
CHRISTIE, Annie Rothwell
  Rothwell, Annie
CHRISTIE, Douglas
  Campbell, Colin
  Durie, Lynn
CHURCH, Elsie
  Parrish, Jean J
CITOVITCH, Enid
  Baldry, Enid
CLAIR, Colin
  Nicholai, C L R
CLAMP, Helen M E
  Leigh, Olivia
CLARK, Alfred Alexander
 Gordon
  Hare, Cyril
CLARK, Charles Heber
  Adeler, Max
CLARK, Dorothy *and*
 McMEEKIN, Isabel
  McMeekin, Clark

CLARK, Douglas
  Ditton, James
CLARK, Frederick Stephen
  Dalton, Clive
CLARK, Mabel Margaret
  Storm, Lesley
CLARK, Maria
  Clark, Mary Lou
CLARK, Marie Catherine Audrey
  Curling, Audrey
CLARK, Marjorie
  Rivers, Georgia
CLARK, Mary Elizabeth *and*
 QUIGLEY, M C
  Clark, Margery
CLARK, Winifred
  Finley, Scott
CLARKE, Brenda
  Honeyman, Brenda
CLARKE, David
  Waldo, Dave
CLARKE, Dorothy Josephine
  Shaw, Josephine
CLARKE, J Calvitt
  Addison, Carol
  Grant, Richard
CLARKE, *Lady*
  Fitzgerald, Errol
CLARKE, Percy A
  Frazer, Martin
  Lander, Dane
  Lytton, Jane
  Nielson, Vernon
CLARKE, Rebecca Sophia
  Sophie, May
CLARKE, Sylvestre
  Buffalo Child Long Lance

37

CLAY, Michael John
  Griffin, John
CLAYTON, *Reverend* F H
  Irishman, An
CLAYTON, Richard H M
  Haggard, William
CLEARY, C V H
  Day, Harvey
  Duncan, A H
  Norris, P E
CLEAVER, Hylton Reginald
  Crunden, Reginald
CLEGG, Paul
  Vale, Keith
CLEMENS, Brian
  O'Grady, Tony
CLEMENS, Paul
  Cadwallader
CLEMENS, Samuel Langhorne
  Twain, Mark
CLEVELY, Hugh Desmond
  Claymore
  Claymore, Tod
CLINE, Norma
  Klose, Norma Cline
CLOPET, Liliane M C
  Bethune, Mary
CLUTTERBUCK, Richard
  Jocelyn, Richard
CLYDE, Leonard Worswick
  Baron, Peter
COAD, Frederick R
  Sosthenes
COATES, Anthony
  Mandeville, D E
COBB, Clayton W
  Patten, J

COBB, Ivo Geikie
  Weymouth, Anthony
COCKBURN, Claud
  Helvick, James
  Pitcairn, Frank
COERR, Eleanor Beatrice
  Hicks, Eleanor
  Page, Eleanor
COFFEY, Edward Hope
  Hope, Edward
COFFMAN, Virginia
  Du Vaul, Virginia
COHEN, Morton N
  Moreton, John
COHEN, Victor
  Caldecott, Veronica
COKE, Desmond
  Blinders, Belinda
COLE, G(eorge) D(ouglas)
  H(oward)
  Cole, Douglas
  Populus
COLE, Lois Dwight
  Dudley, Nancy
  Eliot, Anne
COLE, Margaret A
  Renton, Julia
  Saunders, Ione
COLEMAN, John
  Dexter, John
  Gorman, Ginny
  Hughes, Valerina
  Hughes, Zach
  Kanto, Peter
  Pilgrim, Derral
  Rangely, E R
  Rangely, Olivia
  Van Heller, Marcus

COLEMAN, William Lawrence
  Coleman, Lonnie
COLEMAN-COOKE, John C
  Ford, Langridge
COLES, Albert John
  Stewer, Jan
COLES, Cyril Henry *and*
  MANNING, Adelaide Frances
  Oke
  Coles, Manning
  Gaite, Francis
COLES, Phoebe Catherine
  Fraser, Peter
COLEY, Rex
  Ragged Staff
COLFER, Rebecca B
  R
COLLIE, Ruth
  Stitch, Wilhelmina
COLLIN SMITH, Rodney
  Collin, Rodney
COLLINGS, Edwin
  Bkackwell, John
COLLINGS, I J
  Collings, Jillie
  George, Vicky
COLLINGS, Joan
  Sutherland, Joan
COLLINS, Dale
  Fennimore, Stephen
COLLINS, Mildred
  Collins, Joan
COLLINS, Vere Henry
  Tellar, Mark
COLLINSON OWEN, H
  C O

COLLOMS, Brenda
  Cross, Brenda
  Hughes, Brenda
COMBER, Elizabeth
  Han Suyin
COMBER, Lillian
  Beckwith, Lillian
COMBER, Rose
  Star, Elison
COMPTON, D G
  Compton, Guy
  Lynch, Frances
CONARAIN, Alice Nina
  Bowyer, Nina
  Conarain, Nina
  Hoy, Elizabeth
CONDON, Madeline B
  Haefer, Hanna
CONE, Molly
  More, Caroline
CONE, P C L
  Clapp, Patricia
CONLY, Robert Carroll
  O'Brien, Richard C
CONNER, Reardon
  Connor, Patrick Reardon
CONNOLLY, Cyril
  Palinurus
CONNOR, Joyce Mary
  Marlow, Joyce
CONNOR, *Sir* William
  Cassandra
CONRAD, Isaac
  Conrad, Jack
COOK, Dorothy Mary
  Cameron, D Y
  Clare, Elizabeth

39

COOK, Ida
  Burchell, Mary
COOK, Marjorie Grant
  Grant, Marjorie
  Seaford, Caroline
COOK, Ramona Graham
  Graham, Ramona
COOK, William Everett
  Cook, Will
  Everett, Wade
  Keene, James
  Peace, Frank
  Riordan, Dan
COOKE, C H
  Bickerdyke, John
COOKE, Diana
  Witherby, Diana
COOKSON, Catherine
  Fawcett, Catherine
  Marchant, Catherine
COOLBEAR, Marian H
  Colbere, Hope
COOMBS, Joyce
  Hales, Joyce
  Scobey, Marion
COOPER, Edith E *and*
 BRADLEY, Katherine H
  Field, Michael
COOPER, Edmund
  Avery, Richard
COOPER, Gordon
  Colam, Lance
COOPER, John
  Finch, John
  Lloyd, John
COOPER, John Dean
  Cooper, Jeff

COOPER, John Murray
  Sutherland, William
COOPER, Mae Klein *and*
 KLEIN, Grace
  Farewell, Nina
COPE, *Sir* Zachary
  Zeta
COPELAND, Lewis
  Henry, Lewis C
COPPAGE, George Herman
  Jubilate
COPPEL, Alfred
  Gilman, Robert Cham
  Marin, A C
  Marin, Alfred
COPPER, Dorothy
  Carter, Diana
  Dickens, Irene
  Grant, Carol
  Green, Linda
CORBY, Jane
  Carew, Jean
  Holden, Joanne
CORDES, Theodore K
  Casey, T
  Daedalus
  Erskine-Gray
CORK, Barry
  Causeway, Jane
CORLEY, Edwin *and*
 MURPHY, John
  Buchanan, Patrick
CORNISH, Doris Mary
  Lisle, Mary
CORNWELL, David John Moore
  Le Carré, John
CORRALL, Alice Enid
  Glass, Justine

CORTEZ-COLUMBUS, Robert
 Cimabue
 Kennedy, R C
COSENS, Abner
 Wayfarer
COSTA, Gabriel
 Callisthenes
COTLER, Gordon
 Gordon, Alex
COULSON, John
 Bonett, John
COULSON, Juanita *and*
 BRADLEY, Marion Z
 Wells, John J
COULSON, Robert Stratton *and*
 DE WEESE, T Eugene
 Stratton, Thomas
COULTER, Stephen
 Mayo, James
COURAGE, John
 Goyne, Richard
COURNOS, John
 Courtney, John
 Gault, Mark
COURSE, Pamela
 Becket, Lavinia
 Mansbridge, Pamela
COURTIER, Sidney Hobson
 Chestor, Rui
COURTNEY-BROWNE, Reginald
D S
 Browne, Courtney
COUSINS, Margaret
 Johns, Avery
 Masters, William
 Parrish, Mary
COVE, Joseph Walter
 Gibbs, Lewis

COVERT, Alice Lent
 Dale, Maxine
 Lowell, Elaine
COWARD, Noël
 Whittlebot, Hernia
COWLISHAW, Ranson
 Wash, R
 Woodrook, R A
COWPER, Francis
 Roe, Richard
COX, A B
 Berkeley, Anthony
 Iles, Francis
COX, Edith Muriel
 Goaman, Muriel
COX, Euphrasia Emeline
 Cox, Lewis
 Parsons, Bridget
COX, John
 Cox, Jack
 Roberts, David
COX, Julia
 Julia
COX, William Robert
 Reeve, Joel
COX, William Trevor
 Trevor, William
COXALL, Jack Arthur
 Dawson, Oliver
CRADOCK, Phyllis Nan Sortain
 Cradock, Fanny
 Dale, Frances
CRADOCK, Phyllis Nan Sortain
 and CRADOCK, John
 Bon Viveur
CRAIG, Edward Anthony
 Carrick, Edward

CRAIGIE, Dorothy M
  Craigie, David
CRAIGIE, Pearl Mary Teresa
  Hobbes, John Oliver
CRAINE, John Henry
  Jason
CRAWFORD, Phyllis
  Turner, Josie
CRAWFORD, Sallie
  Trotter, Sallie
CREASEY, Clarence Hamilton
  Cressy, Edward
CREASEY, Jeanne
  Crecy, Jeanne
  Williams, J R
  Williams, Jeanne
CREASEY, John
  Ashe, Gordon
  Cooke, M E
  Cooke, Margaret
  Cooper, Henry St John
  Deane, Norman
  Fecamps, Elise
  Frazer, Robert Caine
  Gill, Patrick
  Halliday, Michael
  Hogarth, Charles
  Hope, Brian
  Hughes, Colin
  Hunt, Kyle
  Mann, Abel
  Manton, Peter
  Marric, J J
  Marsden, James
  Martin, Richard
  Mattheson, Rodney
  Morton, Anthony
  Ranger, Ken

42

CREASEY, J (cont'd)
  Reilly, William K
  Riley, Tex
  York, Jeremy
CREBBIN, Edward Horace
  Sea-wrack
CRICHTON, Eleanor
  McGavin, Moyra
CRICHTON, Kyle
  Forsythe, Robert
CRICHTON, Lucilla Matthew
  Andrews, Lucilla
CRICHTON, Michael
  Hudson, Jeffrey
  Lange, John
CRISP, S E
  Crispie
CRITCHLOW, Dorothy
  Dawson, Jane
CROCCHIOLA, Stanley Francis
  Louis
  Stanley, F
CROFT-COOKE, Rupert
  Bruce, Leo
  Croft, Taylor
CROLY, Jane Cunningham
  June, Jenny
CRONIN, Bernard
  Adair, Dennis
  North, Eric
CRONIN, Brendan Leo
  Cronin, Michael
  Miles, David
CROSBIE, Hugh Provan
  Carrick, John
  Crosbie, Provan
CROSHER, Geoffrey Robins
  Kesteven, G R

CROSS, John Keir
  MacFarlane, Stephen
CROSSEN, Kendell Foster
  Barlay, Bennett
  Chaber, M E
  Foster, Richard
  Monig, Christopher
  Richards, Clay
CROUDACE, Glyn
  Monnow, Peter
CROUNSE, Helen Louise
  Jackson, Joyce
CROWE, *Lady* (Bettina)
  Lum, Peter
CROWLEY, Aleister *see*
 CROWLEY, Edward Alexander
CROWLEY, Edward Alexander
  Abhavananda
  Carr, H D
  Crowley, Aleister
  Fénix, *Comte de*
  Frater, Perdurabo
  Gentleman of the University
    of Cambridge
  Khan, Khaled
  St E A of M and S
  Shivaji, Mahatma Guru Sri
    Paramahansa
  Svareff, *Count* Vladimir
  Therion, The Master
CRUTTENDEN, Nellie
  Jenny Wren
CRYER, Neville
  Fern, Edwin
CUMBERLAND, Marten
  O'Hara, Kevin
CUMMING, Robert Dalziel
  Skookum Chuck

CUMMINGS, Bruce Frederick
  Barbellion, W N P
CUMMINS, Mary Warmington
  Mackie, Alice
  Melville, Jean
CUNNINGHAM, Virginia Myra
  Mundy
  Mundy, V M
CURNOW, Allen
  Whim Wham
CURRIE, *Lady*
  Fane, Violet
CURRY, Colin Thomas
  Douglas, Colin
CURRY, Thomas Albert
  Jefferis, Jeff
CURRY, Winifred J P
  Primrose, Jane
CUST, Barbara Kate
  Fanshaw, Caroline
  Ward, Kate
CUTHBERTSON, James Lister
  C
CUTHRELL, Faith Baldwin
  Baldwin, Faith

§ §

*A man that should call everything
by its right name would hardly
pass the streets without being
knocked down as a common
enemy.*
—*Marquis of Halifax. Works*

§ §

DA CRUZ, Daniel
  Ballentine, John
  Cross, T T
DACHS, David
  Stanley, Dave
DAINTON, William
  Dainton, Courtney
DAKERS, Elaine
  Lane, Jane
DALE, Margaret
  Miller, Margaret J
DALE, R J
  Vinton, V V
DALLY, Ann
  Mullins, Ann
DALRYMPLE-HAY, Barbara *and*
 DALRYMPLE-HAY, John
  Hay, John
DALTON, Gilbert
  Carstairs, Rod
  Norton, Victor
DANIEL, Glyn Edmund
  Rees, Dilwyn
DANIELL, Albert Scott
  Bowood, Richard
  Daniell, David Scott
DANNAY, Frederic
  Nathan, Daniel
DANNAY, Frederic *and*
 LEE, Manfred B
  Queen, Ellery
  Ross, Barnaby
DANSON, Frank Corse
  Dickson, Frank C
DARBY, Edith M
  Greenfield, Bernadette
DAREFF, Hal
  Foley, Scott

DARGAN, Olive
  Burke, Fielding
D'ARLEY, Catherine
  Arley, Catherine
DAUGHTREY, Olive Lydia
  Earle, Olive L
DAUKES, Sidney Herbert
  Fairway, Sidney
DAVENTRY, Leonard John
  Alexander, Martin
DAVID, Julia
  Draco, F
DAVIDSON, Edith May
  May, Roberta E
DAVIDSON, Margaret
  Compere, Mickie
  Davidson, Mickie
DAVIES, Betty Evelyn
  Warwick, Pauline
DAVIES, D Jacob
  Jacob, Herbert Mathias
DAVIES, David Margerison
  Margerison, David
DAVIES, Edith
  Jay, Joan
DAVIES, Hilda A
  Tanis
DAVIES, Joan Howard
  Drake, Joan
DAVIES, John
  Whitaker, Ray
DAVIES, John Evan Weston
  Mather, Berkely
DAVIES, Leslie Purnell
  Berne, Leo
  Blake, Robert
  Bridgeman, Richard
  Evans, Morgan

DAVIES, L P (cont'd)
   Jefferson, Ian
   Peters, Lawrence
   Philips, Thomas
   Thomas, G K
   Vardre, Leslie
   Welch, Rowland
DAVIES, Robertson
   Marchbanks, Samuel
DAVIS, Arthur Hoey
   Rudd, Steele
DAVIS, Burton *and*
 DAVIS, Clare Ogden
   Saunders, Lawrence
DAVIS, Frederick Clyde
   Coombs, Murdo
   Ransome, Stephen
DAVIS, Frederick William
   Campbell, Scott
DAVIS, Hope Hale
   Hale, Hope
DAVIS, Lavinia
   Farmer, Wendell
DAVIS, Lily May *and*
 DAVIS, Rosemary
   Davis, Rosemary L
DAVIS, Lois Carlile
   Lamplaugh, Lois
DAVIS, Martha Wirt
   Arsdale, Wirt Van
DAVIS, Robert Prunier
   Brandon, Joe
DAVIS, Rosemary *and*
 DAVIS, Lily May
   Davis, Rosemary L
DAVIS, Will R
   Wallace, John

DAVISON, Frank Cyril Shaw
   Coalfleet, Pierre
DAWES, Edna
   Dane, Eva
DAWSON, William Henry
   Hawthorne, Ernest H
   Lowndes, George
DAY, George Harold
   Quince, Peter
DAY LEWIS, Cecil
   Blake, Nicholas
DE BANZIE, Eric *and*
 RESSICH, John S M
   Baxter, Gregory
DE BELLET, Liane
   De Facci, Liane
DE CAIRE, Edwin
   Moodie, Edwin
DE CHAIR, Somerset
   Hon Member for X
DE CRISTOFORO, R J
   Cristy, R J
DE FREITAS, Michael
   Michael X
DE FREYNE, George
   Bridges, Victor
DE JONG, David Cornel
   Breola, Tjalmar
DE LA MARE, Walter
   Ramal, Walter
DE LA PASTURE, Edmée E M
   Delafield, E M
DE LAUNAY, André Joseph
   Launay, André
   Launay, Droo
DE LEEUW, Cateau W
   Hamilton, Kay
   Lyon, Jessica

DE MENDELSSOHN, Hilde
  Spiel, Hilde
DE ROSA, Peter
  Boyd, Neil
DE SCHANSCHIEFF, Juliet
  Dymoke
  Dymoke, Juliet
DE VOTO, Bernard Augustine
  August, John
  Hewes, Cady
DE WEESE, T Eugene *and*
  COULSON, Robert Stratton
  Stratton, Thomas
DEAN, Mary
  Mee, Mary
DEAN, Robert George
  Griswold, George
DEE, Stephanie
  Plowman, Stephanie
DEGHY, Guy *and*
  WATERHOUSE, Keith
  Froy, Herald
  Gibb, Lee
DEGRAS, Henry Ernest
  Benney, Mark
DEINDORFER, Robert G
  Bender, Jay
  Dender, Jay
  Greene, Robert
DEL REY, Lester
  St John, Philip
DEL REY, Lester *and*
  POHL, Frederik
  McCann, Edson
DELAFOSSE, Frederick Montague
  Vardon, Roger
DELANEY, Mary Murray
  Lane, Mary D

DELANY, Joseph Francis
  Dane, Joel Y
DELVES-BROUGHTON, Josephine
  Bryan, John
DEMING, Richard
  Franklin, Max
  Moreno, Nick
DENHOLM, David
  Forrest, David
DENNEY, Diana
  Ross, Diana
DENNIS, Geoffrey Pomeroy
  Browne, Barum
DENNIS-JONES, Harold
  Hamilton, Paul
  Hessing, Dennis
DENNISON, Enid
  Lloyd, Willson
DENNISTON, Elinore
  Allan, Dennis
  Foley, Rae
DENNY, Norman George
  Dale, Norman
DENNYS, Elisabeth
  Onslow, Katherine
DENT, Anthony
  Amplegirth, Anthony
  Lampton, Austen
DENTON, John
  Longley, John
DENVIL, Jane Gaskell
  Gaskell, Jane
DERLETH, August William
  Grendon, Stephen
  Heath, Eldon
  Holmes, Kenyon
  Mason, Tally
  West, Michael

DERN, Erolie Pearl
  Courtland, Roberta
  Dern, Peggy
  Gaddis, Peggy
DESMARAIS, Ovide E
  Demaris, Ovid
DEVANEY, Pauline *and*
 APPS, Edwin
  Wraith, John
DEVINE, David McDonald
  Devine, D M
  Devine, Dominic
DEWAR, Hubert Stephen Lowry
  Wessex Redivivus
DEWEY, Thomas Blanchard
  Brandt, Tom
  Wainer, Cord
DICK, Oliver Lawson *and*
 CARRIER, Robert
  Oliver, Robert
DICK-ERIKSON, Cicely Sibyl
 Alexandra
  Dick, Alexandra
  Ericson, Sybil
  Erikson, Charlotte
  Hay, Frances
DICK-HUNTER, Noel
  N D H
DICK-LAUDER, *Sir* George
  Lauder, George Dick
DICKINSON, Anne Hepple
  Hepple, Anne
DICKSON, Emma Wells
  Eveleth, Stanford
DIENES, Zoltan
  Zed
DIETZ, Howard
  Freckles

DILCOCK, Noreen
  Christian, Jill
  Ford, Norrey
  Walford, Christian
DILLARD, Polly Hargis
  Hargis, Pauline
  Hargis, Polly
DILLON, E J
  Lanin, E B
DILNOT, George
  Froest, Frank
DINGLE, Aylward Edward
  Cotterell, Brian
  Sinbad
DINNER, William *and*
 MORUM, William
  Smith, Surrey
DISCH, Thomas M *and*
 SLADEK, John Thomas
  Demijohn, Thom
DIVINE, Arthur Durham
  Divine, David
  Rame, David
DIXON, Arthur
  Whye, Felix
DIXON, Ella Hepworth
  Wynman, Margaret
DOANE, Pelagie
  Hoffner, Dorothy
DODGE, Josephine Daskam
  Bacon, J D
DOHERTY, Ivy Ruby
  Hardwick, Sylvia
DOLBEY, Ethel M
  Hawthorne, E M D
DONALDSON, William
  Root, Henry

47

DONN-BYRNE, Brian Oswald
  Byrne, Donn
DONNELLY, Augustine
  Bullen Bear
DONOVAN, Peter
  P O'D
DONSON, Cyril
  Hartford, Via
  Kidd, Russell
  Mackin, Anita
  Pinder, Chuck
DOOLITTLE, Hilda
  H D
DORLING, Henry Taprell
  Taffrail
DORN, Dean M *and*
 CARLE, C E
  Morgan, Michael
DORR, Julia Caroline
  Thomas, Caroline
DOUGLAS, Archibald C
  Nemo
DOUGLAS, Keith
  Hatred, Peter
DOUGLAS, Mary
  Tew, Mary
DOUGLAS, Norman *and*
 FITZGIBBON, Elsa
  Normyx
DOUGLASS, Percival Ian
  Bear, I D
  Crane, Henry
DOWNEY, Edmund
  Allen, F M
DRACKETT, Phil
  King, Paul

DRAGO, Harry Sinclair
  Ermine, Will
  Lomax, Bliss
DRESSER, Davis
  Baker, Asa
  Blood, Matthew
  Carson, Sylvia
  Culver, Kathryn
  Davis, Don
  Halliday, Brett
  Shelley, Peter
  Wayne, Anderson
DRESSER, Davis *and*
 ROLLINS, Kathleen
  Debrett, Hal
DREW, Jane B
  Fry, Jane
DRIVER, Christopher
  Archestratus
DRUMMOND, Alison
  Schaw, Ruth
DRUMMOND, Cherry
  Evans, Cherry
DRUMMOND, Edith
  Carman, Dulce
DRUMMOND, Edith Victoria
  Chichester
  Stirling, Veda
DRUMMOND, Humphrey
  Ap Evans, Humphrey
DRYHURST, Michael John
  Darling, V H
DU BOIS, Theodora
  McCormick, Theodora
DUDDINGTON, Charles Lionel
  Campbell, Berkeley
  Nightingale, Charles

DUDLEY, Ernest
  Lydecker, J J
DUDLEY-SMITH, Trevor
  Black, Mansell
  Burgess, Trevor
  Fitzalan, Roger
  Hall, Adam
  North, Howard
  Rattray, Simon
  Scott, Warwick
  Smith, Caesar
  Trevor, Elleston
DUFF, Charles
  Chernichewski, Vladimir
DUFF, Douglas Valder
  Mainsail
  Savage, Leslie
  Stanhope, Douglas
  Wickloe, Peter
DUFFIELD, Dorothy Dean
  Duffield, Anne
DUFFY, Agnes Mary
  Vox, Agnes Mary
DUGGAN, Denise Valerie
  Egerton, Denise
DUGGLEBY, Jean Colbeck
  Kennedy, Diana
DUGHMAN, John Karl *and*
 DUGHMAN, Frieda Mae
  Churchill, Luanna
DUKE, Anita
  Hewett, Anita
DUKE, Madelaine
  Donne, Maxim
  Duncan, Alex
DUKENFIELD, William Claude
  Bogle, Charles
  Criblecoblis, Otis

DUKENFIELD, W C (cont'd)
  Fields, W C
  Jeeves, Mahatma Kane
DUNCAN, Actea
  Thomas, Carolyn
DUNCAN, Kathleen
  Simmons, Catherine
  Simmons, Kim
DUNCAN, Robert Lipscomb
  Roberts, James Hall
DUNCAN, Sara Jeanette
  Grafton, Garth
DUNCAN, William Murdoch
  Cassells, John
  Dallas, John
  Graham, Neill
  Locke, Martin
  Malloch, Peter
  Marshall, Lovat
DUNK, Margaret
  Duke, Margaret
DUNKERLEY, Elsie Jeanette
  Oxenham, Elsie Jeanette
DUNKERLEY, William Arthur
  Oxenham, John
DUNLOP, Agnes M R
  Kyle, Elisabeth
  Ralston, Jan
DUNN, Mary
  Faid, Mary
DUNNE, Finlay Peter
  Dooley, Martin
DUNNETT, Dorothy
  Halliday, Dorothy
DUNSING, Dee
  Mowery, Dorothy
DUPUY-MAZUEL, Henri
  Catalan, Henri

Real names

DURBRIDGE, Francis *and*
  MCCONNELL, James Douglas
  Rutherford
  Temple, Paul
DURGNAT, Raymond
  Green, O O
DURRELL, Lawrence
  Norden, Charles
DURST, Paul
  Bannon, Peter
  Chelton, John
  Cochran, Jeff
  Shane, John

EAGAN, Frances W
  Seeker, A
EAGLESTONE, Arthur Archibald
  Dataller, Roger
EAMES, Helen Mary
  Mercury
EARNSHAW, Patricia
  Mann, Patricia
EASTWOOD, Helen B
  Baxter, Olive
  Ramsay, Fay
EBBETT, Eve
  Burfield, Eva
EBBS, Robert
  Pitchford, Harry Ronald
  Severn, Richard
EBERLE, Irmengarde
  Allen, Allyn
  Carter, Phyllis Ann
EBERT, Arthur Frank
  Arthur, Frank
ECCLESHARE, Colin
  O P

EDELSTEIN, Hyman
  Synge, Don
EDEN, Dorothy
  Paradise, Mary
EDGAR, Alfred
  Lyndon, Barrie
EDGLEY, Leslie
  Bloomfield, Robert
EDGLEY, Leslie *and*
  EDGLEY, Mary
  Hastings, Brook
EDMISTON, Helen J M
  Robertson, Helen
EDMONDS, Helen
  Ferguson, Helen
  Kavan, Anna
EDMONDS, Ivy Gordon
  Gordon, Gary
  Gross, Gene
EDMONDSON, Sybil
  Armstrong, Sybil
EDMUNDSON, Joseph
  Burton, Conrad
  Jody, J M
EDWARD, Ann Elizabeth
  West, Anna
EDWARD, Irene
  Barr, Elizabeth
EDWARDES, Michael
  Cassilis, Robert
EDWARDS, Florence
  Edwards, Laurence
  Jolly, Susan
EDWARDS, Frederick Anthony
  Edwards, Charman
  Van Dyke, J
EDWARDS, George Graveley
  Graveley, George

50

EGLETON, Clive
  Tarrant, John
EHRENBERG, Golda
  Scott, Katherine
EHRENBORG, *Mrs* C G
  Trew, Cecil G
EHRLICH, Bettina
  Bettina
EIDEN, Paul *and*
 SABRE, Mel R
  Stagge, Delano
EIKER, Mathilde
  Evermay, March
EISENSTADT-JELEZNOV,
 Mikhail
  Argus, M K
ELDERSHAW, Flora Sydney *and*
 BARNARD, Marjorie Faith
  Eldershaw, M Barnard
ELGIN, Betty
  Kirby, Kate
ELIADES, David and
 WEBB, Robert Forrest
  Forrest, David
ELLERBECK, Rosemary
  L'Estrange, Anna
ELLERMAN, Annie Winifred
  Bryher
  Bryher, Winifred
ELLETT, Harold Pincton
  Burnaby, Nigel
ELLIOT, Andrew George
  MacAndrew, Rennie
ELLIOT, Christopher
  Marriot, John
ELLIOTT-CANNON, Arthur
 Elliott
  Cannon, Elliott

ELLIOTT-CANNON, A E (cont'd)
  Forde, Nicholas
  Martyn, Miles
ELLIS, Oliver
  Briony, Henry
ELLISON, James
  Brother Flavius
ELLISON, Joan
  Robertson, Elspeth
ELTING, Mary
  Brewster, Benjamin
  Cole, Davis
  Tatham, Campbell
ELWART, Joan Frances
  Elwart, Joan Potter
  Trawle, Mary Elizabeth
ELY, George Herbert *and*
 L'ESTRANGE, C James
  Strang, Herbert
EMANUEL, Victor Rousseau
  Egbert, H M
  Rousseau, Victor
EMERSON, Ernest
  Milky White
EMMS, Dorothy
  Charques, Dorothy
ENGEL, Lyle Kenyon
  Kenyon, Larry
  Kenyon, Paul
ENGLISH, Jean Ellen
  French, Ellen Jean
EPSTEIN, Beryl
  Williams, Beryl
EPSTEIN, Beryl *and*
 EPSTEIN, Samuel
  Allen, Adam
  Coe, Douglas

51

EPSTEIN, Samuel
  Campbell, Bruce
ERNST, Paul F
  Edson, George Alden
  Stern, Paul F
ESCHERLICH, Elsa Antonie
  Falk, Elsa
ESCOTT, Jack Leonard
  Scott, Jack S
ESTRIDGE, Robin
  Loraine, Philip
EVANS, Constance May
  Gray, Jane
  O'Nair, Mairi
EVANS, George
  Geraint, George
EVANS, George *and*
 EVANS, Kay
  Bird, Brandon
  Evans, Harris
EVANS, Glyn
  Ifans, Glyn
EVANS, Gwynfil Arthur
  Gwynne, Arthur
  Western, Barry
EVANS, Hilary Agard
  Agard, H E
EVANS, Hugh Austin
  Austin, Hugh
EVANS, Jean
  Shaw, Jane
EVANS, Julia
  Hobson, Polly
EVANS, Kathleen
  Kaye, Evelyn
EVANS, Kay *and* EVANS, George
  Bird, Brandon
  Evans, Harris

EVANS, Kay *and* EVANS, Stuart
  Tracey, Hugh
EVANS, Marguerite Florence
  Barcynska, Hélène, *Countess*
  Sandys, Oliver
EVANS, Stuart *and* EVANS, Kay
  Tracey, Hugh
EVELYN, John Michael
  Underwood, Michael
EVENS, George Bramwell
  Romany
EVERETT, *Mrs* H D
  Douglas, Theo
EVERSON, William Oliver
  Brother Antoninus
EWART, Ernest Andrew
  Cable, Boyd
EWART-BIGGS, Christopher
  Elliott, Charles
EWER, Monica
  Crosbie, Elizabeth
EYERLY, Jeanette *and*
 GRIFFITH, Valeria W
  Griffith, Jeannette
EYLES, Kathleen Muriel
  Tennant, Catherine
EYSSELINCK, Janet Gay
  Burroway, Janet

§ §

What are names but air?
—S. T. Coleridge — Names

§ §

FABRY, Joseph B
  Fabrizius, Peter

FADIMAN, Edwin J
  Mark, Edwina
FAIRBAIRN, R H
  R H F
FAIRBURN, Eleanor
  Carfax, Catherine
FAIRCHILD, William
  Cranston, Edward
FAIRFIELD, Cecily Isabel
  West, Rebecca
FAIRLIE, Gerard
  Sapper
FALK, Katherine *and others*
  Heptagon
FALK, Millicent *and others*
  Heptagon
FALL, William E
  Erimus
FALLA, Frank
  Sarnian
FANTHORPE, Robert Lionel
  Barton, Lee
  Fane, Bron
  Roberts, Lionel
  Thanet, Neil
  Thorpe, Trebor
  Torro, Pel
FANTONI, Barry
  Addio, E I
  Flannel, J C
  Gasket, Bamber
  Krin, Sylvie
  Slagg, Glenda
FANTONI, Barry *and*
 INGRAMS, Richard
  Thribb, E J
FARGUS, Fredrick John
  Conway, Hugh

FARJEON, Eve
  Jefferson, Sarah
FARJEON, Joseph Jefferson
  Swift, Anthony
FARMER, Philip José
  Trout, Kilgore
FARMERS, Eileen Elizabeth
  Lane, Elizabeth
FARQUHAR, Jesse Carlton *Jr*
  Scott, John-Paul
FARRELL, Anne Elisabeth
  Allaben, Anne E
FARRELL, Michael
  Burke, Michael
  Gulliver, Lemuel
FARRIS, John Lee
  Bracken, Steve
FARROW, R
  Vincent, John
FAST, Howard
  Cunningham, E V
  Ericson, Walter
FAST, Julius
  Barnett, Adam
FAUST, Frederick
  Austin, Frank
  Baxter, George Owen
  Bolt, Lee
  Brand, Max
  Butler, Walter C
  Challis, George
  Dawson, Peter
  Dexter, Martin
  Evan, Evin
  Evans, Evan
  Frederick, John
  Frost, Frederick
  Lawton, Dennis

FAUST, F (cont'd)
  M B
  Manning, David
  Morland, Peter Henry
  Owen, Hugh
  Silver, Nicholas
  Uriel, Henry
FAY, E F
  Bounder, The
FAY, Judith
  Nicholson, Kate
FEAGLES, Anita MacRae
  Macrae, Travis
FEAR, William H
  Reynolds, John
FEARING, Kenneth;
  BEDFORD-JONES, Henry *and*
  FRIEDE, Donald
  Bedford, Donald F
FEARN, John Russell
  Statten, Vargo
  Winiki, Ephraim
FEARON, Percy
  Poy
FEEHAN, *Sister* Mary Edward
  Clementia
FEILDING, Dorothy
  Fielding, A E
FEIWEL, Raphael Joseph
  Fyvel, T R
FELDMAN, Eugene P R
  Burroughs, Margaret
FELL, Frederick Victor
  Fredericks, Vic
FELLOWES-GORDON, Ian
  Collier, Douglas
  Gordon, Ian

FELLOWS, Dorothy Alice
  Collyer, Doric
  Hunt, Dorothy
FELSTEIN, Ivor
  Steen, Frank
FELTON, Ronald Oliver
  Welch, Ronald
FENN, Caroline K *and*
  MCGREW, Julia
  McGrew, Fenn
FENN, George Manville
  Manville, George
FENWICK-OWEN, Roderic
  Owen, Roderic
FERGUSON, Ida May
  Fergus, Dyjan
FERGUSON, Marilyn
  Renzelman, Marilyn
FERGUSON, Rachel
  Columbine
  Rachel
FERGUSON, William Blair
  Morton
  Morton, William
FERGUSSON HANNAY, *Lady*
  Leslie, Doris
FERNEYHOUGH, Roger Edmund
  Hart, R W
FETHERSTONHAUGH, Patrick
  William Edward
  Fetherston, Patrick
FETTER, Elizabeth
  Lees, Hannah
FEW, Eunice Beatty
  Few, Betty
FICKLING, Forrest E *and*
  FICKLING, Gloria
  Fickling, G G

FIELD, M J
  Freshfield, Mark
FIELDING, Alexander
  Fielding, Xan
FIELDING, Archibald
  Fielding, Dorothy
FIELDING, Molly Hill
  Field, Hill
FINK, Merton
  Finch, Matthew
  Finch, Merton
FINKEL, George
  Pennage, E M
FINLAY, Ian
  Philaticus
FINLEY, Martha
  Farquharson, Martha
FINN, *Sister* Mary Paulina
  Pine, M S
FINNEY, Jack
  Braden, Walter
FINNIN, Mary
  Hogarth, John
FIRTH, Violet Mary
  Fortune, Dion
FISCHER, Matthias Joseph
  Laurence, Robert
FISH, Robert Lloyd
  Lamprey, A C
  Pike, Robert
  Pike, Robert L
FISHER, Dorothea F C
  Canfield, Dorothy
FISHER, Douglas George
  Douglas, George
FISHER, John
  Piper, Roger

FISHER, Stephen Gould
  Fisher, Steve
  Gould, Stephen
  Lane, Grant
FISHER, Veronica Suzanne
  Veronique
FISHMAN, Jack *and*
  ORGILL, Douglas
  Gilman, J D
FITCHETT, W H
  Vedette
FITZGERALD, Beryl
  Hoffman, Louise
FITZGERALD, Desmond
  Gerald, Daryl
FITZ-GERALD, S J A
  Hannaford, Justin
FITZGERALD, Seymour Vesey
  S V F G
FITZGIBBON, Elsa *and*
  DOUGLAS, Norman
  Normyx
FITZHARDINGE, Joan Margaret
  Phipson, Joan
FITZMAURICE-KELLY, James
  J F-K
FLACK, Isaac Harvey
  Graham, Harvey
FLAGG, John
  Gearon, John
FLANAGAN, Ellen
  Raskin, Ellen
FLANAGAN, James
  Long, Myles
FLANNER, Janet
  Genêt
FLEET, William Henry
  Thistleton, *Hon* Francis

55

FLEISCHER, Anthony
  Hofmeyer, Hans
FLEISHMANN, Helle
  Kuthumi
FLEMING, Ronald
  Fleming, Rhoda
  Frazer, Renee
  Langley, Peter
FLETCHER, Constance
  Fleming, George
FLETCHER, Harry L Verne
  Fletcher, John
  Garden, John
  Hereford, John
FLETCHER, J S
  Son of the Soil
FLEUR, Anne Elizabeth
  Elizabeth, Anne
  Lancaster, A F
  Sari
FLEXNER, Stuart
  Fletcher, Adam
FLOREN, Lee
  Austin, Brett
  Franchon, Lisa
  Hall, Claudia
  Hamilton, Wade
  Harding, Matt
  Lang, Grace
  Nelson, Marguerite
  Sterling, Maria Sandra
  Thomas, Lee
  Turner, Len
  Watson, Will
FLUHARTY, Vernon L
  Carder, Michael
  O'Mara, Jim

FLYNN, *Sir* J A
  Oliver, Owen
FLYNN, Mary
  Livingstone, Margaret
FOCKE, E P W
  Ernest, Paul
FOLSOM, Franklin Brewster
  Brewster, Franklin
  Gorham, Michael
  Nesbit, Troy
FOOT, Michael
  Cassius
FOOT, Michael;
  HOWARD, Peter *and*
  OWEN, Frank
  Cato
FOOTE, Carol
  Odell, Carol
FOOTE, Carol *and* GILL, Travis
  Odell, Gill
FORBES, Deloris Stanton
  Forbes, Stanton
  Wells, Tobias
FORBES, Deloris Stanton *and*
  RYDELL, Helen
  Rydell, Forbes
FORBES, Marcelle Azra
  Morphy, *Countess*
FORD, Corey
  Riddell, John
FORD, T Murray
  Le Breton, Thomas
FORD, T W
  Clay, Weston
  Shott, Abel
FORDE, Claude Marie
  Claude

FORSTER, Reginald Kenneth
  Kendal, Robert
FORSYTHE, Robin
  Dingwall, Peter
FORTE, Christine
  Forster, Christine
FORTIER, Cora B
  Maxine
FOSDICK, Charles Austin
  Castlemon, Harry
FOSTER, Donn
  Saint-Eden, Dennis
FOSTER, George Cecil
  Seaforth
FOSTER, Jess Mary Mardon
  White, Heather
FOSTER, Marian Curtis
  Mariana
FOULDS, Elfrida Vipont
  Vipont, Charles
  Vipont, Elfrida
FOUTS, Edward Lee
  Lee, Edward
FOWKES, Aubrey
  Boy
FOWLER, Eric
  Mardle, Jonathan
FOWLER, Gene
  Long, Peter
FOWLER, Helen
  Foley, Helen
FOWLER, Henry Watson
  Egomet
  Quilibet
  Quillet
FOWLER, Kenneth A
  Brooker, Clark

FOX, Charles
  Jeremy, Richard
FOX, Frank
  Renar, Frank
FOX, Gardner F
  Cooper, Jefferson
  Gardner, Jeffrey
  Kendricks, James
  Matthews, Kevin
FOX, James
  Holmes, Grant
FOX, Mona Alexis
  Brand, Mona
FOX, Norman Arnold
  Sabin, Mark
FOX, Winifred *and others*
  Heptagon
FOXALL, P A
  Vincent, Jim
FRAENKEL, Heinrich
  Assiac
FRANCE-HAYHURST,
  Evangeline
  France, Evangeline
FRANCES, Stephen Daniel
  Janson, Hank
FRANCIS, Arthur Bruce Charles
  Bruce, Charles
FRANCIS, Stephen D
  Williams, Richard
FRANCK, Frederick S
  Fredericks, Frank
FRANK, *Mrs* M J
  A L O M
  Lady of Manitoba, A
FRANK, Waldo David
  Search-Light

FRANKAU, Julia Davis
  Danby, Frank
FRANKAU, Pamela
  Naylor, Eliot
FRANKLIN, Cynthia
  Neville, C J
FRANKLIN, Stella Maria
  Sarah Miles
  Brent, *of Bin Bin*
FRASER-HARRIS, D
  Grange, Ellerton
FRAZEE, Steve
  Jennings, D
FRAZER, James Ian Arbuthnot
  Frazer, Shamus
FREDE, Richard
  Frederics, Jocko
  Macdowell, Frederics
FREEDGOOD, Morton
  Godey, John
FREELING, Nicolas
  Nicolas, F R E
FREEMAN, Gillian
  Elizabeth, von S
  George, Eliot
  S, Elizabeth von
FREEMAN, Kathleen
  Cory, Caroline
  Fitt, Mary
  Wick, Stuart Mary
FREEMAN, R Austin
  Ashdown, Clifford
FREEMAN, R Austin *and*
  PITCAIRN, John James
  Ashdown, Clifford
FREEMANTLE, Brian
  Evans, Jonathan
  Winchester, Jack

FRENCH, Alice
  Thanet, Octave
FREWER, Glyn
  Lewis, Mervyn
FREWIN, Leslie Ronald
  Dupont, Paul
FREY, Charles Weiser
  Findley, Ferguson
FRIEDBERG, Gertrude
  Tonkongy, Gertrude
FRIEDE, Donald;
  FEARING, Kenneth *and*
  BEDFORD-JONES, Henry
  Bedford, Donald F
FRIEDLANDER, Peter
  French, Fergus
FRIEDMAN, Eve Rosemary
  Tibber, Robert
  Tibber, Rosemary
FRIEND, Oscar Jerome
  Jerone, Owen Fox
FROST, C Vernon
  Child, Charles B
FROST, J W
  Glenelg
FROST, Kathleen Margaret
  Merivale, Margaret
FRY, Clodagh Micaela Gibson
  Gavin, Amanda
FRYEFIELD, Maurice P
  Brooks, W A
  Brooks, William Allan
  Holmes, Arnold W
FTYARAS, Louis George
  Alexander, L G
FULLBROOK, Gladys
  Hutchinson, Patricia

FULLER, Edmund
  Amicus Curiae
FULLER, Harold Edgar
  Fuller, Ed
  Fulman, Al
FULLER, Henry B
  Page, Stanton
FULLER, James Franklin
  Ignotus
FULLERTON, Alexander
  Fox, Anthony
FURLONG, Vivienne
  Welburn, Vivienne
FURPHY, Joseph
  Collins, Tom
FYTTON ARMSTRONG, T I
  Gawsworth, John

§ §

James Gatz—that was really, or at least legally, his name.
—F. Scott Fitzgerald. The Great Gatsby

§ §

GADDIS, Peggy
  Craig, Georgia
GAINES, Robert
  Summerscales, Rowland
GALBRAITH, J K
  Epernay, Mark
GALL, Michel
  Richardson, Humphrey
GALLAGHER, Frank
  Hogan, David

GALSWORTHY, John
  Sinjohn, John
GANDLEY, Kenneth Royce
  Jacks, Oliver
  Royce, Kenneth
GANTNER, Neilma B
  Sidney, Neilma
GARBER, Nellia B
  Berg, Ila
GARD, Joyce
  Reeves, Joyce
GARDINER, Alfred George
  Alpha of the Plough
GARDINER, Dorothea Frances
  Frank, Theodore
GARDNER, Erle Stanley
  Corning, Kyle
  Fair, A A
  Green, Charles M
  Kendrake, Carleton
  Kenny, Charles J
  Parr, Robert
  Tillray, Les
GARDNER, Jerome
  Gilchrist, John
GARFIELD, Brian
  Garland, Bennett
  Hawk, Alex
  O'Brian, Frank
  Ward, Jonas
  Wynne, Brian
  Wynne, Frank
GARGILL, Morris *and*
 HEARNE, John
  Morris, John
GARNER, Hugh
  Warwick, Jarvis

GARNETT, David
  Burke, Leda
GARRATT, Alfred
  Garratt, Teddie
GARRETT, Randall
  Bupp, Walter
  Gordon, David
  Langart, Darrel T
GARRETT, Randall *and*
 JANIFER, Laurence M
  Phillips, Mark
GARRETT, Randall *and*
 SILVERBERG, Robert
  Randall, Robert
GARRETT, Winifred Selina
  Dean, Lyn
GARRISON, Webb Black
  Webster, Gary
GARRITY, David James
  Garrity
GARROD, John Williams *and*
 PAYNE, Ronald Charles
  Castle, John
GARVEY, Eric William
  Herne, Eric
GARVIN, Amelia Beers (Warnock)
  Hale, Katherine
GARVIN, J L
  Calehas
GARWOOD, Godfrey Thomas
  Thomas, Gough
GASE, Richard
  Gale, John
GASPAROTTI, Elizabeth
  Seifert, Elizabeth
GASTON, William J
  Bannatyne, Jack

GAUNT, Arthur N
  Nettleton, Arthur
GAUTIER-SMITH, Peter Claudius
  Conway, Peter
GEEN, Clifford
  Berkley, Tom
GEISEL, Theodor Seuss
  Dr Seuss
  Lesieg, Theo
GELB, Norman
  Mallery, Amos
GEORGE, Peter
  Peters, Bryan
GEORGE, Robert Esmonde
  Gordon
  Sencourt, Robert
GERAHTY, Digby George
  Standish, Robert
GERARD, Edwin
  Trooper Gerardy
GERMANO, Peter
  Cord, Barry
  Kane, Jim
GERSHON, Karen
  Tripp, Karen
GERSON, Noel Bertram
  Edwards, Samuel
  Lewis, Paul
  Phillips, Leon
  Vail, Philip
  Vaughan, Carter A
GESSNER, Lynne
  Clarke, Merle
GIBBS, Norah
  Boyd, Prudence
  Garland, Lisette
  Ireland, Noelle
  Merrill, Lynne

GIBBS, N (cont'd)
  Ritchie, Claire
  Shayne, Nina
  Wayne, Heather
  Whittington, Sara
GIBSON, G H
  Ironbark
GIBSON, Walter Brown
  Brown, Douglas
  Grant, Maxwell
GIBSON, William
  Mass, William
GIFFORD, James Noble
  Noble, Emily
  Saxon, John
GILBERT, Ruth Gallard
  Ainsworth, Ruth
GILBERT, William Schwenck
  Bab
  Tomline, F Latour
GILBERTSON, Mildred
  Gilbert, Nan
  Mendel, Jo
GILCHRIST, Alan
  Cowan, Alan
GILDEN, Katya *and*
 GILDEN, Bert
  Gilden, K B
GILDERDALE, Michael
  Flemming, Sarah
GILL, T M
  Sabattis
GILL, Travis *and*
 FOOTE, Carol
  Odell, Gill
GILL, Winifred *and others*
  Heptagon

GILLES, Daniel
  Johnson, Marigold
GILLHAM, Elizabeth Wright
 Enright
  Enright, Elizabeth
GILMER, Elizabeth Meriwether
  Dix, Dorothy
GILZEAN, Elizabeth Houghton
  Houghton, Elizabeth
  Hunton, Mary
GIRDLESTON, A H
  A H G
GITTINGS, Jo
  Manton, Jo
GLASKIN, G M
  Jackson, Neville
GLASSCO, John
  Bayer, Sylvia
  Buffy
  Colman, George
  Colson-Haig, S
  Davignon, Grace
  Eady, W P R
  Eddy, Albert
  Gooch, Silas N
  Henderson, George
  Nudleman, Nordyk
  Okada, Hideki
  Saint-Luc, Jean de
  Underwood, Miles
GLASSCOCK, Anne Bonner
  Bonner, Michael
GLEADOW, Rupert
  Case, Justin
GLEMSER, Bernard
  Napier, Geraldine
GLEN, Duncan Munro
  Munro, Ronald Eadie

61

GLENTON, Stella Lennox
  King, Stella
GLIDDEN, Frederick Dilley
  Short, Luke
GLIDDEN, Jonathan H
  Dawson, Peter
GLOVER, Modwena
  Sedgwick, Modwena
GLUCK, Sinclair
  Danning, Melrod
GOAMAN, Muriel
  Cox, Edith
GODFREY, Frederick M
  Cronheim, F G
GODFREY, Lionel Robert
  Holcombe
  Kennedy, Elliott
  Mitchell, Scott
GODLEY, Robert
  James, Franklin
GOETCHEUS, Carolyn
  Lynn, Carol
GOGGAN, John Patrick
  Patrick, John
GOHM, Douglas Charles
  O'Connell, Robert Frank
GOLBERG, Harry
  Grey, Harry
GOLDBERG, Nathan Ralph
  Ralph, Nathan
GOLDEN, Dorothy
  Dennison, Dorothy
GOLDFRANK, *Mrs* Herbert
  Kay, Helen
GOLDIE, Kathleen Annie
  Fidler, Kathleen
GOLDING, Louise
  Davies, Louise

GOLDMAN, William
  Longbaugh, Harry
GOLDSTON, Robert
  Conroy, Robert
GOLLER, Celia Margaret
  Fremlin, Celia
GOLSWORTHY, Arnold
  Holcombe, Arnold
  Jingle
GOMPERTZ, Martin Louis
  Alan
  Ganpat
GOOD, Edward
  Oyved, Moysheh
GOODAVAGE, Joseph F
  Greystone, Alexander A
  Savage, Steve
GOODCHILD, George
  Dare, Alan
  Reid, Wallace Q
  Templeton, Jesse
GOODE, Arthur Russell
  Russell, Arthur
GOODEY, P E
  Condon, Patricia
GOODMAN, George Jerome W
  Smith, Adam
GOODMAN, George Jerome *and*
  KNOWLTON, Winthrop
  Goodman, Winthrop
GOODSPEED, D J
  McLeish, Dougal
GOODWIN, Geoffrey
  Gemini
  Telstar
  Topicus

GOODWIN, Harold Leland *and*
 HARKINS, Peter J
  Blaine, John
GOODWIN, Suzanne
  Ebel, Suzanne
GOODYEAR, Stephen Frederick
  Taylor, Sam
GOODYKOONTZ, William F
  Goode, Bill
GORDON, Alan Bacchus
  Ordon, A Lang
GORDON, *Reverend* Charles
 William
  Connor, Ralph
GORDON, Gordon *and*
 GORDON, Mildred
  Gordons, The
GORDON, Jan
  Gore, William
GORDON, Robert I
  London, Anne
  London, Robert
GOREY, Edward St John
  Blutig, Eduard
  Grode, Redway
  Weary, Ogdred
  Wodge, Dreary
GOSLING, Veronica
  Henriques, Veronica
GOSSMAN, Oliver
  Clyde, Craig
GOTTLIEBSEN, Ralph Joseph
  Scott, O R
GOTTSCHALK, Laura Riding
  Riding, Laura
GOVAN, Mary Christine
  Allerton, Mary
  Darby, J N

GOWING, Sidney Floyd
  Goodwin, John
GOYDER, Margot *and*
 NEVILLE, Ann
  Neville, Margot
GOYNE, Richard
  Courage, John
GRABER, George Alexander
  Cordell, Alexander
GRAHAM, Charles
  Montrose, David
GRAHAM, James Maxtone
  Anstruther, James
GRAHAM, *Dr* Joan
  Medica
GRAHAM, Maude Fitzgerald
  Graham, Susan
GRAINGER, Francis Edward
  Hill, Headon
GRAMONT, Sanche de
  Morgan, Ted
GRANT, Donald *and*
 WILSON, William
  Ness, K T
GRANT, Hilda Kay
  Grant, Kay
  Hilliard, Jan
GRANT, James Miller
  Balfour, Grant
GRANT, John
  Gash, Jonathan
GRANT, M H
  Linesman
  Scolopax
GRANT, *Lady* Sybil
  Scot, Neil
GRANT, William
  Onlooker

63

GRAVELEY, G C
    Grayson, Daphne
GRAVES, Clotilda Inez Mary
    Dehan, Richard
GRAVES, Robert
    Doyle, John
GRAY, Clement
    Daybreak
GRAY, Dorothy K
    Haynes, Dorothy K
GRAY, K E
    Grant, Eve
GRAY, Lindsay Russell Nixon
    Lemon, Grey
GRAY, Simon
    Reade, Hamish
GRAY, Terence J S
    Wei Wu Wei
GRAYDON, William Murray
    Gordon, William Murray
    Murray, William
GRAYLAND, Valerie M
    Belvedere, Lee
    Subond, Valerie

§ §

*A good name is better than
precious ointment.
Bible. Ecclesiastes, 7.1*

§ §

GREALEY, Tom
    Southworth, Louis
GREAVES, Michael
    Callum, Michael

GREEN, Alan Baer *and*
    BRODIE, Julian Paul
    Denbie, Roger
GREEN, Charles Henry
    Sandhurst, B G
GREEN, Dorothy
    Auchterlonie, Dorothy
GREEN, Elizabeth Sara
    Tresilian, Liz
GREEN, Evelyn Everett
    Adair, Cecil
GREEN, Lalage Isobel
    March, Hilary
    Pulvertaft, Lalage
GREEN, Maxwell
    Cabby with camera
GREEN, Peter
    Delaney, Denis
GREEN, Peter *Canon*
    Artifex
GREEN, T
    Ramsey, Michael
GREENAWAY, Gladys
    Manners, Julia
GREENBERG, Jack
    Greenhill, Jack
GREENBERG, Joanne
    Green, Hannah
GREENE, *Sir* Hugh
    Eleigh, Sebastian
GREENE, Sigrid
    De Lima, Sigrid
GREENE, Ward
    Dudley, Frank
GREENER, William Oliver
    Gerrare, Wirt
GREENHILL, Elizabeth Ann
    Giffard, Ann

GREENLAND, W K
King, W Scott
GREENOUGH, William Parker
Montauban, G de
GREENWOOD, A E
Hawthorne, Marx
GREENWOOD, Augustus George
Archer, Owen
GREENWOOD, Julia E C
Askham, Francis
GREENWOOD, T E
McCabe, Rory
GREER, Germaine
Blight, Rose
GREGG, Hilda
Grier, Sydney C
GREIG, Maysie
Ames, Jennifer
Barclay, Ann
Thompson, Madeline
Warren, Mary D
GRESHAM, Elizabeth F
Grey, Robin
GRIBBEN, James
James, Vincent
GRIBBLE, Leonard Reginald
Browning, Sterry
Cody, Stetson
Denver, Lee
Grant, Landon
Grex, Leo
Grey, Louis
Marlowe, Piers
Muir, Dexter
Sanders, Bruce
GRIERSON, Walter
Enquiring Layman

GRIEVE, Alexander Haig Glanville
Glanville, Alec
GRIEVE, Christopher Murray
MacDiarmid, Hugh
GRIEVESON, Mildred
Flemming, Cardine
Mather, Anne
GRIFFIN, Jonathan
Thurlow, Robert
GRIFFIN, Vivian Cory
Crosse, Victoria
GRIFFITH, Valeria W *and*
EYERLY, Jeannette
Griffith, Jeannette
GRIFFITHS, Aileen Esther
Passmore, Aileen E
GRIFFITHS, Charles
Bold, Ralph
GRIFFITHS, Jack
Griffith, Jack
GRIMSTEAD, Hettie
Manning, Marsha
GRINDAL, Richard
Grayson, Richard
GRINGHUIS, Richard H
Gringhuis, Dirk
GROSSMAN, Judith
Hamilton, Ernest
Merril, Judith
Sharon, Rose
Thorstein, Eric
GROSSMAN, Judith *and*
KORNBLUTH, Cyril M
Judd, Cyril
GRUBER, Frank
Acre, Stephen
Boston, Charles K
Vedder, John K

GUARIENTO, Ronald
  Parks, Ron
GUEST, Enid
  Quin, Shirland
GUEST, Francis Harold
  Spenser, James
GUGGISBERG, *Sir* F G
  Ubique
GUIGO, Ernest Philip
  Holt, E Carleton
GUINNESS, Maurice
  Brewer, Mike
  Gale, Newton
GUIRDHAM, Arthur
  Eaglesfield, Francis
GULICK, Grover C
  Gulick, Bill
GUNN, John Angus Lancaster
  Hall, B
GUTHRIE, Norman Gregor
  Crichton, John
GUTHRIE, P R
  Pain, Barry
GUTHRIE, Thomas Anstey
  Anstey, F
GUYONVARCH, Irene
  Pearl, Irene
GWINN, Christine M
  Kelway, Christine
GWINN, William R
  Randall, William
GWYNN, Audrey
  Thomson, Audrey
GWYNN, Ursula Grace
  Leigh, Ursula
GYE, Harold Frederick Neville
  Gye, Hal
  Hackston, James

HAARER, Alec Ernest
  Shanwa
HADFIELD, Alan
  Dale, Robin
HAGAN, Stelia F
  Hawkins, John
HAIG, Emily Alice
  B L H
  E H
  Field, Robert à
  Hastings, Beatrice
  Longclothes, Ninon de
  Morning, Alice
  Tina, Beatrice
  Triformis, D
HALDANE, Robert Aylmer
  Square, Charlotte
HALE, Ethela Ruth
  (*Mrs* Fellowes)
  Hodgen, J T
HALE, Julian Anthony Stuart
  Stuart, Anthony
HALE, Kathleen
  McClean, Kathleen
HALE, Sylvia
  Barnard, Nancy
HALEY, W J
  Sell, Joseph
HALL, Bennie Caroline
  Hall, Bennet
HALL, Emma L
  St Claire, Yvonne
HALL, Frederick
  Hall, Patrick
HALL, Irene
  Gough, Irene
HALL, Josef Washington
  Close, Upton

HALL, Marie
  Boas, Marie
HALL, Oakley Maxwell
  Manor, Jason
HALL, Verner
  Hustle, Hugh
HAMBLETON, Phyllis MacVean
  Vane, Phillipa
HAMILTON, Alex
  Pooter
HAMILTON, Cecily
  Hamilton, Max
  Rae, Scott
HAMILTON, Charles Harold St
  John
  Clifford, Martin
  Conquest, Owen
  Redway, Ralph
  Richards, Frank
  Richards, Hilda
HAMILTON, Gerald
  Weston, Patrick
HAMILTON, *Sir* George
  Rostrevor
  Rostrevor, George
HAMILTON, Leigh Brackett
  Brackett, Leigh
HAMILTON, Mary A A
  Iconoclast
HAMILTON, Mary Margaret Kaye
  Kaye, Mary Margaret
HAMILTON-WILKES, Edwin
  Hamilton-Wilkes, Monty
  Uncle Monty
HAMMERTON, J A
  J A H
HAMMETT, Dashiell
  Collinson, Peter

HAMMOND, Lawrence
  Francis, Victor
HAMMOND-INNES, Ralph
  Hammond, Ralph
  Innes, Hammond
HAMON, Louis *Count*
  Cheiro
HAMPDEN, John
  Montagu, Robert
HANKINSON, Charles J
  Holland, Clive
HANLEY, Clifford
  Calvin, Henry
HANLEY, Jack
  Harvey, Gene
HANLEY, James
  Bentley, James
  Shone, Patric
HANNA, Frances
  Nichols, Fan
HANNAY, James Owen
  Birmingham, George A
HANZELON, Robert M
  De Hart, Robert
HARBAGE, Alfred
  Kyd, Thomas
HARBAUGH, Thomas Chalmers
  Holmes, *Captain* Howard
HARBINSON-BRYANS, Robert
  Bryans, Robin
  Harbinson, Robert
HARDINGE, George
  Milner, George
HARDINGE, Rex
  Capstan
HARDISON, O B
  Bennett, H O

67

HARDWICK, Mollie
  Atkinson, Mary
HARDWICK, Richard
  Holmes, Rick
  Honeycutt, Richard
HARDY, Jane
  Boileau, Marie
HARDY, Marjorie
  Hardy, Bobbie
HARE, Walter B
  Burns, Mary
HARKINS, Peter
  Adams, Andy
HARKINS, Peter J *and*
 GOODWIN, Harold Leland
  Blaine, John
HARKNETT, Terry
  Gilman, George G
  Hardy, Adam
  Hedges, Joseph
  Pike, Charles R
HARLAND, Henry
  Luska, Sidney
HARMAN, Richard
  Martin, Richard
HARPER, Edith
  Flamank, E
HARRELL, Irene Burk
  Amor, Amos
  Waylan, Mildred
HARRIS, *Mrs* Herbert
  Short, Francis
HARRIS, Ida Fraser
  Proctor, Ida
HARRIS, Joel Chandler
  Uncle Remus

HARRIS, John
  Hebden, Mark
  Hennessy, Max
HARRIS, John Wyndham Parkes
 Lucas Beynon
  Beynon, John
  Harris, John Beynon
  Parkes, Lucas
  Parkes, Wyndham
  Wyndham, John
HARRIS, Marion Rose
  Young, Rose
HARRIS, Mark
  Wiggen, Henry W
HARRIS, Pamela
  Meinikoff, Pamela
HARRIS, Polly Anne Colver
  Colver, Anne
  Harris, Colver
HARRIS, Rona Olive
  O'Harris, Pixie
HARRIS, William
  Harris, Peter
HARRIS-BURLAND, John B
  Burland, Harris
HARRISON, Chester William
  Hickok, Will
HARRISON, Constance Cary
  Refugitta
HARRISON, *Mrs* E E
  Motte, Nel
HARRISON, Elizabeth C
  Cavanna, Betty
  Headley, Elizabeth
HARRISON, Harry
  Dempsey, Hank
HARRISON, J H
  Wynyard, John

HARRISON, John Gilbert
  Gilbert, John
HARRISON, Julia
  Richmond, Fiona
HARRISON, Michael
  Downes, Quentin
  Egremont, Michael
HARRISON, Philip
  Carmichael, Philip
HARRISON, Richard Motte
  Motte, Peter
HARRISON, Susie Frances
  Seranus
HART, Caroline Horowitz
  Winters, Mary K
HARTHOORN, Susanne
  Hart, Suzanne
HARTIGAN, Patrick Joseph
  O'Brien, John
HARTLEY, Ellen R
  Raphael, Ellen
HARTMANN, Helmut Henry
  Seymour, Henry
HARVEY, Charles
  Willoughby, Hugh
HARVEY, John
  Dancer, J B
  Hart, Jon
HARVEY, Margaret Susan Janet
  Michelmore, Susan
HARVEY, Peter Noel
  Day, Adrian
  Peters, Noel
HARVEY, William
  Denovan, Saunders
HASLAM, Nicky
  Hopper, Sam
  Parsons, Paul

HASSON, James
  De Salignac, Charles
HASWELL, C J D
  Foster, George
  Haswell, Jock
HAUCK, Louise Platt
  Landon, Louise
HAUSMAN, Leon Augustus
  Poe, Bernand
HAVERS, Dora
  Gift, Theo
HAWKINS, *Sir* Anthony Hope
  A H
  Hope, Anthony
HAWTON, Hector
  Curzon, Virginia
HAYES, Catherine E Simpson
  Markwell, Mary
  Yukon Bill
HAYES, Herbert Edward Elton
  Elton, H E
HAYNES, John Harold
  Wake, G B
HAYNES DIXON, Margaret
  Rumer
  Godden, Rumer
HAYS, Peter
  Jeffries, Ian
HAZLEWOOD, Rex
  Delta
  Keneu
HEADLEY, Elizabeth
  Allen, Betsy
HEAL, Edith
  Page, Eileen
  Powers, Margaret
HEALD, Tim
  Lancaster, David

HEARD, Henry Fitzgerald
 Heard, Gerald
HEARNE, John *and*
 GARGILL, Morris
 Morris, John
HEAVEN, Constance
 Fecher, Constance
HEBERDEN, Mary Violet
 Leonard, Charles L
HECTOR, Barbara
 Barrie, Hester
HEELIS, Beatrix
 Potter, Beatrix
HEGEDUS, Adam de
 Garland, Rodney
HEILBRUN, Carolyn
 Cross, Amanda
HEINEY, Donald William
 Harris, Macdonald
HEINLEIN, Robert A
 Macdonald, Anson
 Monroe, Lyle
 Saunders, Caleb
HEISS, John Stanger
 Asche, Oscar
HEITNER, Iris
 James, Robert
HEMING, Dempster E
 Dempster, Guy
HEMING, Jack C W
 Western-Holt, J C
HEMINGWAY, Ernest
 Hadley, John
HEMPSTEAD, Charles Edward
 Charles, Edward
HENDERSON, Archibald
 Steele, Erskine

HENDERSON, Donald Landels
 Bridgwater, Donald
 Landels, D H
 Landels, Stephanie
HENDERSON, James Leal
 Currier, Jay L
HENDERSON, James Maddock
 Danvers, Peter
 Jordan, Bryn
HENDERSON, Le Grand
 Le Grand
HENDRY, Frank Coutts
 Shalimar
HENHAM, E J
 Trevena, John
HENKLE, Henrietta
 Buckmaster, Henrietta
HENLEY, Art
 Eric, Kenneth
 Jones, Webb
HENNISSART, Martha *and*
 LATIS, Mary J
 Dominic, R B
 Lathen, Emma
HENSLEY, Sophia Margaret
 Try-Davies, J
HEPBURN, Edith Alice Mary
 Wickham, Anna
HEPBURN, Thomas Nicoll
 Setoun, Gabriel
HEPPELL, Mary
 Clare, Marguerite
 Heppell, Blanche
HERAPATH, Theodora
 Capelle, Anne
HERBERT, *Sir* Alan Patrick
 A P H
 Haddock, Albert

HERBERT, John
  Simple, Peter
HERBERT, Robert Dudley
  Sidney Powys
  Adams, R D
  Alpha Crucis
  R D A
HERMAN, Alan
  Allan, Ted
HERN, Anthony
  Hope, Andrew
HERNDEN, Beryl *and*
  BALFOUR, Eve
  Hearnden, Balfour
HERON-ALLEN, Edward
  Blayre, Christopher
HERRON, Elsie Ellerington
  Elsey, J J
HERTZBERG, Nancy
  Keesing, Nancy
HETHERINGTON, Keith James
  Conway, Keith
  Keith, James
HEUMAN, William
  Kramer, George
HEWETSON, Sara
  Dicant, V L
HEWISON, Robert John Petrie
  Petrie, John
HEWITT, Cecil Rolph
  Rolph, C H
HEWITT, Kathleen Douglas
  Martin, Dorothea
HEWSON, Irene Dale
  Ross, Jean
HEYDON, J K
  Trevarthen, Hal P

HEYER, Georgette
  Martin, Stella
HIBBERT, Eleanor Alice Burford
  Burford, Eleanor
  Carr, Philippa
  Ford, Elbur
  Holt, Victoria
  Kellow, Kathleen
  Plaidy, Jean
  Tate, Ellalice
HIBBS, John
  Blyth, John
HICKEN, Una
  Kindler, Asta
HICKEY, Madelyn E
  De Lacy, Louise
  Eastlund, Madelyn
  Hickey, Lyn
  Sullivan, Eric Harrison
HICKS, E L *Bishop of Lincoln*
  Quartus
HICKS, Tyler Gregory
  Murphy, Louis J
HIGGINBOTHAM, Anne D
  Higginbotham, Anne T
  McIntosh, Ann T
HIGGINS, Charles
  Dall, Ian
HIGGINS, Margaret
  O'Brien, Bernadette
HIGGINSON, Henry Clive
  Theta, Eric Mark
HIGGS, Alec S
  Stansbury, Alec
HIGHSMITH, Patricia
  Morgan, Claire
HILL, Brian
  Magill, Marcus

71

HILL, Douglas
  Hillman, Martin
HILL, *Mrs* E E
  Southern Cross
HILL, Grace
  MacDonald, Marcia
HILL, John Alexander
  Skeever, Jim
HILL, Mavis
  Barrister, A
HILL, Reginald
  Ruell, Patrick
HILLS, Frances E
  Mercer, Frances
HILLSTROM, Joseph
  Hill, Joe
HILLYARD, Mary Dorothea
  Kellway, Mary D
HILTON, James
  Trevor, Glen
HILTON, John Buxton
  Stanley, Warwick
HINCKS, Cyril Malcolm
  Coulsdon, John
  Dayle, Malcolm
  Gee, Osman
  Howard, John M
  Malcolm, Charles
  Malcolm, Ronald
HINES, Dorothea
  De Culwen, Dorothea
HIRD, Neville
  Meyer, Henry J
HIRST, Gillian
  Baxter, Gillian
HISCOCK, Eric
  E H
  Whitefriar

HISCOCK, Leslie
  Marsh, Patrick
HITCHENS, Dolores
  Birkley, Dolan
  Burke, Noel
  Olsen, D B
HITCHIN, Martin
  Mewburn, Martin
HOAR, Peter
  Amberley, Simon
HOAR, Roger Sherman
  Farley, Ralph Milne
HOBSBAWM, E J
  Newton, Francis
HODDER, Alfred
  Walton, Francis
HODDER-WILLIAMS,
  Christopher
  Brogan, James
HODGE, Horace Emerton
  Hodge, Merton
HODGES, Barbara K
  Cambridge, Elizabeth
HODGES, Doris Marjorie
  Hunt, Charlotte
HOFDORP, Pim
  Geerlink, Will
HOFF, Harry Summerfield
  Cooper, William
HOFFENBERG, Mason
  Drake, Hamilton
  Perez, Faustino
HOFFENBERG, Mason *and*
  SOUTHERN, Terry
  Kenton, Maxwell
HOFFMAN, Anita
  Fettsman, Ann

HOGAN, Ray
  Ringold, Clay
HOGAN, Robert Jasper
  Cantrell, Wade B
  Jasper, Bob
HOGARTH, Grace
  Gay, Amelia
HOGARTH, Grace *and*
 NORTON, Alice Mary
  Weston, Allen
HOGBEN, Lancelot Thomas
  Calvin, Kenneth
HOGBIN, Herbert
  Hogbin, Ian
HOGG, Beth
  Grey, Elizabeth
HOGG, Michael
  Simple, Peter
HOGUE, Wilbur Owings
  Shannon, Carl
HOKE, Helen L
  Sterling, Helen
  Troy, Alan
HOLBECHE, Philippa
  Shore, Philippa
HOLDAWAY, Marjorie F
  Japonica
HOLDAWAY, Neville Aldridge
  Temple-Ellis, N A
HOLDEN, J R
  Joystick
HOLDEN, Raymond
  Peckham, Richard
HOLLEY, Marietta
  Jemyma
  Josiah Allen's Wife

HOLLIDAY, Joseph
  Bosco, Jack
  Dale, Jack
HOLLIDAY, Robert Cortes
  Hill, Murray
HOLLIS, Christopher
  Somerset, Percy
HOLLOWS, Norman F *and*
 BRADLEY, Ian
  Duplex
HOLMES, Charles Henry
  Adams, Clayton
HOLMES, Daniel Henry
  Henry, Daniel Jr
HOLMES, Llewellyn Perry
  Hardin, Dave
  Stuart, Matt
HOLMES, Peter
  Fenwick, Peter
HOLMSTROM, John Eric
  Gellert, Roger
HOLROYD, Ethel Mary
  Cookridge, John Michael
  Marshall, Beverley
HOLT, Henry
  Hopkins, Stanley
HOLT, Margaret Van Vechten
  Holt, Rackham
HOME-GALL, Edward Reginald
  Clive, Clifford
  Dale, Edwin
  Hall, Rupert
  Home-Gall, Reginald
HOMERSHAM, Basil Henry
  Manningham, Basil
HOOD, Torrey
  Bevans, Torre
  Torrey, Marjorie

73

ḤOOK, Alfred Samuel
  Colton, A J
HOOK, H Clarke
  Harvey, Ross
HOOKE, Charles W
  Fielding, Howard
HOOKHAM, Margaret Evelyn
  Fonteyn, Margot
HOPE, Charles Evelyn Graham
  Pelham, Anthony
HOPE, Essex
  Smith, Essex
HOPKINS, Robert Sydney
  Rostand, Robert
HOPLEY-WOOLRICH, Cornell
 George
  Hopley, George
  Irish, William
  Woolrich, Cornell
HOPP, Signe
  Zinken
HOPSON, William L
  Sims, John
HORKAN, Nelle Irwin
  Edwards, Ellen
HORLER, Sydney
  Cavendish, Peter
  Heritage, Martin
  Standish, J O
HORNBERGER, H Richard
  Hooker, Richard
HORNBY, John Wilkinson
  Brent, Calvin
  Grace, Joseph
  Hornby, John
  Summers, Gordon
HORNBY, Lesley
  Twiggy
74

HORNE, Geoffrey
  North, Gil
HORSFIELD, Richard Edward
  Gaunt, M B
HOSIE, Stanley William
  Stanley, Michael
HOSKEN, Alice Cecil Seymour
  Stanton, Coralie
HOSKEN, Clifford James Wheeler
  Keverne, Richard
HOSKIN, Cyril Henry
  Rampa, T Lobsang
HOUGH, Richard Alexander
  Carter, Bruce
HOUGH, Stanley Bennett
  Gordon, Rex
  Stanley, Bennett
HOUNSFIELD, Joan
  Wheezy
HOUSEMAN, Lorna
  Westall, Lorna
HOVICK, Rose Louise
  Lee, Gypsy Rose
HOWARD, Felicity
  Longfield, Jo
HOWARD, Herbert Edmund
  Philmore, R
HOWARD, Hilda Glynn
  Glynn-Ward, H
  Glynn-Ward, Hilda
HOWARD, James Arch
  Fisher, Laine
HOWARD, Munroe
  St Clair, Philip
HOWARD, Peter;
 FOOT, Michael *and*
 OWEN, Frank
  Cato

HOWARD, Robert E
  Ervin, Patrick
  Taverel, John
  Walser, Sam
  Ward, Robert
HOWARTH, Patrick John Fielding
  Francis, C D E
HOWE, Doris Kathleen
  Stewart, Kaye
HOWELL, Douglas Nayler
  Hancock, Robert
HOWITT, John Leslie Despard
  Despard, Leslie
HOYT, Edwin Palmer Jr
  Martin, Christopher
HUBBARD, Clifford Lionel Barry
  Canis
HUBBARD, Elbert
  Fra Elbertus
HUBBARD, Frank McKinney
  Hubbard, Kin
  Martin, Abe
HUBBARD, LaFayette Ronald
  Elron
  Engelhardt, Frederick
  Esterbrook, Tom
  Hubbard, L Ron
  La Fayette, Rene
  Northrop, *Captain* B A
  Rachen, Kurt von
HUDLESTON, Gilbert Roger
  Pater, Roger
HUDSON, H Lindsay
  Lindsay, H
HUDSON, William Henry
  Harford, Henry
HUEFFER, Ford Madox
  Ford, Ford Madox

HUFF, Darrell
  Hough, Don
  Nelson, Chris
  West, Mark
HUGGETT, Berthe
  Brook, Esther
HUGHES, Ivy
  Hay, Catherine
HUGHES, Valerie Anne
  Carrington, V
HUGHES, Walter Dudley
  Derventio
HUGHES, Walter Llewellyn
  Walters, Hugh
HUGHES, William
  Northerner
HUGILL, John Anthony
  Crawford
  Crawford, Anthony
HUGILL, Robert
  Gill, Hugh
HULBERT, Joan
  Rostron, Primrose
HULL, Richard
  Sampson, Richard Henry
HUMPHREYS, Eliza M J
  Rita
HUMPHRIES, Adelaide
  Harris, Kathleen
  Way, Wayne
  West, Token
HUMPHRIES, Barry
  Barry
HUMPHRIES, Elsie Mary
  Forrester, Mary
HUMPHRIES, Sydney
  Vane, Michael

75

HUMPHRYS, Leslie George
  Condray, Bruno
  Humphrys, Geoffrey
HUNT, Anna Rebecca Gale
  Berwick, Claude
  Canadienne
HUNT, E Howard
  Baxter, John
  Davis, Gordon
  Dietrich, Robert
  St John, David
HUNT, Katherine Chandler
  Nash, Chandler
HUNT-BODE, Gisele
  Hunt, Diana
HUNTER, Alfred John
  Addiscombe, John
  Brenning, L H
  Dax, Anthony
  Drummond, Anthony
  Hunter, Jean
  Hunter, John
HUNTER, Bluebell Matilda
  Guildford, John
HUNTER, Christine
  Hunter, John
  Steer, Charlotte
HUNTER, Eileen
  Clements, E H
  Laura
HUNTER, Elizabeth
  Chace, Isobel
HUNTER, William R
  Hagen, Brett
HUNTER BLAIR, Pauline *see*
  BLAIR, Pauline Hunter
HUNTINGTON, Helen
  Lynde, H H

HURREN, Bernard
  Nott, Barry
HURT, Edwin Franklin
  Franklin, E
HURWOOD, Bernhardt J
  Knight, Mallory
HUSKINSON, Richard King
  King, Richard
HUTCHINSON, Barbara Beatrice
  Fearn, Roberta
HUTCHINSON, Juliet Mary Fox
  Phoenice, J
HUTCHINSON, Robert Hare
  Hare, Robert
HUTCHISON, Graham Seton
  Seton, Graham
HUTTON, Andrew Nielson
  Olympic
HUXLEY, Julian Sorell
  Balbus
  J S H
HUXTABLE, Marjorie
  Dare, Simon
  Stewart, Marjorie
HUYGHUE, Douglas S
  Eugene
HYDE, Edmund Errol Claude
  Rejje, E
HYDE, Lavender Beryl
  Ashe, Elizabeth
HYMERS, Laura M
  West, Laura M
HYNAM, John
  Kippax, John
HYNDMAN, Jane Andrews
  Wyndham, Lee
HYNDMAN, Robert Utley
  Wyndham, Robert

HYNE, Charles John
  Cutcliffe Wright
    Chesney, Weatherby
    Hyne, C J Cutcliffe
    Hyne, Cutcliffe

IAMS, Samuel H
  Iams, Jack
IBBOTT, Arthur Pearson
  Bertram, Arthur
IDELL, Albert Edward
  Rogers, Phillips
INGAMELLS, F G
  Home Guard
INGRAM-MOORE, Erica
  Marsden, June
INGRAMS, Richard *and*
  FANTONI, Barry
    Thribb, E J
INGRAMS, Richard *and*
  OSMOND, Andrew
    Reid, Philip
INHOFE, Susan Eloise
  Hinton, S E
IRISH, Betty M
  Arthur, Elisabeth
  Bell, Nancy
IRVING, Clifford
  Burkholz, Herbert
  Luckless, John
IRVING, John Treat
  Quod, John
IRWIN, Constance
  Frick, C H
IVISON, Elizabeth
  Towers, Tricia
  Wilson, Elizabeth

§ §

*Sam Johnson is hardly a name
for a great writer.*
—George Bernard Shaw

§ §

JACKSON, Ada Acraman
  Ajax
JACKSON, Caary Paul
  Lochions, Colin
  Paulson, Jack
JACKSON, Charles Philip
  Castle Kains
  Castle, Philip
  Harmodius
  P C
JACKSON, Kathryn
  Hubbard, Joan
JACOB, Naomi
  Gray, Ellington
JACOB, Piers Anthony
  Anthony, Piers
JACOBS, Charles
  Humana, Charles
JACOBS, Helen Hull
  Hull, H Braxton
JACOBS, Thomas Curtis Hicks
  Carstairs, Kathleen
  Curtis, Tom
  Dower, Penn
  Howard, Helen
  Pender, Marilyn
  Pendower, Jacques
  Penn, Ann
JACOT DE BOLNOD, B L
  Jacot, Bernard

77

JAFFE, Gabriel
  Poole, Vivian
JAMES, Charles
  Coronet
JAMES, Florence Alice Price
  Warden, Florence
JAMES, Godfrey Warden
  Broome, Adam
JAMES, J W G
  Norham, Gerald
JAMES, Montague Rhodes
  M R J
JAMESON, Annie Edith
  Buckrose, J E
JAMIESON, Kathleen Florence
  Janes, Kathleen
  Janes, Kathleen F
JANIFER, Laurence M
  Harris, Larry M
JANIFER, Laurence M *and*
  GARRETT, Randall
  Phillips, Mark
JANNER, Greville
  Mitchell, Ewan
JANSEN, Johanna *and*
  CAMPBELL, Margaret
  Bayard, Fred
JANVIER, Margaret Thomson
  Vandegrift, Margaret
JANVIER, Thomas Allibone
  Black, Ivory
JAQUES, Edward Tyrell
  Tearle, Christian
JARRETT, Cora
  Keene, Faraday
JAY, Geraldine
  Jay, Charlotte

JAY, Marion
  Spalding, Lucille
JEFFERIES, Greg
  Collins, Geoffrey
JEFFERIES, Ira
  Morris, Ira J
JEFFERY, Graham
  Brother Graham
JEFFREY-SMITH, May
  Aunt Maysie
  Thornton, Maimee
JEFFRIES, Bruce Graham
  Montague
  Bourne, Peter
  Graeme, Bruce
  Graeme, David
JEFFRIES, Gay
  Graeme, Linda
JEFFRIES, Roderic Graeme
  Alding, Peter
  Ashford, Jeffrey
  Graeme, Roderic
  Hastings, Graham
JELLY, Oliver
  Fosse, Alfred
JENKINS, Alan Charles
  Bancroft, John
JENKINS, Richard
  Burton, Richard
JENKINS, Sara Lucile
  Sargent, Joan
JENKINS, William Fitzgerald
  Leinster, Murray
JENNINGS, E C
  Jay
JENNINGS, Hilda *and others*
  Heptagon

JENNINGS, John Edward
  Baldwin, Bates
  Williams, Joel
JENNINGS, Richard
  W M
JEROME, Owen Fox
  Friend, Oscar Jerome
JERVIS, Vera Murdock Stuart
  England, Jane
JEWETT, Sarah Orne
  Eliot, Alice C
JOHN, Owen
  Bourne, John
JOHNS, Walter T
  Neby, Al
JOHNSON, Annabel I *and*
  JOHNSON, Edgar R
  Johnson, A E
JOHNSON, H
  Robertson, Muirhead
JOHNSON, Henry T
  Thomson, Neil
JOHNSON, Lilian Beatrice
  Johnson, Lee
JOHNSON, Marion
  Masson, Georgina
JOHNSON, Nancy Marr
  Marr, Nancy J
JOHNSON, Pamela Hansford *and*
  STEWART, Neil
  Lombard, Nap
JOHNSON, Victor
  Bell, John
JOHNSON, Virginia Wales
  Cousin Virginia
JOHNSTON, Alexander
  Smith, Spartacus

JOHNSTON, George Henry
  Shane, Martin
JOHNSTON, Mabel Annesley
  Marney, Suzanne
JOHNSTON, Robert Thomson
  Forsyth, R A
JONES, A Miles
  Bullingham, Ann
JONES, Alice
  John, Alix
JONES, Frank H
  Mentor
JONES, Harry Austin
  Jons, Hal
JONES, Jack
  Reynolds, Jack
JONES, Judith Anastasia
  Maro, Judith
JONES, *Lady* Roderick
  Bagnold, Enid
  Lady of Quality
JONES, Le Roi
  Baraka, Imamu Amiri
JONES, Maynard Benedict
  Jones, Nard
JONES, P D
  Denham, Peter
JONES, Robert Maynard
  Jones, Bobi
  Probert, Lowri
  Siôn, Mari
JONES, Susan Carleton
  Carleton-Milecete
  Carleton, S
  Milecete, Helen
JORDAN, June
  Meyer, June

JORDAN, Robert Furneaux
  Player, Robert
JOSCELYN, Archie Lynn
  Archer, A A
  Cody, A R
  Cody, Al
  McKenna, Evelyn
  Westland, Lynn
JOSKE, Neville *and*
 GOYDER, Margot
  Neville, Margot
JOURDAIN, Eleanor F
  Lamont, Frances
JOYCE, James
  Chanel
JUDD, Frederick
  Lester-Rands, A
JUDD, Harrison
  Garrett, Truman
JUDSON, Jeanne
  Hancock, Frances Deane
JUNOR, *Sir* John
  J J

KAGEY, Rudolf
  Steel, Kurt
KAHANE, Jack
  Barr, Cecil
  Carr, Basil
KAHN, H S
  Sackerman, Henry
KALISCH, A
  Crescendo
KAMPF, Harold Bertram
  Kaye, Harold B
KANE, Frank
  Boyd, Frank

KANE, Henry
  McCall, Anthony
KAPLAN, Jean Caryl
  Caryl, Jean
KAPP, Yvonne
  Cloud, Yvonne
KARIG, Walter
  Duncan, Julia K
  Ferris, James Cody
  Patrick, Keats
KATCHAMAKOFF, Atanas
  Shannon, Monica
KATZ, Menke
  Hiat, Elchik
KATZIN, Olga
  Sagittarius
KAUFMAN, Louis
  Keller, Dan
KAY, Ernest
  Ludlow, George
  Random, Alan
KAY, Frederic George
  Gee, Kenneth F
  Howard, George
KAYE, Barrington
  Kaye, Tom
KAYE, Mary Margaret
  Hamilton, Mollie
KAYSER, Ronal
  Clark, Dale
KEANE, Mary Nesta
  Farrell, M J
KEATING, Lawrence Alfred
  Bassett, John Keith
  Thomas, H C
KEATLEY, Sheila
  Avon, Margaret

KECK, Maud *and*
 ORBISON, Roy
  Orbison, Keck
KEDDIE, Margaret Manson
  Auntie Margaret
KEEGAN, Mary Constance
  Heathcott, Mary
  Raymond, Mary
KEELE, Kenneth David
  Cassils, Peter
KEELING, Jill Annette
  Shaw, Jill A
KEEVILL, Henry John
  Allison, Clay
  Alvord, Burt
  Bonney, Bill
  Earp, Virgil
  Harding, Wes
  McLowery, Frank
  Mossman, Burt
  Reno, Mark
  Ringo, Johnny
KELLEY, Audrey *and*
 ROOS, William
  Roos, Kelley
KELLIHER, Dan T *and*
 SECRIST, W G
  Secrist, Kelliher
KELLY, Elizabeth
  Kellier, Elizabeth
  Stevenson, Christine
KELLY, Harold Ernest
  Carson, Lance
  Glinto, Darcy
  Toler, Buck
KELLY, *Mrs* T
  Tennant, Carrie

KEMPF, Pat
  Hunter, Pat
KEMPINSKI, Tom
  Thomas, Gerrard
KENAFICK, Joseph
  Kennedy, James
KENDALL, Carlton Waldo
  Ladnek, Odlaw
KENNEDY, John McFarland
  Verdad, S
KENNEDY, H A
  H A K
KENNEDY, Joseph Charles
  Kennedy, X J
KENNINGTON, Gilbert Alan
  Grant, Alan
  Kennington, Alan
KENSDALE, W E N
  Norwood, Elliott
KENT, Arthur
  Boswell, James
  Bradwell, James
  Du Bois, M
  Granados, Paul
  Stamper, Alex
  Vane, Brett
KENT, Ellen Louisa Margaret
  Margaret
KENWARD, Betty
  Jennifer
KENYON, Fred
  Cumberland, Gerald
KEOGH, M J
  Gumsucker
KERR, D
  Colt, Russ
KERR, Doris Boake
  Boake, Capel

81

KERR, Graham
  Galloping Gourmet, The
KERR, James Lennox
  Dawlish, Peter
  Kerr, Lennox
KERSHAW, John H D
  D'Allenger, Hugh
KETCHUM, Philip
  Saunders, Carl McK
KETTLE, Jocelyn
  Kettle, Pamela
KEVIN, John William
  Ferres, Arthur
KIDD, Walter E
  Pendleton, Conrad
KIEFER, Warren *and*
 MIDDLETON, Harry
  Kiefer, Middleton
KIENZLE, Raymond N
  Ray, Nicholas
KIMBRO, John
  Ashton, Ann
  Bramwell, Charlotte
  Kimbro, Jean
  Kimbrough, Katheryn
KING, Albert
  Albion, Ken
  Bannon, Mark
  Brennan, Walt
  Brent, Catherine
  Bronson, Wade
  Cleveland, Jim
  Conrad, Paul
  Cooper, Craig
  Creedi, Joel
  Dallas, Steve
  Doan, Reece
  Driscoll, Eli

KING, A (cont'd)
  Ford, Wallace
  Foreman, Lee
  Foster, Evan
  Gibson, Floyd
  Gifford, Matt
  Girty, Simon
  Hammond, Brad
  Harlan, Ross
  Harmon, Gil
  Hoffman, Art
  Holland, Tom
  Howell, Scott
  Hoyt, Nelson
  Kane, Mark
  Kelsey, Janice
  Kimber, Lee
  King, Ames
  King, Berta
  King, Christopher
  Mason, Carl
  Muller, Paul
  Ogden, Clint
  Owen, Ray
  Prender, Bart
  Ripley, Alvin
  Santee, Walt
  Scott, Grover
  Shelby, Cole
  Taggart, Dean
  Tyler, Ellis
  Waldron, Simon
  Wallace, Agnes
  Wetzel, Lewis
  Yarbo, Steve
KING, Francis
  Cauldwell, Frank

KING, Frank
  Conrad, Clive
KING, James Clifford
  Fry, Pete
  King, Clifford
KING, John
  Boswell, John
  Kildare, John
KING, Kay
  Holt, Elizabeth
KING-HALL, Stephen
  Etienne
KINGSLEY, Mary
  Malet, Lucas
KIRBY, Derek Amos
  Ladwick, Marty
KIRK, Richard Edmund
  Church, Jeffrey
KIRKHAM, Nellie
  Myatt, Nellie
KIRKPATRICK, *Mrs* Helen
  Gemmill
KIRKUP, James
  James, Andrew
  Terahata, Jun
  Tsuyuki Shigeru
KIRKWOOD, Joyce
  Corlett, Joyce I
KIRWAN, Molly
  Morrow, Charlotte
KIRWAN-WARD, Bernard
  Ward, Kirwan
KITCHIN, F H
  Copplestone, Bennet
KLASS, Philip
  Tenn, William

KLEIN, Grace *and*
  COOPER, Mae Klein
  Farewell, Nina
KLEINHAUS, Theodore John
  Littlejohn, Jon R
KNAPP, Clarence
  Glutz, Ambrose
KNIGHT, Bernard
  Picton, Bernard
KNIGHT, Eric
  Hallas, Richard
KNIGHT, Francis Edgar
  Salter, Cedric
KNIGHT, Kathleen Moore
  Amos, Alan
KNIGHTS, Leslie
  Leslie, Val
KNIPE, Emilie
  Benson, Thérèse
KNIPSCHEER, James M W
  Fox, James M
  Holmes, Grant
KNOTT, William Cecil
  Carol, Bill J
  Knott, Bill
  St Giraud
KNOWLES, Mabel Winifred
  Wynne, May
KNOWLTON, Edward Rogers
  Rogers, Kerk
KNOWLTON, Winthrop *and*
  GOODMAN, George Jerome
  Goodman, Winthrop
KNOX, E V
  Evoe
KNUDSON, Margrethe
  Knudson, Greta

83

KOEFED-NIELSEN, Carl
  Nielsen, Koef
KOESTLER, Arthur
  Costler, *Dr* A
KOFFLER, Camilla
  Ylla
KOHLS, Olive N Allen
  Allen, Dixie
KONINGSBERGER, Hans
  Koning, Hans
KOONTZ, Dean R
  Coffey, Brian
KÖRMENDI, Ferenc
  Julian, Peter
KORNBLUTH, Cyril M
  Corwin, Cecil
  Park, Jordan
KORNBLUTH, Cyril M *and*
  GROSSMAN, Judith
  Judd, Cyril
KORNBLUTH, Cyril M *and*
  POHL, Frederick
  Gottesman, S D
KORZENIOWSKI, Jessie
  Conrad, Jessie
KORZENIOWSKI, Teodor Josef
  Konrad
  Conrad, Joseph
KOSINSKI, Jerzy
  Novak, Joseph
KOUYOUMDJIAN, Dikran
  Arlen, Michael
KOVAR, Edith May
  Lowe, Edith
KRAENZEL, Margaret Powell
  Blue, Wallace
KRASNEY, Samuel A
  Curzon, Sam

KRAUS, Robert
  Hippopotamus, Eugene H
KRECHNIAK, Joseph Marshall
  Marshall, Joseph
KREINER, George
  Bouverie
KRISHNAMURTI, Jiddu
  Alcyone
KRONMILLER, Hildegarde
  Lawrence, Hilda
KUBIS, Patricia Lou
  Scott, Casey
KUMMER, Frederick Arnold
  Fredericks, Arnold
KURNITZ, Harry
  Page, Marco
KUSKIN, Karla Seidman
  Charles, Nicholas
KUTTNER, Henry
  Edmonds, Paul
  Gardner, Noel
  Garth, Will
  Hammond, Keith
  Hastings, Hudson
  Horn, Peter
  Kenyon, Robert O
  Liddell, C H
  Morgan, Scott
  Stoddard, Charles
KUTTNER, Henry *and*
  BARNES, Arthur
  Kent, Kelvin
KUTTNER, Henry *and/or*
  MOORE, C L
  O'Donnell, Lawrence
  Padgett, Lewis

LACOSTE, Guy R *and*
 BINGHAM, E A
  Berton, Guy
LA SPINA, Fanny Greye (Bragg)
 La Spina, Greye
 Putnam, Isra
LAFFEATY, Christina
 Carstens, Netta
 Fortina, Martha
LAFFIN, John
 Dekker, Carl
 Napier, Mark
 Sabre, Dirk
LAIDLER, Graham
 Pont
LAKE, Joe Barry
 Barry, Joe
LAKE, Kenneth Robert
 Boyer, Robert
 King, Arthur
 Roberts, Ken
 Soutter, Fred
LAKRITZ, Esther
 Collingswood, Frederick
 Marion, S T
LAMB, Antonia
 Hellerlamb, Toni
LAMB, Elizabeth Searle
 Mitchell, K L
LAMB, Geoffrey Frederick
 Balaam
LAMB, Mary Montgomerie *see*
 CURRIE, *Lady*
LAMBERT, Hubert Steel
 Marle, T B
LAMBERT, Leslie Harrison
 Alan, A J

LAMBOT, Isobel Mary
 Ingham, Daniel
 Turner, Mary
LAMBURN, John Battersby
 Crompton
 Crompton, John
LAMBURN, Richmal Crompton
 Crompton, Richmal
L'AMOUR, Louis
 Burns, Tex
LAMPMAN, Evelyn
 Bronson, Lynn
LANDELLS, Anne
 Sibley, Lee
LANDELLS, Richard
 Baron, Paul
 Dryden, Keith
 Gaunt, Richard
 Lanzol, Cesare
 Pelham, Randolph
LANDESMAN, Irving Ned
 Landesman, Jay
LANDON, Melville de Lancy
 Lan
 Perkins, Eli
LANDWIRTH, Heinz
 Lind, Jakov
LANE, Kenneth Westmacott
 West, Keith
LANE, *Sir* Ralph Norman
 Angell
 Angell, Norman
LANES, Selma G
 Gordon, Selma
LANGBEHN, Theo
 Lang, Theo
 Piper, Peter

Real names

LANGDON, John
  Gannold, John
LANGDON-DAVIES, John
  James, John
  Nada, John
  Stanhope, John
LANGLEY, Sarah
  Langley, Lee
LANGMAID, Kenneth Joseph
 Robb
  Graham, Peter
  Laing, Kenneth
LANGNER, Lawrence
  Child, Alan
LANIGAN, Richard
  Ex-Journalist
LARBALESTIER, Phillip George
  Archer, G Scott
LARCOMBE, Jennifer Geraldine
  Rees, J Larcombe
LARIAR, Lawrence
  Knight, Adam
  Stark, Michael
LARKINS, William
  Long, Gerry
LARRALDE, Romulo
  Brent, Romney
LASH, William Quinlan
  Quinlan, William
LASKI, Marghanita
  Russell, Sarah
LASKY, Jesse L
  Love, David
  Smeed, Frances
LATHAM, Alison *and*
 LATHAM, Esther
  Latham, Murray

LATHROP, Lorin Andrews
  Gambier, Kenyon
LATIMER, Jonathan
  Coffin, Peter
LATIS, Mary J *and*
 HENISSART, Martha
  Dominic, R B
  Lathen, Emma
LAUGHLIN, Virginia Carli
  Clarke, John
  Laklan, Carli
LAURENCE, Frances Elsie
  Field, Christine
LAVENDER, David Sievert
  Catlin, Ralph
LAVRENCIC, Karl
  Sylvester, Anthony
LAW, Michael
  Kreuzenau, Michael
LAWLOR, Patrick
  Penn, Christopher
LAWRENCE, D H
  Davison, Lawrence H
LAWRENCE, Dulcie
  Hamilton, Judith
  Mace, Margaret
LAWRENCE, Elizabeth
  Bradburne, E S
LAWRENCE, James Duncan
  Lancer, Jack
LAWRENCE, T E
  C D
  C J G
  J C
  Ross, J H
  Shaw, T E
LAWSON, Alfred
  Torroll, G D

LAZARUS, Marguerite
  Gilbert, Anna
LAZENBY, Norman
  Norton, Jed
LE GALLIENNE, Richard
  Logroller
LE RICHE, P J
  Kish
LE ROI, David de Roche
  Roche, John
LEAF, Munro
  Calvert, John
  Mun
LEDERER, Esther Pauline
  Landers, Ann
LEE, Austin
  Austwick, John
  Callender, Julian
LEE, Henry David Cook
  Parios
LEE, Manfred B *and*
 DANNAY, Frederic
  Queen, Ellery
  Ross, Barnaby
LEE, Manning de Villeneuve
  Hatch, Robert
LEE, Marion Van Der Veer
  Lee, Babs
LEE, Maureen
  Northe, Maggie
LEE, Norman
  Armstrong, Raymond
  Corrigan, Mark
  Hobart, Robertson
LEE, Polly Jae
  Lee, Jae Gardiner

LEE HOWARD, L A
  Howard, Leigh
  Krislov, Alexander
LEE-RICHARDSON, James
  Dunne, Desmond
LEEMING, Jill
  Chaney
LEFFINGWELL, Albert
  Chambers, Dana
  Jackson, Giles
LEGMAN, George Alexander
  De La Glannege, Roger-Maxe
  Legman, G
LEHMAN, Paul Evan
  Evan, Paul
LEHMANN, R C
  Toil, Cunnin
LEHRBURGER, Egon
  Larsen, Egon
LEIBER, Fritz
  Lathrop, Francis
LEISK, David Johnson
  Johnson, Crockett
LEITE, George Thurston *and*
 SCOTT, Jody
  Scott, Thurston
LEMIEUX, Kenneth
  Orvis, Kenneth
LEMMON, Laura Lee
  Wilson, Lee
LENANTON, *Lady*
  Lenanton, C
  Oman, Carola
LENT, Blair
  Small, Ernest
LEON, Henry Cecil
  Cecil, Henry
  Maxwell, Clifford

87

LEONARD, John
Cyclops
LEONARD, Lionel Frederick
Lonsdale, Frederick
LESLEY, Peter
Allen, John W Jr
Lesley, J P
LESLIE, Cecilie
Macadam, Eve
LESLIE, Josephine A C
Dick, R A
LESLIE, *Sir* Shane
Ionicos, Ion
LESSER, Milton
Marlowe, Stephen
L'ESTRANGE, C James *and*
ELY, George Herbert
Strang, Herbert
LEVIN, Abraham
George, G S
LEVIN, Bernard
Battle, Felix
Cherryman, A E
Taper
LEVINE, William
Levinrew, Will
LEVY, Julia Ethel
Juliet
LEVY, Newman
Flaccus
LEWIN, Michael Sultan
Furber, Douglas
LEWING, Anthony
Bannerman, Mark
LEWIS, Alfred Henry
Quin, Dan

LEWIS, Charles Bertrand
Quad, M
LEWIS, Clifford *and*
LEWIS, Judith Mary
Berrisford, Judith
LEWIS, Clive Staples
Hamilton, Clive
LEWIS, J R
Lewis, Roy
Springfield, David
LEWIS, Lydia T
Lesbia
LEWIS, Mary Christianna
Berrisford, Mary
Brand, Christianna
Roland, Mary
Thompson, China
LEWIS, Mildred
De Witt, James
LEY, Willy
Willey, Robert
LEYLAND, Eric
Cleaver, Denis
Felmersham, Michael
Fielding, Anthony
Grant, Nesta
Little, Sylvia
Lodge, John
Patterson, Duke
Strangeway, Mark
Tarrant, Elizabeth
Wyatt, Escott
L'HOTELLIER, Alf
Outlaw, The
LIDDELOW, Marjorie Joan
Law, Marjorie J

LIEBERS, Arthur
  Love, Arthur
LIEBLER, Jean Mayer
  Mather, Virginia
LIGHTHALL, William Douw
  Chateauclair, Wilfred
LIGHTNER, A M
  Hopf, Alice L
LILIENTHAL, David Jr
  Ely, David
LILLEY, Peter *and*
  STANSFIELD, Anthony
  Buckingham, Bruce
LILLIE, Gordon W
  Pawnee Bill
LINDHOLM, Anna Chandler
  Fay, Dorothy
LINDSAY, Barbara *and*
  STERNE, E G
  James, Josephine
LINDSAY, Jack
  Meadows, Peter
  Preston, Richard
LINDSAY, Kathleen
  Cameron, Margaret
  Richmond, Mary
LINDSAY, Maurice
  Brock, Gavin
LINEBARGER, Paul
  Smith, Cordwainer
LININGTON, Elizabeth
  Blaisdell, Anne
  Egan, Lesley
  O'Neill, Egan
  Shannon, Dell
LIPKIND, William
  Will

LIPPINCOTT, Sara Jane
  Greenwood, Grace
LIPSCHITZ, *Rabbi* Chaim
  Yerushalmi, Chaim
LIST, Ilka Katherine
  Macduff, Ilka
  Obolensky, Ilka
LITTLE, Cecile Enid
  Ashmore, Jane
LITTLE, Constance *and*
  LITTLE, Gwenyth
  Little, Conyth
LITTLE, D F
  Wessex, Martin
LITTLE, Gwenyth *and*
  LITTLE, Constance
  Little, Conyth
LITTLE, Malcolm
  Malcolm X
LIVERTON, Joan
  Medhurst, Joan
LIVINGSTON, A D
  Delano, Al
LLOYD, Richard Dafydd Vivian
  Llewellyn
  Llewellyn, Richard
LOADER, William
  Nash, Daniel
LOBAUGH, Elma K
  Lowe, Kenneth
LOBLEY, Robert
  Nong
LOCK, Arnold Charles Cooper
  Cooper, Charles
LOCKHART, Arthur John
  Pastor Felix
LOCKIE, Isobel
  Knight, Isobel

89

LOCKRIDGE, Frances Louise *and*
  LOCKRIDGE, Richard
    Richards, Francis
LOCKWOOD, Frank
    Circumlibra
LOEWENGARD, Heidi H F
    Albrand, Martha
    Holland, Katrin
    Lambert, Christine
LOFTS, Norah
    Astley, Juliet
    Curtis, Peter
LOGAN, Olive
    Chroniqueuse
LOGUE, Christopher
    Vicarion, *Count* Palmiro
LOMBINO, Salvatore A
    Cannon, Curt
    Collins, Hunt
    Hannon, Ezra
    Hunter, Evan
    McBain, Ed
    Marsten, Richard
LOMER, Sydney Frederick
  McIllree
    Oswald, Sydney
LONG, Amelia
    Laing, Patrick
    Reynolds, Adrian
    Reynolds, Peter
LONG, Amelia *and*
  McHUGH, Edna
    Coxe, Kathleen Buddington
LONG, Gladys
    Beaton, Jane
LONG, Leonard
    Long, Shirley

LONG, Lily Augusta
    Doubleday, Roman
LONG, Lois
    Lipstick
LONGRIGG, Roger Erskine
    Black, Laura
    Drummond, Ivor
    Erskine, Rosalind
LONGSTREET, Stephen
    Burton, Thomas
    Haggard, Paul
    Ormsbee, David
    Weiner, Henri
LOOKER, Samuel Joseph
    Game Cock
    Pundit, Ephraim
    Wade, Thomas
LOOMIS, Noel Miller
    Miller, Frank
    Water, Silas
LORD, Doreen Mildred Douglas
    Ireland, Doreen
    Lord, Douglas
LORD, Phillips H
    Parker, Seth
LORD, William Wilberforce
    Langstaff, Tristram
LORDE, Andre Geraldin
    Domini, Rey
LORDING, Rowland Edward
    Tiveychoc, A
LORENZ, Frederic
    Holden, Larry
LORIMER, Maxwell
    Wall, Max
LORING, Emilie
    Story, Josephine

LOTHROP, Harriet Mulford
  Sidney, Margaret
LOTTICH, Kenneth
  Conrad, Kenneth
LOVESEY, Peter
  Lear, Peter
LOW, Lois
  Paxton, Lois
LOWELL, Jan *and*
 LOWELL, Robert
  Lowell, J R
LOWNDES, Marie Adelaide Belloc
  Curtin, Philip
LOWTHER, Armstrong John
  Laird
LU KUAN YU
  Luk, Charles
LUARD, William Blaine
  Luard, L
LUCAS, Beryl Llewellyn
  Llewellyn
LUCAS, E V
  E V L
  V V V
LUCAS, Edgar Ernest
  Goodson, Bill
LUCCHETTI, Anthony
  Prescott, John
LUCCOCK, Halford Edward
  Stylites, Simeon
LUCEY, James D
  James, Matthew
LUDLUM, Robert
  Ryder, Jonathan
LUMSDEN, Jean
  Swift, Rachelle

LUNN, *Sir* Arnold
  Croft, Sutton
  Rubicon
LUNN, Hugh Kingsmill
  Kingsmill, Hugh
LUTYENS, Mary
  Wyndham, Esther
LUXMORE, Robert
  Fesenmeyer
LYALL, James Robert
  Patroclus
LYBURN, *Dr* Eric Frederic
 St John
  Doctor Futuer
  Toller
LYLE-SMYTHE, Alan
  Caillou, Alan
LYND, Robert
  Y Y
LYNDS, Dennis
  Arden, William
  Collins, Michael
  Crowe, John
LYNE, Charles
  De Castro, Lyne
LYNES, Daisy Elfreda
  Glyn-Forest, D
LYNN, Elwyn
  Augustus
LYONS, John Benignus
  Fitzwilliam, Michael
LYTLE, *Mrs* W J A
  Berney, Beryl
LYTTLETON, Edith Joan
  Lancaster, G B

§ §

How public, like a frog
To tell your name the livelong day
To an admiring bog.
—Emily Dickinson. Collected
poems

§ §

MABBOTT, Thomas O
  Hunter, M O
McADAM, Constance
  Clyde, Constance
MACALLISTER, Alister
  Brock, Lynn
  Wharton, Anthony
McALMON, Robert
  Urquhart, Guy
MACBETH, Madge Hamilton
  Dill, W S
  Knox, Gilbert
McBRIDE, Robert Medill
  Medill, Robert
  Reid, Marshall
McCALL, Virginia
  Nielson, Virginia
McCARROLL, James
  Dubh, Scian
MACCARTHY, *Sir* Desmond
  Hawk, Affable
McCARTHY, Shaun
  Callas, Theo
  Cory, Desmond
McCARTNEY, R J
  Scott, Bruce
McCHESNEY, Mary F
  Rayter, Joe
92

McCLINTOCK, Marshall
  Duncan, Gregory
  Marshall, Douglas
  Starret, William
MACCLURE, Victor
  Craig, Peter
McCONNELL, James Douglas
  Rutherford
    Rutherford, Douglas
McCONNELL, James Douglas
  Rutherford *and*
  DURBRIDGE, Francis
  Temple, Paul
McCORMICK, Donald
  Deacon, Richard
McCORQUODALE, Barbara
  Hamilton
  Cartland, Barbara
McCUE, Lillian Bueno
  De la Torre, Lillian
McCULLEY, Johnston
  Brien, Raley
  McAlpin, Grant
McCULLOCH, Derek
  Uncle Mac
McCULLOCH, Joseph
  Michaelhouse, John
McCUTCHAN, Philip D
  Galway, Robert Conington
  MacNeil, Duncan
  Wigg, T I G
McDERMOTT, John Richard
  Ryan, J M
McDONALD, Margaret Josephine
  McDonald, Jo
MACDONALD, Philip
  Lawless, Anthony
  Porlock, Martin

MACDONALD, Philip *and*
 MACDONALD, Ronald
  Fleming, Oliver
MACDONALD, Susanne
 MacFarland, Anne
MACDONNELL, A G
 Cameron, John
 Gordon, Neil
MACDONNELL, James Edmond
 Macnell, James
McDOUGALL, E Jean Taylor
 Rolyat, Jane
McDOUGALL, Margaret
 Norah
McELFRESH, Adeline
 Cleveland, John
 Scott, Jane
 Wesley, Elizabeth
McEVOY, Marjorie
 Bond, Gillian
 Harte, Marjorie
McEWEN, Jessie Evelyn
 Fisher, Agnes
McFARLANE, David
 Tyson, Teilo
MACFARLANE, George Gordon
 Miller, Patrick
McFAUL, Frances Elizabeth
 Grand, Sarah
McGARRY, William Rutledge
 Smythe, James P
McGAUGHY, Dudley Dean
 Dean, Dudley
 Owen, Dean
McGEOGH, Andrew
 Paul, Adrian
McGIVERN, William Peter
 Peters, Bill

MACGLASHAN, John
 Glashan, John
McGLOIN, Joseph Thaddeus
 O'Finn, Thaddeus
MACGREGOR, James Murdoch
 McIntosh, J T
MACGREGOR, Mary Esther
 Keith, Marian
MACGREGOR, Miriam
 Pegden, Helen
McGREW, Julia *and*
 FENN, Caroline K
  McGrew, Fenn
McGUINNESS, Bernard
 McGuinness, Brian
McHARGUE, Georgess
 Chase, Alice
 Usher, Margo Scegge
MACHEN, Arthur
 Siluriensis, Leolinus
MACHLIN, Milton
 Jason, William
 Roberts, McLean
McHUGH, Edna *and*
 LONG, Amelia
  Coxe, Kathleen Buddington
McILWAIN, David
 Maine, Charles Eric
 Rayner, Richard
 Wade, Robert
McILWRAITH, Jean Newton
 Forsyth, Jean
McILWRAITH, Maureen Mollie
 Hunter
 Hunter, Mollie
MACINTOSH, Joan
 Blaike, Avona

Real names

McINTOSH, Kinn Hamilton
    Aird, Catherine
MACINTYRE, John
    Brandane, John
MACINTYRE, John Thomas
    O'Neil, Kerry
MACK, Elsie Frances
    Moore, Frances Sarah
MACK, J C O
    Callum Beg
MACKAY, Fulton
    MacBride, Aeneas
MACKAY, James Alexander
    Angus, Ian
MACKAY, Lewis
    Matheson, Hugh
MACKAY, Louis Alexander
    Smalacombe, John
MACKAY, Minnie
    Corelli, Marie
MACKENZIE, *Sir* Edward
    Portsea
MACKENZIE, Joan
    Finnigan, Joan
MACKEOWN, N R
    Giles, Norman
MACKESY, Leonora Dorothy
  Rivers
    Starr, Leonora
McKIBBIN, *Reverend* Archibald
    Cloie, Mack
McKIBBON, John
    Probyn, Elise
MACKIE, Albert David
    Macnib
McKILLOP, Norman
    Beg, Toram

MACKINLAY, Lelia A S
    Grey, Brenda
MACKINNON, Charles Roy
    Conte, Charles
    Donald, Vivian
    Macalpin, Rory
    Montrose, Graham
    Rose, Hilary
    Stuart, Charles
    Torr, Iain
MACKINTOSH, Elizabeth
    Daviot, Gordon
    Tey, Josephine
McLACHLAN, Dan
    McMud, Dok
MACLAREN, James Paterson
    Medicus
McLAREN, Moray David Shaw
    Murray, Michael
MACLEAN, Alistair
    Stuart, Ian
McLEAN, Kathryn
    Forbes, Kathryn
MACLEOD, Charlotte
    Hughes, Matilda
MACLEOD, Ellen
    Anderson, Ella
MACLEOD, Jean Sutherland
    Airlie, Catherine
MACLEOD, Joseph Todd Gordon
    Drinan, Adam
MACLEOD, Robert
    Knox, Bill
MACLEOD-SMITH, D
    Mariner, David
MACMANUS, Anna Johnston
    Carbery, Ethna

McMEEKIN, Isabel *and*
CLARK, Dorothy
McMeekin, Clark
McMILLAN, Donald
Stuart, John Roy
MACMILLAN, Douglas
Cary, D M
McMILLAN, James
Coriolanus
McMORDIE, John Andrew
Shan
McMORDIE, Taber
Channing, Peter
MACMULLAN, Charles W
Kirkpatrick
Munro, C K
McNALLY, Mary Elizabeth
O'Brien, Deirdre
McNAMARA, Barbara Willard
O'Conner, Elizabeth
McNAMARA, Lena
Mack, Evalina
McNAUGHT, Ann Boyce
Gilmour, Ann
MACNEICE, Louis
Malone, Louis
McNEILE, H C
Sapper
McNEILLIE, John
Niall, Ian
McNEILLY, Wilfred
Ballinger, W A
McNEILLY, Wilfred *and*
BAKER, William Howard
Ballinger, W A
McPHEE, Hugh
Phee, Hugh

MACPHERSON, Jessie
Kennie, Jessie
MACQUARRIE, Hector
Cameron, Hector
MACQUEEN, James William
Edwards, James G
MACRORY, Patrick
Greer, Patrick
MACVEAN, Phyllis
Greaves, Gillian
Hambledon, Phyllis
MADDISON, Angela Mary
Banner, Angela
MAGEE, James
Taylor, John
MAGEE, William Kirkpatrick
Eglinton, John
MAGENHEIMER, Cathryn Cecile
Magenheimer, Kay
MAGRAW, Beatrice
Padeson, Mary
MAGRILL, David S
Dalheath, David
MAGUIRE, Robert A J
Taaffe, Robert
MAHONEY, Elizabeth
Mara, Thalia
MAIDEN, Cecil
Cecil, Edward
MAINPRIZE, Don
Rock, Richard
MAINWARING, Daniel
Homes, Geoffrey
MAIR, George Brown
Bok, Kooshti
Macdouall, Robertson
MAIZEL, Clarice Louise
Maizel, Leah

MALLALIEU, J P W
  Pied Piper, The
MALLESON, Lucy
  Gilbert, Anthony
  Meredith, Anne
MALLETTE, Gertrude Ethel
  Gregg, Alan
MALZBERG, Barry
  O'Donnell, K M
MANCHEE, Carol M Cassidy
  Cole, Carol Cassidy
MANFRED, Frederick Feikema
  Feikema, Feike
MANN, George
  Schwarz, Bruno
MANNES, Marya
  Sec
MANNING, Adelaide Frances Oke
and COLES, Cyril Henry
  Coles, Manning
  Gaite, Francis
MANNING, Frederic
  Private 19022
MANNING, Rosemary
  Voyle, Mary
MANNOCK, Laura
  Adair, Sally
  Mannock, Jennifer
  Whetter, Laura
MANNON, Martha *and*
 MANNON, Mary Ellen
  Mannon, M M
MANSELL, *Mrs* C B
  St Clair, Everett
MANTIBAND, James
  Keystone, Oliver
MANTLE, Winifred Langford
  Fellowes, Anne

MANTLE, W L (cont'd)
  Lang, Frances
  Langford, Jane
MAREK, Kurt W
  Ceram, C W
MARKOV, Georgi *and*
 PHILLIPS, David
  St George, David
MARLOWE, Stephen
  Less, Milton
MARQUAND, John Phillips
  Phillips, John
MARQUAND, Leopold
  Burger, John
MARQUES, Susan Lowndes
  Lowndes, Susan
MARRECO, Anne
  Acland, Alice
MARRISON, Leslie William
  Dowley, D M
MARSH, John
  Davis, Julia
  Elton, John
  Harley, John
  Lawrence, Irene
  Marsh, Joan
  Richmond, Grace
  Sawley, Petra
  Ware, Monica
  Woodward, Lillian
MARSHALL, Arthur Hammond
  Marshall, Archibald
MARSHALL, Charles Hunt *and*
 YATES, George Worthing
  Hunt, Peter
MARSHALL, Christabel
  St John, Christopher

MARSHALL, Edison
  Hunter, Hall
MARSHALL, Evelyn
  Bourne, Lesley
  Marsh, J E
  Marsh, Jean
MARSHALL, Margaret
  Smith, Elvet
MARSHALL, Marjorie
  March, Stella
MARSTON, J E
  Jeffrey, E Jeffrey
MARTEAU, F A
  Bride, Jack
  Rameaut, Maurice
MARTEN, J Chisholm
  Lanark, David
MARTENS, Anne Louise
  Kendall, Jane
MARTIN, Charles Morris
  Martin, Chuck
MARTIN, Kingsley
  Critic
MARTIN, Malachi
  Serafian, Michael
MARTIN, Netta
  Ashton, Lucy
MARTIN, Patricia Miles
  Miles, Miska
MARTIN, Reginald Alec
  Cameron, Brett
  Dixon, Rex
  Eliott, E C
  McCoy, Hank
  Martin, Rex
  Martin, Robert
  Martin, Scott

MARTIN, Robert Bernard
  Bernard, Robert
MARTIN, Robert Lee
  Roberts, Lee
MARTIN, *Sir* Theodore
  Bon Gaultier
MARTIN, Timothy
  Tim
MARTIN, Violet Florence
  Ross
  Ross, Martin
MARTINEZ-DELGADO, Luis
  Luimardel
MARTING, Ruth Lenore
  Bailey, Hilea
MARTINN, Paul
  Plaut, Martin
MARTYN, Wyndham
  Grenvil, William
MASCHLER, Tom *and*
  RAPHAEL, Frederic
  Caine, Mark
MASCHWITZ, Eric
  Marvel, Holt
MASON, Arthur Charles
  Scrope, Mason
MASON, Douglas Rankine
  Rankine, Douglas
MASON, F Van Wyck
  Coffin, Geoffrey
  Mason, Frank W
  Weaver, Ward
MASON, Madeline
  Mason, Tyler
MASON, Michael
  Blake, Cameron
MASON, Philip
  Woodruff, Philip

97

MASON, Sydney Charles
  Carr, Charles
  Carr, Elaine
  Hatton, Cliff
  Hayes, Clanton
  Henderson, Colt
  Holmes, Caroline
  Horn, Chester
  Langley, John
  Ledgard, Jake
  Lee, Jesse
  Lomax, Jeff
  Maddern, Stan
  Maine, Sterling
  Mann, Stanley
  Marlow, Phyllis
  Masters, Steve
  Merrick, Spencer
  Stanley, Margaret
MASTERS, Anthony
  Tate, Richard
MASTERS, Edgar Lee
  Ford, Webster
MASTERS, Kelly
  Ball, Zachary
MATHERS, Edward Powys
  Torquemada
MATHESON, Donald H
  Harmston, Donald
MATHEWS, Albert
  Siogvolk, Paul
MATTHEWMAN, Phyllis
  Surrey, Kathryn
MATTHEWS, Clayton
  Moore, Arthur
MATTHEWS, Edwin J
  Saxon

MATTHEWS, James Brander
  Matthews, Brander
  Penn, Arthur
MATTHEWS, Margaret Bryan
  Goodyear, Susan
MATUSOW, Harvey Marshall
  Allenby, Gordon
  Matusow, Marshall
  Muldoon, Omar
  Sadballs, John
MAUGHAM, Robert Cecil
  Romer *Viscount*
  Maugham, Robin
MAVOR, Osborne Henry
  Bridie, James
MAXFIELD, Prudence
  Hill, Prudence
MAXTONE-GRAHAM, Joyce
  Struther, Jan
MAXWELL, Patricia Anne
  Trehearne, Elizabeth
MAXWELL, Violet S
  Maxwell, C Bede
MAY, Elaine
  Dale, Esther
MAY, John
  Duffer, Allan
MAYER, Jane *and*
 SPIEGEL, Clara E
  Jaynes, Clare
MAYNE, Ethel Colburn
  Huntly, Frances E
MAYNE, William J C *and*
 CAESAR, Richard Dynely
  James, Dynely
MAZURE, Alfred Leonardus
  Cullner, Lenard
  Maz

MAZZOCCO, Edward
  Maze, Edward
MEAD, Martha Norburn
  Norburn, Martha
MEAD, Sidney
  Moko
MEAKER, Marijane
  Kerr, M E
  Packer, Vin
MEANS, Mary *and*
 SAUNDERS, Theodore
  Scott, Denis
MEARES, John Willoughby
  Uncut Cavendish
MEARES, Leonard F
  Grover, Marshall
  McCoy, Marshall
MEE, Arthur
  Idris
MEESKE, Marilyn
  Crannach, Henry
MEGAW, Arthur Stanley
  Stanley, Arthur
MEGROZ, R L
  Cumberland, Roy
  Dimsdale, C D
MEHTA, Rustam
  Hartman, Roger
  Martin, R J
MEIGS, Cornelia Lynde
  Aldon, Adair
MEINZER, Helen Abbott
  Abbott, A C
MELIDES, Nicholas
  Macguire, Nicholas
MELLETT, John Calvin
  Brooks, Jonathan

MELLING, Leonard
  Lummins
MELONEY, William
  Frenken-Meloney
  Grant, Margaret
MENZEL, Donald H
  Howard, Don
MERCER, Cecil William
  Yates, Dornford
MEREDITH, Kenneth Lincoln
  Mayo, Arnold
MERTZ, Barbara G
  Michaels, Barbara
  Peters, Elizabeth
METHOLD, Kenneth
  Cade, Alexander
MEYER, Harold Albert
  Merrick, Hugh
MEYER, Jerome Sydney
  Jennings, S M
MEYERS, Roy
  Lethbridge, Rex
MEYNELL, Ester H
  Moorhouse, E Hallam
MEYNELL, Laurence Walter
  Baxter, Valerie
  Eton, Robert
  Ludlow, Geoffrey
  Tring, A Stephen
MEYNELL, Shirley Ruth
  Darbyshire, Shirley
MEYNELL, Wilfred
  Oldcastle, John
MIDDLETON, Harry *and*
 KIEFER, Warren
  Kiefer, Middleton
MIDDLETON, Henry Clement
  Simplex, Simon

MIDDLETON, Maud Barbara
  Walker, Barbara
MIERS, Earl Schenk
  Meredith, David William
MILAM, Lorenzo W
  Allworthy, A W
MILKOMANE, George Alexis
 Milkomanovich
  Bankoff, George
  Borodin, George
  Braddon, George
  Conway, Peter
  Redwood, Alec
  Sava, George
MILLAR, Kenneth
  Macdonald, John
  Macdonald, John Ross
  Macdonald, Ross
MILLAR, Minna
  Collier, Joy
MILLARD, Christopher S
  Mason, Stuart
MILLAY, Edna St Vincent
  Boyd, Nancy
MILLER, Albert
  Mills, Alan
MILLER, Charles Dean
  Von Mueller, Karl
MILLER, Cincinnatus H
  Miller, Joaquin
MILLER, Harriet
  Miller, Olive Thorne
MILLER, J A
  Pook, Peter
MILLER, Lynn
  Captious Critic
MILLER, Mary
  Durack, Mary

MILLER, Mary Britton
  Bolton, Isabel
MILLER, Warren
  Vail, Amanda
MILLER, William *and*
 WADE, Robert
  Masterson, Whit
  Miller, Wade
  Wilmer, Dale
MILLER, Wright
  North, Mark
MILLETT, Nigel
  Oke, Richard
MILLIGAN, Elsie
  Burr, Elsie
MILLS, Algernon Victor
  Latimer, Rupert
MILLS, Hugh Travers
  Travers, Hugh
MILLS, Janet Melanie Ailsa
  Challoner, H K
MILLWARD, Pamela
  Midling, Perspicacity
MILNE, Charles
  Milne, Ewart
MILNER, Alfred, *Vicount*
  Milner
  M
MILNER, Marion
  Field, Joanna
MILTON, Gladys Alexandra
  Carlyle, Anthony
M'ILWRAITH, Jean N
  Forsyth, Jean
MINTO, Frances
  Cowen, Frances
  Hyde, Eaeanor
  Munthe, Frances

MINTO, Mary
  Macqueen, Jay
MITCHELL, Clare May
  Canfield, Cleve
MITCHELL, Donald Grant
  Marvel, Ik
  Timon, John
MITCHELL, Gladys
  Hockaby, Stephen
  Torrie, Malcolm
MITCHELL, Isabel
  Plain, Josephine
MITCHELL, James
  Munro, James
MITCHELL, James Leslie
  Gibbon, Lewis Grassic
MITCHELL, John
  Slater, Patrick
MITCHELL, John Hanlon
  Hanlon, John
MITRINOVIC, Dmitri
  Cosmoi, M M
MIZNER, Elizabeth Howard
  Howard, Elizabeth
MOBERLY, Charlotte Anne
  Elizabeth
  Morison, Elizabeth
MOCKLER, Gretchen
  Travis, Gretchen
MODELL, Merriam
  Piper, Evelyn
MOFFATT, James
  More, J J
MOGRIDGE, Stephen
  Stevens, Jill
MOHAN, Josephine Elizabeth
  Jermonte

MOLESWORTH, *Mrs* Mary
  Louisa Stewart
  Graham, Ennis
MOLLOY, Edward
  Jamieson, Thomas
  Jones, H S
  Ward, Herbert B S
MONGER, Ifor
  Manngian, Peter
  Richards, Peter
MONRO-HIGGS, Gertrude
  Monro, Gavin
MONROE, Donald *and*
  MONROE, Keith
  Keith, Donald
MONTEFIORE, Caroline L
  Eric
MONTGOMERY, Leslie Alexander
  Doyle, Lynn
MONTGOMERY, Robert Bruce
  Crispin, Edmund
MONTGOMERY, Rutherford
  George
  Avery, Al
  Proctor, Everitt
MOORE, Bertha B
  Cannon, Brenda
MOORE, Birkett
  Allegro
MOORE, C L *and/or*
  KUTTNER, Henry
  O'Donnell, Laurence
  Padgett, Lewis
MOORE, Doris Langley
  Gentlewoman, A
MOORE, Harold William
  Roome, Holdar

MOORE, John
Trotwood, John
MOORE, Mary McLeod
Pandora
MOORHOUSE, Herbert Joseph
Moorhouse, Hopkins
MOORHOUSE, Hilda
Vansittart, Jane
MOORHOUSE, Sydney
Langdale, Stanley
Lyndale, Sydney M
MORANT, Harry H
Breaker, The
MORDAUNT, Evelyn May
Mordaunt, Elinor
Riposte, A
MOREAU, David
Merlin, David
MORETTI, Ugo
Drug, Victor
Gouttier, Maurice
Sherman, George
MOREWOOD, Sarah L
Hope, Noel
MORGAN, Brian Stanford
Morgan, Bryan
MORGAN, Charles
Menander
MORGAN, Diana
Blaine, Sara
MORGAN, Murray C
Murray, Cromwell
MORGAN, Thomas Christopher
Muir, John
MORIN, Claire
France, Claire
MORISON, John
Clergyman, A

MORLAND, Nigel
Dane, Mary
Donavan, John
Forrest, Norman
Garnett, Roger
McCall, Vincent
Shepherd, Neal
MORLEY, Leslie Reginald William
Hutchins, Anthony
MORRIS, David
Hall, Martyn T
MORRIS, Jean
O'Hara, Kenneth
MORRIS, John
McGaw, J W
MORRISON, Alistair
Lauder, Afferbeck
MORRISON, Arthur
Hewitt, Martin
MORRISON, Eula A
Delmonico, Andrea
MORRISON, Margaret Mackie
Cost, March
Morrison, Peggy
MORRISON, Thomas
Muir, Alan
MORSE, Anne Christenson
Head, Ann
MORSE, Martha
Wilson, Martha
MORTIMER, John
Lincoln, Geoffrey
MORTIMER, Penelope
Temple, Ann
MORTON, A Q
Kew, Andrew
MORTON, Guy Mainwaring
Traill, Peter

MORTON, J B
  Beachcomber
MORUM, William *and*
 DINNER, William
  Smith, Surrey
MOSS, Robert Alfred
  Moss, Nancy
  Moss, Roberta
MOSTYN, Anita Mary
  Fielding, Ann Mary
MOTT, Edward Spencer
  Gubbins, Nathaniel
  Spencer, Edward
MOTT, J Moldon
  Blackburn, John
MOTTRAM, Ralph Hale
  Marjoram, J
MOUNT, Thomas Ernest
  Cody, Stone
  King, Oliver
MOUNTBATTEN, *Lord* Louis
  Marco
MOUNTCASTLE, Clara H
  Sima, Caris
MOUNTFIELD, David
  Grant, Neil
MOYNIHAN, Cornelius
  Vivian
MUDDOCK, Joyce Emerson
  Donovan, Dick
MUGGESON, Margaret
  Dickinson, Margaret
  Jackson, Everatt
MUIR, Edwin
  Moore, Edward
MUIR, Marie
  Blake, Monica
  Kaye, Barbara

MUIR, Wilhelmina Johnstone
  Muir, Willa
  Scott, Agnes Neill
MULHEARN, Winifred
  Grandma
MULLER, Robert
  Anatole
MUMFORD, A H
  Videns
MUNBY, Arthur Joseph
  Brown, Jones
MUNRO, Hector Hugh
  Saki
MUNRO, Hugh
  Jason
MURFREE, Mary Noailles
  Craddock, Charles Egbert
  Dembry, R Emmet
MURIEL, John
  Dewes, Simon
  Lindsey, John
MURPHY, Charlotte *and*
 MURPHY, Lawrence
  Murphy, C L
MURPHY, Emily Gowan
 (Ferguson)
  Canuck, Janey
  Ferguson, Emily
MURPHY, John *and*
 CORLEY, Edwin
  Buchanan, Patrick
MURPHY, Lawrence *and*
 MURPHY, Charlotte
  Murphy, C L
MURPHY, Lawrence D
  Lawrence, Steven C
MURRAY, Andrew Nicholas
  Islay, Nicholas

MURRAY, Blanche
  Murray, Geraldine
MURRAY, Francis Edwin
  Mair, H Allen
MURRAY, Joan
  Blood, Joan Wilde
MURRAY, Ruth Hilary
  Finnegan, Ruth
MURRAY, Venetia Pauline *and*
  BIRCH, Jack Ernest Lionel
  Flight, Francies
MURRAY, William Waldie
  Orderly Sergeant, The
MURRY, Colin Middleton
  Cowper, Richard
  Murry, Colin
MURRY, Violet
  Arden, Mary
MUSKETT, Netta Rachel
  Hill, Anne
MUSPRATT, Rosalie
  John, Jasper
MUSSI, Mary
  Edgar, Josephine
  Howard, Mary
MUSTO, Barry
  Simon, Robert
MYERS, Mary Cathcart
  Borer, Mary Cathcart
MYSTERY WRITERS OF
  AMERICA INC:
  CALIFORNIA CHAPTER
  Durrant, Theo

NAIR, K K
  Chaitanya, Krishna
NAISMITH, Robert Stevenson
  Stevenson, Robert

NASH, Vaughan *and*
  SMITH, Llewellyn
  Two East Londoners
NEAL, Adeline Phyllis
  Grey, A F
NEEDHAM, Joseph
  Holorenshaw, Henry
NEILD, James Edward
  J E N
  Jaques
  Sly, Christopher
NELMS, Henning
  Talbot, Hake
NELSON, Ethel
  Nina
NELSON, Lawrence
  Trent, Peter
NERNEY, Patrick W
  Nudnick
NETTELL, Richard
  Kenneggy, Richard
NETTZ, Julie
  Julie
NEUBAUER, William Arthur
  Arthur, William
  Garrison, Joan
  Marsh, Rebecca
  Newcomb, Norma
NEVILLE, Alison
  Candy, Edward
NEVILLE, Ann *and*
  GOYDER, Margot
  Neville, Margot
NEVILLE, Derek
  Salt, Jonathan
NEWELL, Robert Henry
  Kerr, Orpheus C

NEWLIN, Margaret
  Rudd, Margaret
NEWMAN, Bernard
  Betteridge, Don
NEWMAN, James Roy
  Stryfe, Paul
NEWMAN, Lyn Lloyd
  Irvine, Lyn
NEWMAN, Mona A J
  Fitzgerald, Barbara
  Stewart, Jean
NEWMAN, Terence
  O'Connor, Dermot
NEWNHAM, Don
  Eden, Matthew
NEWTON, Dwight Bennett
  Bennett, Dwight
NEWTON, H Chance
  Gawain
NEWTON, William
  Jansen, Hank
  Ross, Gene
NEWTON, William Simpson
  Mitcham, Gilroy
  Newton, Macdonald
NICHOLS, *Captain* G H F
  Quex
NICHOLS, Mary Eudora
  Brown, Eve
NICHOLSON, Joan
  Craig, Alison
  Weir, Jonnet
NICHOLSON, Margaret Beda
  Yorke, Margaret
NICHOLSON, Violet
  Hope, Lawrence
NICKSON, Arthur
  Hodson, Arthur

NICKSON, A (cont'd)
  Peters, Roy
  Saunders, John
  Winstan, Matt
NICOL, Eric Patrick
  Jabez
NICOLE, Christopher
  Cade, Robin
  Grange, Peter
  Logan, Mark
  York, Andrew
NICOLL, *Sir* William Robertson
  Clear, Claudius
  Wace, W E
NIELSON, Helen Berniece
  Giles, Kris
NILSON, Annabel
  Nilson, Bee
NISBET, Ulric
  Callaway, Hugh
NISOT, Mavis Elizabeth
  Penmare, William
NOCK, Albert Jay
  Historicus
  Journeyman
NOLAN, Cynthia
  Reed, Cynthia
NOLAN, Frederick
  Christian, Frederick H
NOLAN, William F
  Anmar, Frank
  Cahill, Mike
  Edwards, F E
NOONAN, Robert
  Tressall, Robert
  Tressell, Robert
NORGATE, Walter
  Le Grys, Walter

105

NORMAN, C H
  Stanhope of Chester
NORTH, William
  Rodd, Ralph
NORTHAM, Lois Edgell
  Nelson, Lois
NORTHCOTT, Cecil
  Miller, Mary
NORTON, Alice Mary
  North, Andrew
  Norton, André
NORTON, Alice Mary *and*
  HOGARTH, Grace
  Weston, Allen
NORTON, Marjorie
  Ellison, Marjorie
NORTON, Olive Marion
  Neal, Hilary
  Noon, T R
  Norton, Bess
  Norway, Kate
NORWAY, Nevil Shute
  Shute, Nevil
NORWOOD, Victor George
  Charles
  Banton, Coy
  Baxter, Shane V
  Bowie, Jim
  Brand, Clay
  Cody, Walt
  Corteen, Craig
  Corteen, Wes
  Dangerfield, Clint
  Destry, Vince
  Fargo, Doone
  McCord, Whip
  Rand, Brett
  Russell, Shane

  Shane, Rhondo
  Tressidy, Jim
NOVAK, Cornelius Dan
  Zacharia
  Zacharia, Dan
NOWELL, Elizabeth Cameron
  Clemons, Elizabeth
NUMANO, Allen
  Corenanda, A L A
NURSE, Malcolm Ivan Meredith
  Padmore, George
NUTT, Charles
  Beaumont, Charles
  Grantland, Keith
  Lovehill, C V
  McNutt, Charles
  Phillips, Michael
  Tenneshaw, S M
NUTT, David
  Brand, David
NUTT, Lily Clive
  Arden, Clive
NUTTALL, Anthony
  Allyson, Alan
  Bardsley, Michael
  Curtis, Spencer
  Lenton, Anthony
  Tracey, Grant
  Trent, Lee
  Wells, Tracey
NYE, Nelson Coral
  Colt, Clem
  Denver, Drake C

OAKESHOTT, Edna
  Peters, Jocelyn
OAKLEY, Eric Gilbert
  Capon, Peter

Gregson, Paul
  Scott-Morley, A
OAKLEY, John, *Dean of Manchester*
  Vicesimus
OBENCHAIN, Eliza Caroline
  Hall, Eliza Calvert
O'BRIEN, Conor Cruise
  O'Donnell, Donat
O'CASEY, Sean
  Green Crow, The
  O'Cathasaigh, P
O'CONNOR, Patrick Joseph
  Fiacc, Padraic
O'CONNOR, Richard
  Archer, Frank
  Wayland, Patrick
O'CONNOR, T P
  T P
O'DONOGHUE, Elinor Mary
  Oddie, E M
O'DONOVAN, Michael Francis
  O'Connor, Frank
O'FARRELL, William
  Grew, William
O'FERRALL, Ernest
  Kodak
OGNALL, Leopold Horace
  Carmichael, Harry
  Howard, Harry
  Howard, Hartley
O'GRADY, Elizabeth Anne
  Scollan, E A
O'GRADY, John P
  Culotta, Nino
  O'Grada, Sean
O'HARA, John
  Delaney, Franey

OLD, Phyllis Muriel Elizabeth
  Shiel-Martin
OLD COYOTE, Elnora A
  Old Coyote, Sally
  Wright, Elnora A
  Wright, Sally
OLDFIELD, Claude Houghton
  Houghton, Claude
OLDMEADOW, Ernest James
  Downman, Francis
OLIVER, Amy Roberts
  Onions, Berta
  Ruck, Berta
OLIVER, Doris M
  Hughes, Alison
OLIVER, George
  Onions, Oliver
OLIVER, John Rathbone
  Roland, John
OLNEY, Ellen Warner
  Hayes, Henry
OLSEN, Theodore Victor
  Stark, Joshua
OLSON, Herbert Vincent
  Olsen, Herb
O'MAHONY, Charles Kingston
  Kingston, Charles
O'MALLEY, *Lady*
  Bridge, Ann
O'MORE, Peggy
  Bowman, Jeanne
O'NEILL, Herbert Charles
  Strategicus
O'NEILL, Rose Cecil
  Latham, O'Neill
O'NOLAN, Brian
  An Broc
  Knowall, George

O'NOLAN, B (cont'd)
  Na gCopaleen, Myles
  O'Brien, Flann
OPPENHEIM, E Phillips
  Partridge, Anthony
OPPENHEIMER, Carlota
  Carlota
ORAGE, Alfred James
  A R O
  Congreve, R H
  Orage, A R
  R H C
ORBISON, Roy *and*
 KECK, Maud
  Orbison, Keck
ORDE-WARD, F W
  Williams, F Harald
ORGA, Irfan
  Riza, Ali
ORGILL, Douglas *and*
 FISHMAN, Jack
  Gilman, J D
O'RIORDAN, Conal O'Connell
  Connell, Norreys
ORME, Eve
  Day, Irene
O'ROURKE, Frank
  O'Malley, Frank
ORTON, John Kingsley
  Orton, Joe
  Wellbrook, Edna
ORTON, Thora
  Colson, Thora
OSBERT, Reuben
  Osborn, Reuben
OSBORNE, Dorothy Gladys
  Arthur, Gladys

O'SHAUGHNESSY, Marjorie
  Shaw, Adelaide
OSLER, Eric Richard
  Dick, T
OSMOND, Andrew *and*
 INGRAMS, Richard
  Reid, Philip
OSTERGAARD, Geoffrey
  Gerard, Gaston
OSTLERE, Gordon Stanley
  Gordon, Richard
OSTLERE, Mary
  Gordon, Mary
OSTRANDER, Isabel Egerton
  Chipperfield, Robert Orr
  Fox, David
  Grant, Douglas
OURSLER, Fulton
  Abbot, Anthony
OURSLER, William Charles
  Gallagher, Gale
OUSELEY, G J R
  Disciple of the Master, A
OVERHOLSER, Wayne D
  Daniels, John S
  Leighton, Lee
  Stevens, Dan J
  Wayne, Joseph
OVERY, Jillian P J
  Martin, Gil
  Overy, Martin
ØVSTEDAL, Barbara
  Laker, Rosalind
  Paul, Barbara
OWEN, Dilys
  Edwards, Olwen

OWEN, Frank;
  FOOT, Michael *and*
  HOWARD, Peter
    Cato
OWEN, Jack
    Dykes, Jack
OWENS, Iris
    Daimler, Harriet
OXMAN, Philip
    Peachum, Thomas
OZAKI, Milton K
    Saber, Robert O

§ §

*My name is legion: for we are
many.*
—Bible. Mark, 5.9

§ §

PADGETT, Ron
    Dangerfield, Harlan
    Veitch, Tom
PADLEY, Arthur
    Winn, Patrick
PADLEY, Walter
    Marcus Aurelius
PAGE, Evelyn *and*
  BLAIR, Dorothy
    Scarlett, Roger
PAGE, Gerald W
    Grindle, Carleton
    Pembrooke, Kenneth
PAGE, Norvell W
    Stockbridge, Grant
PAGE, Patricia Kathleen
    Cape, Judith
    Irwin, P K

PAGET, Violet
    Lee, Vernon
PAINE, Lauran Bosworth
    Ainsworthy, Roy
    Allen, Clay
    Almonte, Rosa
    Andrews, A A
    Armour, John
    Bartlett, Kathleen
    Batchelor, Reg
    Beck, Harry
    Bedford, Kenneth
    Benton, Will
    Bosworth, Frank
    Bradford, Will
    Bradley, Concho
    Brennan, Will
    Carrel, Mark
    Carter, Nevada
    Cassady, Claude
    Clarke, Richard
    Clarke, Robert
    Custer, Clint
    Dana, Amber
    Dana, Richard
    Davis, Audrey
    Drexler, J F
    Duchesne, Antoinette
    Durham, John
    Fisher, Margot
    Fleck, Betty
    Frost, Joni
    Glendenning, Donn
    Glenn, James
    Gordon, Angela
    Gorman, Beth
    Hart, Francis
    Hayden, Jay

109

PAINE, L B (cont'd)
  Holt, Helen
  Houston, Will
  Howard, Elizabeth
  Howard, Troy
  Hunt, John
  Ingersol, Jared
  Kelley, Ray
  Ketchum, Jack
  Kilgore, John
  Liggett, Hunter
  Lucas, J K
  Lyon, Buck
  Martin, Bruce ·
  Martin, Tom
  Morgan, Angela
  Morgan, Arlene
  Morgan, Frank
  Morgan, John
  Morgan, Valerie
  O'Connor, Clint
  Pindell, Jon
  St George, Arthur
  Sharp, Helen
  Slaughter, Jim
  Standish, Buck
  Stuart, Margaret
  Thompson, Buck
  Thompson, Russ
  Thorn, Barbara
  Undine, P F
PAINTING, Norman
  Milna, Bruno
PALESTRANT, Simon
  Edward, Stephen
  Stevens, S P
  Strand, Paul E

PALMER, Cecil
  Ludlow, John
PALMER, John Leslie
  Haddon, Christopher
PALMER, John Leslie *and*
  SAUNDERS, Hilary Aidan
  St George
  Beeding, Francis
  Pilgrim, David
PALMER, John Williamson
  Coventry, John
PALMER, Madelyn
  Peters, Geoffrey
PALMER, Paul
  Downing, Century
PALMER, Ray
  Gade, Henry
PALMER, Stuart
  Stewart, Jay
PALMER-ARCHER, Laura M
  Bushwoman
PANIKKAR, Kavalam
  Putra, Kerala
PANOWSKI, Eileen Janet
  Thompson, Eileen
PARCELL, Norman Howe
  Nicholson, John
PARES, Marion
  Campbell, Judith
PARGETER, Edith Mary
  Peters, Ellis
PARKER, Dorothy
  Constant Reader
PARKER, Marion
  Dominic, *Sister* Mary
PARKES, Frank
  Dompo, Kwesi

PARKES, James W
   Hadham, John
PARKES, Terence
   Larry
PARKHILL, Forbes
   Martinez, J D
   Vloto, Otto
PARKINSON, Roger
   Holden, Matthew
PARKS, Georgina
   Gabrielle
PARR, Olive Katherine
   Chase, Beatrice
PARRIS, John
   Lascelles, Alison
PARRY, Hugh J
   Cross, James
PARRY, Margaret G
   Glyn, Megan
PARRY, Michel
   Cassaba, Carlos
   Fury, Nick
   Lee, Steve
   Lovecraft, Linda
   Pendragon, Eric
PARSONS, Anthony
   Nicholls, Anthony
PARSONS, Charles P
   Craven Hill
PARTRIDGE, Bellamy
   Bailey, Thomas
PARTRIDGE, Eric
   Vigilans
PARTRIDGE, Kate Margaret
   Partridge, Sydney
PATERSON, W R
   Swift, Benjamin

PATRICK, Keats
   Karig, Walter
PATRY, M *and*
  WILLIAMS, D F
   Williams, Patry
PATTEN, Gilbert
   Standish, Burt L
PATTERSON, Henry
   Fallon, Martin
   Graham, James
   Higgins, Jack
   Marlowe, Hugh
   Patterson, Harry
PATTERSON, Isabella Innis
   Patterson, Innis
PATTINSON, James
   Ryder, James
PATTINSON, Lee
   Holland, Rosemary
   Maxwell, Ann
   Miller, Ellen
PATTINSON, Nancy
   Asquith, Nan
PATTISON, Andrew Seth P
   Seth, Andrew
PATTISON, Ruth
   Abbey, Ruth
PAUL, Elliot Harold
   Rutledge, Brett
PAUL, Maury
   Benedict, Billy
   Knickerbocker, Cholly
   Madison, Dolly
   Stuyvesant, Polly
PAXTON, Lois
   Low, Dorothy Mackie
PAYNE, Charles J
   Snaffles

111

Real names

PAYNE, Donald Gordon
  Cameron, Ian
  Gordon, Donald
  Marshall, James Vance
PAYNE, Eileen Mary
  Mansell, C R
PAYNE, Pierre Stephen Robert
  Cargoe, Richard
  Horne, Howard
  Payne, Robert
  Young, Robert
PAYNE, Ronald Charles *and*
 GARROD, John William
  Castle, John
PAZ, Magdeleine
  Marx, Magdeleine
PEACH, Edward C
  Ophiel
PEARCE, Brian
  Hussey, Leonard
  Redman, Joseph
PEARCE, Melville Chaning
  Nicodemus
PEARCE, Raymond
  Maplesden, Ray
PEARSON, W T
  Pengreep, William
PECHEY, Archibald Thomas
  Cross, Mark
  Valentine
PECK, Leonard
  Brain, Leonard
PEDLAR, Ann
  Stafford, Ann
PEDRICK-HARVEY, Gale
  Pedrick, Gale
PEED, William Bartlett
  Peek, Bill

PEEL, Frederick *and*
 SIDDLE, Charles
  Slingsby, Rufus
PEEL, Hazel
  Hayman, Hazel
  Peel, Wallis
PEEPLES, Samuel Anthony
  Ward, Brad
PEERS, Edgar Allison
  Truscot, Bruce
PEISER, Maria Lilli
  Palmer, Lilli
PEMBER, William Leonard
  Monmouth, Jack
PEMBER-DEVEREUX, Margaret
 R R
  Devereux, Roy
PENDLETON, Donald Eugene
  Britain, Dan
  Gregory, Stephen
PENNER, Manola J
  Alexander, Jean
PENWARDEN, Helen
  Smith, Jessica
PEOPLE, Granville Church
  Church, Granville
PEPPER, Joan
  Alexander, Joan
PERELMAN, S J
  Namlerep, Sidney
PERKINS, Kenneth
  Phillips, King
PERRY, Clair Willard
  Perry, Clay
PERRY, James Black
  Weir, Logan
PERRY, Martin
  Martyn, Henry

PERRY, Robert
  Marquis, Don
PETAJA, Emil
  Pine, Theodor
PETERS, Arthur A
  Peters, Fritz
PETERS, Robert Louis
  Bridge, John
PETERSON, Corinna
  Cochrane, Corinna
PETERSON, Margaret
  Green, Glint
PETRIE, Rhona
  Duell, Eileen-Marie
PETRONE, Jane Gertrude
  Muir, Jane
PEYTON, Kathleen Wendy *and*
 PEYTON, Michael
  Peyton, K M
PHILIPS, Judson Pentecost
  Pentecost, Hugh
PHILLIPS, David *and*
 MARKOV, Georgi
  St George, David
PHILLIPS, David Graham
  Graham, John
PHILLIPS, Dennis John Andrew
  Challis, Simon
  Chambers, Peter
  Chester, Peter
PHILLIPS, Gerald William
  Huntingdon, John
PHILLIPS, Gordon
  Lucio
PHILLIPS, Horace
  Stanton, Marjorie
PHILLIPS, Hubert
  Caliban

PHILLIPS, H (cont'd)
  Dogberry
  Ninespot
PHILLIPS, Hugh
  Hughes, Philip
PHILLIPS, James Atlee
  Atlee, Philip
PHILLIPS, Olga
  Olga
PHILLIPS, Pauline
  Van Buren, Abigail
PHILLPOTTS, Eden
  Hext, Harrington
PHILPOT, Joseph H
  Lafargue, Philip
PHILPOTT, Alexis Robert
  Pantopuck
PHYSICK, Edward Harold
  Visiak, E H
PICKEN, Mary
  Wells, Jane Warren
PIERCE, Mary Cunningham
  Cunningham, Mary
PIGGOTT, William
  Wales, Hubert
PIKE, Mary Hayden
  Langdon, Mary
  Story, Sydney A J
PILCHER, Rosamunde
  Fraser, Jane
PILLEY, Phil
  Lindley, Gerard
PINTO, Jacqueline
  Blairman, Jacqueline
PIPER, David Towry
  Towry, Peter
PIPER, Evelyn
  Modell, Merriam

113

PITCAIRN, John James *and*
 FREEMAN, R Austin
  Ashdown, Clifford
PLACE, Marian Templeton
  White, Dale
  Whitinger, R D
PLATH, Sylvia
  Lucas, Victoria
PLATT, Edward
  Trent, Paul
PLOMER, William
  D'Arfey, William
  Pagan, Robert
PLUMLEY, Ernest F
  Clevedon, John
PLUMMER, Thomas Arthur
  Sarne, Michael
POCOCK, Tom
  Allcot, Guy
POHL, Frederik
  MacCreigh, James
POHL, Frederik *and*
 DEL REY, Lester
  McCann, Edson
POHL, Frederik *and*
 KORNBLUTH, Cyril M
  Gottesman, S D
POLAND, Dorothy E H
  Farely, Alison
  Hammond, Jane
POLANSKY, Abraham *and*
 WILLSON, Mitchell A
  Hogarth, Emmett
POLIAKOFF, Vladimir
  Augur
POLLEY, Judith Anne
  Hagar, Judith
  Luellen, Valentina

POLWARTH, Gwendoline Mary
  Polwarth, G Marchant
PONSONBY, Doris Almon
  Rybot, Doris
POOLE, Reginald Heber
  Heber, Austin
  Heber, Reginald
  Poole, Michael
PORN, Alice
  Ali-Mar
PORTER, Barbara Conney
  Conney, Barbara
PORTER, Edward
  Harvey, Lyon
PORTER, Eleanor
  Stewart, Eleanor
PORTER, Harold Everett
  Hall, Holworthy
PORTER, Maurice
  Mouthpiece
PORTER, William Sydney
  Henry, O
POSNER, David Louis
  Bourchier, Jules
POSNER, Jacob D
  Dean, Gregory
POSSELT, Eric
  Palmer, Edgar A
POTTER, George William
  Withers, E L
POTTER, Heather
  Jenner, Heather
POTTER, Margaret
  Betteridge, Anne
POU, Genevieve
  Holden, Genevieve
POUND, Ezra
  Adkins, M D

POUND, Ezra (cont'd)
 Atheling, William
 B L
 Dias, B H
 Hall, John
 Helmholtz, Bastien von
 J L
 Janus, Hiram
 Llewmys, Weston
 Maria, Hermann Karl Georg
  Jesus
 Saunders, Abel
 T J V
 Venison, Alfred
POWE, Bruce
 Portal, Ellis
POWELL, Talmage
 McCready, Jack
POWELL-SMITH, Vincent
 Elphinstone, Francis
 Justiciar
 Santa Maria
POWER, *Sir* D'Arcy
 D'A P
POWLEY, *Mrs* A A
 Gene, Marta
PRAFULLA, Das
 Subhadra-Nandan
PRATHER, Richard S
 Knight, David
 Ring, Douglas
PRATT, E B Atkinson
 Blake, Eleanor
PRATT, Fletcher
 Fretcher, George U
PRATT, John
 Winton, John

PRATT, Theodore
 Brace, Timothy
PRATT, William Henry
 Karloff, Boris
PRESLAND, John
 Bendit, Gladys
PREVOST-BATTERSBY, H F
 Prevost, Francis
PRICE, Beverly Joan
 Randell, Beverly
PRICE, Edgar Hoffman
 Daly, Hamlin
PRICE, Jeremie
 Lane, Marvyn
PRICE, Olive
 Cherryholmes, Anne
PRICE-BROWN, John
 Bohn, Eric
 Price-Brown
PRICHARD, H Hesketh *and*
 PRICHARD, Kate Hesketh
 Heron, E *and* H
PRIESTLEY, Clive Ryland
 Ryland, Clive
PRIESTLEY, John Boynton
 Goldsmith, Peter
PRIOR, Mollie
 Roscoe, Janet
PRITCHARD, William Thomas
 Dexter, William
PUDDEPHA, Derek
 Quill
PUECHNER, Ray
 Haddo, Oliver
 Victor, Charles B
PULLEIN-THOMPSON, Christine
 Keir, Christine

PULLEIN-THOMPSON, Denis
  Cannan, Denis
PULLEIN-THOMPSON,
 Josephine Mary
  Cannan, Joanna
  Mann, Josephine
PULLEN, George
  Culpeper, Martin
PULLING, Albert Van Siclen
  Pulling, Pierre
PUNNETT, Margaret *and*
 PUNNETT, Ivor
  Simons, Peter
  Simons, Roger
PURCELL, Victor W W S
  Buttle, Myra
PURDY, Ken
  Prentiss, Karl
PURVES, Frederick
  Lloyd, Joseph M
PYKE, John
  Westlaw, Steven
PYKE, Lillian Maxwell
  Maxwell, Erica

QUENTIN, Dorothy
  Beverly, Linda
QUIBELL, Agatha
  Pearce, A H
QUIGLEY, Aileen
  Fabian, Ruth
  Lindley, Erica
QUIGLEY, M C *and*
 CLARK, Mary Elizabeth
  Clark, Margery
QUIGLY, Elizabeth Pauline
  Elisabeth

QUILLER-COUCH, *Sir* Arthur
  A Q-C
  Q

RABBETS, Thomas G
  St Ebbar
RADCLIFFE, Garnett
  Travers, Stephen
RADETZBY von RADETZ,
 Countess
  Harding, Bertita
RADFORD, Ruby Lorraine
  Bailey, Matilda
  Ford, Marcia
RAE, Hugh Cranford
  Crawford, Robert
  Houston, R B
RAE, Margaret Doris
  Rae, Doris
RAGG, Thomas Murray
  Thomas, Murray
RALEIGH-KING, Robin Victor
 Lethbridge
  Graham, Robin
  King, Robin
RAMAGE, Jennifer
  Mason, Howard
RAME, Maria Louise
  Ouida
RAMSAY, Allan
  Zero
RAMSAY-LAYE, Elizabeth
  Massary, Isabel
RAMSKILL, Valerie
  Brooke, Carol
RANDALL, A E
  Hope, John Francis

RANDOLPH, Georgiana Ann
  Rice, Craig
  Sanders, Daphne
  Venning, Michael
RANDOLPH, Lowell King
  Ran, Kip
RANSFORD, Oliver
  Wylcotes, John
RANSOME, L E
  Chester, Elizabeth
  Melbourne, Ida
  Ransome, Barbara
  Stirling, Stella
RAPHAEL, Chaim
  Davey, Jocelyn
RAPHAEL, Frederic *and*
 MASCHLER, Tom
  Caine, Mark
RASH, Dora
  Wallace, Doreen
RAUBENHEIMER, George H
  Harding, George
RAVENSCROFT, John R
  Ravenscroft, Rosanne
RAWLEY, Callman
  Rakosi, Carl
RAWSON, Clayton
  Merlini, The Great
  Towne, Stuart
RAYMOND, Rene
  Chase, James Hadley
  Docherty, James L
  Grant, Ambrose
  Marshall, Raymond
RAYMOND, Walter
  Cobbleigh, Tom
RAYNER, Augustus Alfred
  Hall, Whyte

RAYNER, Claire
  Brandon, Sheila
  Lynton, Ann
  Martin, Ruth
REACH, James
  Manning, Roy
  West, Tom
READ, Anthony
  Ferguson, Anthony
READ, James
  Bacon, Jeremy
READ, John
  Jan
READE, *Mrs* Frances
  Lawson
  Langworthy, Yolande
REAGAN, Thomas B
  Thomas, Jim
REANEY, James
  Spoonhill
REBACK, Marcus *and*
 CALDWELL, Janet Taylor
  Caldwell, Taylor
  Reiner, Max
REDMAN, Ben Ray
  Lord, Jeremy
REDMAN, William Xavier
  Scarlet, Will
REDMON, Lois
  Rogers, Rachel
REECE, Alys
  Wingfield, Susan
REED, Alexander Wyclif
  Harlequin
REED, Blair
  Ring, Adam
REEMAN, Douglas
  Kent, Alexander

117

REES, Helen
  Oliver, Jane
REES, Joan
  Avery, June
  Bedford, Ann
  Strong, Susan
REEVE, Winifred Babcock
  Watanna, Onoto
REEVE-JONES, Alan
  Lunchbasket, Roger
REEVES, John Morris
  Reeves, James
REID, John
  Caliban
  Toulmin, David
REID, Whitelaw
  Agate
REILLY, Helen K
  Abbey, Kieran
REINFELD, Fred
  Young, Edward
RENFREW, A
  Patterson, Shott
RENNIE, James Alan
  Denver, Boone
RENTOUL, T Laurence
  Gage, Gervais
RESIDE, W J
  Raeside, Juks
RESSICH, John S M *and*
 DE BANZIE, Eric
  Baxter, Gregory
REY, Hans Augusto
  Uncle Gus
REY, Lester Del *and*
 POHL, Frederik
  McCann, Edson

REYNOLDS, Helen Mary
 Greenwood Dickson
  Dickson, Helen
  Reynolds, Dickson
REYNOLDS, John E
  Dexter, Ross
RICCI, Lewis Anselm da Costa
  Bartimeus
RICE, Brian Keith
  Vigilans
RICE, Dorothy
  Borne, D
  Vicary, Dorothy
RICE, Joan
  Hallam, Jay
RICHARDS, Allen
  Rosenthal, Richard A
RICHARDS, James
  Cladpole, Jim
RICHARDS, Ronald C W
  Saddler, K Allen
RICHARDSON, Eileen
  Shane
RICHARDSON, Ethel Henrietta
  Richardson, Henry Handel
RICHARDSON, Gladwell
  Blacksnake, George
  Jones, Calico
  Kent, Pete
  Kildare, Maurice
  O'Riley, Warren
  Warner, Frank
  Winslowe, John R
RICHARDSON, Mary Kathleen
  Norton, S H
RIDDELL, *Mrs* J H
  Hawthorne, Rainey
  Trafford, F G

RIDDLESTON, Charles H
  Drongo, Luke
RIDDOLLS, Brenda H
  English, Brenda H
RIDEAUX, Charles
  Chancellor, John
RIDGE, William Pett
  Simpson, Warwick
RIGONI, Orlando Joseph
  Ames, Leslie
  Wesley, James
RIGSBY, Howard
  Howard, Vechel
RILEY, James Whitcomb
  Johnson, Benjamin F
RIMANOCZY, A
  Eland, Charles
RISTER, Claude
  Billings, Buck
  Holt, Tex
RITCHIE, L Edwin
  Lewis, Voltaire
RIVETT, Edith Caroline
  Carnac, Carol
  Lorac, E C R
ROARK, Garland
  Garland, George
ROBBINS, Clarence Aaron
  Robbins, Tod
ROBBINS, June
  Julie of Colorado Springs
ROBERTS, Cecil
  Beresford, Russell
ROBERTS, Dorothy James
  Mortimer, Peter
ROBERTS, E N
  Newman, Ernest

ROBERTS, Eric
  Robin
ROBERTS, Irene
  Carr, Roberta
  Harle, Elizabeth
  Roberts, Ivor
  Rowland, Iris
  Shaw, Irene
ROBERTS, James
  Horton, Robert J
ROBERTS, Keith J K
  Bevan, Alistair
ROBERTS, Ursula
  Miles, Susan
ROBERTSHAW, James Denis
  Gaunt, Michael
ROBERTSON, Constance Noyes
  Scott, Dana
ROBERTSON, Eileen Arbuthnot
  Robertson, E Arnot
ROBERTSON, Frank Chester
  Crane, Robert
  Field, Frank Chester
  Hill, King
ROBERTSON, James Logie
  Haliburton, Hugh
ROBERTSON, James Robin
  Connell, John
ROBERTSON, Keith
  Keith, Carlton
ROBERTSON, Margery Ellen
  Thorp, Ellen
  Thorp, Morwenna
ROBERTSON, Walter George
  Werrerson, Talbot
ROBERTSON, William
  Strathearn-Hay

119

Real names

ROBEY, Timothy Lester
 Townsend
  Townsend, Timothy
ROBINETT, Stephen
 Hallus, Tak
ROBINS, Denise
 French, Ashley
 Gray, Harriet
 Kane, Julia
 Wright, Francesca
ROBINS, Elizabeth
 Raimond, C E
ROBINSON, H
 Madeoc
ROBINSON, Joan Gale
 Thomas, Joan Gale
ROBINSON, Julien Louis
 Vedey, Julian
ROBINSON, Lewis George
 Limnelius, George
ROBINSON, Patricia *and*
 STEVENSON, Ferdinan
 Macomber, Daria
ROBINSON, Richard Blundell
 Leaderman, George
ROBSON, Norman
 Robb, John
ROCHE, Thomas
 Yes Tor
ROCHESTER, George Ernest
 Gaunt, Jeffrey
ROCKEY, Howard
 Panbourne, Oliver
RODDA, Charles
 Holt, Gavin
RODDA, Charles *and*
 AMBLER, Eric
 Reed, Eliot
120

ROE, Eric
 Roe, Tig
ROE, Ivan
 Savage, Richard
ROETHKE, Theodore
 Rothberg, Winterset
ROGERS, Ruth
 Alexander, Ruth
ROGERSON, James
 Hamilton, Roger
ROHLFS, *Mrs* Anna
 Greene, Anna Katharine
ROLFE, Edwin
 Fuller, Lester
ROLFE, Frederick
 Corvo, *Baron*
ROLLINS, Kathleen *and*
 DRESSER, Davis
 Debrett, Hal
ROLLINS, William
 Stacy, O'Connor
ROMANOFF, Alexander
 Nicholayevitch
 Abdullah, Achmed
ROMLEY, Frederick J
 Romley, Derek
ROOME, Gerald Antony
 Leslie, Colin
ROOS, William
 Rand, William
ROOS, William *and*
 KELLEY, Audrey
 Roos, Kelley
ROPES, Arthur Reed
 Ross, Adrian
ROSCOE, John *and*
 RUSO, Michael
 Roscoe, Mike

ROSE, Alfred
  Reade, Rolf S
ROSE, Alvin Emmanuel
  Pruitt, Alan
ROSE, Elizabeth Jane
  Elizabeth
ROSE, Graham
  Graham, John
ROSE, Ian
  Rose, Robert
ROSE, Mary H
  Maizie
ROSEN, Michael
  Landgrave of Hesse
ROSENBERG, Ethel
  Clifford, Eth
  Penn, Ruth Bonn
ROSENBERG, Henrietta
  Keating, Walter S
ROSENKRANTZ, Linda
  Damiano, Laila
ROSENQUIST, Fingal
  Südorf, Fingal von
ROSENTHAL, Michael D H
  Ross, Michael D H
ROSMAN, Alice Grant
  Rosna
ROSS, Frank Xavier
  Frank, R Jr
ROSS, Isaac
  Ross, George
ROSS, W W Eustace
  E R
ROSS, William Edward Daniel
  Ames, Leslie
  Brooks, Laura Frances
  Colby, Alice
  Colby, Lydia

ROSS, W E D (cont'd)
  Dana, Rose
  Daniels, Jan
  Daniels, Jane
  Dorset, Ruth
  Gilmer, Ann
  McCormack, Charlotte
  Randolph, Ellen
  Randolph, Jane
  Roberts, Dan
  Ross, Clarissa
  Ross, Dan
  Ross, Dana
  Ross, Marilyn
  Ross, W E D
  Rossiter, Jane
  Steele, Tex
  Williams, Rose
ROSS, Zola Helen
  Arre, Helen
  Iles, Bert
ROSSITER, John
  Ross, Jonathan
ROSSNER, Robert
  Ross, Ivan T
ROSTEN, Leo C
  Ross, Leonard Q
ROTH, Arthur
  McGurk, Slater
ROTH, Holly
  Ballard, K G
  Merrill, P J
ROTHERAY, Geoffrey Neville
  Rooke, Dennis
ROTHWELL, Henry Talbot
  Talbot, Henry
ROUSSEAU, Leon
  Strydom, Len

121

ROWE, John Gabriel
  Rowe, Alice E
  Walters, T B
ROWLAND, Donald Sydney
  Adams, Annette
  Bassett, Jack
  Baxter, Hazel
  Benton, Karla
  Berry, Helen
  Brant, Lewis
  Bray, Alison
  Brayce, William
  Brockley, Fenton
  Bronson, Oliver
  Buchanan, Chuck
  Caley, Rod
  Carlton, Roger
  Cleve, Janita
  Court, Sharon
  Craig, Vera
  Craile, Wesley
  Dryden, John
  Fenton, Freda
  Field, Charles
  Kroll, Burt
  Langley, Helen
  Lansing, Henry
  Lant, Harvey
  Lynn, Irene
  McHugh, Stuart
  Madison, Hank
  Mason, Chuck
  Murray, Edna
  Page, Lorna
  Patterson, Olive
  Porter, Alvin
  Random, Alex
  Rimmer, W J

  Rix, Donna
  Rockwell, Matt
  Roscoe, Charles
  Scott, Norford
  Scott, Valerie
  Segundo, Bart
  Shaul, Frank
  Spurr, Clinton
  Stan, Roland
  Stevens, J D
  Suttling, Mark
  Talbot, Kay
  Travers, Will
  Vinson, Elaine
  Walters, Rick
  Webb Neil
RUBEL, James Lyon
  Hayes, Timothy
  Macrae, Mason
RUBENSTEIN, Stanley Jack
  Ar, Esjay
RUBINS, Harold
  Robbins, Harold
RUCHLIS, Hyman
  Barrow, George
RUDNYCKYJ, Jaroslav B
  Bij-Bijchenko
RUMBOLD-GIBBS, Henry St
John C
  Gibbs, Henry
  Harvester, Simon
  Saxon, John
RUNBECK, Margaret Lee
  McKinley, Karen
RUNDLE, Anne
  Lamont, Marianne
  Marshall, Joanne
  Sanders, Jeanne

RUNYAN, Alfred Damon
  Runyon, Damon
RURIC, Peter
  Cain, Paul
RUSH, Noel
  Garnett, David S
  Lee, David
RUSO, Michael *and*
  ROSCOE, John
  Roscoe, Mike
RUSSELL, Elizabeth Mary
  Countess
  Elizabeth
RUSSELL, George William
  A E
RUSSELL, Henry George
  Minicam
RUSSELL, Shirley
  King, Stephanie
  Vernon, Marjorie
RUSSELL, Ursula D'Ivry
  D'Ivry, Ursula
RUSTERHOLTZ, Winsome Lucy
  Turvey, Winsome
RUTLEDGE, Nancy
  Bryson, Leigh
RYALL, William Bolitho
  Bolitho, William
RYAN, John D
  Brother Ernest
RYAN, Paul William
  Finnegan, Robert
RYDBERG, Ernie
  Brouillette, Emil
  McCary, Reed
RYDELL, Helen *and*
  FORBES, Deloris Stanton
  Rydell, Forbes

RYDER, M L
  Lawson, Michael
RYDER, Vera
  Cook, Vera
  Mortimer, June
RYNNE, Alice
  Curtayne, Alice
RYWELL, Martin
  Hemingway, Taylor
  Sears, Deane

SABRE, Mel R *and*
  EIDEN, Paul
  Stagg, Delano
SAINT, Dora Jessie
  Read, Miss
SAINT-HILAIRE, P B
  Pavitra
SAINT INNOCENT, Marquis of
  Kahler, Woodland
ST JOHN, Wylly Folk
  Fox, Eleanor
  Larson, Eve
  Pierce, Katherine
  Vincent, Mary Keith
  Williams, Michael
SAKLATVALA, Beram
  Marsh, Henry
SALMON, Annie Elizabeth
  Ashley, Elizabeth
  Martin, Nancy
SALMON, Geraldine Gordon
  Sarasin, J G
SALMON, P R
  Panlake, Richard
SALSBURY, Nate
  Ireland, Baron

123

SALTZMANN, Sigmund
  Salten, Felix
SAMACHSON, Joseph
  Miller, John
  Morrison, William
SAMBROT, William Anthony
  Ayes, Anthony
SAMMAN, Fern
  Powell, Fern
SAMPSON, Richard Henry
  Hull, Richard
SAMUELSON-SANDVID, Dorothy
  Dorfy
SANDERSON, Douglas
  Brett, Martin
  Douglas, Malcolm
SANDES, John
  Oriel
SANDFORD, Christopher
  Dansdorf, Chrysilla von
SANDFORD, Matthew
  Matt
SANDOZ, Mari
  Macumber, Mari
SANDS, Leo G
  Craig, Lee
  Helmi, Jack
  Herman, Jack
  Meuron, Skip
SARGENT, Genevieve
  Ginger
SASSOON, Siegfried
  Kain, Saul
  Lyre, Pinchbeck
  S S
  Sigma Sashûn

SATHERLEY, David *and*
  WHITEHAND, James
  Whitehand, Satherley
SAUNDERS, Ann Loreille
  Cox-Johnson, Ann
SAUNDERS, Hilary Aidan St
  George *and*
  PALMER, John Leslie
  Beeding, Francis
  Pilgrim, David
SAUNDERS, Jean
  Innes, Jean
SAUNDERS, Margaret Bell
  Bell, Margaret
SAUNDERS, Margaret Marshall
  Saunders, Marshall
SAUNDERS, Theodore *and*
  MEANS, Mary
  Scott, Denis
SAVAGE, Lee
  Stewart, Logan
SAVAGE, Mildred
  Barrie, Jane
SAWKINS, Raymond Harold
  Forbes, Colin
  Raine, Richard
SAXON, Sophia
  Jarrett, Kay
SAYER, Nancy Margetts
  Bradfield, Nancy
SAYER, Walter William
  Quiroule, Pierre
SAYERS, Dorothy L
  Leigh, Johanna
SAYERS, James D
  James, Dan
SCHAAF, M B
  Goffstein, M B

SCHIFF, Sydney
  Hudson, Stephen
SCHISGALL, Oscar
  Hardy, Stuart
SCHMIDT, James Norman
  Norman, James
SCHNEIDER, Daniel Edward
  Taylor, Daniel
SCHNEIDER, Monica Maria
  Oliver, Frances
SCHOENFELD, Eugene L
  Pocrates, *Dr* Hip
SCHOFIELD, Sylvia Anne
  Matheson, Sylvia A
  Mundy, Max
SCHONFIELD, Hugh Joseph
  Fielding, Hubert
  Hegesippus
SCHREINER, Olive Emilie Albertina
  Iron, Ralph
SCHUBE, Purcell G
  Mee
SCHÜTZE, Gladys Henrietta
  Leslie, Henrietta
  Mendl, Gladys
SCOBIE, Stephen Arthur Cross
  Waverley, John
SCOTT, Elise Aylen
  Aylen, Elise
SCOTT, Evelyn
  Souza, Ernest
SCOTT, Hilda R
  Smith, Harriet
SCOTT, Hugh Stowell
  Merriman, Henry Seton
SCOTT, Jody *and*
  LEITE, George Thurston
  Scott, Thurston

SCOTT, Leslie
  Cole, Jackson
  Leslie, A
  Leslie, A Scott
  Scott, Bradford
SCOTT, Marian Gallagher
  Oliver, Gail
SCOTT, Mary E
  Graham, Jean
SCOTT, Peter Dale
  Greene, Adam
  Sproston, John
SCOTT, Rose Laure
  Buckley, Eunice
SCOTT, William Matthew
  Scott, Will
  Watt, William
SCOTT, Winifred Mary
  Wynne, Pamela
SCOTT-HANSEN, Olive
  Murrell, Shirley
SCROGGIE, Marcus Graham
  Cathode Ray
SEAMAN, Elizabeth C
  Bly, Nellie
SEAMAN, *Sir* Owen
  Nauticus
  O S
SEARLE, M E
  Eirene
  M E S
SEAVER, Richard
  Mole, Oscar
SEAWELL, Molly Elliot
  Davis, Foxcroft
SEBENTHALL, Roberta
  Kruger, Paul

125

SEBLEY, Frances Rae
  Jeffs, Rae
SECCOMBE, Thomas
  T S
SECRIST, W G *and*
  KELLIHER, Dan T
  Secrist, Kelliher
SEEDO, Sonia
  Fuchs, Sonia
SEID, Ruth
  Sinclair, Jo
SELCAMM, George
  Machlis, Joseph
SELDES, Gilbert Vivian
  Johns, Foster
SELDON TRUSS, Leslie
  Selmark, George
SERAILLIER, Anne
  Rogers, Anne
SERNER, Gunnar
  Heller, Frank
SERVADIO, Gaia
  Mostyn-Owen, Gaia
SERWICHER, Kurt
  Kasznar, Kurt
SEUFFERT, Muriel
  Faulkner, Mary
  Seuffert, Muir
SEWALL, Robert
  Abbott, Bruce
  Lamont, Wood C
SHACKLETON, Edith
  Heald, Edith
SHAFFER, Anthony *and*
  SHAFFER, Peter
  Anthony, Peter
SHAMBROOK, Rona
  Randall, Rona

SHANN, Renée
  Gaye, Carol
  Pent, Katherine
SHAROT, Angela
  Lansbury, Angela
SHARP, *Sir* Henry
  Ainsworth, Oliver
SHARP, Ian
  Judge, The
SHARP, William
  Macleod, Fiona
SHAW, Charles
  Singer, Bant
SHAW, George Bernard
  Corno di Bassetto
  G B S
SHAW, Howard
  Howard, Colin
SHAW, Jane
  Gillespie, Jane
SHEA, Patrick
  Laughlin, P S
SHECKLEY, Robert
  O'Donnevan, Finn
SHELDON, Alice B
  Sheldon, Raccoona
  Tiptree, James *Jr*
SHELDON, Peter
  Gaddes, Peter
SHELLABARGER, Samuel
  Esteven, John
  Loring, Peter
SHEPPARD, John Hamilton
  George
  Creek, Nathan
SHERIDAN, Elsie Lee
  Cromwell, Elsie
  Gordon, Jane

SHERIDAN, E L (cont'd)
  Lee, Elsie
SHERIDAN, H B
  Sherry, Gordon
SHERMAN, Frank Dempster
  Carmen, Felix
SHIEL, M P *and*
  TRACY, Louis
  Holmes, Gordon
SHIELDS, George Oliver
  Coquina
SHIPMAN, Natalie
  Arthur, Phyllis
SHIRLEY, Edith
  Australia Jane
SHIRREFFS, Gordon D
  Donalds, Gordon
  Gordon, Stewart
  Maclean, Art
SHOLL, Anna McClure
  Corson, Geoffrey
SHORTT, Charles Rushton
  Rushton, Charles
SHURA, Mary Francis
  Craig, Mary
SHUTE, Evan Vere
  Jameson, Vere
SIDDLE, Charles *and*
  PEEL, Frederick
  Slingsby, Rufus
SIDEBOTHAM, Herbert
  Candidus
  Scrutator
  Student of Politics, A
  Student of War, A
SIEGEL, Doris
  Wells, Susan

SILVERBERG, Robert
  Chapman, Walker
  Drummond, Walter
  Jorgenson, Ivar
  Knox, Calvin
  Knox, Calvin M
  Osborne, David
  Sebastian, Lee
SILVERBERG, Robert *and*
  GARRETT, Randall
  Randall, Robert
SILVETTE, Herbert
  Dogbolt, Barnaby
SIM, Katharine Phyllis
  Nuraini
SIMMONDS, Michael Charles
  Essex, Frank
  Simmonds, Mike
SIMMONS, J S A
  Cromie, Stanley
  Montgomery, Derek
SIMONDS, Peter
  Greaves, Richard
SIMONS, Katherine Drayton
  Mayrant
  Mayrant, Drayton
SIMPSON, Anthony McVay
  Warren, Tony
SIMPSON, Bertram L
  Weale, B Putnam
SIMPSON, Evan John
  John, Evan
SIMPSON, John Frederick
  Norman Hampson
  Hampson, John
SIMPSON, Keith
  Bailey, Guy

127

SIMS, George Robert
 Dagonet
SIMSON, Eric Andrew
 Kirk, Laurence
SINCLAIR, Bertha Muzzy
 Bower, B M
SINCLAIR, Kathleen Henrietta
 Knight, Brigid
SINGER, Isaac Bashevis
 Bashevis, Isaac
 Warshofsky, Isaac
SINGER, James Hyman
 Singer, Burns
SINGH, Gopal
 Dardi
SIZER, Laurence
 Laurier, Don
SKIDELSKY, Simon Jasha
 Simon, S J
SKINNER, Conrad Arthur
 Maurice, Michael
SKINNER, June O'Grady
 O'Grady, Rohan
SKUES, George Edward
 Mackenzie
 Seaforth
SLADEK, John Thomas *and*
 DISCH, Thomas M
 Demijohn, Thom
SLANEY, George Wilson
 Woden, George
SLATER, Ernest
 Gwynne, Paul
SLATER, James
 Capitalist
SLATER, Montagu
 Johns, Richard

SLAUGHTER, Frank Gill
 Terry, C V
SLAVITT, David
 Sutton, Henry
SLESAR, Henry
 Leslie, O H
SLOCUM, Edward Mark
 Edwinson, Edmund
SLOGGETT, Nellie
 Cornwall, Nellie
SMALL, Austin J
 Seamark
SMITH, Alfred Aloysius
 Horn, Trader
SMITH, Charles H
 Arp, Bill
SMITH, Dorothy Gladys
 Anthony, C L
 Smith, Dodie
SMITH, Edgar
 Mason, Michael
SMITH, Edward Ernest
 Lindall, Edward
SMITH, Edward Percy
 Percy, Edward
SMITH, Elizabeth Thomasina
 Meade
 Meade, L T
SMITH, Ernest Bramah
 Bramah, Ernest
SMITH, Florence Margaret
 Smith, Stevie
SMITH, Frances C
 Smith, Jean
SMITH, Frank E
 Craig, Jonathan
SMITH, Frederick E
 Farrell, David

SMITH, G M
  Grey, Steele
SMITH, George
  Smith, Clyde
SMITH, Goldwin
  Bystander, A
SMITH, H Everard
  Everard, Henry
SMITH, Helen Zenna
  Price, Evadne
SMITH, June Johns
  Johns, June
SMITH, Lillian M
  Warner, Leigh
SMITH, Lily
  Wanderer
SMITH, Llewellyn *and*
 NASH, Vaughan
  Two East Londoners
SMITH, Margaret Ruth
  Seranne, Ann
SMITH, Marjorie Seymour
  Fearn, Elena
SMITH, Mary
  Drewery, Mary
SMITH, Norman Edward Mace
  Sheraton, Neil
  Shore, Norman
SMITH, Robert
  Chattan, Robert
SMITH, Robert Charles
  Charles, Robert
  Leader, Charles
SMITH, Rodney Collin *see*
 COLLIN SMITH, Rodney
SMITH, Sarah
  Stretton, Hesba

SMITH, Sidney Wallace
  Brodie, Gordon
SMITH, Walter Chalmers
  Knott, Hermann
  Orwell
SMITHELLS, Doreen
  Boscawen, Linda
SMITHERS, Leonard
  Neaniskos
SMITHIES, Muriel
  Howe, Muriel
  Nash, Newlyn
  Redmayne, Barbara
SMITTER, Eliott-Burton
  Hadley, Leila
SNODGRASS, W D
  Gardons, S S
  McConnell, Will
  Prutkov, Kozma
SNOW, Donald Clifford
  Fall, Thomas
SNOW, Charles Horace
  Averill, H C
  Ballew, Charles
  Hardy, Russ
  Lee, Ranger
  Marshall, Gary
  Smith, Wade
  Wills, Chester
SNOW, Helen Foster
  Wales, Nym
SNYDER, Louis Leo
  Nordicus
SODERBERG, Percy Measday
  Archer, S E
SOLOMON, Samuel
  Moolson, Melusa

129

SOMERVILLE, Edith Oenone
   Graham, Viva
   Herring, Geilles
   Somerville
SOUSTER, Raymond
   Holmes, Raymond
SOUTER, Helen Greig
   Aunt Kate
SOUTHERN, Terry *and*
 HOFFENBERG, Mason
   Kenton, Maxwell
SOUTHWOLD, Stephen
   Bell, Neil
   Martens, Paul
   Miles
SPECK, Gerald Eugene
   Kepps, Gerald
   Science Investigator
   Stone, Eugene
SPEICHER, Helen Ross *and*
 BORLAND, Kathryn K
   Abbott, Alice
   Land, Jane *and* Ross
SPENCE, William Duncan
   Bowden, Jim
   Ford, Kirk
   Rogers, Floyd
   Spence, Duncan
SPENDER, Stephen
   S H S
SPEWACK, Samuel
   Abbott, A A
SPICER, Bart *and*
 SPICER, Betty Coe
   Barbette, Jay
SPIEGEL, Clara E *and*
 MAYER, Jane
   Jaynes, Clare

SPILLANE, Frank Morrison
   Spillane, Mickey
SPINELLI, Grace
   Spinelli, Marcos
SPIRO, Edward H
   Cookridge, E H
SPOONER, Peter Alan
   Mellor, Michael
   Peters, Alan
   Rennie, Jack
   Underwood, Keith
SPRATLING, Walter Norman
   Sparlin, W
SPRIGG, Christopher St John
   Caudwell, Christopher
SPRING, Howard
   R H S
SPROAT, Iain Macdonald
   Penn, Richard
SPROULE, Howard
   Sproule, Wesley
SQUIBBS, H W Q
   Quirk
SQUIRE, *Sir* John Collings
   Eagle, Solomon
STACEY, P M de Cosqueville
   De Cosqueville, Pierre
   Shelton, Michael
STAFFORD, Muriel
   Sauer, Muriel S
STAMP, Roger
   Mingston, R Gresham
STANIER, Maida
   Culex
STANLEY, Nora Kathleen Begbie
   Stange, Nora K
STANNARD, Eliza Vaughan
   Winter, John Strange

STANSFIELD, Anthony *and*
  LILLEY, Peter
    Buckingham, Bruce
STANTON-HOPE, W E
  Hope, Stanton
STAPLES, Reginald Thomas
  Brewster, Robin
  Stevens, Robert Tyler
STARK, Raymond
  Norwood, John
STARKEY, James Sullivan
  O'Sullivan, Seumas
STARR, Richard
  Essex, Richard
  Richards, Stella
STATON-BEVAN, William
  Norman
  Abbey, Staton
STEARN, John Theodor
  Stern, John
STEARNS, Myron Morris
  Amid, John
STEELE, Mary Quintard Govan
  Gage, Wilson
STEELE, Patricia M V
  Joudry, Patricia
STEELE, Robert V P
  Thomas, Lately
STEFFAN, Alice Jacqueline
  Steffan, Jack
STEFFENS, Arthur Joseph
  Hardy, Arthur S
STEIN, Aaron Marc
  Bagby, George
  Bagby, George A
  Stone, Hampton
STEIN, Gertrude
  Toklas, Alice B

STEPHEN, Joyce Alice
  Thomas, J Bissell
STEPHENS, Donald Ryder
  Sinderby, Donald
STEPHENS, Eve
  Anthony, Evelyn
STEPHENS, James
  Esse, James
STERN, David
  Sterling, Peter
STERN, Elisabeth Gertrude
  Morton, Leah
STERN, Frederick Martin
  Martin, Frederick
STERN, James
  St James, Andrew
STERN, Philip Van Doren
  Storme, Peter
STERNE, E G
  Broun, Emily
STERNE, E G *and*
  LINDSAY, Barbara
    James, Josephine
STEVENS, Frances Moyer
  Hale, Christopher
STEVENS, Henry Charles
  Garry, Stephen
  Mann, John
STEVENSON, Edward I P
  Mayne, Xavier
STEVENSON, Ferdinan *and*
  ROBINSON, Patricia
    Macomber, Daria
STEVENSON, James Patrick
  Radyr, Tomos
STEWART, Alfred Walter
  Connington, J J

131

STEWART, Dorothy Mary
  Elgin, Mary
STEWART, James L
  Granger, Stewart
STEWART, John Innes
  Mackintosh
  Innes, Michael
STEWART, Kenneth Livingston
  Livingston, Kenneth
STEWART, Neil *and*
 JOHNSON, Pamela Hansford
  Lombard, Nap
STICKLAND, Louise Annie
 Beatrice
  Somers, J L
STICKLAND, M E
  Stand, Marguerite
STINE, George Harry
  Correy, Lee
STITT, James M
  Brunswick, James
STOBO, *Reverend* Edward
 John
  Aletheia
STOCKFORD, Lela E
  Hamilton-Stockford, Joan
STOCKS, Mary *and others*
  Heptagon
STODDARD, Charles Warren
  Pepperwood, Pip
STODDARD, William Osborn
  Forrest, *Colonel* Cris
STODDART, Jane T
  Lorna
STOE, M
  Bazagonov, M S
STOFFER, Edith G
  Ross, Deborah

STOKER, Alan
  Evans, Alan
STOKES, Francis William
  Everton, Francis
STOKES, Manning Lee
  Ludwell, Bernice
  Manning, Lee
STOLL, Dennis Gray
  Craig, Denys
STONE, Grace Zaring
  Vance, Ethel
STONE, Irving
  Tennenbaum, Irving
STONEBRAKER, Florence
  Shepard, Fern
  Stuart, Florence
STONEHAM, Charles Thurley
  Thurley, Norgrove
STONEHOUSE, Patricia Ethel
  Russell, Lindsay
STONIER, George
  Whitebait, William
STONOR, Oliver
  Bishop, Morchard
STOPPARD, Tom
  Boot, William
STORY, Rosamond Mary
  Jeskins, Richard
  Lee, Charles H
  Lindsay, Josephine
  Tracy, Catherine
  Woods, Ross
STOTT, Mary
  Jacques
STOUTENBURG, Adrien
  Kendall, Lace
STRACHAN, Gladys Elizabeth
  Bill

STRAITON, Edward Cornock
  Vet, T V
STRATEMEYER, Edward
  Bonehill, Ralph
  Winfield, Allen
  Winfield, Arthur M
STREATFEILD, Noel
  Scarlett, Susan
STREET, Cecil John Charles
  Burton, Miles
  Rhode, John
STRONG, Anna Louise
  Anise
STRONG, Charles Stanley
  Stanley, Chuck
STRUNSKY, Simeon
  Patient Observer, The
STUART, Dorothy Margaret
  D M S
STUART, Hector A
  Caliban
STUART, Vivian Alex
  Allen, Barbara
  Finlay, Fiona
  Stuart, Alex
  Stuart, V A
STUART-HEATON, Peter
  Heaton, Peter
STUART-JERVIS, Charles
  Edward
  Coysh, Edward
STUBBS, Harry Clement
  Clement, Hal
STUBBS, Jean
  Darby, Emma
  March, Emma
STUDDERT, Annie
  Rixon, Annie

STURE-VASA, Mary
  O'Hara, Mary
STURGES, Mary d'Este
  Virakam, Soror
STURGIS, Justin
  Burgess, Gelett
STURT, George
  Bourne, George
STURTZEL, Howard Allison
  Annixter, Paul
STURTZEL, Jane L
  Annixter, Jane
STYLES, Showell
  Carr, Glyn

§ §

What song the Syrens sang, or
what name Achilles assumed,
though puzzling questions, are
not beyond all conjecture.
—Sir Thomas Browne. Urn burial

§ §

SUDDABY, William Donald
  Griff, Alan
SULLIVAN, Edward Alan
  Murray, Sinclair
SUMMERS, Hollis
  Hollis, Jim
SUMMERSCALES, Rowland
  Gaines, Robert
SUMMERTON, Margaret
  Roffman, Jan
SUTTON, Graham
  Marsden, Anthony

SUTTON, Margaret
  Sutton, Rachel B
SUTTON, Phyllis Mary
  Riches, Phyllis
SVEINSSON, Solveig
  Rivers, Ronda
SWAN, Annie S
  Lyall, David
  Orchard, Evelyn
SWARD, Robert S
  Dr Soft
SWATRIDGE, Irene M M
  Chandos, Fay
  Lance, Leslie
  Mossop, Irene
  Storm, Virginia
  Tempest, Jan
SWATRIDGE, Irene M M *and*
 SWATRIDGE, Charles John
  Charles, Theresa
SWEET, John
  Kim
SWETENHAM, Violet Hilda
  Drummond, Violet Hilda
SWINNERTON, Frank
  Pure Simon
SYMINGTON, David
  Halliday, James
SYMONDS, E M
  Paston, George
SYMONS, Dorothy G
  Groves, Georgina

TABER, Clarence Wilbur
  Job, Modern
TABORI, Paul
  Hefner, Paul

TABORI, P (cont'd)
  Stafford, Peter
  Stevens, Christopher
TAIT, Dorothy
  Fairburn, Ann
TAIT, Euphemia Margaret
  Ironside, John
TAIT, George B
  Barclay, Alan
TAMES, Richard Lawrence
  Lawrence, James
TANNER, Edward Everett
  Dennis, Patrick
  Rowans, Virginia
TATE, George
  Armstrong, George
TATHAM, Laura
  Martin, John
  Phipps, Margaret
TATTERSALL, Muriel Joyce
  Wand, Elizabeth
TAYLOR, Bert Leston
  B L T
TAYLOR, Constance Lindsay
  Cullingford, Guy
TAYLOR, Deems
  Smeed
TAYLOR, Kamala
  Markandaya, Kamala
TAYLOR, Phoebe Atwood
  Tilton, Alice
TAYLOR, Roland
  Gill, Stanley
TAYLOR, Stephana Vere
  Benson, S Vere
TAYLOR, Sybil
  Tremayne, Sydney

TAYLOR, Thomas Hilhouse
  Taylor, Toso
TEAGUE, John Jessop
  Gerard, Morice
TEGNER, Henry
  Northumbrian Gentleman
  Ruffles
TEILHET, Darwin le Ora
  Fisher, Cyrus
  Fisher, Cyrus T
TELENGA, Suzette
  Yorke, Susan
TELLER, Neville
  Owen, Edmund
TENNYSON, Margaret
  Forrest, Carol
TERHUNE, Mary Virginia
  Harland, Marion
TERKEL, Louis
  Terkel, Studs
TETLEY, Edith Madeline
  Weetwood, E M
TETTMAR, Betty Eileen
  Spence, Betty E
THAYER, Emma Redington
  Thayer, Lee
THAYER, Tiffany Ellsworth
  Doe, John
  Ellsworth, Elmer
THIMBLETHORPE, June
  Thorpe, Sylvia
THIRKELL, Angela
  Parker, Leslie
THOM, William Albert Strang
  Morrison, J Strang
THOMAS, Edward
  Eastaway, Edward

THOMAS, Edward Llewellyn
  Gordon
  Gordon, Don
THOMAS, Ernest Lewys
  Vaughan, Richard
THOMAS, Eugene
  Grey, Donald
THOMAS, John Oram
  Oram, John
THOMAS, Mary
  Thomas, Tay
THOMAS, Reg
  Preston, Jane
THOMAS, Robert Richard
  Howerd, Gareth
THOMAS, Ronald Wills
  Wills, Ronald
THOMAS, Ross
  Bleeck, Oliver
THOMAS, Stanley A C
  Wyandotte, Steve
THOMAS, Walter Dill Jr
  Dill, Walter
THOMASHOWER, Dorothy
  Thomas, Dorothy
THOMPSON, A M
  Dangle
THOMPSON, Antony Allert
  Alban, Antony
THOMPSON, Arthur Leonard
  Bell
  Clifford, Francis
THOMPSON, Edward Anthony
  Lejeune, Anthony
THOMPSON, George Selden
  Selden, George
THOMPSON, Harlan
  Holt, Stephen

135

THOMPSON, J W M
  Quince, Peter
THOMPSON, Phyllis
  Morgan, Phyllis
  Rose, Phyllis
THOMSON, Christine Campbell
  Alexander, Dair
THOMSON, Daisy
  Roe, M S
  Thomson, Jon H
THORNE, Isabel Mary
  Villiers, Elizabeth
THORNETT, Ernest Basil
 Charles
  Penny, Rupert
THORP, Joseph
  T
THORPE, John
  Campbell, Duncan
  Centaur
  Scott, Douglas
THORPE-CLARK, Mavis
  Latham, Mavis
TICHBORNE, Henry
  Sundowner
TIERNEY, John
  James, Brian
TILLETT, Dorothy Stockbridge
  Strange, John Stephen
TILLEY, E D
  Tilley, Gene
TILSLEY, Frank
  X Y Z
TITUS, Eve
  Lord, Nancy
TODD, Barbara Euphan
  Euphan

TODD, John Murray
  Fox, John
TODD, Ruthven Campbell
  Campbell, R T
TOFANI, Louise E
  Theophany
TOMLIN, Eric
  Stuart, Frederick
TOMLINSON, Joshua Leonard
  Linson
TONKIN, C B
  Pledger, P J
TOOHEY, Barbara *and*
  BIERMANN, June
  Bennett, Margaret
TORDAY, Ursula
  Allardyce, Paula
  Blackstock, Charity
  Blackstock, Lee
  Keppel, Charlotte
TORREY, Ware
  Crosby, Lee
TORSVAN, Traven
  Traven, B
TOWNSEND, George Alfred
  Gath
TOWNSEND, Joan
  Pomfret, Joan
TOWNSEND, Mary Ashley
  Ashley, Mary
  Xariffa
TRACY, Donald Fiske
  Fuller, Roger
TRACY, Louis *and*
  SHIEL, M P
  Holmes, Gordon
TRALINS, S Robert
  Bixby, Ray Z

TRALINS, S R (cont'd)
King, Norman A
O'Shea, Sean
O'Toole, Rex
Tralins, Bob
Tralins, Robert S
Traube, Ruy
TRANTER, Nigel
Tredgold, Nye
TRENT, Ann
Carlton, Ann
Crosse, Elaine
Desana, Dorothy
Sernicoli, Davide
TREWIN, J C
J C T
TRIEM, Paul Ellsworth
Ellsworth, Paul
TRIMBLE, Chloe Maria
Gartner, Chloe
TRIMBLE, Louis
Brock, Stuart
Travis, Gerry
TRIMMER, Eric
Jameson, Eric
TRIPP, H Alker
Hoe, Lee
TRIPP, Kathleen
Loewenthal, Karen
TRIPP, Miles Barton
Brett, John Michael
TRIPPE, Peter
Peters, Geoffrey
TROCCHI, Alexander
De Las Lunas, Carmencita
Lengel, Frances
TROUBETZKOI, *Princess*
Rives, Amelia

TROWBRIDGE, John Townsend
Creyton, Paul
TRUAX, Rhoda
Wyngard, Rhoda
TRUMAN, Marcus George
Beckett, Mark
TRUMBO, Dalton
Abbott, *Dr* John
Demaine, C F
Doyle, Emmett
Fincher, Beth
Flexman, Theodore
Jackson, Sam
Rich, Robert
TRUPO, Anthony
Norvell, Anthony
TRUSS, Leslie Seldon *see*
SELDON TRUSS, Leslie
TUBB, E C
Grey, Charles
Guthrie, Alan
Holt, George
Maddox, Carl
West, Douglas
Wilding, Eric
TUCK, John Erskine
Erskine, John T
TUCKER, Agnes
Carruth, Agnes K
TUCKER, James
Craig, David
TUCKER, William Joseph
Scorpio
TULLETT, Denis John
Dee, John
Melmoth
Sutton, John

TUNLEY, Roul
  Boyd, Edward
TURNBULL, Dora Amy
  Wentworth, Patricia
TURNER, John Victor
  Hume, David
TURNER, Lida Larrimore
  Larrimore, Lida
TURNER, Philip
  Chance, Stephen
TURNGREN, Annette
  Hopkins, A T
TURTON-JONES, Edith
  Gillespie, Susan
TUTE, Warren
  Warren, Andrew
TYLER-WHITTLE, Michael
 Sidney
  Whittle, Tyler

UHR, Elizabeth
  Stern, Elizabeth
ULLYETT, Kenneth
  Bentley, W J
UNDERWOOD, Mavis Eileen
  Kilpatrick, Sarah
UNETT, John
  Preston, James
UNWIN, David Storr
  Severn, David
UPCHURCH, Boyd
  Boyd, John
UPWARD, Edward Falaise
  Chalmers, Allen
URELL, William Francis
  Francis, William

UREN, Malcolm
  Malcolm, John
  Matelot
URIS, Auren
  Auren, Paul
URQUHART, Macgregor
  Hart, Max
USHER, Frank Hugh
  Franklin, Charles
  Lester, Frank
USHER, John Gray
  Gray, Christopher
UTTLEY, Alice Jane
  Uttley, Alison

VACZEK, Louis C
  Hardin, Peter
VAHEY, John George Haslette
  Clandon, Henrietta
  Haslette, John
  Lang, Anthony
  Loder, Vernon
  Mowbray, John
  Proudfoot, Walter
VAN DEVENTER, Emma M
  Lynch, Lawrence L
VAN ESSEN, W
  Serjeant, Richard
VAN SILLER, Hilda
  Siller, Van
VAN ZELLER, Claud H
  Brother Choleric
  Venning, Hugh
VANCE, John Holbrook
  Holbrook, John
  Vance, Jack
VANN, Gerald
  Oke, Simon

VAUGHAN, *Lady* Auriel
  Malet, Oriel
VAUGHAN, Owen
  Rhoscomyl, Owen
VEITCH, Thomas
  Kentigern, John
VENABLES, Terry *and*
 WILLIAMS, Gordon Maclean
  Yuill, P B
VENN, Mary Eleanor
  Adrian, Mary
VENNARD, Alexander Vindex
  Bowyang, Bill
  Reid, Frank
VERNER, Christopher Stuart
  Chase, Lesley
VERNON, Kathleen Rose
  Dixon, Lesley
  Vernon, Kay
VERWER, Johanne
  Johanson, Elizabeth
  Verwer, Hans
VESEY, Ernest Blakeman
  Lewis, Ernest
VICKERS, Roy
  Durham, David
  Kyle, Sefton
  Spencer, John
VICTOR, Metta Victoria
 Fuller
  Regester, Seeley
VIDAL, Gore
  Box, Edgar
VIERECK, George Sylvester
  Corners, George F
VILLIERS, David Hugh
  Buckingham, David

VINCIGUERRA, Frances
  Winwar, Francis
VINING, Charles A M
  R T L
VINING, Elizabeth Gray
  Gray, Elizabeth Janet
VINTER, Helen
  Smith, Naomi
VIVIAN, Evelyn Charles H
  Cannell, Charles
  Mann, Jack
  Vivian, E Charles
VLASTO, John Alexander
  Alexander, John
  Remenham, John
VOELKER, John Donaldson
  Traver, Robert
VOLK, Gordon
  Knotts, Raymond
VOSS, Vivian
  Vee, Roger
VULLIAMY, Colwyn Edward
  Rolls, Anthony
  Teg, Twm

WACE, M A
  Golden Gorse
WADDEL, Charles Carey
  Carey, Charles
WADDELL, Martin
  Sefton, Catherine
WADDELL, Samuel
  Mayne, Rutherford
WADDINGTON, Miriam
  Merritt, E B

WADE, Robert *and*
  MILLER, William
    Masterson, Whit
    Miller, Wade
WADE, Rosalind
  Carr, Catharine
WAGENKNECHT, Edward
  Charles
    Forrest, Julian
WAGNER, Margaret Dale
  Wagner, Peggy
WAINHOUSE, Austryn
    Audiart
    Casavini, Pieralissandro
WAINWRIGHT, Gordon Ray
  Gordon, Ray
WAINWRIGHT, John
  Ripley, Jack
WALDO, Edward Hamilton
  Hunter, E Waldo
  Sturgeon, Theodore
  Waldo, E Hunter
WALDRON, Corbin A
  Cal, Dakota
WALKER, David Esdaile
  Esdaile, David
WALKER, Edith
  Trafford, Jean
  Walker, Jean Brown
WALKER, Emily Kathleen
  Ash, Pauline
  Barry, Eileen
  Devon, Sara
  Foster, Delia
  Lawson, Christine
  Lester, Jane
  Mayne, Cora
  Murray, Jill

WALKER, E K (cont'd)
  Tilbury, Quenna
  Treves, Kathleen
  Vincent, Heather
  Vincent, Honor
  Winchester, Kay
WALKER, Irma Ruth
  Walker, Ira
WALKER, John
  Thirlmere, Rowland
WALKER, Kenneth Macfarlane
  Macfarlane, Kenneth
WALKER, Lucy
  Sanders, Dorothy Lucy
WALKER, Peter Norman
  Coram, Christopher
  Ferris, Tom
  Manton, Paul
WALKER, Rowland
  Kenworthy, Hugh
WALKER, Roy
  Oliver, Roy
WALKER, Stella Archer
  Archer-Batten, S
WALKER, W Sylvester
  Coo-ee
WALKERLEY, Rodney L de
  Burgh
    Athos
WALL, John W
  Sarban
WALLACE, Elizabeth Virginia
  Wallace, Betty
WALLACE, Henry
  Uncle Henry
WALLACE, John
  Texas Ranger

WALLACE, Lewis Alexander
  M B Oxon
WALLACE, Penelope
  Halcrow, Penelope
WALLER, Leslie
  Cody, C S
  Mann, Patrick
WALLIS, Geraldine
  Campbell, Hope
WALLIS, Peter
  York, Peter
WALMSLEY, Arnold
  Roland, Nicholas
WALSH, James Morgan
  Carew, John
  Hill, H Haverstock
WALTER, Dorothy Blake
  Blake, Katherine
  Blake, Kay
  Ross, Katherine
  Walter, Katherine
  Walter, Kay
WALTON, John *and*
  BRIGHOUSE, Harold
  Conway, Olive
WALZ, Audrey
  Bonnamy, Francis
WANNAN, John Fearn
  Fearn, John
WARBURG, James Paul
  Paul, James
WARD, Arthur Sarsfield
  Rohmer, Sax
WARD, Robert Spencer
  King, Evan
WARE, Eugene Fitch
  Ironquill

WARNER, Geoffrey John
  Johns, Geoffrey
WARREN, Edward Perry
  Raile, Arthur Lyon
WARREN, John Russell
  Coverack, Gilbert
WARRINER, Thurman
  Kersey, John
  Troy, Simon
WATERHOUSE, Keith *and*
  DEGHY, Guy
  Froy, Herald
  Gibb, Lee
WATERS, John
  Warner, Jack
WATERS, Rosemary Elizabeth
  Horstmann, Rosemary
WATFORD, Joel
  Essex, Jon
WATKINS, Alex
  Linklater, Lane
WATKINS-PITCHFORD, Denys
  James
  B B
WATNEY, Bernard
  Dolley, Marcus J
WATSON, Adam
  Scipio
WATSON, Albert Ernest
  Watson, Andrew
WATSON, Elliot Grant
  Lovegood, John
WATSON, Jack Charles
  Wauchope
  Chrystie, Edward M
WATSON, James Wreford
  Wreford, James

Real names

WATSON, John
　Maclaren, Ian
WATSON, Julia
　De Vere, Jane
　Hamilton, Julia
WATSON, R A
　Cromarty, Deas
WATT, Alexander Peter
　Fordham
　Fraser, Peter
WATT, Esme
　Jeans, Angela
WATTS, Edgar John Palmer
　Palmer, John
WATTS, Peter Christopher
　Chisholm, Matt
　James, Cy
　Owen, Tom
WAUGH, Hillary Baldwin
　Grandower, Elissa
　Taylor, H Baldwin
　Walker, Harry
WAY, Elizabeth Fenwick
　Fenwick, Elizabeth
WAYE, Ellen
　Jose, Ellen J
WEALE, Anne
　Blake, Andrea
WEAVER, Harriet Shaw
　Wright, Josephine
WEBB, Charles Henry
　Paul, John
WEBB, Dorothy Anna
　March, Jermyn
WEBB, Godfrey E C
　England, Norman
　Godfrey, Charles

WEBB, Jack
　Farr, John
　Grady, Tex
WEBB, Jean Frances
　Hamill, Ethel
WEBB, Richard Wilson *and*
　WHEELER, Hugh Callingham
　Patrick, Q
　Quentin, Patrick
　Stagge, Jonathan
WEBB, Robert Forrest *and*
　ELIADES, David
　Forrest, David
WEBB, Ruth Enid
　Morris, Ruth
WEBBE, Gale Dudley
　Cole, Stephen
WEBSTER, Alice Jane
　Chandler
　Webster, Jean
WEBSTER, Owen
　Pilgrim, Adam
WEEKES, Agnes Russell
　Pryde, Anthony
WEEKS, *Lady* Constance Avard
　Tomkinson, Constance
WEES, Frances Shelley
　Shelley, Frances
WEI, Rex
　Williams, Rex
WEIGHTMAN, Archibald John
　Stuart, Alan
WEINBAUM, Stanley Grauman
　Jessel, John
　Stanley, Marge
WEINER, Margery
　Lake, Sarah

WEINSTEIN, Nathan Wallenstein
  West, Nathanael
WEIR, Rosemary
  Bell, Catherine
  Green, R
WELCH, Colin
  Simple, Peter
WELDON, A E
  Macnamara, Brinsley
WELLS, Carolyn
  Wright, Rowland
WELLS, H G
  Bliss, Reginald
WELLS, Helen
  Lewis, Francine
WELLS, Lee Edwin
  Poole, Richard
WENZ, Paul
  Warrego, Paul
WERNER, Elsa Jane
  Bedford, A N
  Bedford, Annie North
  Hill, Monica
  Nast, Elsa Ruth
  Werner, Jane
WERTENBAKER, Lael Tucker
  Tucker, Lael
WEST, Betty Bowen
  Bowen, Betty
WEST, G A
  Kap-o-Kaslo
WEST, Gertrude
  West, Trudy
WEST, Morris
  East, Morris
  Morris, Julian
WEST-WATSON, Keith Campbell
  Campbell, Keith

WESTHEIMER, David
  Smith, Z Z
WESTLAKE, Donald Edwin
  Coe, Tucker
  Stark, Richard
WESTMARLAND, Ethel Louisa
  Courtney, Christine
  Elliott, Ellen
WESTMORELAND, Vera
Gertrude
  Elysian, Anne
WHALLEY, Dorothy
  Cowlin, Dorothy
WHARMBY, Margot
  Winn, Alison
WHARTON, Michael
  Simple, Peter
WHEAR, Rachel
  Low, Rachel
WHEELER, Hugh Callingham
and WEBB, Richard Wilson
  Patrick Q
  Quentin, Patrick
  Stagge, Jonathan
WHELAN, Jerome Bernard
  Brien, R N
WHELPTON, Eric
  Lyte, Richard
WHEWAY, John
  Armitage, Hazel
WHIBLEY, Charles
  Thersites
WHISH, Violet E
  Swift, Stella
WHITBY, Anthony Charles
  Lesser, Anthony
WHITE, Alan
  Fraser, James

143

WHITE, Celia
  Tustin, Elizabeth
WHITE, Frank James
  Stewart-Hargreaves, E H I
WHITE, Herbert Oliver
  Martyn, Oliver
WHITE, Pauline Arnold
  Arnold, Pauline
WHITE, Stanhope
  Dan Bana
  Sabiad
WHITE, Stanley
  Krull, Felix
  White, James Dillon
WHITE, William Anthony P
  Boucher, Anthony
  Holmes, H H
WHITE, William Hale
  Rutherford, Mark
WHITEHAND, James *and*
 SATHERLEY, David
  Whitehand, Satherley
WHITEHOUSE, Arthur George
 Joseph
  Whitehouse, Arch
WHITEING, Richard
  Thorn, Whyte
WHITEMAN, William Meredith
  Turner, C John
WHITEFIELD, John
  Pilio, Gerone
WHITFIELD, Raoul
  Decolta, Ramon
WHITFORD, Joan
  Ford, Barry
  Oldham, Hugh R
WHITNEY, Julie
  Yulya

144

WHITSON, John Harvey
  Garland, Luke
  Hazelton, *Captain*
  Hazelton, *Colonel*
  Merriwell, Frank
  Sewell, Arthur
  Sims, *Lieut* A K
  Steel, Robert
  Steele, Addison
  Stevens, Maurice
  Williams, Russell
WHITTEN, Wilfred
  John o'London
WHITTET, George Sorley
  Kerr, John O'Connell
  Monkland, George
WHITTINGTON, Harry
  Harrison, Whit
  Holland, Kel
  Myers, Harriet Kathryn
  Philips, Steve
  Stuart, Clay
  Wells, Hondo
  White, Harry
  Whitney, Hallam
WIBBERLEY, Leonard Patrick
 O'Connor
  Holton, Leonard
  O'Connor, Patrick
  Webb, Christopher
WICKER, Tom
  Connolly, Paul
WICKSTEED, Margaret Hope
  Hope, Margaret
WIEDENBECK, Emilie Agnes
  Mable, Peter
WIGGINS, David
  Priestley, Robert

WIGGLESWORTH, Martin
 Worth, Martin
WIGHT, J A
 Herriot, James
WILBY, Basil
 Knight, Gareth
WILCOX, Harry
 Derby, Mark
WILCOXEN, Harriett
 Harriett
WILD, Dora Mary
 Broome, Dora
WILD, Reginald
 Edwards, Leonard
WILDING, Philip
 Fraser, Jefferson
 Haynes, John Robert
 Marshall, Lloyd
 Russell, Erle
 Stanton, Borden
 Stewart, Logan
 Stuart, Logan
WILKES-HUNTER, Richard
 Douglas, D
 Douglas, Shane
 Farr, C
 Gray, Adrian
 Mitchell, Kerry
WILKINS, Mary Louise
 Calhoun, Mary
WILKINSON, A G
 Desor, Réné
WILKINSON, Louis Umfreville
 Marlow, Louis
WILKINSON, Percy F H
 Wilkinson, Tim
WILLANS, Angela
 Grant, Mary

WILLARD, Josiah Flynt
 Flynt, Josiah
WILLETT, Franciscus
 McKern, Pat
WILLIAMS, Carol Elizabeth
 Fenner, Carol
WILLIAMS, D F *and*
 PATRY, M
 Williams, Patry
WILLIAMS, Edward John
 Farrer, E Maxwell
WILLIAMS, Gordon Maclean *and*
 VENABLES, Terry
 Yuill, P B
WILLIAMS, Guy Richard Owen
 Guinness, Owen
 Woolland, Henry
WILLIAMS, Jay
 Delving, Michael
WILLIAMS, Kathryn
 Vinson, Kathryn
WILLIAMS, Margaret Wetherby
 Erskine, Margaret
 Williams, Wetherby
WILLIAMS, Meurig
 Carrington, Michael
WILLIAMS, Ned
 Harbin, Robert
WILLIAMS, Peggy Eileen
 Arabella
 Evans, Margiad
WILLIAMS, Robert Moore
 Browning, John S
WILLIAMSON, Ellen Douglas
 Douglas, Ellen
WILLIAMSON, Ethel
 Veheyne, Cherry

145

WILLIAMSON, Jack
  Stewart, Will
WILLIAMSON, Leila Isobel
  Orme, Eve
WILLIAMSON, Lydia Buckland
  Sorace, Richard
WILLIAMSON, Thames Ross
  Dagonet, Edward
  Fleming, Waldo
  Morgan, De Wolfe
  Saltar the Mongol
  Smith, S S
  Trent, Gregory
WILLIS, Corinne
  Denning, Patricia
WILLIS, George Anthony
 Armstrong
  A A
  Armstrong, Anthony
WILLIS, Priscilla D
  Adams, Mary Scott
WILLOUGHBY-HIGSON, Philip
 John
  Higson, P J W
WILLSON, Mitchell A *and*
 POLANSKY, Abraham
  Hogarth, Emmett
WILMOT, Frank Leslie
 Thomson
  Maurice, Furnley
WILMOT, James Reginald
  Trevor, Ralph
WILSON, Albert
  Wilson, Yates
WILSON, Alec
  Ulster Imperialist
WILSON, Andrew James
  Wilson, Snoo

WILSON, Arthur
  Dalry
WILSON, Christine
  Geach, Christine
  Lowing, Anne
  Neil, Frances
WILSON, Desemea
  Patrick, Diana
WILSON, Florence Roma Muir
  Marichaud, Alphonse
  Wilson, Romer
WILSON, Helen
  Wilson, Holly
WILSON, John
  Stripper
WILSON, John Anthony Burgess
  Burgess, Anthony
  Kell, Joseph
  Wilson, John Burgess
WILSON, Robert McNair
  Wynne, Anthony
WILSON, Viva
  Viva
WILSON, William *and*
 GRANT, Donald
  Ness, K T
WILTON, Charles Edward
  Anglo-Austral
WIMHURST, Cecil Gordon Eugene
  Brent, Nigel
WINCHELL, Prentice
  Collans, Dev
  De Bekker, Jay
  Dean, Spencer
  St Clair, Dester
  Sterling, Stewart
WINDER, Mavis Areta
  Areta, Mavis

WINDER, M A (cont'd)
  Winder, Mavis
  Wynder, Mavis Areta
WINKWORTH, Derek W
  5029
WINNINGTON, Richard
  Ross, John
WINTER, Bevis
  Bocca, Al
  Cagney, Peter
  Hill, Bennet
  Shayne, Gordon
WINTER, C H
  Riverina
WINTERFIELD, Henry
  Michael, Manfred
WINTERS, Bayla
  Winters, Bernice
WINTERTON, Paul
  Bax, Roger
  Garve, Andrew
  Somers, Paul
WINTHROP, Bud Robert
  Flanagan, Bud
WINTRINGHAM, Tom
  Gracchus
WIRT, Mildred
  Bell, Frank
  Clark, Joan
  West, Dorothy
WISE, Arthur
  McArthur, John
WITCOMBE, Rick
  Marker, Clare
WOHL, Ludwig von
  De Wohl, Louis
WOLFF, William
  Martindale, Spencer

WOLFSON, Victor
  Dodge, Langdon
WOLLHEIM, Donald A
  Grinnell, David
WOOD, Christopher
  Dixon, Rosie
  Grape, Oliver
  Lea, Timothy
  May, Jonathan
WOOD, Grace Ashley
  Ancilla
WOOD, James
  McLeod, Finlay
  Stuart, Gordon
WOOD, John James O'Hara
  Dee, R K
WOOD, Lilian Catherine
  Cymry Bach
WOOD, Patricia E W
  Ross, Patricia
WOOD, Samuel Andrew
  Temple, Robin
WOOD, Violet
  Wood, Quality
WOODCOCK, E Page
  Uncle Reg
WOODFORD, Irene-Cecile
  Barrie, Jane
  Goff, Madeleine
  Lee, Veronica
  Woodford, Cecile
WOODHAM-SMITH, Cecil
  Gordon, Janet
WOODRICH, Mary Neville
  Neville, Mary
WOODROFFE, *Sir* John G
  Avalon, Arthur

WOODS, Margery Hilton
  Hilton, Margery
WOODS, Olwen
  Woods, Jonah
WOOLFOLK, Josiah Pitts
  Britt, Sappho Henderson
  Kennedy, Howard
  Sayre, Gordon
  Woodford, Jack
WOOLLEY, Catherine
  Thayer, Jane
WOOLSEY, Sarah Chauncey
  Coolidge, Susan
WORBOYS, Anne Eyre
  Eyre, Annette
WORDINGHAM, James A
  Dare, Michael
WORNER, Philip A I
  Incledon, Philip
  Sylvester, Philip
WORNUM, Miriam
  Dennis, Eve
WORRELL, Everil
  Monett, Lireve
WORSLEY, T C
  Lister, Richard
WORTHINGTON-STUART,
  Brian Arthur
  Meredith, Peter
  Stuart, Brian
WORTHLEY, R G
  Viola
WORTHY, Brian Johnson
  Johnson, Brian
WORTIS, Avi
  Avi

WORTS, George F
  Brent, Loring
WRAITH, W J
  Alexander, Walter
WRIGHT, Elinor
  Lyon, Elinor
WRIGHT, George T
  Wright, Ted
WRIGHT, John
  Wright, Wade
WRIGHT, Marjory Beatrice
  Pilgrim
WRIGHT, Mary
  Bawn, Mary
WRIGHT, R L Gerard
  Bristowe, Edwin
WRIGHT, Ronald Selby
  Radio Padre
WRIGHT, Sydney Fowler
  Fowler, Sydney
WRIGHT, Willard Huntington
  Van Dine, S S
WURMBRAND, Richard
  Moses, Ruben
WYLER, Rose
  Thayer, Peter
WYLLIE, James McLeod
  Barras Seer
WYND, Oswald
  Black, Gavin
WYNDHAM LEWIS, D B
  Beachcomber
  Shy, Timothy
WYNNE-TYSON, Esme
  De Morny, Peter

YARDUMIAN, Miryam
  Miryam
YATES, Alan Geoffrey
  Brown, Carter
YATES, George Worthing *and*
 MARSHALL, Charles Hunt
  Hunt, Peter
YATES, Raymond Francis
  Hall, Borden
YAUKEY, Grace
  Spencer, Cornelia
YELLOT, Barbara Leslie
  Jordan, Barbara Leslie
YIN, Leslie Charles Bowyer
  Charteris, Leslie
YOCKEY, Francis Parker
  Varange, Ulick
YONGE, Charlotte Mary
  Aunt Charlotte
YORKE, Henry Vincent
  Green, Henry
YOSELOFF, Thomas
  Young, Thomas
YOUD, Samuel
  Christopher, John
  Ford, Hilary
  Godfrey, William
  Graaf, Peter
  Nichols, Peter
  Rye, Anthony
YOUNG, Agnes
  Young, Agatha
YOUNG, Eric Brett
  Leacroft, Eric
YOUNG, Ernest
  Gilcraft

YOUNG, Ernest A
  Rockwood, Harry
YOUNG, Janet Randall
  Randall, Janet
  Young, Jan
YOUNG, Nedrick
  Douglas, Nathan
YOUNG, Phyllis Brett
  Young, Kendal
YOUNG, Robert
  Hill, Rabin
YOUNGER, Elizabeth
  Hely, Elizabeth
YOUNGER, William Anthony
  Mole, William

ZAFFO, George J
  Stewart, Scott
ZALBERG, Daniel
  Daniel, S
ZARCHY, Harry
  Lewis, Roger
ZEHNDER, Meinrad
  Martin, Anthony
ZELAZNY, Roger
  Denmark, Harrison
ZILLIACUS, Konni
  Covenanter
  Diplomaticus
  Vigilantes
  Williams, Roth
ZIM, Sonia
  Bleeker, Sonia
ZIMMER, Maude Files
  Baird, Maude F
  Fileman, Nan

Real names

ZIMMERMAN, Robert Allen
  Dylan, Bob
ZINBERG, Len
  Lacy, Ed
ZINSSER, Hans
  R S

ZORZA, Victor
  Kremlinologist
ZUBER, Mary E L
  Rowlands, Lesley

Pseudonyms

§ §

'What's the use of their having names', the Gnat said, 'if they won't answer to them? —Lewis Carroll. Through the looking glass

§ §

A A
  Willis, George Anthony
    Armstrong
A A B
  Baumann, Arthur A
A E
  Russell, George William
A H
  Hawkins, *Sir* Anthony Hope
A H G
  Girdleston, A H
A L O M
  Frank, *Mrs* M J
A P H
  Herbert, *Sir* Alan Patrick
A Q-C
  Quiller-Couch, *Sir* Arthur
A R O
  Orage, Alfred James

ABBEY, Kieran
  Reilly, Helen K
ABBEY, Ruth
  Pattison, Ruth
ABBEY, Staton
  Staton-Bevan, William Norman
ABBOT, Anthony
  Oursler, Fulton
ABBOTT, A A
  Spewack, Samuel
ABBOTT, A C
  Meinzer, Helen Abbott
ABBOTT, Alice
  Borland, Kathryn K *and*
  Speicher, Helen Ross
ABBOTT, Bruce
  Sewall, Robert
ABBOTT, *Dr* John
  Trumbo, Dalton
ABBOTT, Johnston
  Ashworth, Edward
    Montague
ABDULLAH, Achmed
  Romanoff, Alexander
    Nicholayevitch
ABERCROMBIE, Patricia Barnes
  Barnes, Patricia
ABHAVANANDA
  Crowley, Edward Alexander

151

ACHARYA, Pundit
  Bhattacharya, Basudeb
ACLAND, Alice
  Marreco, Anne
ACRE, Stephen
  Gruber, Frank
ADAIR, Cecil
  Green, Evelyn Everett
ADAIR, Dennis
  Cronin, Bernard
ADAIR, Hazel
  Addis, Hazel Iris
ADAIR, Sally
  Mannock, Laura
ADAMS, Andy
  Harkins, Peter
ADAMS, Annette
  Rowland, Donald Sydney
ADAMS, Bart
  Bingley, David Ernest
ADAMS, Clayton
  Holmes, Charles Henry
ADAMS, Mary Scott
  Willis, Priscilla D
ADAMS, R D
  Herbert, Robert Dudley
    Sidney Powys
ADDIO, E I
  Fantoni, Barry
ADDISCOMBE, John
  Hunter, Alfred John
ADDISON, Carol
  Clarke, J Calvitt
ADELER, Max
  Clark, Charles Heber
ADKINS, M D
  Pound, Ezra

ADRIAN, Mary
  Venn, Mary Eleanor
AGARD, H E
  Evans, Hilary Agard
AGATE
  Reid, Whitelaw
AINSWORTH, Harriet
  Cadell, Elizabeth
AINSWORTH, Oliver
  Sharp, *Sir* Henry
AINSWORTH, Patricia
  Bigg, Patricia Nina
AINSWORTH, Ruth
  Gilbert, Ruth Gallard
AINSWORTHY, Roy
  Paine, Lauran Bosworth
AIRD, Catherine
  McIntosh, Kinn Hamilton
AIRLIE, Catherine
  Macleod, Jean Sutherland
AJAX
  Jackson, Ada Acraman
AKENS, Floyd
  Baum, Lyman Frank
ALAIN
  Brustlein, Daniel
ALAN, A J
  Lambert, Leslie Harrison
ALAN, Jane
  Chisholm, Lilian
ALAN, Marjorie
  Bumpus, Doris Marjorie
ALBAN, Antony
  Thompson, Antony Allert
ALBERT, Ned
  Braun, Wilbur
ALBION, Ken
  King, Albert

ALBRAND, Martha
  Loewengard, Heidi H F
ALCYONE
  Krishnamurti, Jiddu
ALDEN, Jack
  Barrows, Marjorie
ALDING, Peter
  Jeffries, Roderic Graeme
ALDON, Adair
  Meigs, Cornelia Lynde
ALETHEIA
  Stobo, *Reverend* Edward John
ALEXANDER, Dair
  Thomson, Christine Campbell
ALEXANDER, Jean
  Penner, Manola J
ALEXANDER, Joan
  Pepper, Joan
ALEXANDER, John
  Vlasto, John Alexander
ALEXANDER, L G
  Ftyaras, Louis George
ALEXANDER, Martin
  Daventry, Leonard John
ALEXANDER, Ruth
  Rogers, Ruth
ALEXANDER, Walter
  Wraith, W J
ALGOL
  Bretherton, C H
ALI-MAR
  Porn, Alice
ALIEN
  Baker, Louisa Alice
ALIKI
  Brandenberg, Alyce Christina
ALIUNAS
  Baronas, Aloyzas

ALLABEN, Anne E
  Farrell, Anne Elisabeth
ALLAN, Dennis
  Denniston, Elinore
ALLAN, Luke
  Amy, William Lacey
ALLAN, Ted
  Herman, Alan
ALLARDYCE, Paula
  Torday, Ursula
ALLCOT, Guy
  Pocock, Tom
ALLEGRO
  Moore, Birkett
ALLEN, Adam
  Epstein, Beryl *and*
  Epstein, Samuel
ALLEN, Allyn
  Eberle, Irmengarde
ALLEN, Barbara
  Stuart, Vivian Alex
ALLEN, Betsy
  Headley, Elizabeth
ALLEN, Clay
  Paine, Lauran Bosworth
ALLEN, Dixie
  Kohls, Olive N Allen
ALLEN, Eric
  Allen-Ballard, Eric
ALLEN, F M
  Downey, Edmund
ALLEN, John W Jr
  Lesley, Peter
ALLEN, Ronald
  Ayckbourne, Alan
ALLEN, Steve
  Allen, Stephen Valentine

153

ALLENBY, Gordon
  Matusow, Harvey Marshall
ALLERTON, Mark
  Cameron, William Ernest
ALLERTON, Mary
  Govan, Mary Christine
ALLISON, Clay
  Keevil, Henry John
ALLWORTHY, A W
  Milam, Lorenzo W
ALLYSON, Alan
Nuttall, Anthony
ALMONTE, Rosa
  Paine, Lauran Bosworth
ALPHA CRUCIS
  Herbert, Robert Dudley
  Sidney Powys
ALPHA OF THE PLOUGH
  Gardiner, Alfred George
ALTHEA
  Braithwaite, Althea
ALVORD, Burt
  Keevill, Henry John
AMBERLEY, Richard
  Bourquin, Paul
AMBERLEY, Simon
  Hoar, Peter
AMES, Felicia
  Burden, Jean
AMES, Jennifer
  Greig, Maysie
AMES, Leslie
  Rigoni, Orlando Joseph
AMES, Leslie
  Ross, William Edward
  Daniel
AMICUS CURIAE
  Fuller, Edmund

AMID, John
  Stearns, Myron Morris
AMIS, Breton
  Best, Rayleigh Breton Amis
AMOR, Amos
  Harrell, Irene Burk
AMOS, Alan
  Knight, Kathleen Moore
AMPHIBIAN
  Aston, *Sir* George
AMPLEGIRTH, Anthony
  Dent, Anthony
AN BROC
  O'Nolan, Brian
ANATOLE
  Muller, Robert
ANAUTA
  Blackmore, Anauta
ANCILLA
  Wood, Grace Ashley
ANDERS, Rex
  Barrett, Geoffrey John
ANDERSON, Ella
  Macleod, Ellen
ANDERSON, Rachel
  Bradby, Rachel
ANDOM, R
  Barrett, Alfred Walter
ANDREWS, A A
  Paine, Lauran Bosworth
ANDREWS, Lucilla
  Crichton, Lucilla Matthew
ANDRÉZEL, Pierre
  Blixen-Finecke, Karen
  Christine *Baroness*
ANGELL, Norman
  Lane, *Sir* Ralph Norman
  Angell

ANGLO-AUSTRAL
  Wilton, Charles Edward
ANGUS, Ian
  Mackay, James Alexander
ANISE
  Strong, Anna Louise
ANMAR, Frank
  Nolan, William F
ANNIXTER, Jane
  Sturtzel, Jane L
ANNIXTER, Paul
  Sturtzel, Howard Allison
ANSTEY, F
  Guthrie, Thomas Anstey
ANSTRUTHER, James
  Graham, James Maxtone
ANTHONY, C L
  Smith, Dorothy Gladys
ANTHONY, Charles
  Akerman, Anthony Charles
ANTHONY, Evelyn
  Stephens, Eve
ANTHONY, John
  Beckett, Ronald Brymer
ANTHONY, Peter
  Shaffer, Anthony *and*
  Shaffer, Peter
ANTHONY, Piers
  Jacob, Piers Anthony
ANTONINUS, BROTHER
  Everson, William Oliver
AP EVANS, Humphrey
  Drummond, Humphrey
AR, Esjay
  Rubinstein, Stanley Jack
ARCHER, A A
  Joscelyn, Archie

ARCHER, Frank
  O'Connor, Richard
ARCHER, G Scott
  Larbalestier, Phillip George
ARCHER, Owen
  Greenwood, Augustus George
ARCHER, S E
  Soderberg, Percy Measday
ARCHER-BATTEN, S
  Walker, Stella Archer
ARCHESTRATUS
  Driver, Christopher
ARDEN, Clive
  Nutt, Lily Clive
ARDEN, Mary
  Murry, Violet
ARDEN, William
  Lynds, Dennis
ARESBYS, The
  Bamberger, Helen R *and*
  Bamberger, Raymond
ARETA, Mavis
  Winder, Mavis Areta
ARGUS, M K
  Eisenstadt-Jaleznov, Mikhail
ARIEL
  Arden, Adrian
ARION
  Chesterton, G K
ARLEN, Michael
  Kouyoumdjian, Dikran
ARLEY, Catherine
  D'Arley, Catherine
ARMITAGE, Hazel
  Wheway, John
ARMOUR, John
  Paine, Lauran Bosworth

ARMSTRONG, Anthony
  Willis, George Anthony
  Armstrong
ARMSTRONG, George
  Tate, George
ARMSTRONG, Raymond
  Lee, Norman
ARMSTRONG, Sybil
  Edmondson, Sybil
ARMSTRONG, Warren
  Bennett, William E
ARNOLD, Pauline
  White, Pauline Arnold
ARNOLD, Wilcox
  Aitken, Andrew
ARP, Bill
  Smith, Charles H
ARRE, Helen
  Ross, Zola Helen
ARSDALE, Wirt Van
  Davis, Martha Wirt
ARTHUR, Burt
  Arthur, Herbert
ARTHUR, Elisabeth
  Irish, Betty M
ARTHUR, Frank
  Ebert, Arthur Frank
ARTHUR, Gavin
  Arthur, Chester Alan
ARTHUR, Gladys
  Osborne, Dorothy Gladys
ARTHUR, Phyllis
  Shipman, Natalie
ARTHUR, William
  Baker, William Howard
ARTHUR, William
  Neubauer, William Arthur

ARTIFEX
  Green, *Canon* Peter
ASCHE, Oscar
  Heiss, John Stanger
ASCOTT, Adelie
  Bobin, John W
ASH, Fenton
  Atkins, Frank A
ASH, Pauline
  Walker, Emily Kathleen
ASHDOWN, Clifford
  Freeman, R Austin *and*
  Pitcairn, John James
ASHE, Elizabeth
  Hyde, Lavender Beryl
ASHE, Gordon
  Creasey, John
ASHE, Susan
  Best, Carol Anne
ASHFORD, Jeffrey
  Jeffries, Roderic Graeme
ASHLEY, Elizabeth
  Salmon, Annie Alizabeth
ASHLEY, Fred
  Atkins, Frank A
ASHLEY, Mary
  Townsend, Mary Ashley
ASHMORE, Jane
  Little, Cecile Enid
ASHTON, A B
  Basch, Ernst
ASHTON, Ann
  Kimbro, John
ASHTON, E B
  Basch, Ernst
ASHTON, E E
  Basch, Ernst

ASHTON, Lucy
  Martin, Netta
ASKHAM, Francis
  Greenwood, Julia E C
ASQUITH, Nan
  Pattinson, Nancy
ASSIAC
  Fraenkel, Heinrich
ASTLEY, Juliet
  Lofts, Norah
ATHELING, William
  Pound, Ezra
ATHELING, William *Jr*
  Blish, James
ATHOS
  Walkerley, Rodney L de Burgh
ATKINSON, Mary
  Hardwick, Mollie
ATLEE, Philip
  Phillips, James Atlee
AUBREY, Frank
  Atkins, Frank A
AUCHTERLONIE, Dorothy
  Green, Dorothy
AUDIART
  Wainhouse, Austryn
AUGUR
  Poliakoff, Vladimir
AUGUST, John
  De Voto, Bernard Augustine
AUGUSTUS
  Lynn, Elwyn
AULD, Philip
  Burns, Bernard
AUNT CHARLOTTE
  Yonge, Charlotte Mary
AUNT DAISY
  Basham, Daisy

AUNT EVA
  Bilsky, Eva
AUNT KATE
  Souter, Helen Greig
AUNT MAYSIE
  Jeffrey-Smith, May
AUNTIE MARGARET
  Keddie, Margaret Manson
AUREN, Paul
  Uris, Auren
AUSTIN, Brett
  Floren, Lee
AUSTIN, Frank
  Faust, Frederick
AUSTIN, Hugh
  Evans, Hugh Austin
AUSTRALIA JANE
  Shirley, Edith
AUSTRALIANUS
  Back, Karl John
AUSTWICK, John
  Lee, Austin
AVALON, Arthur
  Woodroffe, *Sir* John G
AVERILL, H C
  Snow, Charles Horace
AVERY, Al
  Montgomery, Rutherford
  George
AVERY, June
  Rees, Joan
AVERY, Richard
  Cooper, Edmund
AVI
  Wortis, Avi
AVON, Margaret
  Keatley, Sheila

AWDRY, R C
  Charles, Richard
AYE, John
  Atkinson, John
AYES, Anthony
  Sambrot, William Anthony
AYLEN, Elise
  Scott, Elise Aylen
AYRES, Paul
  Aarons, Edward Sidney

§ §

*'The case of the prisoner Leon
Trotsky—which', he said, giving
Sippy the eye again, 'I am strongly
inclined to think an assumed and
fictitious name—is more serious.'
—P. G. Wodehouse. Carry on,
Jeeves*

§ §

B B
  Watkins-Pitchford, Denys
  James
B B B
  Buckham, Bernard
B L
  Pound, Ezra
B L H
  Haig, Emily Alice
B L T
  Taylor, Bert Leston
BAB
  Gilbert, William Schwenck
BACH, Sebastian
  Andrews, John Arthur

BACHELOR OF ARTS, A
  Bentley, Phyllis
BACK-BACK
  Brown, Kay
BACON, J D
  Dodge, Josephine Daskam
BACON, Jeremy
  Read, James
BAGBY, George
  Stein, Aaron Marc
BAGBY, George A
  Stein, Aaron Marc
BAGNOLD, Enid
  Jones, *Lady* Roderick
BAILEY, Guy
  Simpson, Keith
BAILEY, Hilea
  Marting, Ruth Lenore
BAILEY, Matilda
  Radford, Ruby Lorraine
BAILEY, Thomas
  Partridge, Bellamy
BAIRD, Maude F
  Zimmer, Maude Files
BAKER, Asa
  Dresser, Davis
BALAAM
  Lamb, Geoffrey Frederick
BALBUS
  Huxley, Julian Sorell
BALDRY, Enid
  Citovich, Enid
BALDWIN, Bates
  Jennings, John Edward
BALDWIN, Faith
  Cuthrell, Faith Baldwin
BALFOUR, Grant
  Grant, James Miller

BALL, Zachary
  Masters, Kelly
BALLARD, K G
  Roth, Holly
BALLARD, P D
  Ballard, Willis Todhunter
BALLARD, Todhunter
  Ballard, Willis Todhunter
BALLENTINE, John
  Da Cruz, Daniel
BALLEW, Charles
  Snow, Charles Horace
BALLINGER, W A
  Baker, William Howard
BALLINGER, W A
  Baker, William Howard *and*
  McNeilley, Wilfred
BALLINGER, W A
  McNeilly, Wilfred
BAMFYLDE, Walter
  Bevan, Tom
BANA, Dan
  White, Stanhope
BANCROFT, John
  Jenkins, Alan Charles
BANKOFF, George
  Milkomane, George Alexis
  Milkomanovich
BANNATYNE, Jack
  Gaston, William J
BANNER, Angela
  Maddison, Angela Mary
BANNERMAN, Mark
  Lewing, Anthony
BANNON, Mark
  King, Albert
BANNON, Peter
  Durst, Paul

BANTON, Coy
  Norwood, Victor George
  Charles
BARAK, Michael
  Bar-Zohar, Michael
BARAKA, Imamu Amiri
  Jones, Le Roi
BARBELLION, W N P
  Cummings, Bruce Frederick
BARBER, Antonia
  Anthony, Barbara
BARBETTE, Jay
  Spicer, Bart and
  Spicer, Betty Coe
BARCLAY, Alan
  Tait, George B
BARCLAY, Ann
  Greig, Maysie
BARCYNSKA, Hélène *Countess*
  Evans, Marguerite Florence
BARDSLEY, Michael
  Nuttall, Anthony
BARKER, Jack
  Barker, Michael
BARLAY, Bennett
  Crossen, Kendell Foster
BARLING, Charles
  Barling, Muriel Vere
BARNARD, Nancy
  Hale, Sylvia
BARNETT, Adam
  Fast, Julius
BARNWELL, J O
  Caruso, Joseph
BARON, Paul
  Landells, Richard
BARON, Peter
  Clyde, Leonard Worswick

159

BARON, Willie
  Bryant, Baird
BARR, Cecil
  Kahane, Jack
BARR, Elisabeth
  Edward, Irene
BARRAS SEER
  Wyllie, James McLeod
BARRATT, Robert
  Beeton, D R
BARRIE, Hester
  Hector, Barbara
BARRIE, Jane
  Savage, Mildred
BARRIE, Jane
  Woodford, Irene-Cecile
BARRINGTON, E
  Beck, Lily Adams
BARRINGTON, Maurice
  Brogan, Denis
BARRINGTON, P V
  Barling, Muriel Vere
BARRINGTON, Pamela
  Barling, Muriel Vere
BARRISTER, A
  Hill, Mavis
BARROW, George
  Ruchlis, Hyman
BARRY
  Humphries, Barry
BARRY, Ann
  Byers, Amy
BARRY, Charles
  Bryson, Charles
BARRY, Eileen
  Walker, Emily Kathleen
BARRY, Jocelyn
  Bowden, Jean

BARRY, Joe
  Lake, Joe Barry
BARTIMEUS
  Ricci, Lewis Anselm da Costa
BARTLETT, Kathleen
  Paine, Lauran Bosworth
BARTLETT, Laura
  Baum, Lyman Frank
BARTON, Jack
  Chadwick, Joseph
BARTON, Lee
  Fanthorpe, Robert Lionel
BASHEVIS, Isaac
  Singer, Isaac Bashevis
BASSETT, Jack
  Rowland, Donald Sydney
BASSETT, John Keith
  Keating, Lawrence Alfred
BASUDEB, Sree
  Bahttacharya, Basudeb
BATCHELOR, Reg
  Paine, Lauran Bosworth
BATTLE, Felix
  Levin, Bernard
BAWN, Mary
  Wright, Mary
BAX, Roger
  Winterton, Paul
BAXTER, George Owen
  Faust, Frederick
BAXTER, Gillian
  Hirst, Gillian
BAXTER, Gregory
  Ressich, John S M *and*
  De Banzie, Eric
BAXTER, Hazel
  Rowland, Donald Sydney

BAXTER, John
　Hunt, E Howard
BAXTER, Olive
　Eastwood, Helen B
BAXTER, Shane V
　Norwood, Victor George
　　Charles
BAXTER, Valerie
　Meynell, Laurence Walter
BAYARD, Fred
　Campbell, Margaret *and*
　Jansen, Johanna
BAYER, Oliver Weld
　Bayer, Eleanor *and*
　Bayer, Leo
BAYER, Sylvia
　Glassco, John
BAYLISS, Timothy
　Baybars, Taner
BAZAGANOV, M S
　Stoe, M
BEA, Empy
　Babcock, Maurice P
BEACHCOMBER
　Morton, J B
BEACHCOMBER
　Wyndham Lewis, D B
BEAR, Bullen
　Donnelly, Augustine
BEAR, I D
　Douglass, Percival Ian
BEATON, George
　Brenan, Edward Fitzgerald
BEATON, Jane
　Long, Gladys
BEATTY, Baden
　Casson, Frederick

BEAUMONT, Charles
　Nutt, Charles
BECK, Allen
　Cave, Hugh Barnett
BECK, Christopher
　Bridges, Thomas Charles
BECK, Harry
　Paine, Lauran Bosworth
BECKET, Lavinia
　Course, Pamela
BECKETT, Mark
　Truman, Marcus George
BECKWITH, Lillian
　Comber, Lillian
BEDFORD, A N
　Werner, Elsa Jane
BEDFORD, Ann
　Rees, Joan
BEDFORD, Annie North
　Werner, Elsa Jane
BEDFORD, Donald F
　Bedford-Jones, Henry;
　Friede, Donald *and*
　Fearing, Kenneth
BEDFORD, Kenneth
　Paine, Lauran Bosworth
BEE
　Boshell, Gordon
BEECH, Margaret
　Barclay, Vera C
BEEDING, Francis
　Saunders, Hilary Aidan
　St George *and*
　Palmer, John Leslie
BEG, Callum
　Mack, J C O
BEG, Toram
　McKillop, Norman

161

BELL, Catherine
  Weir, Rosemary
BELL, Frank
  Wirt, Mildred
BELL, John
  Johnson, Victor
BELL, Josephine
  Ball, Doris Bell Collier
BELL, Leigh
  Bell, Alison Clare Harvey
BELL, Margaret
  Saunders, Margaret Bell
BELL, Nancy
  Irish, Betty M
BELL, Neil
  Southwold, Stephen
BELLAIRS, George
  Blundell, Harold
BELLMAN, Walter
  Barrett, Hugh Gilchrist
BELVEDERE, Lee
  Grayland, Valerie M
BENARY-ISBERT, Margot
  Benary, Margot
BENDER, Jay
  Deindorfer, Robert G
BENDIT, Gladys
  Presland, John
BENEDICT, Billy
  Paul, Maury
BENNETT, Dwight
  Newton, Dwight Bennett
BENNETT, H O
  Hardison, O B
BENNETT, Margaret
  Toohey, Barbara *and*
    Biermann, June

BENNEY, Mark
  Degras, Henry Ernest
BENSON, Adam
  Bingley, David Ernest
BENSON, S Vere
  Taylor, Stephana Vere
BENSON, Thérèse
  Knipe, Emilie
BENTINCK, Ray
  Best, Rayleigh Breton Amis
BENTLEY, James
  Hanley, James
BENTLEY, W J
  Ullyett, Kenneth
BENTON, Karla
  Rowland, Donald Sydney
BENTON, Will
  Paine, Lauran Bosworth
BERESFORD, Russell
  Roberts, Cecil
BERG, Ila
  Garber, Nellia B
BERGER, Helen
  Bamberger, Helen R
BERKELEY, Anthony
  Cox, A B
BERKLEY, Tom
  Geen, Clifford
BERNARD
  Boggs, Helen
BERNARD, Robert
  Martin, Robert Bernard
BERNE, Leo
  Davies, Leslie Purnell
BERNEY, Beryl
  Lytle, *Mrs* W J A
BERRINGTON, John
  Brownjohn, Alan

BERRISFORD, Judith
  Lewis, Clifford *and*
  Lewis, Judith May
BERRISFORD, Mary
  Lewis, Mary Christianna
BERRY, Erick
  Best, Allena
BERRY, Helen
  Rowland, Donald Sydney
BERRY, Matilda
  Beauchamp, Kathleen
  Mansfield
BERTON, Guy
  La Coste, Guy R *and*
  Bingham, E A
BERTRAM, Arthur
  Ibbott, Arthur Pearson
BERWICK, Claude
  Hunt, Anna Rebecca Gale
BETHUNE, Mary
  Clopet, Liliane M C
BETTERIDGE, Anne
  Potter, Margaret
BETTERIDGE, Don
  Newman, Bernard
BETTINA
  Ehrlich, Bettina
BEVAN, Alistair
  Roberts, Keith J K
BEVANS, Torre
  Hood, Torrey
BEVERLY, Linda
  Quentin, Dorothy
BEXAR, Phil
  Borg, Philip Anthony John
BEYNON, John
  Harris, John Wyndham
  Parkes Lucas Beynon

BICKERDYKE, John
  Cooke, C H
BIELY, Andrey
  Bugaev, Boris Nikolaevich
BIJ-BIJCHENKO, B
  Rudnyckyj, Jaroslav B
BILL
  Strachan, Gladys Elizabeth
BILL, Margaret
  Saunders, Margaret Bill
BILLINGS, Buck
  Rister, Claude
BIRD, Brandon
  Evans, George *and*
  Evans, Kay
BIRD, Lilian
  Barradell-Smith, Walter
BIRD, Richard
  Barradell-Smith, Walter
BIRKENHEAD, Edward
  Birkenhead, Elijah
BIRKLEY, Dolan
  Hitchens, Dolores
BIRMINGHAM, George A
  Hannay, James Owen
BISHOP, Morchard
  Stonor, Oliver
BIXBY, Ray Z
  Tralins, S Robert
BIZET, George
  Bisset-Smith, G T
BLACK, Gavin
  Wynd, Oswald
BLACK, Ivory
  Janvier, Thomas Allibone
BLACK, Jack
  Ames, R F

BLACK, Jett
  Black, Oliver
BLACK, Kitty
  Black, Dorothy
BLACK, Laura
  Longrigg, Roger Erskine
BLACK, Lionel
  Barker, Dudley
BLACK, Mansell
  Dudley-Smith, Trevor
BLACK, Veronica
  Black, Maureen
BLACKBURN, John
  Mott, J Moldon
BLACKBURN, Martin
  Allfree, P S
BLACKER, Hereth
  Chalke, Herbert
BLACKLIN, Malcolm
  Chambers, Aidan
BLACKSNAKE, George
  Richardson, Gladwell
BLACKSTOCK, Charity
  Torday, Ursula
BLACKSTOCK, Lee
  Torday, Ursula
BLACKWELL, John
  Collings, Edwin
BLAIKE, Avona
  Macintosh, Joan
BLAINE, James
  Avallone, Michael Angelo *Jr*
BLAINE, Jeff
  Barrett, Geoffrey John
BLAINE, John
  Goodwin, Harold Leland *and*
    Harkins, Peter J

BLAINE, Sara
  Morgan, Diana
BLAIR
  Blair-Fish, Wallace Wilfred
BLAIR, Frank
  Buckby, Samuel
BLAIRMAN, Jacqueline
  Pinto, Jacqueline
BLAISDELL, Anne
  Linington, Elizabeth
BLAKE
  Adam, Ronald
BLAKE, Andrea
  Weale, Anne
BLAKE, Cameron
  Mason, Michael
BLAKE, Eleanor
  Pratt, E B Atkinson
BLAKE, Katherine
  Walter, Dorothy Blake
BLAKE, Kay
  Walter, Dorothy Blake
BLAKE, Monica
  Muir, Marie
BLAKE, Nicholas
  Day Lewis, Cecil
BLAKE, Robert
  Davis, Leslie Purnell
BLAKE, Vanessa
  Brown, May
BLAKE, William
  Blech, William James
BLAKE, William James
  Blech, William James
BLAND, E
  Bland, *Mrs* Edith
  (Nesbit)

BLAND, Fabian
Bland, *Mrs* Edith (Nesbit)
and Bland, Hubert
BLAND, *Mrs* Hubert
Bland, *Mrs* Edith (Nesbit)
BLAND, Jennifer
Bowden, Jean
BLAUTH, Christopher
Blauth-Muszkowski, Peter
BLAYRE, Christopher
Heron-Allen, Edward
BLEECK, Oliver
Thomas, Ross
BLEEKER, Sonia
Zim, Sonia
BLIGHT, Rose
Greer, Germaine
BLINDERS, Belinda
Coke, Desmond
BLINKHOALIE
Allison, William
BLISS, Adam
Burkhardt, Eve *and*
Burkhardt, Robert
Ferdinand
BLISS, Reginald
Wells, H G
BLIXEN, Karen
Blixen-Finecke, Karen
Christence *Baroness*
BLOOD, Joan Wilde
Murray, Joan
BLOOD, Matthew
Dresser, Davis
BLOOMFIELD, Robert
Edgley, Leslie
BLUE, Wallace
Kraenzel, Margaret Powell

BLUNDELL, Peter
Butterworth, Frank Nestle
BLUTIG, Eduard
Gorey, Edward St John
BLY, Nellie
Seaman, Elizabeth C
BLYTH, John
Hibbs, John
BOAKE, Capel
Kerr, Doris Boake
BOAS, Marie
Hall, Marie
BOCCA, Al
Winter, Bevis
BODEN, Hilda
Bodenham, Hilda
BOGLE, Charles
Dukenfield, William Claude
BOHN, Eric
Price-Brown, John
BOILEAU, Marie
Hardy, Jane
BOK, Kooshti
Mair, George Brown
BOLD, Ralph
Griffiths, Charles
BOLDREWOOD, Rolf
Browne, Thomas Alexander
BOLITHO, Ray D
Blair, Dorothy
BOLITHO, William
Ryall, William Bolitho
BOLSTER, Evelyn
Bolster, *Sister* M Angela
BOLT, Ben
Binns, Ottwell
BOLT, Lee
Faust, Frederick

165

BOLTON, Isabel
  Miller, Mary Britton
BON GAULTIER
  Martin, *Sir* Theodore
BON VIVEUR
  Cradock, Phyllis Nan Sortain
  and Cradock, John
BOND, Gillian
  McEvoy, Marjorie
BONEHILL, Ralph
  Stratemeyer, Edward
BONETT, Emery
  Carter, Felicity Winifred
BONETT, John
  Coulson, John
BONNAMY, Francis
  Walz, Audrey
BONNER, Michael
  Glasscock, Anne Bonner
BONNER, Parker
  Ballard, Willis Todhunter
BONNEY, Bill
  Keevill, Henry John
BOON, August
  Breton-Smith, Clare
BOOT, William
  Stoppard, Tom
BORDEN, Leo
  Borden, Deal
BORER, Mary Cathcart
  Myers, Mary Cathcart
BORG, Jack
  Borg, Philip Anthony John
BORLAND, Hal
  Borland, Harold Glen
BORNE, D
  Rice, Dorothy

BORODIN, George
  Milkomane, George Alexis
  Milkomanovich
BORTH, Willan G
  Bosworth, Willan George
BOSCAWEN, Linda
  Smithells, Doreen
BOSCO, Jack
  Holliday, Joseph
BOSTON, Charles K
  Gruber, Frank
BOSWELL, James
  Kent, Arthur
BOSWELL, John
  King, John
BOSWORTH, Frank
  Paine, Lauran Bosworth
BOUCHER, Anthony
  White, William Anthony P
BOUNDER, THE
  Fay, E F
BOURCHIER, Jules
  Posner, David Louis
BOURNE, George
  Sturt, George
BOURNE, John
  John, Owen
BOURNE, Lesley
  Marshall, Evelyn
BOURNE, Peter
  Jeffries, Bruce Graham
  Montague
BOUVERIE
  Kreiner, George
BOVEE, Ruth
  Paine, Lauran Bosworth
BOWDEN, Jim
  Spence, William

BOWEN, Betty
West, Betty Bowen
BOWEN, Elenore Sith
Bohannan, Laura M Smith
BOWEN, Marjorie
Campbell, Gabrielle Margaret
Vere
BOWER, B M
Sinclair, Bertha Muzzy
BOWERS, *Mrs* J Milton
Bierce, Ambrose
BOWIE, Jim
Norwood, Victor George
Charles
BOWIE, Sam
Ballard, Willis Todhunter
BOWMAN, Jeanne
O'More, Peggy
BOWOOD, Richard
Daniell, Albert Scott
BOWYER, Nina
Conarain, Alice Nina
BOX, Edgar
Vidal, Gore
BOY
Fowkes, Aubrey
BOWYANG, Bill
Vennard, Alexander Vindex
BOYD, Edward
Tunley, Roul
BOYD, Frank
Kane, Frank
BOYD, John
Upchurch, Boyd
BOYD, Nancy
Millay, Edna St Vincent
BOYD, Neil
De Rosa, Peter

BOYD, Prudence
Gibbs, Norah
BOYER, Robert
Lake, Kenneth Robert
BRACE, Timothy
Pratt, Theodore
BRACKEN, Steve
Farris, John Lee
BRACKETT, Leigh
Hamilton, Leigh Brackett
BRADBURNE, E S
Lawrence, Elizabeth
BRADDON, George
Milkomane, George Alexis
Milkomanovich
BRADEN, Walter
Finney, Jack
BRADFIELD, Nancy
Sayer, Nancy Margetts
BRADFORD, De Witt
Blossom, D Bradford
BRADFORD, Will
Paine, Lauren Bosworth
BRADLEY, Concho
Paine, Lauren Bosworth
BRADLEY, Shelland
Birt, Francis Bradley
BRADWELL, James
Kent, Arthur
BRAHMS, Caryl
Abrahams, Doris Caroline
BRAIN, Leonard
Peck, Leonard
BRAMAH, Ernest
Smith, Ernest Bramah
BRAMWELL, Charlotte
Kimbro, John

BRAND, Christianna
  Lewis, Mary Christianna
BRAND, Clay
  Norwood, Victor George
  Charles
BRAND, David
  Nutt, David
BRAND, Max
  Faust, Frederick
BRAND, Mona
  Fox, Mona Alexis
BRANDANE, John
  Macintyre, John
BRANDON, Bruce
  Braun, Wilbur
BRANDON, Curt
  Bishop, Curtis Kent
BRANDON, Joe
  Davis, Robert Prunier
BRANDON, Sheila
  Rayner, Claire
BRANDT, Tom
  Dewey, Thomas Blanchard
BRANT, Lewis
  Rowland, Donald Sydney
BRAY, Alison
  Rowland, Donald Sydney
BRAYCE, William
  Rowland, Donald Sydney
BREAKER, THE
  Morant, Harry H
BRECK, Vivian
  Breckenfeld, Vivian Gurney
BRENAN, Gerald
  Brenan, Edward Fitzgerald
BRENDA
  Castle Smith, *Mrs* G

BRENNAN, Walt
  King, Albert
BRENNAN, Will
  Paine, Lauran Bosworth
BRENNING, L H
  Hunter, Alfred John
BRENT, *of Bin Bin*
  Franklin, Stella Maria Sarah
  Miles
BRENT, Calvin
  Hornby, John Wilkinson
BRENT, Catherine
  King, Albert
BRENT, Loring
  Worts, George F
BRENT, Nigel
  Wimhurst, Cecil Gordon
  Eugene
BRENT, Romney
  Larralde, Romulo
BREOLA, Tjalmar
  De Jong, David Cornel
BRETT, John Michael
  Tripp, Miles Barton
BRETT, Martin
  Sanderson, Douglas
BRETT, Michael
  Brett, Leslie Frederick
BRETT, Rosalind
  Blair, Kathryn
BREWER, Mike
  Guinness, Maurice
BREWSTER, Benjamin
  Elting, Mary
BREWSTER, Franklin
  Folsom, Franklin Brewster
BREWSTER, Robin
  Staples, Reginald Thomas

BRIDE, Jack
Marteau, F A
BRIDGE, Ann
O'Malley, *Lady*
BRIDGE, John
Peters, Robert Louis
BRIDGEMAN, Richard
Davies, Leslie Purnell
BRIDGER, Adam
Bingley, David Ernest
BRIDGES, Tom
Bridges, Thomas Charles
BRIDGES, Victor
De Freyne, George
BRIDGWATER, Donald
Henderson, Donald Landels
BRIDIE, James
Mavor, Osborne Henry
BRIEN, R N
Whelan, Jerome Bernard
BRIEN, Raley
McCulley, Johnston
BRIGGS, Philip
Briggs, Phyllis
BRINSMEAD, H F
Brinsmead, Hesba
BRIONY, Henry
Ellis, Oliver
BRISTOWE, Edwin
Wright, R L Gerrard
BRITAIN, Dan
Pendleton, Donald Eugene
BRITT, Sappho Henderson
Woolfolk, Josiah Pitts
BROCK, Gavin
Lindsay, Maurice
BROCK, Lynn
Macallister, Alister

BROCK, Stuart
Trimble, Louis
BROCKLEY, Fenton
Rowland, Donald Sydney
BRODIE, Gordon
Smith, Sidney Wallace
BROGAN, James
Hodder-Williams, Christopher
BRONSON, Lynn
Lampman, Evelyn
BRONSON, Oliver
Rowland, Donald Sydney
BRONSON, Wade
King, Albert
BROOK, Barnaby
Brooks, Collin
BROOK, Esther
Huggett, Berthe
BROOK, Peter
Chovil, Alfred Harold
BROOKE, Carol
Ramskill, Valerie
BROOKER, Clark
Fowler, Kenneth A
BROOKS, Jonathan
Mellett, John Calvin
BROOKS, Laura Frances
Ross, William Edward Daniel
BROOKS, W A
Fryefield, Maurice P
BROOKS, William Allan
Fryefield, Maurice P
BROOME, Adam
James, Godfrey Warden
BROOME, Dora
Wild, Dora Mary
BROTHER ANTONINUS
Everson, William Oliver

169

BROTHER CHOLERIC
 Van Zeller, Claud H
BROTHER ERNEST
 Ryan, John D
BROTHER FLAVIUS
 Ellison, James
BROTHER GRAHAM
 Jeffrey, Graham
BROUILLETTE, Emil
 Rydberg, Ernie
BROUN, Emily
 Sterne, E G
BROWN, Carter
 Yates, Alan Geoffrey
BROWN, Douglas
 Gibson, Walter Brown
BROWN, Eve
 Nichols, Mary Eudora
BROWN, Jones
 Munby, Arthur Joseph
BROWN, Mandy
 Brown, May
BROWN, Marel
 Brown, Margaret Elizabeth
 Snow
BROWNE, Barum
 Dennis, Geoffrey Pomeroy
BROWNE, Courtney
 Courtney-Browne, Reginald
 D S
BROWNING, John
 Brown, John
BROWNING, John S
 Williams, Robert Moore
BROWNING, Sterry
 Gribble, Leonard Richard
BRUCE, Charles
 Francis, Arthur Bruce Charles

BRUCE, Leo
 Croft-Cooke, Rupert
BRUNSWICK, James
 Stitt, James M
BRYAN, John
 Delves-Broughton, Josephine
BRYANS, Robin
 Harbinson-Bryans, Robert
BRYHER
 Ellerman, Annie Winifred
BRYHER, Winifred
 Ellerman, Annie Winifred
BRYSON, Leigh
 Rutledge, Nancy
BUCHANAN, Chuck
 Rowland, Donald Sydney
BUCHANAN, Patrick
 Corley, Edwin *and*
  Murphy, John
BUCKINGHAM, Bruce
 Lilley, Peter *and*
  Stansfield, Anthony
BUCKINGHAM, David
 Villiers, David Hugh
BUCKLEY, Eunice
 Scott, Rose Laure
BUCKMASTER, Henrietta
 Henkle, Henrietta
BUCKROSE, J E
 Jameson, Annie Edith
BUDD, Jackson
 Budd, William John
BUFFALO CHILD LONG
 LANCE
 Clarke, Sylvestre
BUFFY
 Glassco, John

BULLEN BEAR
  Donnelly, Augustine
BULLINGHAM, Ann
  Jones, A Miles
BUPP, Walter
  Garrett, Randall
BURCHELL, Mary
  Cook, Ida
BURFIELD, Eva
  Ebbett, Eve
BURFORD, Eleanor
  Hibbert, Eleanor Alice
    Burford
BURGEON, G A L
  Barfield, Arthur Owen
BURGER, John
  Marquand, Leopold
BURGESS, Anthony
  Wilson, John Anthony
    Burgess
BURGESS, Gelett
  Sturgis, Justin
BURGESS, Trevor
  Dudley-Smith, Trevor
BURKE, Edmund
  Boggs, Winifred
BURKE, Fielding
  Dargan, Olive
BURKE, Jonathan
  Burke, John Frederick
BURKE, Leda
  Garnett, David
BURKE, Michael
  Farrell, Michael
BURKE, Noel
  Hitchens, Dolores
BURKE, Shifty
  Benton, Peggie

BURLAND, Harris
  Harris-Burland, John B
BURKHOLZ, Herbert
  Irving, Clifford
BURNABY, Nigel
  Ellett, Harold Pincton
BURNS, Bobby
  Burns, Vincent
BURNS, Elizabeth
  Behanna, Gertrude Florence
BURNS, Mary
  Hare, Walter B
BURNS, Sheila
  Bloom, Ursula
BURNS, Tex
  L'Amour, Louis
BURR, Elsie
  Milligan, Elsie
BURROUGHS, Margaret
  Feldman, Eugene P R
BURROWAY, Janet
  Eysselinck, Janet Gay
BURTON, Conrad
  Edmundson, Joseph
BURTON, Miles
  Street, Cecil John Charles
BURTON, Richard
  Jenkins, Richard
BURTON, Thomas
  Longstreet, Stephen
BUSHWOMAN
  Palmer-Archer, Laura M
BUSTOS DOMECQ, Honorio
  Borges, Jorge Luis *and*
    Bioy-Casares, Adolfo
BUTLER, Ivan
  Beuttler, Edward I O

171

BUTLER, Joan
  Alexander, Robert William
BUTLER, Richard
  Allbeury, Theo Edward
  le Bouthillier
BUTLER, Richard
  Butler, Arthur Ronald
BUTLER, Walter C
  Faust, Frederick
BUTTLE, Myra
  Purcell, Victor W W S
BYRNE, Donn
  Donn-Byrne, Brian Oswald
BYROM, James
  Bramwell, James Guy
BYSTANDER, A
  Smith, Goldwin

C
Cuthbertson, James Lister
C D
  Lawrence, T E
C J G
  Lawrence, T E
C O
  Collinson Owen, H
CABBY WITH CAMERA
  Green, Maxwell
CABLE, Boyd
  Ewart, Ernest Andrew
CABOCHON, Francis
  Allan, Philip Bertram Murray
CADE, Alexander
  Methold, Kenneth
CADE, Robin
  Nicole, Christopher
CADWALLADER
  Clemens, Paul
172

§ §

A self-made man may prefer a
self-made name.
—*Judge Learned Hand*

§ §

CAGNEY, Peter
  Winter, Bevis
CAHILL, Mike
  Nolan, William F
CAILLOU, Alan
  Lyle-Smythe, Alan
CAILLOUX, Pousse
  Bethell, Leonard Arthur
CAIN, Paul
  Ruric, Peter
CAINE, Mark
  Maschler, Tom *and*
    Raphael, Frederic
CAL, Dakota
  Waldron, Corbin A
CALDECOTT, Veronica
  Cohen, Victor
CALDWELL, Elinor
  Breton-Smith, Clare
CALEHAS
  Garvin, J L
CALEY, Rod
  Rowland, Donald Sydney
CALHOUN, Mary
  Wilkins, Mary Louise
CALIBAN
  Phillips, Hubert
CALIBAN
  Reid, John

CALIBAN
  Stuart, Hector A
CALLAHAN, John
  Chadwick, Joseph
CALLAS, Theo
  McCarthy, Shaun
CALLAWAY, Hugh
  Nisbet, Ulric
CALLENDER, Julian
  Lee, Austin
CALLISTHENES
  Costa, Gabriel
CALLUM, Michael
  Greaves, Michael
CALLUM BEG
  Mack, J C O
CALVERT, John
  Leaf, Munro
CALVIN, Henry
  Hanley, Clifford
CALVIN, Kenneth
  Hogben, Lancelot Thomas
CAM
  Campbell, Barbara Mary
CAMBRIDGE, Elizabeth
  Hodges, Barbara K
CAMDEN, Richard
  Beeston, L J
CAMERON, Brett
  Martin, Reginald Alec
CAMERON, D Y
  Cook, Dorothy Mary
CAMERON, Hector
  Macquarrie, Hector
CAMERON, Ian
  Payne, Donald Gordon
CAMERON, John
  Macdonell, A G

CAMERON, Margaret
  Lindsay, Kathleen
CAMPBELL, Berkeley
  Duddington, Charles Lionel
CAMPBELL, Bruce
  Epstein, Samuel
CAMPBELL, Colin
  Christie, Douglas
CAMPBELL, Duncan
  Thorpe, John
CAMPBELL, Hope
  Wallis, Geraldine
CAMPBELL, Judith
  Pares, Marion
CAMPBELL, Keith
  West-Watson, Keith Campbell
CAMPBELL, R T
  Todd, Ruthven Campbell
CAMPBELL, Scott
  Davis, Frederick William
CAMPBELL, Stuart
  Campbell, Sydney George
CAMPION, Sarah
  Alpers, Mary Rose
CANADIENNE
  Hunt, Anna Rebecca Gale
CANAWAY, Bill
  Canaway, W H
CANDIDUS
  Brogan, Colm
CANDIDUS
  Sidebotham, Herbert
CANDY, Edward
  Neville, Alison
CANFIELD, Cleve
  Mitchell, Clare May
CANFIELD, Dorothy
  Fisher, Dorothea F C

CANIS
  Hubbard, Clifford Lionel
  Barry
CANNAN, Denis
  Pullein-Thompson, Denis
CANNAN, Joanna
  Pullein-Thompson, Josephine
  Mary
CANNELL, Charles
  Vivian, Evelyn Charles H
CANNON, Brenda
  Moore, Bertha B
CANNON, Curt
  Lombino, Salvatore A
CANNON, Elliott
  Elliott-Cannon, Arthur
  Elliott
CANTRELL, Wade B
  Hogan, Robert Jasper
CANUCK, Abe
  Bingley, David Ernest
CANUCK, Janey
  Murphy, Emily Gowan
  (Ferguson)
CANUSI, Jose
  Barker, S Omar
CANYON, Claudia
  Anderson, Betty
CAPE, Judith
  Page, Patricia Kathleen
CAPELLE, Anne
  Herapath, Theodora
CAPITALIST
  Slater, James
CAPON, Peter
  Oakley, Eric Gilbert
CAPP, Al
  Caplin, Alfred Gerald

CAPSTAN
  Hardinge, Rex
CAPTIOUS CRITIC
  Miller, Lynn
CARBERY, Ethna
  MacManus, Anna Johnston
CARDER, Michael
  Fluharty, Vernon L
CAREW, Jean
  Corby, Jane
CAREW, John
  Walsh, James Morgan
CAREW, Tim
  Carew, John Mohun
CAREY, Charles
  Waddel, Charles Carey
CAREY, James
  Carew-Slater, Harold James
CARFAX, Catherine
  Fairburn, Eleanor
CARGOE, Richard
  Payne, Pierre Stephen
  Robert
CARLETON, Janet
  Adam Smith, Janet
  Buchanan
CARLETON, S
  Jones, Susan Carleton
CARLETON-MILECETE
  Jones, Susan Carleton
CARLOTA
  Oppenheimer, Carlota
CARLTON, Ann
  Trent, Ann
CARLTON, Roger
  Rowland, Donald Sydney
CARLYLE, Anthony
  Milton, Gladys Alexandra

CARMAN, Dulce
  Drummond, Edith
CARMEN, Felix
  Sherman, Frank Dempster
CARMICHAEL, Harry
  Ognall, Leopold Horace
CARMICHAEL, Philip
  Harrison, Philip
CARNAC, Carol
  Rivett, Edith Caroline
CARNEGIE, Sacha
  Carnegie, Raymond Alexander
CAROL, Bill J
  Knott, William Cecil
CARP, Augustus
  Bashford, *Sir* Henry Howarth
CARR, Basil
  Kahane, Jack
CARR, Catherine
  Wade, Rosalind
CARR, Charles
  Mason, Sydney Charles
CARR, Christopher
  Benson, Arthur Christopher
CARR, Elaine
  Mason, Sydney Charles
CARR, Glyn
  Styles, Showell
CARR, H D
  Crowley, Edward Alexander
CARR, Philippa
  Hibbert, Eleanor Alice
    Burford
CARR, Roberta
  Roberts, Irene
CARREL, Mark
  Paine, Lauran Bosworth

CARRICK, Edward
  Craig, Edward Anthony
CARRICK, John
  Crosbie, Hugh Provan
CARRINGTON, Michael
  Williams, Meurig
CARRINGTON, V
  Hughes, Valerie Anne
CARROLL, Martin
  Carr, Margaret
CARRUTH, Agnes K
  Tucker, Agnes
CARSON, Anthony
  Brooke, Peter
CARSON, Lance
  Kelly, Harold Ernest
CARSON, Sylvia
  Dresser, Davis
CARSTAIRS, Kathleen
  Jacobs, Thomas Curtis Hicks
CARSTAIRS, Rod
  Dalton, Gilbert
CARSTENS, Netta
  Laffeaty, Christina
CARTER, Ann
  Brooks, Ann
CARTER, Anne
  Brooks, Ann
CARTER, Bruce
  Hough, Richard Alexander
CARTER, Diana
  Copper, Dorothy
CARTER, John L
  Carter, Compton Irving
CARTER, Nevada
  Paine, Lauran Bosworth
CARTER, Nick
  Avallone, Michael Angelo *Jr*

175

CARTER, Nick
  Carter, Bryan
CARTER, Phyllis Ann
  Eberle, Irmengarde
CARTLAND, Barbara
  McCorquodale, Barbara
  Hamilton
CARVER, Dave
  Bingley, David Ernest
CARY, Arthur
  Cary, Joyce
CARY, D M
  Macmillan, Douglas
CARYL, Jean
  Kaplan, Jean Caryl
CASAVINI, Pieralessandro
  Wainhouse, Austryn
CASE, Justin
  Cave, Hugh Barnett
CASE, Justin
  Gleadow, Rupert
CASEY, Mart
  Casey, Michael T *and*
  Casey, Rosemary
CASEY, T
  Cordes, Theodor K
CASSADY, Claude
  Paine, Lauran Bosworth
CASSANDRA
  Connor, *Sir* William
CASSELLS, John
  Duncan, William Murdoch
CASSILIS, Robert
  Edwardes, Michael
CASSILS, Peter
  Keele, Kenneth David
CASSIUS
  Foot, Michael
176

CASTLE, Douglas
  Brown, John Ridley
CASTLE, John
  Payne, Ronald Charles *and*
  Garrod, John William
CASTLE, Philip
  Jackson, Charles Philip
  Castle Kains
CASTLEMON, Harry
  Fosdick, Charles Austin
CATALAN, Henri
  Dupuy-Mazuel, Henri
CATHODE RAY
  Scroggie, Marcus Graham
CATLIN, Ralph
  Lavender, David Sievert
CATO
  Foot, Michael;
  Howard, Peter *and*
  Owen, Frank
CATTO, Max
  Catto, Maxwell Jeffrey
CAUDWELL, Christopher
  Sprigg, Christopher St John
CAULDWELL, Frank
  King, Francis
CAUSEWAY, Jane
  Cork, Barry
CAVANNA, Betty
  Harrison, Elizabeth C
CAVENDISH
  Brown, E
CAVENDISH, Peter
  Horler, Sydney
CECIL, Edward
  Maiden, Cecil
CECIL, Henry
  Leon, Henry Cecil

CELTICUS
  Bevan, Aneurin
CENSOR
  Bunce, Oliver Bell
CENTAUR
  Thorpe, John
CERAM, C W
  Marek, Kurt W
CHABER, M E
  Crossen, Kendell Foster
CHACE, Isobel
  Hunter, Elizabeth
CHAITANYA, Krishna
  Nair, K K
CHALLIS, George
  Faust, Frederick
CHALLIS, Simon
  Phillips, Dennis John
  Andrew
CHALLONER, H K
  Mills, Janet Melanie Ailsa
CHALMERS, Allen
  Upward, Edward Falaise
CHALON, Jon
  Chaloner, John Seymour
CHAMBERS, Dana
  Leffingwell, Albert
CHAMBERS, Peter
  Phillips, Dennis John
  Andrew
CHANAIDH, Fear
  Campbell, John Lorne
CHANCE, Jonathan
  Chance, John Newton
CHANCE, Stephen
  Turner, Philip
CHANCELLOR, John
  Rideaux, Charles

CHANDOS, Fay
  Swatridge, Irene M M
CHANEL
  Joyce, James
CHANEY
  Leeming, Jill
CHANNEL, A R
  Catherall, Arthur
CHANNING, Peter
  McMordie, Taber
CHAPMAN, Marison
  Chapman, Mary I *and*
  Chapman, John Stanton
CHAPMAN, Walker
  Silverberg, Robert
CHARLES, Edward
  Hempstead, Charles Edward
CHARLES, Franklin
  Adams, Cleve Franklin
CHARLES, Frederick
  Ashford, F C
CHARLES, Nicholas
  Kuskin, Karla Seidman
CHARLES, Robert
  Smith, Robert Charles
CHARLES, Theresa
  Swatridge, Charles John *and*
  Swatridge, Irene M M
CHARQUES, Dorothy
  Emms, Dorothy
CHARTERIS, Leslie
  Yin, Leslie Charles Bowyer
CHASE, Alice
  McHargue, Georgess
CHASE, Beatrice
  Parr, Olive Katherine
CHASE, James Hadley
  Raymond, Rene

177

CHASE, Lesley
  Verner, Christopher Stuart
CHATEAUCLAIR, Wilfred
  Lighthall, William Douw
CHATHAM, Larry
  Bingley, David Ernest
CHATTAN, Robert
  Smith, Robert
CHEETHAM, Hal
  Cheetham, James
CHEIRO
  Hamon, Louis *Count*
CHELTON, John
  Durst, Paul
CHERNICHEWSKI, Vladimir
  Duff, Charles
CHERRYHOLMES, Anne
  Price, Olive
CHERRYMAN, A E
  Levin, Bernard
CHESHAM, Henry
  Bingley, David Ernest
CHESHIRE, Giff
  Cheshire, Gifford Paul
CHESNEY, Weatherby
  Hyne, Charles John Cutliffe
  Wright
CHESTER, Elizabeth
  Ransome, L E
CHESTER, Peter
  Phillips, Dennis John
  Andrew
CHESTOR, Rui
  Courtier, Sidney Hobson
CHICHESTER
  Drummond, Edith Victoria
CHILD, Alan
  Langner, Laurence

CHILD, Charles B
  Frost, C Vernon
CHIPPERFIELD, Robert Orr
  Ostrander, Isabel Egerton
CHISHOLM, Matt
  Watts, Peter Christopher
CHOLERIC, BROTHER
  Van Zeller, Claude H
CHRISTIAN, Frederick H
  Nolan, Frederick
CHRISTIAN, Jill
  Dilcock, Noreen
CHRISTOPHER, John
  Youd, Samuel
CHRONIQUEUSE
  Logan, Olive
CHRYSTIE, Edward M
  Watson, Jack Charles
  Wauchope
CHU FENG
  Blofeld, John
CHUB, Sergeant
  Abrahamson, Maurice Noel
CHURCH, Granville
  People, Granville Church
CHURCH, Jeffrey
  Kirk, Richard Edmund
CHURCHILL, Luanna
  Dughman, John Karl *and*
  Dughman, Frieda Mae
CIRCUMLIBRA
  Lockwood, Frank
CLADPOLE, Jim
  Richards, James
CLAIRE, Keith
  Andrews, Claire *and*
  Andrews, Keith

CLANDON, Henrietta
  Vahey, John George
    Haslette
CLAPP, Patricia
  Cone, P C L
CLARE, Elizabeth
  Cook, Dorothy Mary
CLARE, Helen
  Blair, Pauline Hunter
CLARE, Marguerite
  Heppell, Mary
CLARK, Dale
  Kayser, Ronal
CLARK, Joan
  Wirt, Mildred
CLARK, Margery
  Clark, Mary Elizabeth *and*
    Quigley, M C
CLARK, Mary Lou
  Clark, Maria
CLARKE, John
  Laughlin, Virginia Carli
CLARKE, Merle
  Gessner, Lynne
CLARKE, Pauline
  Blair, Pauline Hunter
CLARKE, Richard
  Paine, Lauran Bosworth
CLARKE, Robert
  Paine, Lauran Bosworth
CLAUDE
  Forde, Claude Marie
CLAUGHTON-JAMES, James
  Bentley, James W B
CLAY, Bertha M
  Braeme, Charlotte Monica
CLAY, Weston
  Ford, T W

CLAYMORE, Tod
  Clevely, Hugh Desmond
    Claymore
CLEAR, Claudius
  Nicoll, *Sir* William Robertson
CLEAVER, Denis
  Leyland, Eric
CLEMENT, Hal
  Stubbs, Harry Clement
CLEMENTIA
  Feehan, *Sister* Mary Edward
CLEMENTS, E H
  Hunter, Eileen
CLEMONS, Elizabeth
  Nowell, Elizabeth Cameron
CLEO ET ANTHONY
  Anthony, Edward
CLERGYMAN, A
  Morison, John
CLERIHEW, E
  Bentley, Edmund Clerihew
CLEVE, Janita
  Rowland, Donald Sydney
CLEVEDON, John
  Plumley, Ernest F
CLEVELAND, Jim
  King, Albert
CLEVELAND, John
  McElfresh, Adeline
CLIFFORD, Eth
  Rosenberg, Ethel
CLIFFORD, Francis
  Thompson, Arthur Leonard
    Bell
CLIFFORD, John
  Bayliss, John Clifford

CLIFFORD, Martin
  Hamilton, Charles Harold
  St John
CLINTON, Jeff
  Bickham, Jack Miles
CLIVE, Clifford
  Home-Gall, Edward
  Reginald
CLIVE, William
  Bassett, Ronald
CLOIE, Mack
  McKibbin, *Reverend*
  Archibald
CLOSE, Upton
  Hall, Josef Washington
CLOUD, Yvonne
  Kapp, Yvonne
CLYDE, Constance
  MacAdam, Constance
CLYDE, Craig
  Gossman, Oliver
COALFLEET, Pierre
  Davison, Frank Cyril Shaw
COBBER, Lance Corporal
  Adcock, A St John
COBBLEIGH, Tom
  Raymond, Walter
COCHRAN, Jeff
  Durst, Paul
COCHRANE, Corinna
  Peterson, Corinna
COCKIN, Joan
  Burbridge, Edith Joan
CODY, A R
  Joscelyn, Archie Lynn
CODY, Al
  Joscelyn, Archie Lynn

CODY, C S
  Waller, Leslie
CODY, Stetson
  Gribble, Leonard Reginald
CODY, Stone
  Mount, Thomas Ernest
CODY, Walt
  Norwood, Victor George
  Charles
COE, Douglas
  Epstein, Beryl *and*
  Epstein, Samuel
COE, Tucker
  Westlake, Donald Edwin
COFFEY, Brian
  Koontz, Dean R
COFFIN, Geoffrey
  Mason, F Van Wyck
COFFIN, Peter
  Latimer, Jonathan
COIGNARD, John
  Barach, Alvan Leroy
COLAM, Lance
  Cooper, Gordon
COLBERE, Hope
  Coolbear, Marian H
COLBY, Alice
  Ross, William Edward
  Daniel
COLBY, Lydia
  Ross, William Edward
  Daniel
COLE, Ann Kilborn
  Callahan, Claire
COLE, Carol Cassidy
  Manchee, Carol M Cassidy
COLE, Davis
  Elting, Mary

COLE, Douglas
　Cole, G(eorge) D(ouglas)
　　H(oward)
COLE, Jackson
　Scott, Leslie
COLE, Richard
　Barrett, Geoffrey John
COLE, Stephen
　Webbe, Gale Dudley
COLEMAN, Lonnie
　Coleman, William Lawrence
COLES, Manning
　Manning, Adelaide Frances
　　Oke *and*
　　Coles, Cyril Henry
COLLANS, Dev
　Winchell, Prentice
COLLIER, Douglas
　Fellowes-Gordon, Ian
COLLIER, Joy
　Millar, Minna
COLLIN, Rodney
　Collin Smith, Rodney
COLLINGS, Jillie
　Collings, I J
COLLINGSWOOD, Frederick
　Lakritz, Esther
COLLINS, D
　Bulleid, H A V
COLLINS, Geoffrey
　Jefferies, Greg
COLLINS, Hunt
　Lombino, Salvatore A
COLLINS, Joan
　Collins, Mildred
COLLINS, Michael
　Lynds, Dennis

COLLINS, Tom
　Furphy, Joseph
COLLINSON, Peter
　Hammett, Dashiell
COLLYER, Doric
　Fellows, Dorothy Alice
COLMAN, George
　Glassco, John
COLSON, Thora
　Orton, Thora
COLSON-HAIG, S
　Glassco, John
COLT, Clem
　Nye, Nelson Coral
COLT, Russ
　Kerr, D
COLTMAN, Will
　Bingley, David Ernest
COLTON, A J
　Hook, Alfred Samuel
COLTON, Mel
　Braham, Hal
COLUMBINE
　Ferguson, Rachel
COLVER, Anne
　Harris, Polly Anne Colver
COMFORT, Montgomery
　Campbell, Ramsay
COMPERE, Mickie
　Davidson, Margaret
COMPTON, Frances Snow
　Adams, Henry
COMPTON, Guy
　Compton, D G
COMRADE, Robert W
　Brooks, Edwy Searles

181

COMYNS, Barbara
  Carr, Barbara Irene Veronica
  Comyns
CONARAIN, Nina
  Conarain, Alice Nina
CONDON, Patricia
  Gooden, P E
CONDRAY, Bruno
  Humphrys, Leslie George
CONGREVE, R H
  Orage, Alfred James
CONISTON, Ed
  Bingley, David Ernest
CONNELL, John
  Robertson, James Robin
CONNELL, Norreys
  O'Riordan, Conal O'Connell
CONNEY, Barbara
  Porter, Barbara Conney
CONNINGTON, J J
  Stewart, Alfred Walter
CONNOLLY, Paul
  Wicker, Tom
CONNOR, Patrick Reardon
  Conner, Reardon
CONNOR, Ralph
  Gordon, *Reverend* Charles
  William
CONQUEST, Owen
  Hamilton, Charles Harold
  St John
CONRAD, Brenda
  Brown, Zenith
CONRAD, Clive
  King, Frank
CONRAD, Jack
  Conrad, Isaac

CONRAD, Jessie
  Korzeniowski, Jessie
CONRAD, Joseph
  Korzeniowski, Teodor Józef
  Konrad
CONRAD, Kenneth
  Lottich, Kenneth
CONRAD, Paul
  King, Albert
CONROY, Jim
  Chadwick, Joseph
CONROY, Robert
  Goldston, Robert
CONSTANT READER
  Parker, Dorothy
CONTE, Charles
  Mackinnon, Charles Roy
CONWAY, Celine
  Blair, Kathryn
CONWAY, Hugh
  Fargus, Frederick John
CONWAY, Keith
  Hetherington, Keith James
CONWAY, Laura
  Ansle, Dorothy Phoebe
CONWAY, Olive
  Walton, John *and*
  Brighouse, Harold
CONWAY, Peter
  Gautier-Smith, Peter Claudius
CONWAY, Peter
  Milkomane, George Alexis
  Milkomanovich
CONWAY, Troy
  Avallone, Michael Angelo Jr
COO-EE
  Walker, W Sylvester

COOK, John Estes
  Baum, Lyman Frank
COOK, Vera
  Ryder, Vera
COOK, Will
  Cook, William Everett
COOKE, M E
  Creasey, John
COOKE, Margaret
  Creasey, John
COOKRIDGE, E H
  Spiro, Edward H
COOKRIDGE, John Michael
  Holroyd, Ethel Mary
COOLIDGE, Susan
  Woolsey, Sarah Chauncey
COOMBS, Murdo
  Davis, Frederick Clyde
COOPER, Charles
  Lock, Arnold Charles Cooper
COOPER, Craig
  King, Albert
COOPER, Henry St John
  Creasey, John
COOPER, Jeff
  Cooper, John Dean
COOPER, Jefferson
  Fox, Gardner F
COOPER, William
  Hoff, Harry Summerfield
COPPLESTONE, Bennet
  Kitchin, F H
COQUINA
  Shields, George Oliver
CORAM, Christopher
  Walker, Peter Norman
CORBY, Dan
  Catherall, Arthur

CORD, Barry
  Germano, Peter
CORDELL, Alexander
  Graber, George Alexander
CORELLI, Marie
  Mackay, Minnie
CORENANDA, A L A
  Numano, Allen
CORIOLANUS
  McMillan, James
CORLETT, Joyce I
  Kirkwood, Joyce
CORNERS, George F
  Viereck, George Sylvester
CORNING, Kyle
  Gardner, Erle Stanley
CORNO DI BASSETTO
  Shaw, George Bernard
CORNWALL, Nellie
  Sloggett, Nellie
CORONET
  James, Charles
CORREY, Lee
  Stine, George Harry
CORRIGAN, Mark
  Lee, Norman
CORSON, Geoffrey
  Sholl, Anna McClure
CORTEEN, Craig
  Norwood, Victor George
  Charles
CORTEEN, Wes
  Norwood, Victor George
  Charles
CORVO, *Baron*
  Rolfe, Frederick
CORWIN, Cecil
  Kornbluth, Cyril M

183

CORY, Caroline
  Freeman, Kathleen
CORY, Desmond
  McCarthy, Shaun
COSMOI, M M
  Mitrinovič, Dmitrí
COST, March
  Morrison, Margaret Mackie
COSTLER, *Dr* A
  Koestler, Arthur
COSTS
  Booth, John Bennion
COTTERELL, Brian
  Dingle, Aylward Edward
COULSDON, John
  Hincks, Cyril Malcolm
COURAGE, John
  Goyne, Richard
COURT, Sharon
  Rowland, Donald Sydney
COURTLAND, Roberta
  Dern, Erolie Pearl
COURTNEY, Christine
  Westmarland, Ethel Louisa
COURTNEY, John
  Cournos, John
COUSIN VIRGINIA
  Johnson, Virginia Wales
COVENANTER
  Zilliacus, Konni
COVENTRY, John
  Palmer, John Williamson
COVERACK, Gilbert
  Warren, John Russell
COWAN, Alan
  Gilchrist, Alan
COWEN, Frances
  Minto, Frances

COWLIN, Dorothy
  Whalley, Dorothy
COWPER, Richard
  Murry, Colin Middleton
COX, Edith
  Goaman, Muriel
COX, Jack
  Cox, John
COX, Lewis
  Cox, Euphrasia Emeline
COXE, Kathleen Buddington
  Long, Amelia R *and*
  McHugh, Edna
COX-JOHNSON, Ann
  Saunders, Ann Loreille
COYSH, Edward
  Stuart-Jervis, Charles Edward
CRAD, Joseph
  Ansell, Edward Clarence
  Trelawney
CRADDOCK, Charles Egbert
  Murfee, Mary Noailles
CRADOCK, Fanny
  Cradock, Phyllis Nan Sortain
CRAIG, A A
  Anderson, Poul
CRAIG, Alison
  Nicholson, Joan
CRAIG, David
  Tucker, James
CRAIG, Denys
  Stoll, Dennis Gray
CRAIG, Georgia
  Gaddis, Peggy
CRAIG, Jennifer
  Brambleby, Ailsa
CRAIG, Jonathan
  Smith, Frank E

CRAIG, John Eland
  Chipperfield, Joseph E
CRAIG, Lee
  Sands, Leo G
CRAIG, Mary
  Shura, Mary Francis
CRAIG, Peter
  MacClure, Victor
CRAIG, Vera
  Rowland, Donald Sydney
CRAIGIE, David
  Craigie, Dorothy M
CRAILE, Wesley
  Rowland, Donald Sydney
CRANE, Henry
  Douglass, Percival Ian
CRANE, Robert
  Robertson, Frank Chester
CRANNACH, Henry
  Meeske, Marilyn
CRANSTON, Edward
  Fairchild, William
CRAVEN HILL
  Parsons, Charles P
CRAWFORD, Anthony
  Hugill, John Anthony Crawford
CRAWFORD, Robert
  Rae, Hugh Cranford
CRECY, Jeanne
  Creasey, Jeanne
CREEDI, Joel
  King, Albert
CREEK, Nathan
  Sheppard, John Hamilton
  George
CRESCENDO
  Kalisch, A

CRESSY, Edward
  Creasey, Clarence Hamilton
CRESTON, Dormer
  Baynes, Dorothy Julia
CREYTON, Paul
  Trowbridge, John Townsend
CRIBLECOBLIS, Otis
  Dukenfield, William Claude
CRICHTON, John
  Guthrie, Norman Gregor
CRICKETER
  Cardus, *Sir* Neville
CRISPIE
  Crisp, S E
CRISPIN, Edmund
  Montgomery, Robert Bruce
CRISPIN, Suzy
  Cartwright, Justin
CRISTY, R J
  De Cristoforo, R J
CRITCHIE, Estil
  Burks, Arthur J
CRITIC
  Martin, Kingsley
CROFT, Sutton
  Lunn, *Sir* Arnold
CROFT, Taylor
  Croft-Cooke, Rupert
CROMARTY, Deas
  Watson, R A
CROMIE, Stanley
  Simmons, J S A
CROMPTON, John
  Lamburn, John Battersby
  Crompton
CROMPTON, Richmal
  Lamburn, Richmal Crompton

185

CROMWELL, Elsie
 Sheridan, Elsie Lee
CRONHEIM, F G
 Godfrey, Frederick M
CRONIN, Michael
 Cronin, Brendan Leo
CROSBIE, Elizabeth
 Ewer, Monica
CROSBIE, Provan
 Crosbie, Hugh Provan
CROSBY, Lee
 Torrey, Ware
CROSS, Amanda
 Heilbrun, Carolyn
CROSS, Brenda
 Colloms, Brenda
CROSS, James
 Parry, Hugh J
CROSS, Mark
 Pechey, Archibald Thomas
CROSS, Nancy
 Baker, Anne
CROSS, T T
 Da Cruz, Daniel
CROSSE, Elaine
 Trent, Ann
CROSSE, Victoria
 Griffin, Vivian Cory
CROWE, John
 Lynds, Dennis
CROWLEY, Aleister
 Crowley, Edward Alexander
CRUMPET, Peter
 Buckley, Fergus Reid
CRUNDEN, Reginald
 Cleaver, Hylton Reginald
CULEX
 Stanier, Maida

CULLINGFORD, Guy
 Taylor, Constance Lindsay
CULLNER, Lenard
 Mazure, Alfred Leonardus
CULOTTA, Nino
 O'Grady, John P
CULPEPER, Martin
 Pullen, George
CULVER, Kathryn
 Dresser, Davis
CUMBERLAND, Gerald
 Kenyon, Fred
CUMBERLAND, Roy
 Mégroz, R L
CUNNINGHAM, E V
 Fast, Howard
CUNNINGHAM, Mary
 Pierce, Mary Cunningham
CUNNINGHAM, Ray
 Arthur, Frances Browne
CURLING, Audrey
 Clark, Marie Catherine Audrey
CURNOW, Frank
 Atkinson, Frank
CURRIER, Jay L
 Henderson, James Leal
CURRY, Avon
 Bowden, Jean
CURTAYNE, Alice
 Rynne, Alice
CURTIN, Philip
 Lowndes, Marie Adelaide
  Belloc
CURTIS, Peter
 Lofts, Norah
CURTIS, Spencer
 Nuttall, Anthony

CURTIS, Tom
  Jacobs, Thomas Curtis Hicks
CURZON, Sam
  Krasney, Samuel A
CURZON, Virginia
  Hawton, Hector
CUSTER, Clint
  Paine, Lauran Bosworth
CLYCOPS
  Leonard, John
CYMRY BACH
  Wood, Lilian Catherine
CYNICUS
  Anderson, Martin

§ §

*Why 'WM'? No-one knows. But
those were the initials Richard
Jennings chose to write under
and used for forty years.
Perhaps he was paying respects
to William Morris.
—Hugh Cudlipp. Publish and
be damned*

§ §

D'A P
  Power, *Sir* D'Arcy
D M S
  Stuart, Dorothy Margaret
DAEDALUS
  Cordes, Theodor K
DAGONET
  Sims, George Robert
DAGONET, Edward
  Williamson, Thames Ross

DAIMLER, Harriet
  Owens, Iris
DAINTON, Courtney
  Dainton, William
DALE, Edwin
  Home-Gall, Edward Reginald
DALE, Esther
  May, Elaine
DALE, Frances
  Cradock, Phyllis Nan Sortain
DALE, Jack
  Holliday, Joseph
DALE, Maxine
  Covert, Alice Lent
DALE, Norman
  Denny, Norman George
DALE, Robin
  Hadfield, Alan
DALEY, Bill
  Appleman, John Alan
DALHEATH
  Magrill, David S
DALL, Ian
  Higgins, Charles
DALLAS, John
  Duncan, William Murdoch
DALLAS, Steve
  King, Albert
D'ALLENGER, Hugh
  Kershaw, John H D
DALRY
  Wilson, Arthur
DALTON, Clive
  Clark, Frederick Stephen
DALTON, Priscilla
  Avallone, Michael Angelo Jr
DALY, Hamlin
  Price, Edgar Hoffman

187

D'AMBROSIO, Raymond
  Brosia, D M
DAMIANO, Laila
  Rosenkrantz, Linda
DAN BANA
  White, Stanhope
DANA, Amber
  Paine, Lauran Bosworth
DANA, Richard
  Paine, Lauran Bosworth
DANA, Rose
  Ross, William Edward Daniel
DANBY, Frank
  Frankau, Julia Davis
DANCER, J B
  Harvey, John
DANE, Clemence
  Ashton, Winifred
DANE, Eva
  Dawes, Edna
DANE, Joel Y
  Delany, Joseph Francis
DANE, Mark
  Avallone, Michael Angelo Jr
DANE, Mary
  Morland, Nigel
DANFORTH, Paul M
  Allen, John E
DANGERFIELD, Clint
  Norwood, Victor George
    Charles
DANGERFIELD, Harlan
  Padgett, Ron
DANGLE
  Thompson, A M
DANIEL, S
  Zalberg, Daniel

DANIELL, David Scott
  Daniell, Albert Scott
DANIELS, Jan
  Ross, William Edward Daniel
DANIELS, Jane
  Ross, William Edward Daniel
DANIELS, John S
  Overholser, Wayne D
DANNING, Melrod
  Gluck, Sinclair
DANSDORF, Chrysilla von
  Sandford, Christopher
DANVERS, Jack
  Casseleyr, Camille
DANVERS, Peter
  Henderson, James Maddock
DARBY, Catherine
  Black, Maureen
DARBY, Emma
  Stubbs, Jean
DARBY, J N
  Govan, Mary Christine
DARBYSHIRE, Shirley
  Meynell, Shirley Ruth
DARDI
  Singh, Gopal
DARE, Alan
  Goodchild, George
DARE, Michael
  Wordingham, James A
DARE, Simon
  Huxtable, Marjorie
D'ARFEY, William
  Plomer, William
DARLING, V H
  Dryhurst, Michael John
DARLINGTON, Con
  Best, Carol Anne

DATALLER, Roger
  Eaglestone, Arthur Archibald

DAVEY, Jocelyn
  Raphael, Chaim

DAVID, Jay
  Adler, Bill

DAVIDSON, Mickie
  Davidson, Margaret

DAVIES, Louise
  Golding, Louise

DAVIES, Lucian
  Beeston, L J

DAVIGNON, Grace
  Glassco, John

DAVIOT, Gordon
  Mackintosh, Elizabeth

DAVIS, Audrey
  Paine, Lauran Bosworth

DAVIS, Don
  Dresser, Davis

DAVIS, Foxcroft
  Seawell, Molly Elliot

DAVIS, Gordon
  Hunt, E Howard

DAVIS, Julia
  Marsh, John

DAVIS, Rosemary L
  Davis, Lily May *and*
  Davis, Rosemary

DAVIS, Stratford
  Bolton, Miriam

DAVISON, Lawrence H
  Lawrence, D H

DAWLISH, Peter
  Kerr, James Lennox

DAWSON, Jane
  Critchlow, Dorothy

DAWSON, Michael
  Boyle, John Howard Jackson

DAWSON, Oliver
  Coxall, Jack Arthur

DAWSON, Peter
  Faust, Frederick

DAWSON, Peter
  Glidden, Jonathan H

DAX, Anthony
  Hunter, Alfred John

DAY, Adrian
  Harvey, Peter Noel

DAY, Harvey
  Cleary, C V H

DAY, Irene
  Orme, Eve

DAY, Lionel
  Black, Ladbroke Lionel Day

DAYBREAK
  Gray, Clement

DAYLE, Malcolm
  Hincks, Cyril Malcolm

DE BEKKER, Jay
  Winchell, Prentice

DE CASTRO, Lyne
  Lyne, Charles

DE COSQUEVILLE, Pierre
  Stacey, P M de Cosqueville

DE CULWEN, Dorothea
  Hines, Dorothea

DE FACCI, Liane
  De Bellet, Liane

DE GRAEFF, Allen
  Blaustein, Albert P

DE HART, Robert
  Hanzelon, Robert M

DE LA GLANNEGE, Roger-Maxe
  Legman, George Alexander

189

DE LA TORRE, Lillian
McCue, Lillian Bueno
DE LACY, Louise
Hickey, Madeyln E
DE LAS LUNAS, Carmencita
Trocchi, Alexander
DE LAUBE
Cardena, Clement
DE LIMA, Sigrid
Greene, Sigrid
DE MORNY, Peter
Wynne-Tyson, Esme
DE PRE, Jean-Anne
Avallone, Michael Angelo Jr
DE SALIGNAC, Charles
Hasson, James
DE VERE, Jane
Watson, Julia
DE WITT, James
Lewis, Mildred
DE WOHL, Louis
Wohl, Ludwig von
DEACON, Richard
McCormick, Donald
DEAN, Dudley
McGaughy, Dudley Dean
DEAN, Gregory
Posner, Jacob D
DEAN, Lyn
Garret, Winifred Selina
DEAN, Spencer
Winchell, Prentice
DEANE, Norman
Creasey, John
DEBORAH, Leonard
Abbott, Harold Daniel

DEBRETT, Hal
Dresser, Davis *and*
Rollins, Kathleen
DECOLTA, Ramon
Whitfield, Raoul
DEE, John
Tullett, Denis John
DEE, R K
Wood, John James O'Hara
DEHAN, Richard
Graves, Clotilda Inez Mary
DEKKER, Carl
Laffin, John
DELAFIELD, E M
De la Pasture, Edmée E M
DELANEY, Denis
Green, Peter
DELANEY, Franey
O'Hara, John
DELANO, Al
Livingston, A D
DELL, Belinda
Bowden, Jean
DELMONICO, Andrea
Morrison, Eula A
DELTA
Hazlewood, Rex
DELVING, Michael
Williams, Jay
DEMAINE, C F
Trumbo, Dalton
DEMAREST, Anne
Bond, Florence D F
DEMAREST, Doug
Barker, Will
DEMARIS, Ovid
Desmarais, Ovide E

DEMBRY, R Emmet
  Murfree, Mary Noailles
DEMIJOHN, Thom
  Disch, Thomas M *and*
  Sladek, John Thomas
DEMPSEY, Hank
  Harrison, Harry
DEMPSTER, Guy
  Heming, Dempster E
DENBIE, Roger
  Brodie, Julian Paul *and*
  Green, Alan Baer
DENDER, Jay
  Deindorfer, Robert G
DENHAM, Peter
  Jones, P D
DENMARK, Harrison
  Zelazny, Roger
DENNING, Patricia
  Willis, Corinne
DENNIS, Eve
  Wornum, Miriam
DENNIS, Patrick
  Tanner, Edward Everett
DENNISON, Dorothy
  Golden, Dorothy
DENOVAN, Saunders
  Harvey, William
DENVER, Boone
  Rennie, James Alan
DENVER, Drake C
  Nye, Nelson Coral
DENVER, Lee
  Gribble, Leonard Reginald
DERBY, Mark
  Wilcox, Harry
DERMOTT, Stephen
  Bradbury, Parnell

DERN, Peggy
  Dern, Erolie Pearl
DERVENTIO
  Hughes, Walter Dudley
DESANA, Dorothy
  Trent, Ann
DESOR, René
  Wilkinson, A G
DESPARD, Leslie
  Howitt, John Leslie Despard
DESTRY, Vince
  Norwood, Victor George
  Charles
DEVEREUX, Roy
  Pember-Devereux, Margaret
  R R
DEVINE, D M
  Devine, David McDonald
DEVINE, Dominic
  Devine, David McDonald
DEVON, Sara
  Walker, Emily Kathleen
DEWDNEY, Peter
  Brock, Alan St Hill
DEWES, Simon
  Muriel, John
DEXTER, John
  Coleman, John
DEXTER, Martin
  Faust, Frederick
DEXTER, Ross
  Reynolds, John E
DEXTER, William
  Pritchard, William Thomas
DIAS, B H
  Pound, Ezra
DICANT, V L
  Hewetson, Sara

191

DICK, Alexandra
  Dick-Erikson, Cicely Sibyl
  Alexandra
DICK, R A
  Leslie, Josephine A C
DICK, T
  Osler, Eric Richard
DICKENS, Irene
  Copper, Dorothy
DICKINSON, Frankie
  Brownlee, Frances
DICKINSON, Margaret
  Muggeson, Margaret
DICKSON, Carr
  Carr, John Dickson
DICKSON, Carter
  Carr, John Dickson
DICKSON, Frank C
  Danson, Frank Corse
DICKSON, Helen
  Reynolds, Helen Mary
  Greenwood Dickson
DIETRICH, Robert
  Hunt, E Howard
DIGGES, Jeremiah
  Berger, Josef
DILL, W S
  Macbeth, Madge Hamilton
DILL, Walter
  Thomas, Walter Dill Jr
DIMSDALE, C D
  Mégroz, R L
DINESEN, Isak
  Blixen-Finecke, Karen
  Christence *Baroness*
DINGWALL, Peter
  Forsythe, Robin

DIPLOMAT
  Carter, John Franklin
DIPLOMATICUS
  Zilliacus, Konni
DISCIPLE OF THE MASTER,
A
  Ouseley, G J R
DITTON, James
  Clark, Douglas
DIVINE, David
  Divine, Arthur Durham
D'IVRY, Ursula
  Russell, Ursula d'Ivry
DIX, Dorothy
  Gilmer, Elizabeth Meriwether
DIXON, Lesley
  Vernon, Kathleen Rose
DIXON, Rex
  Martin, Reginald Alec
DIXON, Rosie
  Wood, Christopher
DIXON, Ruth
  Barrows, Marjorie
DOAN, Reece
  King, Albert
DOCHERTY, James L
  Raymond, Rene
DR A
  Asimov, Isaac
DOCTOR FUTUER
  Lyburn, *Dr* Eric Frederic
  St John
DR SEUSS
  Geisel, Theodor Seuss
DR SOFT
  Sward, Robert S
DODGE, Langdon
  Wolfson, Victor

DODGE, Steve
  Becker, Stephen David
DOE, John
  Thayer, Tiffany Ellsworth
DOGBERRY
  Phillips, Hubert
DOGBOLT, Barnaby
  Silvette, Herbert
DOLBERG, Alexander
  Burg, David
DOLLEY, Marcus J
  Watney, Bernard
DOMINI, Rey
  Lorde, Andre Geraldin
DOMINIC, *Sister* Mary
  Parker, Marion
DOMINIC, R B
  Latis, Mary J *and*
    Hennissart, Martha
DOMPO, Kwesi
  Parkes, Frank
DONALD, Vivian
  Mackinnon, Charles Roy
DONALDS, Gordon
  Shirreffs, Gordon D
DONAVAN, John
  Morland, Nigel
DONNE, Jack
  Bloom, Jack Don
DONNE, Maxim
  Duke, Madelaine
DONOVAN, Dick
  Muddock, Joyce Emerson
DOOLEY, Martin
  Dunne, Finley Peter
DORFY
  Samuelson-Sandvid, Dorothy

DORMAN, Luke
  Bingley, David Ernest
DORSET, Ruth
  Ross, William Edward Daniel
DOUBLEDAY, Roman
  Long, Lily Augusta
DOUGLAS, Albert
  Armstrong, Douglas
DOUGLAS, Colin
  Currie, Colin Thomas
DOUGLAS, D
  Wilkes-Hunter, Richard
DOUGLAS, Ellen
  Williamson, Ellen Douglas
DOUGLAS, George
  Brown, George Douglas
DOUGLAS, George
  Fisher, Douglas George
DOUGLAS, Malcolm
  Sanderson, Douglas
DOUGLAS, Nathan
  Young, Nedrick
DOUGLAS, Noel
  Chetham-Strode, Warren
DOUGLAS, O
  Buchan, Anna
DOUGLAS, Shane
  Wilkes-Hunter, Richard
DOUGLAS, Theo
  Everett, *Mrs* H D
DOWER, Penn
  Jacobs, Thomas Curtis
  Hicks
DOWLEY, D M
  Marrison, Leslie William
DOWNES, Quentin
  Harrison, Michael

193

DOWNING, Century
  Palmer, Paul
DOWNMAN, Francis
  Oldmeadow, Ernest James
DOYLE, Emmett
  Trumbo, Dalton
DOYLE, John
  Graves, Robert
DOYLE, Lynn
  Montgomery, Leslie Alexander
DRACO, F
  David Julia
DRAKE, Hamilton
  Hoffenberg, Mason
DRAKE, Joan
  Davies, Joan Howard
DRAKE, Winifred
  Bryant, Denny
DRAX, Peter
  Addis, E E
DREWERY, Mary
  Smith, Mary
DREXLER, J F
  Paine, Lauran Bosworth
DRINAN, Adam
  Macleod, Joseph Todd Gordon
DRISCOLL, Eli
  King, Albert
DRONGO, Luke
  Riddleston, Charles H
DRUG, Victor
  Moretti, Ugo
DRUMMOND, Anthony
  Hunter, Alfred John
DRUMMOND, Ivor
  Longrigg, Roger Erskine
DRUMMOND, John
  Chance, John Newton

DRUMMOND, Violet Hilda
  Swetenham, Violet Hilda
DRUMMOND, Walter
  Silverberg, Robert
DRURY, C M
  Abrahall, Clare Hoskyns
DRURY, Clare
  Abrahall, Clare Hoskyns
DRYDEN, John
  Rowland, Donald Sydney
DRYDEN, Keith
  Landells, Richard
DU BOIS, M
  Kent, Arthur
DU VAUL, Virginia
  Coffman, Virginia
DUBH, Scian
  McCarroll, James
DUCHESNE, Antoinette
  Paine, Lauran Bosworth
DUDLEY, Frank
  Greene, Ward
DUDLEY, Nancy
  Cole, Lois Dwight
DUELL, Eileen-Marie
  Petrie, Rhona
DUFFER, Allan
  May, John
DUFFIELD, Anne
  Duffield, Dorothy Dean
DUKE, Margaret
  Dunk, Margaret
DUNCAN, A H
  Cleary, C V H
DUNCAN, Alex
  Duke, Madelaine
DUNCAN, Gregory
  McClintock, Marshall

DUNCAN, Jane
  Cameron, Elizabeth Jane
DUNCAN, Julia K
  Karig, Walter
DUNNE, Desmond
  Lee-Richardson, James
DUNNE, Lyell
  Bundey, Ellen Milne
DUPLEX
  Bradley, Ian *and*
  Hollows, Norman F
DUPONT, Paul
  Frewin, Leslie Ronald
DURACK, Mary
  Miller, Mary
DURHAM, David
  Vickers, Roy
DURHAM, John
  Paine, Lauran Bosworth
DURIE, Lynn
  Christie, Douglas
DURRANT, Theo
  Mystery Writers of America
  Inc; California Chapter
DYKES, Jack
  Owen, Jack
DYLAN, Bob
  Zimmerman, Robert Allen
DYMOKE, Juliet
  De Schanschieff, Juliet
  Dymoke

E H
  Haig, Emily Alice
E H
  Hiscock, Eric
E H A
  Aitken, E H

E M B
  Barton, Emily Mary
E R
  Ross, W W Eustace
E V L
  Lucas, E V
EADY, W P R
  Glassco, John
EAGLE, Solomon
  Squire, *Sir* John Collings
EAGLESFIELD, Francis
  Guirdham, Arthur
EARLE, Olive L
  Daughtrey, Olive Lydia
EARP, Virgil
  Keevill, Henry John
EAST, Michael
  West, Morris
EAST, Roger
  Burford, Roger d'Este
EASTAWAY, Edward
  Thomas, Edward
EASTERTIDE
  Blagbrough, Harriet
EASTLUND, Madelyn
  Hickey, Madelyn E
EBEL, Suzanne
  Goodwin, Suzanne
EDDY, Albert
  Glassco, John
EDEN, Bob
  Burkhardt, Eve *and*
  Burkhardt, Robert
  Ferdinand
EDEN, Matthew
  Newnham, Don
EDGAR, Icarus Walter
  Bishop, Stanley

EDGAR, Josephine
  Mussi, Mary
EDMONDS, Charles
  Carrington, Charles
EDMONDS, Paul
  Kuttner, Henry
EDSON, George Alden
  Ernst, Paul F
EDWARD, Stephen
  Palestrant, Simon
EDWARDS, Charman
  Edwards, Frederick Anthony
EDWARDS, Ellen
  Horkan, Nelle Irwin
EDWARDS, F E
  Nolan, William F
EDWARDS, James G
  Macqueen, James William
EDWARDS, June
  Bhatia, June
EDWARDS, Laurence
  Edwards, Florence
EDWARDS, Leonard
  Wild, Reginald
EDWARDS, Olwen
  Owen, Dilys
EDWARDS, Samuel
  Gerson, Noel Bertram
EDWINSON, Edmund
  Slocum, Edward Mark
EFF, B
  Carney, Jack
EGAN, Lesley
  Linington, Elizabeth
EGBERT, H M
  Emanuel, Victor Rousseau
EGERTON, Denise
  Duggan, Denise Valerie

EGERTON, George
  Bright, Mary C
EGLINTON, John
  Magee, William Kirkpatrick
EGOMET
  Fowler, Henry Watson
EGREMONT, Michael
  Harrison, Michael
EIRENE
  Searle, M E
ELAND, Charles
  Rimanoczy, A
ELDERSHAW, M Barnard
  Barnard, Marjorie Faith *and*
  Eldershaw, Flora Sydney
ELEIGH, Sebastian
  Greene, *Sir* Hugh
ELGIN, Mary
  Stewart, Dorothy Mary
ELIOT, Alice C
  Jewett, Sarah Orne
ELIOT, Anne
  Cole, Lois Dwight
ELIOTT, E C
  Martin, Reginald Alec
ELISABETH
  Quigley, Elizabeth Pauline
ELIZABETH
  Rose, Elizabeth Jane
ELIZABETH
  Russell, Elizabeth Mary
  Countess
ELIZABETH, Anne
  Fleur, Anne Elizabeth
ELIZABETH VON S
  Freeman, Gillian
ELLIOTT, Charles
  Ewart-Biggs, Christopher

ELLIOTT, Ellen
  Westmarland, Ethel Louisa
ELLISON, Marjorie
  Norton, Marjorie
ELLSWORTH, Elmer
  Thayer, Tiffany Ellsworth
ELLSWORTH, Paul
  Trien, Paul Ellsworth
ELPHINSTONE, Francis
  Powell-Smith, Vincent
ELRON
  Hubbard, Lafayette Ronald
ELSEY, J J
  Herron, Elsie Ellerington
ELSNA, Hebe
  Ansle, Dorothy Phoebe
ELTON, H E
  Hayes, Herbert Edward Elton
ELTON, John
  Marsh, John
ELWART, Joan Potter
  Elwart, Joan Frances
ELY, David
  Lilienthal, David Jr
ELYSIAN, Anne
  Westmoreland, Vera Gertrude
EMMETT STREET
  Behan, Brendan
EMSLEY, Clare
  Plummer, Clare
ENGELHARDT, Frederick
  Hubbard, Lafayette Ronald
ENGLAND, Edith M
  Anders, Edith Mary
ENGLAND, Jane
  Jervis, Vera Murdock Stuart
ENGLAND, Norman
  Webb, Godfrey E C

ENGLISH, Brenda H
  Riddolls, Brenda H
ENQUIRING LAYMAN
  Grierson, Walter
ENRIGHT, Elizabeth
  Gillham, Elizabeth Wright
  Enright
EPERNAY, Mark
  Galbraith, J K
EPHESIAN
  Bechoffer Roberts, C E
ERIC
  Montefiore, Caroline L
ERIC, Kenneth
  Henley, Art
ERICSON, Sybil
  Dick-Erikson, Cicely Sybil
  Alexandra
ERICSON, Walter
  Fast, Howard
ERIKSON, Charlotte
  Dick-Erikson, Cicely Sibyl
  Alexandra
ERIMUS
  Fall, William E
ERMINE, Will
  Drago, Harry Sinclair

§ §

*'My own Ernest! I felt from the
start that you could have no other
name.' —Oscar Wilde. The
Importance of being Ernest*

§ §

ERNEST, Paul
  Focke, E P W

ERSKINE, Douglas
  Buchan, John Stuart
ERSKINE, John T
  Tuck, John Erskine
ERSKINE, Margaret
  Williams, Margaret Wetherby
ERSKINE, Rosalind
  Longrigg, Roger Erskine
ERSKINE-GRAY
  Cordes, Theodor K
ERVIN, Patrick
  Howard, Robert E
ESDAILE, David
  Walker, David Esdaile
ESMOND, Harriet
  Burk, John Frederick
ESSE, James
  Stephens, James
ESSEX, Frank
  Simmonds, Michael Charles
ESSEX, Jon
  Watford, Joel
ESSEX, Mary
  Bloom, Ursula
ESSEX, Richard
  Starr, Richard
ESTERBROOK, Tom
  Hubbard, Lafayette Ronald
ESTEVEN, John
  Shellabarger, Samuel
ESTORIL, Jean
  Allan, Mabel Esther
ETIENNE
  King-Hall, Stephen
ETON, Robert
  Meynell, Laurence Walter
EUGENE
  Huyghue, Douglas S
198

EUPHAN
  Todd, Barbara Euphan
EUSTACE, Robert
  Barton, Eustace Robert
EVAN, Evin
  Faust, Frederick
EVAN, Paul
  Lehman, Paul Evan
EVANS, Alan
  Stoker, Alan
EVANS, Cherry
  Drummond, Cherry
EVANS, Evan
  Faust, Frederick
EVANS, Harris
  Evans, George *and*
  Evans, Kay
EVANS, John
  Browne, Howard
EVANS, Jonathan
  Freemantle, Brian
EVANS, Margiad
  Williams, Peggy Eileen
  Arabella
EVANS, Morgan
  Davies, Leslie Purnell
EVELETH, Stanford
  Dickson, Emma Wells
EVERARD, Henry
  Smith, H Everard
EVERETT, Wade
  Cook, William Everett
EVERMAY, March
  Eiker, Mathilde
EVERTON, Francis
  Stokes, Francis William
EVOE
  Knox, E V

EX-JOURNALIST
 Lanigan, Richard
EX-PRIVATE X
 Burrage, Alfred M
EYE WITNESS
 Archibald, Edith Jessie
EYRE, Annette
 Worboys, Anne Eyre

F P A
 Adams, Franklin Pierce
FABIAN, Ruth
 Quigley, Aileen
FABIAN, Warner
 Adams, Samuel Hopkins
FABRIZIUS, Peter
 Fabry, Joseph B
FAGYAS, Maria
 Bush-Fekete, Marie Ilona
FAID, Mary
 Dunn, Mary
FAIR, A A
 Gardner, Erle Stanley
FAIRBURN, Ann
 Tait, Dorothy
FAIRLESS, Michael
 Barber, Margaret Fairless
FAIRWAY, Sidney
 Daukes, Sidney Herbert
FALK, Elsa
 Escherlich, Elsa Antonie
FALL, Thomas
 Snow, Donald Clifford
FALLON, George
 Bingley, David Ernest
FALLON, Martin
 Patterson, Henry

FAN-FAN
 Blackburn, Victoria Grace
FANE, Bron
 Fanthorpe, Robert Lionel
FANE, Violet
 Currie, *Lady*
FANSHAWE, Caroline
 Cust, Barbara Kate
FARELY, Alison
 Poland, Dorothy E H
FAREWELL, Nina
 Klein, Grace *and*
  Cooper, Mae Klein
FARGO, Doone
 Norwood, Victor George
  Charles
FARLEY, Ralph Milne
 Hoar, Roger Sherman
FARMER, Wendell
 Davis, Lavinia
FARQUHARSON, Martha
 Finley, Martha
FARR, C
 Wilkes-Hunter, Richard
FARR, John
 Webb, Jack
FARRELL, David
 Smith, Frederick E
FARRELL, M J
 Keane, Mary Nesta
FARRER, E Maxwell
 Williams, Edward John
FAULKNER, Mary
 Seuffert, Muriel
FAWCETT, Catherine
 Cookson, Catherine
FAWKES, Guy
 Benchley, Robert

FAY, Dorothy
  Lindholm, Anna Chandler
FEARN, Elena
  Smith, Marjorie Seymour
FEARN, John
  Wannan, John Fearn
FEARN, Roberta
  Hutchinson, Barbara Beatrice
FECAMPS, Elise
  Creasey, John
FECHER, Constance
  Heaven, Constance
FEIKEMA, Feike
  Manfred, Frederick Feikema
FELIX, Pastor
  Lockhart, Arthur John
FELLOWES, Anne
  Mantle, Winifred Langford
FELMERSHAM, Michael
  Leyland, Eric
FEMORA
  Brodey, Jim
FENIX, *Comte de*
  Crowley, Edward Alexander
FENNER, Carol
  Williams, Carol Elizabeth
FENNIMORE, Stephen
  Collins, Dale
FENTON, Freda
  Rowland, Donald Sydney
FENWICK, Elizabeth
  Way, Elizabeth Fenwick
FENWICK, Peter
  Holmes, Peter
FERGUS, Dyjan
  Ferguson, Ida May
FERGUSON, Anthony
  Read, Anthony

FERGUSON, Emily
  Murphy, Emily Gowan
  (Ferguson)
FERGUSON, Helen
  Edmonds, Helen
FERN, Edwin
  Cryer, Neville
FERNWAY, Peggy
  Braun, Wilbur
FERRAND, Georgina
  Castle, Brenda
FERRARS, E X
  Brown, Morna D
FERRARS, Elizabeth
  Brown, Morna D
FERRES, Arthur
  Kevin, John William
FERRIS, James Cody
  Karig, Walter
FERRIS, Tom
  Walker, Peter Norman
FESENMEYER
  Luxmore, Robert
FETHERSTON, Patrick
  Fetherstonhaugh, Patrick
  William Edward
FETTSMAN, Ann
  Hoffman, Anita
FEW, Betty
  Few, Eunice Beatty
FIACC, Padraic
  O'Connor, Patrick Joseph
FICKLING, G G
  Fickling, Forrest E *and*
  Fickling, Gloria
FIDLER, Kathleen
  Goldie, Kathleen Annie

FIELD, Charles
Rowland, Donald Sydney
FIELD, Christine
Laurence, Frances Elsie
FIELD, Frank Chester
Robertson, Frank Chester
FIELD, Hill
Fielding, Molly Hill
FIELD, Joanna
Milner, Marion
FIELD, Michael
Bradley, Katherine H *and*
Cooper, Edith E
FIELD, Robert à
Haig, Emily Alice
FIELDING, A E
Feilding, Dorothy
FIELDING, Ann Mary
Mostyn, Anita Mary
FIELDING, Anthony
Leyland, Eric
FIELDING, Dorothy
Fielding, Archibald
FIELDING, Gabriel
Barnsley, Alan G
FIELDING, Howard
Hooke, Charles W
FIELDING, Hubert
Schonfield, Hugh Joseph
FIELDING, Xan
Fielding, Alexander
FIELDS, W C
Dukenfield, William Claude
FILEMAN, Nan
Zimmer, Maude Files
FINCH, John
Cooper, John

FINCH, Matthew
Fink, Merton
FINCH, Merton
Fink, Merton
FINCHER, Beth
Trumbo, Dalton
FINDLATER, Richard
Bain, Kenneth Bruce
Findlater
FINDLEY, Ferguson
Frey, Charles Weiser
FINKELL, Max
Catto, Maxwell Jeffrey
FINLAY, Fiona
Stuart, Vivian Alex
FINLEY, Scott
Clark, Winifred
FINNEGAN, Robert
Ryan, Paul William
FINNEGAN, Ruth
Murray, Ruth Hilary
FINNIGAN, Joan
Mackenzie, Joan
FISHER, Agnes
McEwen, Jessie Evelyn
FISHER, Clay
Allen, Henry
FISHER, Cyrus T
Teilhet, Darwin le Ora
FISHER, Laine
Howard, James Arch
FISHER, Margot
Paine, Lauran Bosworth
FISHER, Steve
Fisher, Stephen Gould
FISKE, Tarleton
Bloch, Robert

201

FITT, Mary
  Freeman, Kathleen
FITZALAN, Roger
  Dudley-Smith, Trevor
FITZGERALD, Barbara
  Newman, Mona A J
FITZGERALD, Errol
  Clarke, *Lady*
FITZGERALD, *Capt* Hugh
  Baum, Lyman Frank
FITZWILLIAM, Michael
  Lyons, John Benignus
5029
  Winkworth, Derek W
FLACCUS
  Levy, Newman
FLAMANK, E
  Harper, Edith
FLANAGAN, Bud
  Winthrop, Bud Robert
FLANNEL, J C
  Fantoni, Barry
FLAVIUS, BROTHER
  Ellison, James
FLECK, Betty
  Paine, Lauran Bosworth
FLEMING, George
  . Fletcher, Constance
FLEMING, Harry
  Bird, William Henry Fleming
FLEMING, Oliver
  MacDonald, Philip *and*
  MacDonald, Ronald
FLEMING, Rhoda
  Fleming, Ronald
FLEMING, Waldo
  Williamson, Thames Ross

FLEMMING, Cardine
  Grieveson, Mildred
FLEMMING, Sarah
  Gilderdale, Michael
FLETCHER, Adam
  Flexner, Stuart
FLETCHER, David
  Barber, Dulan Friar
FLETCHER, George U
  Pratt, Fletcher
FLETCHER, John
  Fletcher, Harry L Verne
FLEXMAN, Theodore
  Trumbo, Dalton
FLIGHT, Francies
  Birch, Jack Ernest Lionel *and*
  Murray, Venetia Pauline
FLYING OFFICER X
  Bates, H E
FLYNT, Josiah
  Willard, Josiah Flynt
FOLEY, Helen
  Fowler, Helen
FOLEY, Rae
  Denniston, Elinore
FOLEY, Scott
  Dareff, Hal
FOLKE, Will
  Bloch, Robert
FONTEYN, Margot
  Hookham, Margaret Evelyn
FORBES, Colin
  Sawkins, Raymond Harold
FORBES, Kathryn
  McLean, Kathryn
FORBES, Stanton
  Forbes, Deloris Stanton

FORD, Barry
  Whitford, Joan
FORD, Elbur
  Hibbert, Eleanor Alice
  Burford
FORD, Ford Madox
  Hueffer, Ford Madox
FORD, Hilary
  Youd, Samuel
FORD, Kirk
  Spence, William Duncan
FORD, Langridge
  Coleman-Cooke, John C
FORD, Leslie
  Brown, Zenith
FORD, Marcia
  Radford, Ruby Lorraine
FORD, Norrey
  Dilcock, Noreen
FORD, Wallace
  King, Albert
FORD, Webster
  Masters, Edgar Lee
FORDE, Nicholas
  Elliott-Cannon, Arthur
  Elliott
FORDEN, James
  Barlow, James
FOREMAN, Lee
  King, Albert
FORREST, Carol
  Tennyson, Margaret
FORREST, *Colonel* Cris
  Stoddard, William Osborn
FORREST, David
  Denholm, David

FORREST, David
  Eliades, David *and*
  Webb, Robert Forrest
FORREST, Julian
  Wagenknecht, Edward
FORREST, Norman
  Morland, Nigel
FORRESTER, Mary
  Humphries, Elsie Mary
FORSTER, Christine
  Forte, Christine
FORSYTH, Jean
  McIlwraith, Jean Newton
FORSYTH, R A
  Johnston, Robert Thomson
FORSYTHE, Robert
  Crichton, Kyle
FORTINA, Martha
  Laffeaty, Christina
FORTUNE, Dion
  Firth, Violet Mary
FOSSE, Alfred
  Jelly, Oliver
FOSTER, Delia
  Walker, Emily Kathleen
FOSTER, Evan
  King, Albert
FOSTER, George
  Haswell, C J D
FOSTER, Richard
  Crossen, Kendell Foster
FOUGASSE
  Bird, Cyril Kenneth
FOWLER, Sydney
  Wright, Sydney Fowler
FOX, Anthony
  Fullerton, Alexander

FOX, David
  Ostrander, Isabel Egerton
FOX, Eleanor
  St John, Wylly Folk
FOX, James M
  Knipscheer, James M W
FOX, John
  Todd, John Murray
FOX, Petronella
  Balogh, Penelope
FOX, Sebastian
  Bullett, Gerald
FRA ELBERTUS
  Hubbard, Elbert
FRANCE, Claire
  Morin, Claire
FRANCE, Evangeline
  France-Hayhurst, Evangeline
FRANCHON, Lisa
  Floren, Lee
FRANCIS, C D E
  Howarth, Patrick John
  Fielding
FRANCIS, Victor
  Hammond, Lawrence
FRANCIS, William
  Urell, William Francis
FRANK, R Jr
  Ross, Frank Xavier
FRANK, Theodore
  Gardiner, Dorothea Frances
FRANKLIN, Charles
  Usher, Frank Hugh
FRANKLIN, E
  Hurt, Edwin Franklin
FRANKLIN, Eugene
  Bandy, Eugene Franklin Jr

FRANKLIN, Jay
  Carter, John Franklin
FRANKLIN, Max
  Deming, Richard
FRASER, Alex
  Brinton, Henry
FRASER, James
  White, Alan
FRASER, Jane
  Pilcher, Rosamunde
FRASER, Jefferson
  Wilding, Philip
FRASER, Peter
  Coles, Phoebe Catherine
FRASER, Peter
  Watt, Alexander Peter
  Fordham
FRATER PERDURABO
  Crowley, Edward Alexander
FRAZER, Martin
  Clarke, Percy A
FRAZER, Renee
  Fleming, Ronald
FRAZER, Robert Caine
  Creasey, John
FRAZER, Shamus
  Frazer, James Ian
  Arbuthnot
FRECKLES
  Dietz, Howard
FREDERICK, John
  Faust, Frederick
FREDERICKS, Arnold
  Kummer, Frederick Arnold
FREDERICKS, Frank
  Franck, Frederick S
FREDERICKS, Vic
  Fell, Frederick Victor

FREDERICS, Jocko
  Frede, Richard
FREMLIN, Celia
  Goller, Celia Margaret
FRENCH, Ashley
  Robins, Denise
FRENCH, Ellen Jean
  English, Jean Ellen
FRENCH, Fergus
  Friedlander, Peter
FRENCH, Paul
  Asimov, Isaac
FRENKEN-MELONEY
  Meloney, William
FRESHFIELD, Mark
  Field, M J
FREUGON, Ruby
  Ashby, Rubie Constance
FREYER, Frederic
  Ballinger, William Sanborn
FRICK, C H
  Irwin, Constance
FRIEND, Oscar Jerome
  Jerome, Owen Fox
FROEST, Frank
  Dilnot, George
FROME, David
  Brown, Zenith
FROST, Frederick
  Faust, Frederick
FROST, Joni
  Paine, Lauran Bosworth
FROY, Herald
  Deghy, Guy *and*
  Waterhouse, Keith
FRY, Jane
  Drew, Jane B

FRY, Pete
  King, James Clifford
FUCHS, Sonia
  Seedo, Sonia
FULLER, Ed
  Fuller, Harold Edgar
FULLER, Lester
  Rolfe, Edwin
FULLER, Roger
  Tracy, Donald Fiske
FULMAN, Al
  Fuller, Harold Edgar
FURBER, Douglas
  Lewin, Michael Sultan
FURY, Nick
  Parry, Michel
FUTUER, *Dr*
  Lyburn, Dr Eric St John
FYVEL, T R
  Feiwel, Raphael Joseph

G B S
  Shaw, George Bernard
G K C
  Chesterton, G K
GABRIELLE
  Parks, Georgina
GADDES, Peter
  Sheldon, Peter
GADDIS, Peggy
  Dern, Erolie Pearl
GADE, Henry
  Palmer, Ray
GAGE, Gervais
  Rentoul, T Laurence
GAGE, Wilson
  Steele, Mary Quintard Govan

GAINES, Robert
  Summerscales, Rowland
GAITE, Francis
  Manning, Adelaide Frances
  Oke *and* Coles, Cyril Henry
GALE, John
  Gase, Richard
GALE, Newton
  Guinness, Maurice
GALLAGHER, Gale
  Oursler, William Charles
GALLOPING GOURMET, THE
  Kerr, Graham
GALWAY, Robert Conington
  McCutchan, Philip D
GAME COCK
  Looker, Samuel Joseph
GAMBIER, Kenyon
  Lathrop, Lorin Andrews
GANNOLD, John
  Langdon, John
GANPAT
  Gompertz, Martin Louis Alan
GARDEN, John
  Fletcher, Harry L Verne
GARDNER, Nancy Bruff
  Bruff, Nancy
GARDNER, Jeffrey
  Fox, Gardner
GARDNER, Noel
  Kuttner, Henry
GARDONS, S S
  Snodgrass, W D
GARFORD, James
  Blackburn, James Garford
GARLAND, Bennett
  Garfield, Brian

GARLAND, George
  Roark, Garland
GARLAND, Lisette
  Gibbs, Norah
GARLAND, Luke
  Whitson, John Harvey
GARLAND, Madge
  Ashton, *Lady*
GARLAND, Rodney
  Hegedus, Adam de
GARNETT, David S
  Rush, Noel
GARNETT, Roger
  Morland, Nigel
GARRATT, Teddie
  Garratt, Alfred
GARRETT, Truman
  Judd, Harrison
GARRISON, Joan
  Neubauer, William Arthur
GARRITY
  Garrity, David James
GARRY, Stephen
  Stevens, Henry Charles
GARSTANG, Basil
  Brereton, John Le Gay
GARTH, Cecil
  Carlton, Grace
GARTH, Will
  Kuttner, Henry
GARTNER, Chloe
  Trimble, Chloe Maria
GARVE, Andrew
  Winterton, Paul
GASH, Jonathan
  Grant, John
GASKELL, Jane
  Denvil, Jane Gaskell

GASKET, Bamber
  Fantoni, Barry
GATE, A G
  Anthony, Edward
GATH
  Townsend, George Alfred
GAULT, Mark
  Cournos, John
GAUNT, Jeffrey
  Rochester, George Ernest
GAUNT, M B
  Horsfield, Richard Edward
GAUNT, Michael
  Robertshaw, James Denis
GAUNT, Richard
  Landells, Richard
GAVIN, Amanda
  Fry, Clodagh Micaela Gibson
GAWAIN
  Newton, H Chance
GAWSWORTH, John
  Fytton-Armstrong, T I
GAY, Amelia
  Hogarth, Grace
GAYE, Carol
  Shann, Renée
GAYLE, Newton
  Guinness, Maurice
GEACH, Christine
  Wilson, Christine
GEARON, John
  Flagg, John
GEE, Kenneth F
  Kay, Frederick George
GEE, Osman
  Hincks, Cyril Malcolm
GEERLINK, Will
  Hofdorp, Pim

GEISEL, Eva
  Bornemann, Eva
GELLERT, Roger
  Holmstrom, John Eric
GEMINI
  Goodwin, Geoffrey
GEMMILL
  Kirkpatrick, *Mrs* Helen
GENE, Marta
  Powley, *Mrs* A A
GENET
  Flanner, Janet
GENTLEMAN OF THE
  UNIVERSITY OF CAMBRIDGE
  ˙ Crowley, Edward Alexander
GENTLEWOMAN, A
  Moore, Doris Langley
GEORGE, Daniel
  Bunting, D G
GEORGE, Eliot
  Freeman, Gillian
GEORGE, Eugene
  Chevalier, Paul Eugene George
GEORGE, G S
  Levin, Abraham
GEORGE, Jonathan
  Burke, John Frederick
GEORGE, Vicky
  Collings, I J
GERAINT, George
  Evans, George
GERALD, Daryl
  Fitzgerald, Desmond
GERARD, Gaston
  Ostergaard, Geoffrey
GERARD, Morice
  Teague, John Jessop

207

GERARDY, *Trooper*
  Gerard, Edwin
GERRARE, Wirt
  Greener, William Oliver
GIBB, Lee
  Deghy, Guy *and*
  Waterhouse, Keith
GIBBON, Lewis Grassic
  Mitchell, James Leslie
GIBBS, Henry
  Rumbold-Gibbs, Henry St
    John C
GIBBS, Lewis
  Cove, Joseph Walter
GIBBS, Mary Ann
  Bidwell, Marjory Elizabeth
    Sarah
GIBSON, Floyd
  King, Albert
GIFFARD, Ann
  Greenhill, Elizabeth Ann
GIFFIN, Frank
  Carter, Ernest
GIFFORD, Matt
  King, Albert
GIFT, Theo
  Havers, Dora
GILBERT, Anna
  Lazarus, Marguerite
GILBERT, Anthony
  Malleson, Lucy
GILBERT, John
  Harrison, John Gilbert
GILBERT, Nan
  Gilbertson, Mildred
GILCHRIST, John
  Gardner, Jerome

GILCRAFT
  Young, Ernest
GILDEN, K B
  Gilden, Katya *and*
  Gilden, Bert
GILES, Kris
  Nielson, Helen Berniece
GILES, Norman
  Mackeown, N R
GILL, Hugh
  Hugill, Robert
GILL, Patrick
  Creasey, John
GILL, Stanley
  Taylor, Roland
GILLESPIE, Jane
  Shaw, Jane
GILLESPIE, Susan
  Turton-Jones, Edith C
GILMAN, Dorothy
  Butters, Dorothy Gilman
GILMAN, George G
  Harknett, Terry
GILMAN, J D
  Fishman, Jack *and*
  Orgill, Douglas
GILMAN, Robert Cham
  Coppel, Alfred
GILMER, Ann
  Ross, William Edward Daniel
GILMOUR, Ann
  McNaught, Ann Boyce
GILROONEY
  Cassidy, Robert John
GINGER
  Sargent, Genevieve
GIRTY, Simon
  King, Albert

GLANVILLE, Alec
  Grieve, Alexander Haig
  Glanville
GLASHAN, John
  MacGlashan, John
GLASS, Justine
  Corrall, Alice Enid
GLENDENNING, Donn
  Paine, Lauran Bosworth
GLENELG
  Frost, J W
GLENN, James
  Paine, Lauran Bosworth
GLINTO, Darcy
  Kelly, Harold Ernest
GLUTZ, Ambrose
  Knapp, Clarence
GLYN, Megan
  Parry, Margaret G
GLYN-FOREST, D
  Lynes, Daisy Elfreda
GLYNN-WARD, H
  Howard, Hilda Glynn
GLYNN-WARD, Hilda
  Howard, Hilda Glynn
GOAMAN, Muriel
  Cox, Edith Muriel
GODDEN, Rumer
  Haynes Dixon, Margaret
  Rumer
GODEY, John
  Freedgood, Morton
GODFREY, Charles
  Webb, Godfrey E C
GODFREY, William
  Youd, Samuel
GOFF, Madeleine
  Woodford, Irene-Cecile

GOFFSTEIN, M B
  Schaaf, M B
GOLDEN GORSE
  Wace, M A
GOLDSMITH, Peter
  Priestley, John Boynton
GOOCH, Silas N
  Glassco, John
GOODE, Bill
  Goodykoontz, William F
GOODMAN, Winthrop
  Goodman, George Jerome
  and Knowlton, Winthrop
GOODSON, Bill
  Lucas, Edgar Ernest
GOODWIN, John
  Gowing, Sidney Floyd
GOODYEAR, Susan
  Matthews, Margaret Bryan
GORDON, Alex
  Cutler, Gordon
GORDON, Angela
  Paine, Lauran Bosworth
GORDON, David
  Garrett, Randall
GORDON, Don
  Thomas, Edward Llewellyn
  Gordon
GORDON, Donald
  Payne, Donald Gordon
GORDON, Gary
  Edmonds, Ivy Gordon
GORDON, Glenda
  Beadle, Gwyneth Gordon
GORDON, Ian
  Fellowes-Gordon, Ian
GORDON, Jane
  Sheridan, Elsie Lee

209

GORDON, Janet
  Woodham-Smith, Cecil
GORDON, Keith
  Bailey, Gordon
GORDON, Lew
  Baldwin, Gordon C
GORDON, Mary
  Ostlere, Mary
GORDON, Neil
  Macdonell, A G
GORDON, Ray
  Wainwright, Gordon Ray
GORDON, Rex
  Hough, Stanley Bennett
GORDON, Richard
  Ostlere, Gordon Stanley
GORDON, Selma
  Lanes, Selma G
GORDON, Stewart
  Shirreffs, Gordon D
GORDON, William Murray
  Graydon, William Murray
GORDONS, THE
  Gordon, Gordon *and*
    Gordon, Mildred
GORE, William
  Gordon, Jan
GORHAM, Michael
  Folsom, Franklin Brewster
GORMAN, Beth
  Paine, Lauran Bosworth
GORMAN, Ginny
  Coleman, John
GOTTESMAN, S D
  Kornbluth, Cyril M *and*
    Pohl, Frederik
GOUGH, Irene
  Hall, Irene

GOULD, Alan
  Canning, Victor
GOULD, Stephen
  Fisher, Stephen Gould
GOUTTIER, Maurice
  Moretti, Ugo
GOYNE, Richard
  Courage, John
GRAAF, Peter
  Youd, Samuel
GRACCHUS
  Wintringham, Tom
GRACE, Joseph
  Hornby, John Wilkinson
GRADY, Tex
  Webb, Jack
GRAEME, Bruce
  Jeffries, Bruce Graham
    Montague
GRAEME, David
  Jeffries, Bruce Graham
    Montague
GRAEME, Linda
  Jeffries, Gay
GRAEME, Roderic
  Jeffries, Roderic Graeme
GRAFTON, Garth
  Duncan, Sara Jeanette
GRAHAM, BROTHER
  Jeffrey, Graham
GRAHAM, Ennis
  Molesworth, *Mrs* Mary
    Louisa Stewart
GRAHAM, Harvey
  Flack, Isaac Harvey
GRAHAM, James
  Patterson, Henry

GRAHAM, Jean
  Scott, Mary E
GRAHAM, John
  Phillips, David Graham
GRAHAM, John
  Rose, Graham
GRAHAM, Neill
  Duncan, William Murdoch
GRAHAM, Peter
  Abraham, Peter L
GRAHAM, Peter
  Langmaid, Kenneth Joseph
    Robb
GRAHAM, Ramona
  Cook, Ramona Graham
GRAHAM, Robin
  Raleigh-King, Robin Victor
    Lethbridge
GRAHAM, Scott
  Black, Hazleton
GRAHAM, Susan
  Graham, Maud Fitzgerald
GRAHAM, Viva
  Somerville, Edith Oenone
GRAMMATICUS
  Blaiklock, Edward
GRANADOS, Paul
  Kent, Arthur
GRAND, Sarah
  McFaul, Frances Elizabeth
GRANDMA
  Mulhearn, Winifred
GRANDOWER, Elissa
  Waugh, Hillary Baldwin
GRANGE, Ellerton
  Fraser-Harris, D
GRANGE, Peter
  Nicole, Christopher

GRANGER, Stewart
  Stewart, James L
GRANT, Alan
  Kennington, Gilbert Alan
GRANT, Ambrose
  Raymond, Rene
GRANT, Carol
  Copper, Dorothy
GRANT, Douglas
  Ostrander, Isabel Egerton
GRANT, Eve
  Gray, K E
GRANT, Jane
  Blackburn, Barbara
GRANT, Kay
  Grant, Hilda Kay
GRANT, Landon
  Gribble, Leonard Reginald
GRANT, Margaret
  Meloney, William
GRANT, Marjorie
  Cook, Marjorie Grant
GRANT, Mary
  Willans, Angela
GRANT, Maxwell
  Gibson, Walter Brown
GRANT, Neil
  Mountfield, David
GRANT, Nesta
  Leyland, Eric
GRANT, Richard
  Clarke, J Calvitt
GRANTLAND, Keith
  Nutt, Charles
GRAPE, Oliver
  Wood, Christopher
GRAVELEY, George
  Edwards, George Graveley

211

GRAY, Adrian
  Wilkes-Hunter, Richard
GRAY, Berkeley
  Brooks, Edwy Searles
GRAY, Christopher
  Usher, John Gray
GRAY, Elizabeth Janet
  Vining, Elizabeth Gray
GRAY, Ellington
  Jacob, Naomi
GRAY, Harriet
  Robins, Denise
GRAY, Jane
  Evans, Constance May
GRAY, Jonathan
  Adams, Herbert
GRAYSON, Daphne
  Graveley, G C
GRAYSON, David
  Baker, Ray Stannard
GRAYSON, Richard
  Grindal, Richard
GREAVES, Gillian
  Macvean, Phyllis
GREAVES, Richard
  Simonds, Peter
GREEN, Charles M
  Gardner, Erle Stanley
GREEN, Glint
  Peterson, Margaret
GREEN, Hannah
  Greenberg, Joanne
GREEN, Henry
  Yorke, Henry Vincent
GREEN, Linda
  Copper, Dorothy
GREEN, O O
  Durgnat, Raymond

GREEN, R
  Weir, Rosemary
GREEN CROW, THE
  O'Casey, Sean
GREENE, Adam
  Scott, Peter Dale
GREENE, Anna Katharine
  Rohlfs, *Mrs* Anna
GREENE, Robert
  Deindorfer, Robert G
GREENFIELD, Bernadette
  Darby, Edith M
GREENHALGH, Katherine
  Bobin, John W
GREENHILL, Jack
  Greenberg, Jack
GREENWOOD, Grace
  Lippincott, Sara Jane
GREER, Patrick
  Macrory, Patrick
GREGG, Alan
  Mallette, Gertrude Ethel
GREGORY, Stephen
  Pendleton, Donald Eugene
GREGSON, Paul
  Oakley, Eric Gilbert
GREIG, Maysie
  Ames, Jennifer
GRENDON, Stephen
  Derleth, August William
GRENVIL, William
  Martyn, Wyndham
GREW, William
  O'Farrell, William
GREX, Leo
  Gribble, Leonard Reginald
GREY, A F
  Neal, Adeline Phyllis

GREY, Brenda
  Mackinlay, Lelia A S
GREY, Charles
  Tubb, E C
GREY, Donald
  Thomas, Eugene
GREY, Elizabeth
  Hogg, Beth
GREY, Harry
  Golberg, Harry
GREY, Louis
  Gribble, Leonard Reginald
GREY, Robin
  Gresham, Elizabeth F
GREY, Rowland
  Brown, L Rowland
GREY, Steele
  Smith, G M
GREY OWL
  Belaney, Archie
GREYSTONE, Alexander A
  Goodavage, Joseph F
GRIER, Sydney C
  Gregg, Hilda
GRIFF, Alan
  Suddaby, William Donald
GRIFFIN, John
  Clay, Michael John
GRIFFITH, Jack
  Griffiths, Jack
GRIFFITH, Jeannette
  Eyerly, Jeannette *and*
  Griffith, Valeria W
GRILE, Dod
  Bierce, Ambrose
GRINDLE, Carleton
  Page, Gerald W

GRINGHUIS, Dirk
  Gringhuis, Richard H
GRINNELL, David
  Wollheim, Donald A
GRISWOLD, George
  Dean, Robert George
GROSS, Gene
  Edmonds, Ivy Gordon
GROUPE, Darryl R
  Bunch, David R
GROVER, Marshall
  Meares, Leonard F
GROVES, Georgina
  Symons, Dorothy G
GUBBINS, Nathaniel
  Mott, Edward Spencer
GUILDFORD, John
  Hunter, Bluebell Matilda
GUINNESS, Owen
  Williams, Guy Richard
GULICK, Bill
  Gulick, Grover C
GULLIVER, Lemuel
  Farrell, Michael
GUMSUCKER
  Keogh, M J
GUN BUSTER
  Austin, John *and*
  Austin, Richard
GUNN, Victor
  Brooks, Edwy Searles
GURNEY, David
  Bair, Patrick
GUTHRIE, Alan
  Tubb, E C
GUTHRIE, John
  Brodie, John

213

GWYNNE, Arthur
  Evans, Gwynfil Arthur
GWYNNE, Nell
  Boggs, Helen
GWYNNE, Paul
  Slater, Ernest
GYE, Hal
  Gye, Harold Frederick Neville

§ §

Caro nome che il mio cor
Festi primo palpitar.
—G. Verdi; F. Piave. Rigoletto

§ §

H A K
  Kennedy, H A
H D
  Doolittle, Hilda
HAAS, Carola
  Catalani, Victoria
HACKSTON, James
  Gye, Harold Frederick Neville
HADDO, Oliver
  Puechner, Ray
HADDOCK, Albert
  Herbert, *Sir* Alan Patrick
HADDON, Christopher
  Palmer, John Leslie
HADDOW, Leigh
  Best, Rayleigh Breton
   Amis
HADHAM, John
  Parkes, James W
HADLEY, John
  Hemingway, Ernest

HADLEY, Leila
  Smitter, Eliott-Burton
HAEFER, Hanna
  Condon, Madeline
HAGAR, Judith
  Polley, Judith Anne
HAGEN, Brett
  Hunter, William R
HAGGARD, Paul
  Longstreet, Stephen
HAGGARD, William
  Clayton, Richard H M
HAGON, Priscilla
  Allan, Mabel Esther
HALCROW, Penelope
  Wallace, Penelope
HALE, Christopher
  Stevens, Frances Moyer
HALE, Hope
  Davis, Hope Hale
HALE, Katherine
  Garvin, Amelia Beers
   (Warnock)
HALES, Joyce
  Coombs, Joyce
HALIBURTON, Hugh
  Robertson, James Logie
HALIFAX, Clifford
  Beaumont, *Dr* Edgar
HALL, Adam
  Dudley-Smith, Trevor
HALL, B
  Gunn, John Angus Lancaster
HALL, Bennett
  Hall, Bennie Caroline
HALL, Borden
  Yates, Raymond Francis

214

HALL, Claudia
Floren, Lee
HALL, Eliza Calvert
Obenchain, Eliza Caroline
HALL, Holworthy
Porter, Harold Everett
HALL, John
Pound, Ezra
HALL, Martyn T
Morris, David
HALL, Patrick
Hall, Frederick
HALL, Rupert
Home-Gall, Edward Reginald
HALL, Whyte
Rayner, Augustus Alfred
HALLAM, Jay
Rice, Joan
HALLARD, Peter
Catherall, Arthur
HALLAS, Richard
Knight, Eric
HALLIDAY, Brett
Dresser, Davis
HALLIDAY, Dorothy
Dunnett, Dorothy
HALLIDAY, James
Symington, David
HALLIDAY, Michael
Creasey, John
HALLUS, Tak
Robinett, Stephen
HAMBLEDON, Phyllis
Macvean, Phyllis
HAMILL, Ethel
Webb, Jean Frances
HAMILTON, Clive
Lewis, Clive Staples

HAMILTON, Ernest
Grossman, Judith
HAMILTON, Judith
Lawrence, Dulcie
HAMILTON, Julia
Watson, Julia
HAMILTON, Kay
De Leeuw, Cateau W
HAMILTON, Max
Hamilton, Cecily
HAMILTON, Michael
Chetham-Strode, Warren
HAMILTON, Mollie
Kaye, Mary Margaret
HAMILTON, Paul
Dennis-Jones, Harold
HAMILTON, Roger
Rogerson, James
HAMILTON, Wade
Floren, Lee
HAMILTON, William
Canaway, W H
HAMILTON-STOCKFORD, Joan
Stockford, Lela E
HAMILTON-WILKES, Monty
Hamilton-Wilkes, Edwin
HAMMOND, Brad
King, Albert
HAMMOND, Jane
Poland, Dorothy E H
HAMMOND, Keith
Kuttner, Henry
HAMMOND, Ralph
Hammond-Innes, Ralph
HAMPSON, John
Simpson, John Frederick
Norman Hampson

215

HAN SUYIN
  Comber, Elizabeth
HANCOCK, Frances Deane
  Judson, Jeanne
HANCOCK, Robert
  Howell, Douglas Nayler
HANLON, John
  Mitchell, John Hanlon
HANNAFORD, Justin
  Fitz-Gerald, S J A
HANNON, Ezra
  Lombino, Salvatore A
HARBIN, Robert
  Williams, Ned
HARBINSON, Robert
  Harbinson-Bryans, Robert
HARDEN, Verna Loveday
  Bentley, Verna Bessie
HARDIN, Dave
  Holmes, Llewellyn Perry
HARDIN, Peter
  Vaczek, Louis C
HARDING, Bertita
  Radetzby von Radetz,
    Countess
HARDING, George
  Raubenheimer, George H
HARDING, Matt
  Floren, Lee
HARDING, Richard
  Boulton, A Harding
HARDING, Wes
  Keevill, Henry John
HARDWICK, Sylvia
  Doherty, Ivy Ruby
HARDY, Adam
  Harknett, Terry

HARDY, Arthur S
  Steffens, Arthur Joseph
HARDY, Bobbie
  Hardy, Marjorie
HARDY, Russ
  Snow, Charles Horace
HARDY, Stuart
  Schisgall, Oscar
HARE, Cyril
  Clark, Alfred Alexander
    Gordon
HARE, Robert
  Hutchinson, Robert Hare
HARFORD, Henry
  Hudson, William Henry
HARGIS, Pauline
  Dillard, Polly Hargis
HARGIS, Polly
  Dillard, Polly Hargis
HARLAN, Ross
  King, Albert
HARLAND, Marion
  Terhune, Mary Virginia
HARLE, Elizabeth
  Roberts, Irene
HARLEQUIN
  Reed, Alexander Wyclif
HARLEY, John
  Marsh, John
HARMODIUS
  Jackson, Charles Philip Castle
    Kains
HARMON, Gill
  King, Albert
HARMSTON, Donald
  Matheson, Donald H
HARPER, Daniel
  Brossard, Chandler

HARPOLE, James
  Abraham, James Johnston
HARRIETT
  Wilcoxen, Harriett
HARRIS, Colver
  Harris, Polly Anne Colver
HARRIS, John Beynon
  Harris, John Wyndham Parkes
  Lucas Beynon
HARRIS, Kathleen
  Humphries, Adelaide
HARRIS, Larry M
  Janifer, Laurence M
HARRIS, Macdonald
  Heiney, Donald William
HARRIS, Peter
  Harris, William
HARRISON, Whit
  Whittington, Harry
HART, Francis
  Paine, Lauran Bosworth
HART, Jon
  Harvey, John
HART, Max
  Urquhart, Macgregor
HART, R W
  Ferneyhough, Roger Edmund
HART, Susanne
  Harthoorn, Susanne
HARTE, Marjorie
  McEvoy, Marjorie
HARTFORD, Via
  Donson, Cyril
HARTMAN, Roger
  Mehta, Rustam
HARTWELL, Nancy
  Callahan, Claire Wallis

HARVESTER, Simon
  Rumbold-Gibbs, Henry St
    John C
HARVEY, Gene
  Hanley, Jack
HARVEY, Lyon
  Porter, Edward
HARVEY, Rachel
  Bloom, Ursula
HARVEY, Ross
  Hook, H Clarke
HASLETTE, John
  Vahey, John George
    Haslette
HASSAN i SABBAH
  Butler, Bill
HASTINGS, Beatrice
  Haig, Emily Alice
HASTINGS, Brook
  Edgley, Leslie *and*
  Edgley, Mary
HASTINGS, Graham
  Jeffries, Roderic Graeme
HASTINGS, Hudson
  Kuttner, Henry
HASWELL, Jock
  Haswell, C J D
HATCH, Robert
  Lee, Manning de Villeneuve
HATRED, Peter
  Douglas, Keith
HATTON, Cliff
  Mason, Sydney Charles
HAWK, Affable
  MacCarthy, *Sir* Desmond
HAWK, Alex
  Garfield, Brian

217

HAWKES, John
  Burne, Clendennin Talbot
HAWKEYE
  Carlisle, R H
HAWKINS, John
  Hagan, Stelia F
HAWTHORNE, E M D
  Dolbey, Ethel M
HAWTHORNE, Ernest H
  Dawson, William Henry
HAWTHORNE, Marx
  Greenwood, A E
HAWTHORNE, Rainey
  Riddell, *Mrs* J H
HAY, Catherine
  Hughes, Ivy
HAY, Frances
  Dick-Erikson, Cicely Sibyl
    Alexandra
HAY, Ian
  Beith, John Hay
HAY, John
  Dalrymple-Hay, Barbara *and*
    Dalrymple-Hay, John
HAYDEN, Jay
  Paine, Lauran Bosworth
HAYES, Clanton
  Mason, Sydney Charles
HAYES, Evelyn
  Bethell, Mary
HAYES, Henry
  Olney, Ellen Warner
HAYES, Timothy
  Rubel, James Lyon
HAYMAN, Hazel
  Peel, Hazel
HAYNES, Dorothy K
  Gray, Dorothy K

HAYNES, John Robert
  Wilding, Philip
HAZARD, Laurence
  Barr, Patricia
HAZELTON, *Captain*
  Whitson, John Harvey
HAZELTON, Colonel
  Whitson, John Harvey
HEAD, Ann
  Morse, Anne Christenson
HEAD, Matthew
  Canaday, John
HEADLEY, Elizabeth
  Harrison, Elizabeth C
HEALD, Edith
  Shackleton, Edith
HEARD, Gerald
  Heard, Henry Fitzgerald
HEARNDEN, Balfour
  Balfour, Eve *and*
    Hernden, Beryl
HEATH, Eldon
  Derleth, August W
HEATH, Veronica
  Blackett, Veronica
HEATHCOTT, Mary
  Keegan, Mary Constance
HEATON, Peter
  Stuart-Heaton, Peter
HEBDEN, Mark
  Harris, John
HEBER, Austin
  Poole, Reginald Heber
HEBER, Reginald
  Poole, Reginald Heber
HEDGES, Joseph
  Harknett, Terry

HEDLEY, Frank
  Barker, Clarence Hedley
HEFNER, Paul
  Tabori, Paul
HEGESIPPUS
  Schonfield, Hugh Joseph
HELLER, Frank
  Serner, Gunnar
HELLERLAMB, Toni
  Lamb, Antonia
HELMHOLTZ, Bastien von
  Pound, Ezra
HELMI, Jack
  Sands, Leo G
HELVICK, James
  Cockburn, Claud
HELY, Elizabeth
  Younger, Elizabeth
HEMINGWAY, Percy
  Addleshaw, Percy
HEMINGWAY, Taylor
  Rywell, Martin
HENDERSON, Colt
  Mason, Sydney Charles
HENDERSON, George
  Glassco, John
HENDERSON, Sylvia
  Ashton-Warner, Sylvia
HENNESSY, Max
  Harris, John
HENRIQUES, Veronica
  Gosling, Veronica
HENRY, B A
  Abrahams, Henry B
HENRY, Daniel Jr
  Holmes, Daniel Henry
HENRY, Lewis C
  Copeland, Lewis

HENRY, O
  Porter, William Sydney
HENRY, Will
  Allen, Henry
HEPPELL, Blanche
  Heppell, Mary
HEPPLE, Anne
  Dickinson, Anne Hepple
HEPTAGON
  Charlton, Joan; Falk,
    Katherine; Falk, Millicent;
    Fox, Winifred; Gill,
    Winifred; Jennings, Hilda
    and Stocks, Mary
HEREFORD, John
  Fletcher, Harry L Verne
HERITAGE, A J
  Addis, Hazel Iris
HERITAGE, Martin
  Horler, Sydney
HERMAN, Jack
  Sands, Leo G
HERMAN, William
  Bierce, Ambrose
HERMES
  Canaway, W H
HERNE, Eric
  Garvey, Eric William
HERNE, Huxley
  Brooker, Bertram
HERON, E *and* H
  Prichard, H Hesketh *and*
    Prichard, Kate Hesketh
HERRING, Geilles
  Somerville, Edith Oenone
HERRIOT, James
  Wight, J A

219

HESSING, Dennis
  Dennis-Jones, Harold
HEWES, Cady
  De Voto, Bernard Augustine
HEWETT, Anita
  Duke, Anita
HEWITT, Martin
  Morrison, Arthur
HEXT, Harrington
  Phillpotts, Eden
HIAT, Elchik
  Katz, Menke
HICKEY, Lyn
  Hickey, Madelyn E
HICKOK, Will
  Harrison, Chester William
HICKS, Eleanor
  Coerr, Eleanor Beatrice
HIGGINBOTHAM, Anne T
  Higginbotham, Anne D
HIGGINS, Jack
  Patterson, Henry
HIGSON, P J W
  Willoughby-Higson, Philip
  John
HILL, Anne
  Muskett, Netta Rachel
HILL, Bennet
  Winter, Bevis
HILL, Craven
  Parsons, Charles P
HILL, H Haverstock
  Walsh, James Morgan
HILL, Headon
  Grainger, Francis Edward
HILL, Joe
  Hillstrom, Joseph

HILL, King
  Robertson, Frank Chester
HILL, Monica
  Werner, Elsa Jane
HILL, Murray
  Holliday, Robert Cortes
HILL, Prudence
  Maxfield, Prudence
HILL, Rabin
  Young, Robert
HILLIARD, Jan
  Grant, Hilda Kay
HILLMAN, Martin
  Hill, Douglas
HILTON, Margery
  Woods, Margery Hilton
HIN ME GEONG
  Armitage, John
HINDE, Thomas
  Chitty, *Sir* Thomas Willes
HINDIN, Nathan
  Bloch, Robert
HINTON, S E
  Inhofe, Susan Eloise
HIPPOPOTAMUS, Eugene H
  Kraus, Robert
HISTORICUS
  Nock, Albert Jay
HOBART, Robertson
  Lee, Norman
HOBBES, John Oliver
  Craigie, Pearl Mary Teresa
HOBSON, Polly
  Evans, Julia
HOCKABY, Stephen
  Mitchell, Gladys
HODGE, Merton
  Hodge, Horace Emerton

HODGEN, J T
  Hale, Ethela Ruth (*Mrs*
  Fellowes)
HODSON, Arthur
  Nickson, Arthur
HOE, Leigh
  Tripp, H Alker
HOFFMAN, Art
  King, Albert
HOFFMAN, Louise
  Fitzgerald, Beryl
HOFFNER, Dorothy
  Doane, Pelagie
HOFMEYER, Hans
  Fleischer, Anthony
HOGAN, David
  Gallagher, Frank
HOGARTH, Charles
  Creasy, John
HOGARTH, Emmett
  Wilson, Mitchell *and*
  Polansky, Abraham
HOGARTH, John
  Finnin, Mary
HOGBIN, Ian
  Hogbin, Herbert
HOLBROOK, John
  Vance, John Holbrook
HOLCOMBE, Arnold
  Golsworthy, Arnold
HOLDEN, Genevieve
  Pou, Genevieve
HOLDEN, Joanne
  Corby, Jane
HOLDEN, Larry
  Lorenz, Frederic
HOLDEN, Matthew
  Parkinson, Roger

HOLLAND, Clive
  Hankinson, Charles J
HOLLAND, Elizabeth
  Baxter, Elizabeth
HOLLAND, Katrin
  Loewengard, Heidi H F
HOLLAND, Kel
  Whittington, Harry
HOLLAND, Rosemary
  Pattinson, Lee
HOLLAND, Tom
  King, Albert
HOLLIS, Jim
  Summers, Hollis
HOLMES, Arnold W
  Fryefield, Maurice P
HOLMES, *Captain* Howard
  Harbaugh, Thomas Chalmers
HOLMES, Caroline
  Mason, Sydney Charles
HOLMES, Gordon
  Shiel, M P *and* Tracy, Louis
HOLMES, Grant
  Fox, James
HOLMES, Grant
  Knipscheer, James M W
HOLMES, H H
  White, William Anthony P
HOLMES, Kenyon
  Derleth, August W
HOLMES, Raymond
  Souster, Raymond
HOLMES, Rick
  Hardwick, Richard
HOLORENSHAW, Henry
  Needham, Joseph
HOLT, E Carleton
  Guigo, Ernest Philip

221

HOLT, Elizabeth
King, Kay
HOLT, Gavin
Rodda, Charles
HOLT, George
Tubb, E C
HOLT, Helen
Paine, Lauran Bosworth
HOLT, Rackham
Holt, Margaret Van Vechten
HOLT, Stephen
Thompson, Harlan
HOLT, Tex
Rister, Claude
HOLT, Victoria
Hibbert, Eleanor Alice
Burford
HOLTON, Leonard
Wibberley, Leonard Patrick
O'Connor
HOME, Michael
Bush, Christopher
HOME-GALL, Reginald
Home-Gall, Edward Reginald
HOME GUARD
Ingamells, F G
HOMES, Geoffrey
Mainwaring, Daniel
HON MEMBER FOR X
De Chair, Somerset
HONEYCUTT, Richard
Hardwick, Richard
HONEYMAN, Brenda
Clarke, Brenda
HOOKER, Richard
Hornberger, H Richard
HOOLEY, Teresa
Butler, Teresa Mary

HOPE, Andrew
Hern, Anthony
HOPE, Anthony
Hawkins, *Sir* Anthony Hope
HOPE, Brian
Creasey, John
HOPE, Edward
Coffey, Edward Hope
HOPE, John Francis
Randall, A E
HOPE, Lawrence
Nicholson, Violet
HOPE, Margaret
Wicksteed, Margaret Hope
HOPE, Noel
Morewood, Sarah L
HOPE, Stanton
Stanton-Hope, W E
HOPF, Alice
Lightner, A M
HOPKINS, A T
Turngreen, Annette
HOPKINS, Stanley
Holt, Henry
HOPLEY, George
Hopley-Woolrich, Cornell
George
HOPPER, Sam
Haslam, Nicky
HORN, Chester
Mason, Sydney Charles
HORN, Peter
Kuttner, Henry
HORN, Trader
Smith, Alfred Aloysius
HORNBY, John
Hornby, John Wilkinson

HORNE, Howard
  Payne, Pierre Stephen Robert
HORSLEY, David
  Bingley, David Ernest
HORSTMANN, Rosemary
  Waters, Rosemary Elizabeth
HORTON, Robert J
  Roberts, James
HOUGH, Don
  Huff, Darrell
HOUGHTON, Claude
  Oldfield, Claude Houghton
HOUGHTON, Elizabeth
  Gilzean, Elizabeth Houghton
HOUSE, Brant
  Chadwick, Paul
HOUSTON, R B
  Rae, Hugh Cranford
HOUSTON, Will
  Paine, Lauran Bosworth
HOWARD, Colin
  Shaw, Howard
HOWARD, Don
  Menzel, Donald H
HOWARD, Elizabeth
  Mizner, Elizabeth Howard
HOWARD, Elizabeth
  Paine, Lauran Bosworth
HOWARD, George
  Kay, Frederic George
HOWARD, Harry
  Ognall, Leopold Horace
HOWARD, Hartley
  Ognall, Leopold Horace
HOWARD, Helen
  Jacobs, Thomas Curtis Hicks
HOWARD, John M
  Hincks, Cyril Malcolm

HOWARD, Keble
  Bell, John Keble
HOWARD, Leigh
  Lee Howard, L A
HOWARD, Mary
  Mussi, Mary
HOWARD, Troy
  Paine, Lauran Bosworth
HOWARD, Vechel
  Rigsby, Howard
HOWE, Muriel
  Smithies, Muriel
HOWELL, Scott
  King, Albert
HOWERD, Gareth
  Thomas, Robert Richard
HOY, Elizabeth
  Conarain, Alice Nina
HOYT, Nelson
  King, Albert
HUBBARD, Joan
  Jackson, Kathryn
HUBBARD, Kin
  Hubbard, Frank McKinney
HUBBARD, L Ron
  Hubbard, Lafayette Ronald
HUBERT
  Bland, Hubert
HUDSON, Jeffrey
  Crichton, Michael
HUDSON, Stephen
  Schiff, Sydney
HUGGINS, Ruth Mabel
  Arthur, Ruth M
HUGHES, Alison
  Oliver, Doris M
HUGHES, Brenda
  Colloms, Brenda

223

HUGHES, Colin
  Creasey, John
HUGHES, Matilda
  Macleod, Charlotte
HUGHES, Philip
  Phillips, Hugh
HUGHES, Terence
  Best, Rayleigh Breton Amis
HUGHES, Valerina
  Coleman, John
HUGHES, Zach
  Coleman, John
HULL, H Braxton
  Jacobs, Helen Hull
HULL, Richard
  Sampson, Richard Henry
HUMANA, Charles
  Jacobs, Charles
HUME, David
  Turner, John Victor
HUME, Frances
  Buckland-Wright, Mary
HUMPHRYS, Geoffrey
  Humphrys, Leslie George
HUNT, Charlotte
  Hodges, Doris Marjorie
HUNT, Diana
  Hunt-Bode, Gisele
HUNT, Dorothy
  Fellows, Dorothy Alice
HUNT, Harrison
  Ballard, Willis Todhunter
HUNT, John
  Paine, Lauran Bosworth
HUNT, Kyle
  Creasey, John

HUNT, Peter
  Yates, George Worthing *and*
  Marshall, Charles Hunt
HUNTER, Alison
  Blair, Norma Hunter
HUNTER, E Waldo
  Waldo, Edward Hamilton
HUNTER, Evan
  Lombino, Salvatore
HUNTER, George
  Ballard, Willis Todhunter
HUNTER, Hall
  Marshall, Edison
HUNTER, Jean
  Hunter, Alfred John
HUNTER, John
  Ballard, Willis Todhunter
HUNTER, John
  Hunter, Alfred John
HUNTER, John
  Hunter, Christine
HUNTER, M O
  Mabbott, Thomas O
HUNTER, Mollie
  McIlwraith, Maureen Mollie
  Hunter
HUNTER, Pat
  Kempf, Pat
HUNTINGDON, John
  Phillips, Gerald William
HUNTLY, Frances E
  Mayne, Ethel Colborn
HUNTON, Mary
  Gilzean, Elizabeth Houghton
HUNGERFORD, Pixie
  Brinsmead, Hesba
HUSSEY, Leonard
  Pearce, Brian

HUSSINGTREE, Martin
  Baldwin, Oliver
HUSTLE, Hugh
  Hall, Verner
HUTCHINS, Anthony
  Morley, Leslie Reginald
  William
HUTCHINSON, Anne
  Burnett, Hallie
HUTCHINSON, Patricia
  Fullbrook, Gladys
HYDE, Eleanor
  Minto, Frances
HYNE, C J Cutliffe
  Hyne, Charles John Cutliffe
  Wright
HYNE, Cutliffe
  Hyne, Charles John Cutliffe
  Wright

I B
  Brown, Ivor
IAMS, Jack
  Iams, Samuel H
ICONOCLAST
  Hamilton, Mary A A
IDRIS
  Mee, Arthur
IFANS, Glyn
  Evans, Glyn
IGNOTUS
  Fuller, James Franklin
ILES, Bert
  Ross, Zola Helen
ILES, Francis
  Cox, A B
INCLEDON, Philip
  Worner, Philip A I

INGERSOL, Jared
  Paine, Lauran Bosworth
INGHAM, Daniel
  Lambot, Isobel Mary
INGRAM, Martin
  Campbell, Alice Ormond
INNES, Hammond
  Hammond-Innes, Ralph
INNES, Jean
  Saunders, Jean
INNES, Michael
  Stewart, John Innes
  Mackintosh
IONICUS, Ion
  Leslie, *Sir* Shane
IOTA
  Caffyn, Kathleen M
IRELAND, Baron
  Salsbury, Nate
IRELAND, Doreen
  Lord, Doreen Mildred
  Douglas
IRELAND, Noelle
  Gibbs, Norah
IRISH, William
  Hopley-Woolrich, Cornell
  George
IRISHMAN, AN
  Clayton, *Reverend* F H
IRON, Ralph
  Schreiner, Olive Emilie
  Albertina
IRONBARK
  Gibson, G H
IRONQUILL
  Ware, Eugene Fitch
IRONSIDE, John
  Tait, Euphemia Margaret

IRVINE, Lyn
  Newman, Lyn Lloyd
IRVING, Robert
  Adler, Irving
IRWIN, P K
  Page, Patricia Kathleen
ISLAY, Nicholas
  Murray, Andrew Nicholas

J A H
  Hammerton, J A
J C
  Lawrence, T E
J C T
  Trewin, J C
J E N
  Neild, James Edward
J F-K
  Fitzmaurice-Kelly, James
J J
  Junor, *Sir* John
J L
  Pound, Ezra
J S H
  Huxley, Julian Sorell
JABEZ
  Nicol, Eric Patrick
JACKS, Oliver
  Gandley, Kenneth Royce
JACKSON, Everatt
  Muggeson, Margaret
JACKSON, Giles
  Leffingwell, Albert
JACKSON, Joyce
  Crounse, Helene Louise
JACKSON, Neville
  Glaskin, G M

JACKSON, Sam
  Trumbo, Dalton
JACKSON, Wallace
  Budd, William John
JACKSTAFF
  Bennett, J J
JACOB, Herbert Mathias
  Davies, D Jacob
JACOT, Bernard
  Jacot de Bolnod, B L
JACQUES
  Stott, Mary
JAMES, Andrew
  Kirkup, James
JAMES, Brian
  Tierney, John
JAMES, Cy
  Watts, Peter Christopher
JAMES, Dan
  Sayers, James D
JAMES, Dynely
  Mayne, William J C *and*
  Caesar, Richard Dynely
JAMES, Franklin
  Godley, Robert
JAMES, John
  Langdon-Davies, John
JAMES, Josephine
  Lindsay, Barbara *and*
  Sterne, E G
JAMES, Matthew
  Lucey, James D
JAMES, Robert
  Heitner, Iris
JAMES, Vincent
  Gribben, James
JAMESON, Eric
  Trimmer, Eric

JAMESON, Vere
  Shute, Evan Vere
JAMIESON, Thomas
  Molloy, Edward
JAN
  Read, John
JANES, Kathleen
  Jamieson, Kathleen Florence
JANES, Kathleen F
  Jamieson, Kathleen Florence
JANICE
  Brustlein, Janice
JANSEN, Hank
  Newton, William
JANSON, Hank
  Frances, Stephen Daniel
JANUS, Hiram
  Pound, Ezra
JAPONICA
  Holdaway, Marjorie F
JAQUES
  Neild, James Edward
JARDIN, Rex
  Burkhardt, Eve *and*
  Burkhardt, Robert
  Ferdinand
JARRETT, Kay
  Saxon, Sophia
JASON
  Craine, John Henry
JASON
  Munro, Hugh
JASON, William
  Machlin, Milton
JASPER, Bob
  Hogan, Robert Jasper
JAY
  Jennings, E C

JAY, Charlotte
  Jay, Geraldine
JAY, Joan
  Davies, Edith
JAY, Simon
  Alexander, Colin James
JAYNES, Clare
  Spiegel, Clara E *and*
  Mayer, Jane
JEANS, Angela
  Watt, Esme
JEEVES, Mahatma Kane
  Dukenfield, William Claude
JEFFERIES, Ian
  Hays, Peter
JEFFERIS, Jeff
  Curry, Thomas Albert
JEFFERSON, Ian
  Davies, Leslie Purnell
JEFFERSON, Sarah
  Farjeon, Eve
JEFFERY, E Jeffery
  Marston, J E
JEFFORD, Bat
  Bingley, David Ernest
JEFFRIES, Jeff
  Boatfield, Jeffrey
JEFFS, Rae
  Sebley, Frances Rae
JEMONTE
  Mohan, Josephine Elizabeth
JEMYMA
  Holley, Marietta
JENNER, Heather
  Potter, Heather
JENNIFER
  Kenward, Betty

JENNINGS, D
  Frazee, Steve
JENNINGS, S M
  Meyer, Jerome Sydney
JENNY WREN
  Cruttenden, Nellie
JEREMY, Richard
  Fox, Charles
JEROME, Owen Fox
  Friend, Oscar Jerome
JESKINS, Richard
  Story, Rosamond Mary
JESSEL, John
  Weinbaum, Stanley Grauman
JINGLE
  Golsworthy, Arnold
JOB, Modern
  Taber, Clarence Wilbur
JOCELYN, Richard
  Clutterbuck, Richard
JODY, J M
  Edmundson, Joseph
JOHANSON, Elizabeth
  Verwer, Johanne
JOHN, A SUFFOLK HERD
 BOY
  Brundle, John
JOHN, Alix
  Jones, Alice
JOHN, Evan
  Simpson, Evan John
JOHN, Jasper
  Muspratt, Rosalie
JOHN, Salisbury
  Caute, David
JOHN O'LONDON
  Whitten, Wilfred

JOHN O'THE NORTH
  Browne, Harry T
JOHNS, Avery
  Cousins, Margaret
JOHNS, Foster
  Seldes, Gilbert Vivian
JOHNS, Geoffrey
  Warner, Geoffrey John
JOHNS, Hilary
  Barraud, E M
JOHNS, June
  Smith, June Johns
JOHNS, Richard
  Slater, Montagu
JOHNSON, A E
  Johnson, Annabel J *and*
  Johnson, Edgar R
JOHNSON, Benjamin F
  Riley, James Whitcomb
JOHNSON, Brian
  Worthy, Brian Johnson
JOHNSON, Crockett
  Leisk, David Johnson
JOHNSON, Lee
  Johnson, Lilian Beatrice
JOHNSON, Marigold
  Gilles, Daniel
JOHNSON, W Bolingbroke
  Bishop, Morris Gilbert
JOLLY, Susan
  Edwards, Florence
JONES, Bobi
  Jones, Robert Maynard
JONES, Bradshaw
  Bradshaw-Jones,
  Malcolm Henry
JONES, Calico
  Richardson, Gladwell

JONES, Clara
  Baldwin, Dorothy
JONES, Joanna
  Burke, John Frederick
JONES, H S
  Molloy, Edward
JONES, Nard
  Jones, Maynard Benedict
JONES, Webb
  Henley, Art
JONS, Hal
  Jones, Harry Austin
JORDAN, Barbara Leslie
  Yellot, Barbara Leslie
JORDAN, Bryn
  Henderson, James Maddock
JORDAN, Neil
  Barker, E M
JORGENSON, Ivar
  Silverberg, Robert
JOSE, Ellen J
  Waye, Ellen
JOSIAH ALLEN'S WIFE
  Holley, Marietta
JOUDRY, Patricia
  Steele, Patricia M V
JOURNEYMAN
  Nock, Albert Jay
JOYCE, Thomas
  Cary, Joyce
JOYSTICK
  Holden, J R
JUBILATE
  Coppage, George Herman
JUDD, Cyril
  Grossman, Judith *and*
    Kornbluth, Cyril M

JUDGE, THE
  Sharp, Ian
JULIA
  Cox, Julia
JULIAN, Peter
  Körmendi, Ferens
JULIE
  Nettz, Julie
JULIE OF COLORADO
  SPRINGS
  Robbins, June
JULIET
  Levy, Julia Ethel
JUNE, Jenny
  Croly, Jane Cunningham
JUNIOR SUB
  Beith, John Hay
JUSTICIAR
  Powell-Smith, Vincent

K B
  Baker, Kate
KAHLER, Woodland
  Saint Innocent, *Marquis of*
KAIN, Saul
  Sassoon, Siegfried
KAJAR
  Bowen, Reuben
KANE, Jim
  Germano, Peter
KANE, Julia
  Robins, Denise
KANE, Mark
  King, Albert
KANE, Wilson
  Bloch, Robert
KANTO, Peter
  Coleman, John

229

KAP-O-KASLO
West, G A
KARAGEORGE, Michael
Anderson, Poul
KARIG, Walter
Patrick, Keats
KARLOFF, Boris
Pratt, William Henry
KASZNAR, Kurt
Serwicher, Kurt
KAVAN, Anna
Edmonds, Helen
KAVANAGH, Dan
Barnes, Julian
KAY, Helen
Goldfrank, *Mrs* Herbert
KAY, Wallace
Arter, Wallace E
KAYE, Barbara
Muir, Marie
KAYE, Evelyn
Evans, Kathleen
KAYE, Harold B
Kampf, Harold Bertram
KAYE, Mary Margaret
Hamilton, Mary Margaret
Kaye
KAYE, Tom
Kaye, Barrington
KEATING, Walter S
Rosenberg, Henrietta
KEENE, Carolyn
Adams, Harriet S (*after*
Edward Stratemeyer)
KEENE, Carolyn
Stratemeyer, Edward
KEENE, Faraday
Jarrett, Cora

KEENE, Frances W
Casman, Frances White
KEENE, James
Cook, William Everett
KEESING, Nancy
Hertzberg, Nancy
KEIR, Christine
Pullein-Thompson, Christine
KEITH, Carlton
Robertson, Keith
KEITH, David
Steegmuller, Francis
KEITH, Donald
Monroe, Donald *and*
Monroe, Keith
KEITH, James
Hetherington, Keith James
KEITH, Marian
MacGregor, Mary Ester
KELL, Joseph
Wilson, John Anthony Burgess
KELLER, Dan
Kaufman, Louis
KELLEY, Ray
Paine, Lauran Bosworth
KELLIER, Elizabeth
Kelly, Elizabeth
KELLOW, Kathleen
Hibbert, Eleanor Alice
Burford
KELLWAY, Mary D
Hillyard, Mary Dorothy
KELSEY, Janice
King, Albert
KELWAY, Christine
Gwinn, Christine M
KENDAL, Robert
Forster, Reginald Kenneth

KENDALL, Jane
  Martens, Anne Louise
KENDALL, Lace
  Stoutenburg, Adrien
KENDRAKE, Carleton
  Gardner, Erle Stanley
KENDRICKS, James
  Fox, Gardner F
KENEU
  Hazlewood, Rex
KENNEDY, Diana
  Duggleby, Jean Colbeck
KENNEDY, Elliott
  Godfrey, Lionel Robert
  Holcombe
KENNEDY, Howard
  Woolfolk, Josiah Pitts
KENNEDY, James
  Kenafick, Joseph
KENNEDY, Milward
  Burge, Milward Rodon
  Kennedy
KENNEDY, R C
  Cortez-Columbus, Robert
  Cimabue
KENNEDY, X J
  Kennedy, Joseph Charles
KENNEGGY, Richard
  Nettell, Richard
KENNIE, Jessie
  Macpherson, Jessie
KENNINGTON, Alan
  Kennington, Gilbert Alan
KENNY, Charles J
  Gardner, Erle Stanley
KENT, Alexander
  Reeman, Douglas

KENT, David
  Birney, Hoffman
KENT, Kelvin
  Kuttner, Henry *and*
  Barnes, Arthur
KENT, Pete
  Richardson, Gladwell
KENT, Simon
  Catto, Maxwell Jeffrey
KENTIGERN, John
  Veitch, Thomas
KENTON, Maxwell
  Southern, Terry *and*
  Hoffenberg, Mason
KENWORTHY, Hugh
  Walker, Rowland
KENYON, Larry
  Engel, Lyle Kenyon
KENYON, Paul
  Engel, Lyle Kenyon
KENYON, Robert O
  Kuttner, Henry
KEPPEL, Charlotte
  Torday, Ursula
KEPPS, Gerald E
  Speck, Gerald Eugene
KERBY, Susan Alice
  Burton, Alice Elizabeth
KERR, Ben
  Ard, William
KERR, Carole
  Carr, Margaret
KERR, John O'Connell
  Whittet, George Sorley
KERR, Lennox
  Kerr, James Lennox
KERR, M E
  Meaker, Marijane

231

KERR, Orpheus C
  Newell, Robert Henry
KERSEY, John
  Warriner, Thurman
KESTEVEN, G R
  Crosher, Geoffrey Robins
KETCHUM, Jack
  Paine, Lauran Bosworth
KETTLE, Pamela
  Kettle, Jocelyn
KEVERNE, Richard
  Hosken, Clifford James
    Wheeler
KEW, Andrew
  Morton, A Q
KEYES, Gordon
  Bedford-Jones, Henry
KEYSTONE, Oliver
  Mantiband, James
KHAN, Khaled
  Crowley, Edward Alexander
KIDD, Russell
  Donson, Cyril
KIEFER, Middleton
  Middleton, Harry *and*
    Kiefer, Warren
KILBOURN, Matt
  Barrett, Geoffrey John
KILDARE, John
  King, John
KILDARE, Maurice
  Richardson, Gladwell
KILGORE, John
  Paine, Lauran Bosworth
KILPATRICK, Sarah
  Underwood, Mavis Eileen
KIM
  Sweet, John

KIMBER, Lee
  King, Albert
KIMBRO, Jean
  Kimbro, John
KIMBROUGH, Katheryn
  Kimbro, John
KINDLER, Asta
  Hicken, Una
KING, Ames
  King, Albert
KING, Arthur
  Cain, Arthur Homer
KING, Arthur
  Lake, Kenneth Robert
KING, Berta
  King, Albert
KING, Charles
  Avenell, Donne
KING, Christopher
  King, Albert
KING, Clifford
  King, James Clifford
KING, Evan
  Ward, Robert Spencer
KING, Kennedy
  Brown, George Douglas
KING, Norman A
  Tralins, S Robert
KING, Oliver
  Mount, Thomas Ernest
KING, Paul
  Drackett, Phil
KING, Reefe
  Barker, Albert H
KING, Richard
  Huskinson, Richard King

KING, Robin
  Raleigh-King, Robin Victor
    Lethbridge
KING, Sampson
  Bennett, Arnold
KING, Stella
  Glenton, Stella Lennox
KING, Stephanie
  Russell, Shirley
KING, W Scott
  Greenland, W K
KINGSLEY, Laura
  Bennett, Dorothy
KINGSMILL, Hugh
  Lunn, Hugh Kingsmill
KINGSTON, Charles
  O'Mahony, Charles Kingston
KINGSTON, Syd
  Bingley, David Ernest
KINNOCH, R G B
  Barclay, George
KINSEY-JONES, Brian
  Ball, Brian N
KIPPAX, John
  Hynam, John
KIRBY, Kate
  Elgin, Betty
KIRK, Laurence
  Simson, Eric Andrew
KISH
  Le Riche, P J
KLAXON
  Bower, John Graham
KLOSE, Norma Cline
  Cline, Norma
KNICKERBOCKER, Cholly
  Paul, Maury

KNIGHT, Adam
  Lariar, Lawrence
KNIGHT, Brigid
  Sinclair, Kathleen Henrietta
KNIGHT, David
  Prather, Richard
KNIGHT, Gareth
  Wilby, Basil
KNIGHT, Isobel
  Lockie, Isobel
KNIGHT, Mallory
  Hurwood, Bernhardt J
KNOTT, Bill
  Knott, William Cecil
KNOTT, Hermann
  Smith, Walter Chalmers
KNOTTS, Raymond
  Volk, Gordon
KNOWALL, George
  O'Nolan, Brian
KNOX, Bill
  Macleod, Robert
KNOX, Calvin
  Silverberg, Robert
KNOX, Gilbert
  Macbeth, Madge Hamilton
KNUDSEN, Greta
  Knudsen, Margrethe
KODAK
  O'Ferrall, Ernest
KONING, Hans
  Koningsberger, Hans
KRAMER, George
  Heuman, William
KREMLINOLOGIST
  Zorza, Victor
KREUZENAU, Michael
  Law, Michael

233

KRIN, Sylvie
  Fantoni, Barry
KRISLOV, Alexander
  Lee Howard, L A
KROLL, Burt
  Rowland, Donald Sydney
KRUGER, Paul
  Sebenthall, Roberta
KRULL, Felix
  White, Stanley
KUTHUMI
  Fleishmann, Helle
KYD, Thomas
  Harbage, Alfred
KYLE, Elisabeth
  Dunlop, Agnes M R
KYLE, Sefton
  Vickers, Roy

§ §

*What good can it do an ass to be
called a lion?*
—Thomas Fuller. Gnomologia

§ §

L L
  Barry, John Arthur
LA FAYETTE, Rene
  Hubbard, Lafayette Ronald
LA SPINA, Greye
  La Spina, Fanny Greye (Bragg)
LACY, Ed
  Zinberg, Len
LADNEK, Odlaw
  Kendall, Carlton Waldo

LADWICK, Marty
  Kirby, Derek Amos
LADY OF MANITOBA, A
  Frank, *Mrs* M J
LADY OF QUALITY
  Jones, *Lady* Roderick
LAFARGUE, Philip
  Philpot, Joseph H
LAING, Kenneth
  Langmaid, Kenneth Joseph
    Robb
LAING, Patrick
  Long, Amelia R
LAIRD
  Lowther, Armstrong John
LAKE, Sarah
  Weiner, Margery
LAKER, Rosalind
  Øvstedal, Barbara
LAKLAN, Carli
  Laughlin, Virginia Carli
LAMBERT, Christine
  Loewengard, Heidi H F
LAMONT, Frances
  Jourdain, Eleanor F
LAMONT, Marianne
  Rundle, Anne
LAMONT, N B
  Barnitt, Nedda Lemmon
LAMONT, Wood C
  Sewall, Robert
LAMPLAUGH, Lois
  Davis, Lois Carlile
LAMPREY, A C
  Fish, Robert Lloyd
LAMPTON, Austen
  Dent, Anthony

LAN
Landon, Melville de Lancey
LANARK, David
Marten, J Chisholm
LANCASTER, A F
Fleur, Anne Elizabeth
LANCASTER, David
Heald, Tim
LANCASTER, G B
Lyttleton, Edith Joan
LANCASTER, Vicky
Ansle, Dorothy Phoebe
LANCE, Leslie
Swatridge, Irene M M
LANCE CORPORAL COBBER
Adcock, A St John
LANCER, Jack
Lawrence, James Duncan
LAND, Jane *and* Ross
Borland, Kathryn K *and*
Speicher, Helen Ross
LANDELS, D H
Henderson, Donald Landels
LANDELS, Stephanie
Henderson, Donald Landels
LANDER, Dane
Clarke, Percy A
LANDERS, Ann
Lederer, Esther Pauline
LANDESMAN, Jay
Landesman, Irving Ned
LANDGRAVE OF HESSE
Rosen, Michael
LANDIS, John
Bell, Gerard
LANDON, Louise
Hauck, Louise Platt

LANE, Carla
Barrett, Romana
LANE, Elizabeth
Farmers, Eileen Elizabeth
LANE, Grant
Fisher, Stephen Gould
LANE, Jane
Dakers, Elaine
LANE, Marvyn
Price, Jeremie
LANE, Mary D
Delaney, Mary Murray
LANG, Anthony
Vahey, John George
Haslette
LANG, Frances
Mantle, Winifred Langford
LANG, Grace
Floren, Lee
LANG, Theo
Langbehn, Theo
LANGART, Darrel T
Garrett, Randall
LANGDALE, Stanley
Moorhouse, Sydney
LANGDON, Mary
Pike, Mary Hayden
LANGE, John
Crichton, Michael
LANGFORD, Jane
Mantle, Winifred Langford
LANGLEY, Helen
Rowland, Donald Sydney
LANGLEY, John
Mason, Sydney Charles
LANGLEY, Lee
Langley, Sarah

235

LANGLEY, Peter
  Fleming, Ronald
LANGSTAFF, Tristram
  Lord, William Wilberforce
LANGWORTHY, Yolande
  Reade, *Mrs* Frances Lawson
LANIN, E B
  Dillon, E J
LANSBURY, Angela
  Sharot, Angela
LANSING, Henry
  Rowland, Donald Sydney
LANT, Harvey
  Rowland, Donald Sydney
LANZOL, Cesare
  Landells, Richard
LAREDO, Johnny
  Cesar, Gene
LARRIMORE, Lida
  Turner, Lida Larrimore
LARRY
  Parkes, Terence
LARSEN, Egon
  Lehrburger, Egon
LARSON, Eve
  St John, Wylly Folk
LASCELLES, Alison
  Parris, John
LATHAM, Mavis
  Thorpe-Clark, Mavis
LATHAM, Murray
  Latham, Alison *and*
  Latham, Esther
LATHAM, O'Neill
  O'Neill, Rose Cecil
LATHEN, Emma
  Latis, Mary J *and*
  Hennissart, Martha

LATHROP, Francis
  Leiber, Fritz
LATIMER, Rupert
  Mills, Algernon Victor
LAUDER, Afferbeck
  Morrison, Alistair
LAUDER, George Dick
  Dick-Lauder, *Sir* George
LAUGHLIN, P S
  Shea, Patrick
LAUNAY, André
  De Launay, André Joseph
LAUNAY, Droo
  De Launay, André Joseph
LAURA
  Hunter, Eileen
LAURENCE, Robert
  Fischer, Matthias Joseph
LAURIER, Don
  Sizer, Laurence
LAVINGTON, Hubert
  Carrington, Hereward
LAW, Marjorie J
  Liddelow, Marjorie Joan
LAWLESS, Anthony
  MacDonald, Philip
LAWRENCE, Bertram
  Bloxham, John Francis
LAWRENCE, Hilda
  Kronmiller, Hildegarde
LAWRENCE, Irene
  Marsh, John
LAWRENCE, James
  Tames, Richard Lawrence
LAWRENCE, Steven C
  Murphy, Lawrence D
LAWSON, Christine
  Walker, Emily Kathleen

LAWSON, Michael
  Ryder, M L
LAWTON, Dennis
  Faust, Frederick
LE BRETON, Thomas
  Ford, T Murray
LE CARRÉ, John
  Cornwell, David John
  Moore
LE GRAND
  Henderson, Le Grand
LE GRYS, Walter
  Norgate, Walter
LEA, Timothy
  Wood, Christopher
LEACROFT, Eric
  Young, Eric Brett
LEADER, Charles
  Smith, Robert Charles
LEADERMAN, George
  Robinson, Richard Blundell
LEAR, Peter
  Lovesey, Peter
LEDGARD, Jake
  Mason, Sydney Charles
LEE, Andrew
  Auchincloss, Louis
LEE, Babs
  Lee, Marion Van Der Veer
LEE, Charles H
  Story, Rosamond Mary
LEE, David
  Rush, Noel
LEE, Edward
  Fouts, Edward Lee
LEE, Elsie
  Sheridan, Elsie Lee

LEE, Gypsy Rose
  Hovick, Rose Louise
LEE, Jae Gardiner
  Lee, Polly Jae
LEE, Jesse
  Mason, Sydney Charles
LEE, Ranger
  Snow, Charles Horace
LEE, Rowena
  Bartlett, Marie
LEE, Steve
  Parry, Michel
LEE, Vernon
  Paget, Violet
LEE, Veronica
  Woodford, Irene-Cecile
LEE, William
  Burroughs, William
LEES, Hannah
  Fetter, Elizabeth
LEES, Marguerite
  Baumann, Margaret
LEGMAN, G
  Legman, George Alexander
LEIGH, Johanna
  Sayers, Dorothy L
LEIGH, Olivia
  Clamp, Helen M E
LEIGH, Ursula
  Gwynn, Ursula Grace
LEIGHTON, Lee
  Overholser, Wayne D
LEINSTER, Murray
  Jenkins, William Fitzgerald
LEJEUNE, Anthony
  Thompson, Edward Anthony
LEMON, Grey
  Gray, Lindsay Russell Nixon

237

LENANTON, C
  Lananton, *Lady*
LENGEL, Frances
  Trocchi, Alexander
LENTON, Anthony
  Nuttall, Anthony
LEO, Alan
  Allan, Frederick William
LEODHAS, Sorche Nic
  Alger, Leclaire Gowans
LEONA
  Button, Margaret
LEONARD, Charles L
  Heberden, Mary Violet
LEONID
  Bosworth, Willan George
LESBIA
  Lewis, Lydia T
LESIEG, Theo
  Geisel, Theodor Seuss
LESLEY, J P
  Lesley, Peter
LESLIE, A
  Scott, Leslie
LESLIE, A Scott
  Scott, Leslie
LESLIE, Colin
  Roome, Gerald Antony
LESLIE, Doris
  Fergusson Hannay, *Lady*
LESLIE, Henrietta
  Schütze, Gladys Henrietta
LESLIE, O H
  Slesar, Henry
LESLIE, Val
  Knights, Leslie
LESS, Milton
  Marlowe, Stephen

LESSER, Anthony
  Whitby, Anthony Charles
LESTER, Frank
  Usher, Frank Hugh
LESTER, Jane
  Walker, Emily Kathleen
LESTER-RANDS, A
  Judd, Frederick
L'ESTRANGE, Anna
  Ellerbeck, Rosemary
LETHBRIDGE, Olive
  Banbury, Olive Lethbridge
LETHBRIDGE, Rex
  Meyers, Roy
LEVINREW, Will
  Levine, William
LEWIS, Ernest
  Vesey, Ernest Blakeman
LEWIS, Francine
  Wells, Helen
LEWIS, Lange
  Beynon, Jane
LEWIS, Mervyn
  Frewer, Glyn
LEWIS, Paul
  Gerson, Noel Bertram
LEWIS, Roger
  Zarchy, Harry
LEWIS, Roy
  Lewis, J R
LEWIS, Voltaire
  Ritchie, L Edwin
LIDDELL, C H
  Kuttner, Henry
LIGGETT, Hunter
  Paine, Lauran Bosworth

238

LIMNELIUS, George
  Robinson, Lewis George
LINCOLN, Geoffrey
  Mortimer, John
LINCOLN, John
  Cardif, Maurice
LIND, Jakov
  Landwirth, Heinz
LINDALL, Edward
  Smith, Edward Ernest
LINDLEY, Erica
  Quigley, Aileen
LINDLEY, Gerard
  Pilley, Phil
LINDSAY, H
  Hudson, H Lindsay
LINDSAY, Josephine
  Story, Rosamond Mary
LINDSAY, Lee
  Barre, Jean
LINDSEY, John
  Muriel, John
LINESMAN
  Grant, M H
LINKLATER, Lane
  Watkins, Alex
LINSON
  Tomlinson, Joshua Leonard
LINTER, Lavender
  Alexander, John McKnight
LIPSTICK
  Long, Lois
LISLE, Mary
  Cornish, Doris Mary
LISTER, Richard
  Worsley, T C

LITTLE, Conyth
  Little, Gwenyth *and*
  Little, Constance
LITTLE, Sylvia
  Leyland, Eric
LITTLEJOHN, Jon R
  Kleinhaus, Theodore John
LIVINGSTON, Kenneth
  Stewart, Kenneth Livingston
LIVINGSTONE, Margaret
  Flynn, Mary
LLEWELLYN
  Lucas, Beryl Llewellyn
LLEWELLYN, Richard
  Lloyd, Richard Dafydd Vivian
  Llewellyn
LLEWMYS, Weston
  Pound, Ezra
LLOYD, Charles
  Birkin, Charles
LLOYD, John
  Cooper, John
LLOYD, Joseph M
  Purves, Frederick
LLOYD, Wallace
  Algie, James
LLOYD, Willson
  Dennison, Enid
LOCHIONS, Colin
  Jackson, Caary Paul
LOCKE, Martin
  Duncan, William Murdoch
LODER, Vernon
  Vahey, John George Haslette
LODGE, John
  Leyland, Eric
LOEWENTHAL, Karen
  Tripp, Kathleen

LOGAN, Agnes
  Adams, Agnes
LOGAN, Mark
  Nicole, Christopher
LOGROLLER
  Le Gallienne, Richard
LOMAX, Bliss
  Drago, Harry Sinclair
LOMAX, Jeff
  Mason, Sydney Charles
LOMBARD, Nap
  Johnson, Pamela Hansford *and*
  Stewart, Neil
LONDON, Anne
  Gordon, Robert I
LONDON, Robert
  Gordon, Robert I
LONG, Gerry
  Larkins, William
LONG, Myles
  Flanagan, James
LONG, Peter
  Fowler, Gene
LONG, Shirley
  Long, Leonard
LONGBAUGH, Harry
  Goldman, William
LONGCLOTHES, Ninon de
  Haig, Emily Alice
LONGFIELD, Jo
  Howard, Felicity
LONGLEY, John
  Denton, John
LONSDALE, Frederick
  Leonard, Lionel Frederick
LORAC, E C R
  Rivett, Edith Caroline

LORAINE, Philip
  Estridge, Robin
LORD, Douglas
  Lord, Doreen Mildred Douglas
LORD, Jeremy
  Redman, Ben Ray
LORD, Nancy
  Titus, Eve
LORING, Peter
  Shellabarger, Samuel
LORNA
  Stoddart, Jane T
LORNE, Charles
  Brand, Charles Neville
LORRAINE, Anne
  Chisholm, Lilian
LOVE, Arthur
  Liebers, Arthur
LOVE, David
  Lasky, Jesse L
LOVECRAFT, Linda
  Parry, Michel
LOVEGOOD, John
  Watson, Elliot Grant
LOVEHILL, C B
  Nutt, Charles
LOVELACE, Linda
  Boreman, Linda
LOVELL, Ingraham
  Bacon, Josephine Dodge
LOW, Dorothy Mackie
  Paxton, Lois
LOW, Rachel
  Whear, Rachel
LOWE, Edith
  Kovar, Edith May
LOWE, Kenneth
  Lobaugh, Elma K

LOWELL, Elaine
  Covert, Alice Lent
LOWELL, J R
  Lowell, Jan *and*
  Lowell, Robert
LOWING, Anne
  Wilson, Christine
LOWNDES, George
  Dawson, William Henry
LOWNDES, Susan
  Marques, Susan Lowndes
LOXMITH, John
  Brunner, John
LUARD, L
  Luard, William Blaine
LUCAS, J K
  Paine, Lauran Bosworth
LUCAS, Victoria
  Plath, Sylvia
LUCIO
  Phillips, Gordon
LUCKLESS, John
  Irving, Clifford
LUDLOW, George
  Kay, Ernest
LUDLOW, Geoffrey
  Meynell, Laurence Walter
LUDLOW, John
  Palmer, Cecil
LUDWELL, Bernice
  Stokes, Manning Lee
LUELLEN, Valentina
  Polley, Judith Anne
LUIMARDEL
  Martinez-Delgado, Luis
LUK, Charles
  Lu Kuan Yu

LUM, Peter
  Crowe, *Lady* (Bettina)
LUMMINS
  Melling, Leonard
LUNCHBASKET, Roger
  Reeve-Jones, Alan
LUSKA, Sidney
  Harland, Henry
LYALL, David
  Swan, Annie S
LYALL, Edna
  Bayly, Ada Ellen
LYDECKER, J J
  Dudley, Ernest
LYMINGTON, John
  Chance, John Newton
LYNCH, Eric
  Bingley, David Ernest
LYNCH, Frances
  Compton, D G
LYNCH, Lawrence L
  Van Deventer, Emma M
LYNDALE, Sydney M
  Moorhouse, Sydney
LYNDE, J H
  Huntington, Helen
LYNDON, Barrie
  Edgar, Alfred
LYNN, Carol
  Goetcheus, Carolyn
LYNN, Irene
  Rowland, Donald Sydney
LYNN, Margaret
  Battye, Gladys
LYNN, Stephen
  Bradbury, Parnell
LYNTON, Ann
  Rayner, Claire

241

LYON, Buck
  Paine, Lauran Bosworth
LYON, Elinor
  Wright, Elinor
LYON, Jessica
  De Leeuw, Cateau W
LYRE, Pinchbeck
  Sassoon, Siegfried
LYTE, Richard
  Whelpton, Eric
LYTTON, Jane
  Clarke, Percy A

§ §

*'But still it would be a confusion',
Berenice insisted. 'Suppose we
all suddenly change to entirely
different names. Nobody would
ever know who anybody was
talking about.'
—Carson McCullers. The
member of the wedding*

§ §

M
  Milner, Alfred, *Viscount
    Milner*
M B
  Faust, Frederick
M B OXON
  Wallace, Lewis Alexander
M E S
  Searle, M E
M R J
  James, Montague Rhodes

MABLE, Peter
  Wiedenbeck, Emilie Agnes
MACADAM, Eve
  Leslie, Cecilie
McALPIN, Grant
  McCulley, Johnston
MACALPIN, Rory
  Mackinnon, Charles Roy
MACANDREW, Rennie
  Elliot, Andrew George
McARTHUR, John
  Wise, Arthur
McBAIN, Ed
  Lombino, Salvatore A
MACBRIDE, Aeneas
  MacKay, Fulton
McCABE, Cameron
  Borneman, Ernest
McCABE, Rory
  Greenwood, T E
McCALL, Anthony
  Kane, Henry
McCALL, Isabel
  Boyd, Elizabeth Orr
McCALL, Vincent
  Morland, Nigel
McCANN, Edson
  Del Rey, Lester *and*
  Pohl, Frederik
McCARY, Reed
  Rydberg, Ernie
McCLEAN, Kathleen
  Hale, Kathleen
McCONNELL, Will
  Snodgrass, W D
McCORD, Whip
  Norwood, Victor George
    Charles

McCORMACK, Charlotte
 Ross, William Edward Daniel
McCORMICK, Theodora
 Du Bois, Theodora
McCOY, Hank
 Martin, Reginald Alec
McCOY, Malachy
 Caulfield, Max
McCOY, Marshall
 Meares, Leonard F
McCREADY, Jack
 Powell, Talmage
MACCREIGH, James
 Pohl, Frederik
MACDIARMID, Hugh
 Grieve, Christopher Murray
MACDONALD, Anson
 Heinlein, Robert A
MACDONALD, Jo
 Macdonald, Margaret
 Josephine
MACDONALD, John
 Millar, Kenneth
MACDONALD, John Ross
 Millar, Kenneth
MACDONALD, Marcia
 Hill, Grace
MACDONALD, Ross
 Millar, Kenneth
MACDOUALL, Robertson
 Mair, George Brown
MACDOWELL, Frederics
 Frede, Richard
MACDUFF, Ilka
 List, Ilka Katherine
MACE, Margaret
 Lawrence, Dulcie

MACEY, Carn
 Barrett, Geofrey John
MACFARLAND, Anne
 MacDonald, Susanne
MACFARLANE, Kenneth
 Walker, Kenneth Macfarlane
MACFARLANE, Stephen
 Cross, John Keir
McGAVIN, Moyra
 Crichton, Eleanor
McGAW, J M
 Morris, John
McGILL, Ian
 Allegro, John Marco
McGREW, Fenn
 McGrew, Julia *and*
 Fenn, Caroline K
McGUINNESS, Brian
 McGuinness, Bernard
MACGUIRE, Nicolas
 Melides, Nicholas
McGURK, Slater
 Roth, Arthur
MACHLIS, Joseph
 Selcamm, George
McHUGH, Stuart
 Rowland, Donald Sydney
McINTOSH, Ann T
 Higginbotham, Anne D
McINTOSH, J T
 Macgregor, James Murdoch
MACK, Evalina
 McNamara, Lena
McKENZIE, Paige
 Blood, Marje
McKENNA, Evelyn
 Joscelyn, Archie Lynn

McKERN, Pat
  Willett, Franciscus
MACKIE, Alice
  Cummins, Mary Warmington
MACKIN, Anita
  Donson, Cyril
McKINLEY, Karen
  Runbeck, Margaret Lee
MACLAREN, Ian
  Watson, John
MACLEAN, Art
  Shirreffs, Gordon D
MACLEAN, Barry
  Chosack, Cyril
MACLEAN, Christina
  Casement, Christina
McLEISH, Dougal
  Goodspeed, D J
MACLEOD, Finlay
  Wood, James
MACLEOD, Fiona
  Sharp, William
MACLEODHAS, Sorche
  Alger, Leclaire Gowans
McLOWERY, Frank
  Keevill, Henry John
McMASTER, Alison
  Baker, Marjorie
McMEEKIN, Clark
  Clark, Dorothy *and*
    McMeekin, Isabel
McMUD, Dok
  McLachlan, Dan
MACNAMARA, Brinsley
  Weldon, A E
MACNEIL, Duncan
  McCutchan, Philip D

MACNEIL, Neil
  Ballard, Willis Todhunter
McNEILL, Janet
  Alexander, Janet
MACNELL, James
  MacDonnell, James Edmond
MACNIB
  Mackie, Albert David
McNUTT, Charles
  Nutt, Charles
MACOMBER, Daria
  Stevenson, Ferdinan *and*
    Robinson, Patricia
MACQUEEN, Jay
  Minto, Mary
MACRAE, Hawk
  Barker, Albert H
MACRAE, Mason
  Rubel, James Lyon
MACRAE, Travis
  Feagles, Anita MacRae
MACTYRE, Paul
  Adam, Robin
MACUMBER, Mari
  Sandoz, Mari
MADDERN, Stan
  Mason, Sydney Charles
MADDOX, Carl
  Tubb, E C
MADEOC
  Robinson, H
MADGETT, Naomi Long
  Andrews, Naomi Cornelia
MADISON, Dolly
  Paul, Maury
MADISON, Hank
  Rowland, Donald Sydney

MAGENHEIMER, Kay
  Magenheimer, Cathryn Cecile
MAGILL, Marcus
  Hill, Brian
MAGNUS, Gerald
  Bowman, Gerald
MAGRISKA, Hélène *Countess*
  Brockies, Enid Florence
MAINE, Charles Eric
  McIlwain, David
MAINE, Stirling
  Mason, Sydney Charles
MAINSAIL
  Duff, Douglas Valder
MAIR, H Allen
  Murray, Francis Edwin
MAIZEL, Leah
  Maizel, Clarice Louise
MAIZIE
  Rose, Mary H
MALCOLM, Charles
  Hincks, Cyril Malcolm
MALCOLM, John
  Batt, Malcolm John
MALCOLM, John
  Uren, Malcolm
MALCOLM, Ronald
  Hincks, Cyril Malcolm
MALCOLM X
  Little, Malcolm
MALET, Lucas
  Kingsley, Mary
MALET, Oriel
  Vaughan, *Lady* Auriel
MALLERY, Amos
  Gelb, Norman
MALLOCH, Peter
  Duncan, William Murdoch

MALLORY, Jay
  Carey, Joyce
MALLOWEN, Agatha Christie
  Christie, *Dame* Agatha
MALONE, Louis
  MacNeice, Louis
MANDEVILLE, D E
  Coates, Anthony
MANN, Abel
  Creasey, John
MANN, Deborah
  Bloom, Ursula
MANN, Jack
  Vivian, Evelyn Charles H
MANN, John
  Stevens, Henry Charles
MANN, Josephine
  Pullein-Thompson, Josephine
  Mary
MANN, Patricia
  Earnshaw, Patricia
MANN, Patrick
  Waller, Leslie
MANN, Stanley
  Mason, Sydney Charles
MANNERS, Julia
  Greenaway, Gladys
MANNGIAN, Peter
  Monger, Ifor
MANNING, David
  Faust, Frederick
MANNING, Lee
  Stokes, Manning Lee
MANNING, Marsha
  Grimstead, Hettie
MANNING, Roy
  Reach, James

MANNINGHAM, Basil
  Homersham, Basil Henry
MANNOCK, Jennifer
  Mannock, Laura
MANNON, M M
  Mannon, Martha *and*
  Mannon, Mary Ellen
MANOR, Jason
  Hall, Oakley Maxwell
MANSBRIDGE, Pamela
  Course, Pamela
MANSELL, C R
  Payne, Eileen Mary
MANSFIELD, Katherine
  Beauchamp, Kathleen
  Mansfield
MANTON, Jo
  Gittings, Jo
MANTON, Paul
  Walker, Peter Norman
MANTON, Peter
  Creasey, John
MANVILLE, George
  Fenn, George Manville
MAO
  Addis, Hazel Iris
MAPLESDEN, Ray
  Pearce, Raymond
MARA, Thalia
  Mahoney, Elizabeth
MARCH, Emma
  Stubbs, Jean
MARCH, Hilary
  Green, Lalage Isobel
MARCH, Jermyn
  Webb, Dorothy Anna
MARCH, Stella
  Marshall, Marjorie

MARCH, William
  Campbell, William Edward
  March
MARCHANT, Catherine
  Cookson, Catherine
MARCHBANKS, Samuel
  Davies, Robertson
MARCO
  Mountbatten, *Lord* Louis
MARCUS AURELIUS
  Padley, Walter
MARDLE, Jonathan
  Fowler, Eric
MARGARET
  Kent, Ellen Louisa Margaret
MARGERISON, David
  Davies, David Margerison
MARIA, Hermann Karl Georg
  Jesus
  Pound, Ezra
MARIANA
  Foster, Marian Curtis
MARICHAUD, Alphonse
  Wilson, Florence Roma Muir
MARIN, A C
  Coppel, Alfred
MARIN, Alfred
  Coppel, Alfred
MARINER, David
  Macleod-Smith, D
MARION, S T
  Lakritz, Esther
MARJORAM, J
  Mottram, Ralph Hale
MARK, David
  Buitenkant, Nathan
MARK, Edwina
  Fadiman, Edwin J

MARK, Matthew
  Babcock, Frederic
MARKANDAYA, Kamala
  Taylor, Kamala
MARKER, Clare
  Witcombe, Rick
MARKHAM, Robert
  Amis, Kingsley
MARKWELL, Mary
  Hayes, Catherine E Simpson
MARLE, T B
  Lambert, Hubert Steel
MARLIN, Roy
  Ashmore, Basil
MARLOW, Joyce
  Connor, Joyce Mary
MARLOW, Louis
  Wilkinson, Louis Umfreville
MARLOW, Phyllis
  Mason, Sydney Charles
MARLOWE, Hugh
  Patterson, Henry
MARLOWE, Piers
  Gribble, Leonard Reginald
MARLOWE, Stephen
  Lesser, Milton
MARNEY, Suzanne
  Johnston, Mabel Annesley
MARO, Judith
  Jones, Judith Anastasia
MARQUIS, Don
  Perry, Robert
MARR, Nancy J
  Johnson, Nancy Marr
MARRIC, J J
  Butler, William Vivian
    ('writing as')

MARRIC, J J
  Creasey, John
MARRIOT, John
  Elliot, Christopher
MARSDEN, Anthony
  Sutton, Graham
MARSDEN, James
  Creasey, John
MARSDEN, June
  Ingram-Moore, Erica
MARSH, Henry
  Saklatvala, Beram
MARSH, J E
  Marshall, Evelyn
MARSH, Jean
  Marshall, Evelyn
MARSH, Joan
  Marsh, John
MARSH, Patrick
  Hiscock, Leslie
MARSH, Rebecca
  Neubauer, William Arthur
MARSHAL, James
  Bounds, Sydney J
MARSHALL, Archibald
  Marshall, Arthur Hammond
MARSHALL, Beverley
  Holroyd, Ethel Mary
MARSHALL, Douglas
  McClintock, Marshall
MARSHALL, Gary
  Snow, Charles Horace
MARSHALL, James Vance
  Payne, Donald Gordon
MARSHALL, Joanne
  Rundle, Anne
MARSHALL, Joseph
  Krechniak, Joseph Marshall

247

MARSHALL, Lloyd
  Wilding, Philip
MARSHALL, Lovat
  Duncan, William Murdoch
MARSHALL, Raymond
  Raymond, Rene
MARSTEN, Richard
  Lombino, Salvatore A
MARTELL, James
  Bingley, David Ernest
MARTENS, Paul
  Southwold, Stephen
MARTIN, Abe
  Hubbard, Frank McKinney
MARTIN, Ann
  Best, Carol Ann
MARTIN, Anthony
  Zehnder, Meinrad
MARTIN, Bruce
  Paine, Lauran Bosworth
MARTIN, Christopher
  Hoyt, Edwin Palmer Jr
MARTIN, Chuck
  Martin, Charles Morris
MARTIN, Dorothea
  Hewitt, Kathleen Douglas
MARTIN, Frederick
  Stern, Frederick Martin
MARTIN, Gil
  Overy, Jillian P J
MARTIN, John
  Tatham, Laura
MARTIN, Nancy
  Salmon, Annie Elizabeth
MARTIN, Peter
  Chaundler, Christine
MARTIN, R J
  Mehta, Rustam

MARTIN, Rex
  Martin, Reginald Alec
MARTIN, Richard
  Creasey, John
MARTIN, Richard
  Harman, Richard
MARTIN, Robert
  Martin, Reginald Alec
MARTIN, Ruth
  Rayner, Claire
MARTIN, Scott
  Martin, Reginald Alec
MARTIN, Stella
  Heyer, Georgette
MARTIN, Tom
  Paine, Lauran Bosworth
MARTINDALE, Spencer
  Wolff, William
MARTINEZ, J D
  Parkhill, Forbes
MARTON, Francesca
  Bellasis, Margaret Rosa
MARTYN, Don
  Borbolla, Barbara
MARTYN, Henry
  Perry, Martin
MARTYN, Miles
  Elliott-Cannon, Arthur Elliott
MARTYN, Oliver
  White, Herbert Oliver
MARVEL, Holt
  Maschwitz, Eric
MARVEL, Ik
  Mitchell, Donald Grant
MARX, Magdeleine
  Paz, Magdeleine
MASON, Carl
  King, Albert

MASON, Chuck
  Rowland, Donald Sydney
MASON, Frank W
  Mason, F Van Wyck
MASON, Howard
  Ramage, Jennifer
MASON, Michael
  Smith, Edgar
MASON, Stuart
  Millard, Christopher S
MASON, Tally
  Derleth, August William
MASON, Tyler
  Mason, Madeline
MASS, William
  Gibson, William
MASSARY, Isabel
  Ramsay-Laye, Elizabeth P
MASSEY, Charlotte
  Cabriani, Vincent
MASSON, Georgina
  Johnson, Marion
MASTERS, Robert V
  Boehm, David Alfred
MASTERS, Steve
  Mason, Sydney Charles
MASTERS, William
  Cousins, Margaret
MASTERSON, Whit
  Wade, Robert *and*
  Miller, William
MATELOT
  Uren, Malcolm
MATHER, Anne
  Grieveson, Mildred
MATHER, Berkely
  Davies, John Evan Weston

MATHER, Virginia
  Liebler, Jean Mayer
MATHESON, Hugh
  Mackay, Lewis
MATHESON, Sylvia A
  Schofield, Sylvia Anne
MATT
  Sandford, Matthew
MATTHESON, Rodney
  Creasey, John
MATTHEWS, Anthony
  Barker, Dudley
MATTHEWS, Brander
  Matthews, James Brander
MATTHEWS, Kevin
  Fox, Gardner F
MATUSOW, Marshall
  Matusow, Harvey Marshall
MAUGHAM, Robin
  Maugham, Robert Cecil Romer
  Viscount
MAURICE, Furnley
  Wilmot, Frank Leslie
  Thomson
MAURICE, Michael
  Skinner, Conrad Arthur
MAXINE
  Fortier, Cora B
MAXTON, Anne
  Best, Allena
MAXWELL, Ann
  Pattinson, Lee
MAXWELL, C Bede
  Maxwell, Violet S
MAXWELL, Clifford
  Leon, Henry Cecil
MAXWELL, Erica
  Pyke, Lillian Maxwell

MAXWELL, Peter
Cave, Peter
MAXWELL, Vicky
Worboys, Anne Ayre
MAY, Jonathan
Wood, Christopher
MAY, Roberta E
Davidson, Edith May
MAYBURY, Anne
Buxton, Anne
MAYHEW, Elizabeth
Bear, Joan E
MAYNE, Cora
Walker, Emily Kathleen
MAYNE, Rutherford
Waddell, Samuel
MAYNE, Xavier
Stevenson, Edward I P
MAYO, Arnold
Meredith, Kenneth Lincoln
MAYO, James
Coulter, Stephen
MAYRANT, Drayton
Simons, Katherine Drayton
Mayrant
MAZ
Mazure, Alfred Leonardus
MAZE, Edward
Mazzocco, Edward
MEADE, L T
Smith, Elizabeth Thomasina
Meade
MEADOWS, Peter
Lindsay, Jack
MEDHURST, Joan
Liverton, Joan
MEDICA
Malleson, Joan Graeme

MEDICUS
MacLaren, James Paterson
MEDILL, Robert
McBride, Robert Medill
MEE
Schube, Purcell G
MEE, Mary
Dean, Mary
MEIKLE, Clive
Brooks, Jeremy
MEINIKOFF, Pamela
Harris, Pamela
MELBOURNE, Ida
Ransome, L E
MELLOR, Michael
Spooner, Peter Alan
MELMOTH
Tullett, Denis John
MELVILLE, Alan
Caverhill, William Melville
MELVILLE, Jean
Cummins, Mary Warmington
MELVILLE, Jennie
Butler, Gwendolyn
MELVILLE, Lewis
Benjamin, Lewis S
MENANDER
Morgan, Charles
MENDEL, Jo
Bond, Gladys Baker
MENDEL, Jo
Gilbertson, Mildred
MENDL, Gladys
Schütze, Gladys Henrietta
MENTOR
Jones, Frank H
MERCER, Frances
Hills, Frances E

MERCURY
  Eames, Helen Mary
MEREDITH, Anne
  Malleson, Lucy
MEREDITH, David William
  Miers, Earl Schenk
MEREDITH, Hal
  Blyth, Harry
MEREDITH, Peter
  Worthington-Stuart, Brian Arthur
MERIVALE, Margaret
  Frost, Kathleen Margaret
MERLIN, David
  Moreau, David
MERLINI, The Great
  Rawson, Clayton
MERRICK, Hugh
  Meyer, Harold Albert
MERRICK, Spencer
  Mason, Sydney Charles
MERRIL, Judith
  Grossman, Judith
MERRILL, Lynne
  Gibbs, Norah
MERRILL, P J
  Roth, Holly
MERRIMAN, Chad
  Cheshire, Gifford Paul
MERRIMAN, Henry Seton
  Scott, Hugh Stowell
MERRITT, E B
  Waddington, Miriam
MERRIWELL, Frank
  Whitson, John Harvey
METCALF, Suzanne
  Baum, Lyman Frank
METHUEN, John
  Bell, John Keble

MEURON, Skip
  Sands, Leo G
MEWBURN, Martin
  Hitchin, Martin
MEYER, Henry J
  Hird, Neville
MEYER, June
  Jordan, June
MIALL, Robert
  Burke, John Frederick
MICHAEL, Manfred
  Winterfield, Henry
MICHAEL X
  De Freitas, Michael
MICHAELHOUSE, John
  McCulloch, Joseph
MICHAELS, Barbara
  Mertz, Barbara
MICHAELS, Steve
  Avallone, Michael Angelo Jr
MICHELMORE, Susan
  Harvey, Margaret Susan Janet
MIDLING, Perspicacity
  Millward, Pamela
MILBURN, Cynthia
  Brooks, Ann
MILECETE, Helen
  Jones, Susan Carleton
MILES
  Southwold, Stephen
MILES, David
  Cronin, Brendan Leo
MILES, John
  Bickham, Jack Miles
MILES, Miska
  Martin, Patricia Miles
MILES, Susan
  Roberts, Ursula

251

MILKY WHITE
  Emerson, Ernest
MILLBURN, Cynthia
  Brooks, Ann
MILLER, Ellen
  Pattinson, Lee
MILLER, Frank
  Loomis, Noel Miller
MILLER, Joaquin
  Miller, Cincinnatus H
MILLER, John
  Samachson, Joseph
MILLER, Marc
  Baker, Marcell Genée
MILLER, Margaret J
  Dale, Margaret
MILLER, Mary
  Northcott, Cecil
MILLER, Olive Thorne
  Miller, Harriet
MILLER, Patrick
  Macfarlane, George Gordon
MILLER, Wade
  Miller, William *and*
    Wade, Robert
MILLS, Alan
  Miller, Albert
MILLS, Martin
  Boyd, Martin à Beckett
MILLS, Osmington
  Brooks, Vivian Collin
MILNA, Bruno
  Painting, Norman
MILNE, Ewart
  Milne, Charles
MILNER, George
  Hardinge, George

MINGSTON, R Gresham
  Stamp, Roger
MINICAM
  Russell, Henry George
MINIER, Nelson
  Baker, Laura
MIRYAM
  Yardumian, Miryam
MISS READ
  Saint, Dora Jessie
MITCHAM, Gilroy
  Newton, William Simpson
MITCHELL, Ewan
  Janner, Greville
MITCHELL, K L
  Lamb, Elizabeth Searle
MITCHELL, Kerry
  Wilkes-Hunter, Richard
MITCHELL, Scott
  Godfrey, Lionel Robert
    Holcombe
MO, Manager
  Cassity, June
MODELL, Merriam
  Piper, Evelyn
MODERN JOB
  Taber, Clarence Wilbur
MOKO
  Mead, Sidney
MOLE, Oscar
  Seaver, Richard
MOLE, William
  Younger, William Anthony
MONETT, Lireve
  Worrell, Everill
MONIG, Christopher
  Crossen, Kendell Foster

MONKLAND, George
  Whittet, George Sorley
MONMOUTH, Jack
  Pember, William Leonard
MONNOW, Peter
  Croudace, Glyn
MONRO, Gavin
  Monro-Higgs, Gertrude
MONROE, Lyle
  Heinlein, Robert A
MONTAGU, Robert
  Hampden, John
MONTAUBON, G DE
  Greenough, William Parker
MONTGOMERY, Derek
  Simmons, J S A
MONTROSE
  Adams, Charles William
    Dunlop
MONTROSE, David
  Graham, Charles
MONTROSE, Graham
  Mackinnon, Charles Roy
MONTROSE, James St David
  Appleman, John Alan
MONTROSS, David
  Backus, Jean L
MOODIE, Edwin
  De Caire, Edwin
MOOLSON, Melusa
  Solomon, Samuel
MOORE, Arthur
  Matthews, Clayton
MOORE, Edward
  Muir, Edwin
MOORE, Frances Sarah
  Mack, Elsie Frances

MOORE, Rosalie
  Brown, Rosalie
MOORHOUSE, E Hallam
  Meynell, Esther H
MOORHOUSE, Hopkins
  Moorhouse, Herbert Joseph
MORDAUNT, Elinor
  Mordaunt, Evelyn May
MORE, Caroline
  Cone, Molly
MORE, Euston
  Bloomer, Arnold
MORE, J J
  Moffatt, James
MORECAMBE, Eric
  Bartholomew, John Eric
MORENO, Nick
  Deming, Richard
MORESBY, Louis
  Beck, Lily Adams
MORETON, John
  Cohen, Morton N
MORGAN, Angela
  Paine, Lauran Bosworth
MORGAN, Arlene
  Paine, Lauran Bosworth
MORGAN, Bryan
  Morgan, Brian Stanford
MORGAN, Carol McAfee
  Appleby, Carol McAfee
MORGAN, Claire
  Highsmith, Patricia
MORGAN, De Wolfe
  Williamson, Thames Ross
MORGAN, Frank
  Paine, Lauran Bosworth
MORGAN, John
  Paine, Lauran Bosworth

253

MORGAN, Michael
  Carle, C E *and*
  Dorn, Dean M
MORGAN, Phyllis
  Thompson, Phyllis
MORGAN, Scott
  Kuttner, Henry
MORGAN, Ted
  Gramont, Sanche de
MORGAN, Valerie
  Paine, Lauran Bosworth
MORISON, Elizabeth
  Moberly, Charlotte Anne
   Elizabeth
MORLAND, Peter Henry
  Faust, Frederick
MORNING, Alice
  Haig, Emily Alice
MORPHY, *Countess*
  Forbes, Marcelle Azra
MORRIS, Ira J
  Jefferies, Ira
MORRIS, John
  Hearne, John *and*
  Gargill, Morris
MORRIS, Julian
  West, Morris
MORRIS, Ruth
  Webb, Ruth Enid
MORRIS, Sara
  Burke, John Frederick
MORRISON, J Strang
  Thom, William Albert
   Strang
MORRISON, Peggy
  Morrison, Margaret Mackie
MORRISON, William
  Samachson, Joseph

MORROW, Betty
  Bacon, Elizabeth
MORROW, Charlotte
  Kirwan, Molly
MORTIMER, June
  Ryder, Vera
MORTIMER, Peter
  Roberts, Dorothy James
MORTON, Anthony
  Creasey, John
MORTON, Leah
  Stern, Elisabeth Gertrude
MORTON, William
  Ferguson, William Blair
   Morton
MOSES, Ruben
  Wurmbrand, Richard
MOSS, Nancy
  Moss, Robert Alfred
MOSS, Roberta
  Moss, Robert Alfred
MOSSMAN, Burt
  Keevill, Henry John
MOSSOP, Irene
  Swatridge, Irene M M
MOSTYN-OWEN, Gaia
  Servadio, Gaia
MOTTE, Nel
  Harrison, *Mrs* E E
MOTTE, Peter
  Harrison, Richard Motte
MOUTHPIECE
  Porter, Maurice
MOWBRAY, John
  Vahey, John George Haslette
MOWERY, Dorothy
  Dunsing, Dee

MOYES, Robin
  Bateman, Robert Moyes
MUIR, Alan
  Morrison, Thomas
MUIR, Dexter
  Gribble, Leonard Reginald
MUIR, Jane
  Petrone, Jane Gertrude
MUIR, John
  Morgan, Thomas Christopher
MUIR, Willa
  Muir, Wilhelmina Johnstone
MULDOON, Omar
  Matusow, Harvey Marshall
MULLER, Pauñ
  King, Albert
MULLINS, Ann
  Dally, Ann
MUN
  Leaf, Munro
MUNDY, Max
  Schofield, Sylvia Anne
MUNDY, V M
  Cunningham, Virginia Myra
    Mundy
MUNRO, C K
  Macmullan, Charles W
    Kirkpatrick
MUNRO, James
  Mitchell, James
MUNRO, Ronald Eadie
  Glen, Duncan Munro
MUNROE, R
  Cheyne, *Sir* Joseph
MUNTHE, Frances
  Minto, Frances

MURPHY, C L
  Murphy, Charlotte *and*
  Murphy, Lawrence
MURPHY, Louis J
  Hicks, Tyler Gregory
MURRAY, Cromwell
  Morgan, Murray C
MURRAY, Edna
  Rowland, Donald Sydney
MURRAY, Geraldine
  Murray, Blanche
MURRAY, Jill
  Walker, Emily Kathleen
MURRAY, Michael
  McLaren, Moray David
    Shaw
MURRAY, Sinclair
  Sullivan, Edward Alan
MURRAY, William
  Graydon, William Murray
MURRELL, Shirley
  Scott-Hansen, Olive
MURRY, Colin
  Murry, Colin Middleton
MYATT, Nellie
  Kirkham, Nellie
MYERS, Harriet Kathryn
  Whittington, Harry

N D H
  Dick-Hunter, Noel
N I
  Camm, Frederick James
N O B
  Bettany, F G
NA gCOPALEEN
  O'Nolan, Brian

255

NADA, John
  Langdon-Davies, John
NAMLEREP, Sidney
  Perelman, S J
NAPIER, Geraldine
  Glemser, Bernard
NAPIER, Mark
  Laffin, John
NASH, Chandler
  Hunt, Katherine Chandler
NASH, Daniel
  Loader, William
NASH, Newlyn
  Smithies, Muriel
NASH, Simon
  Chapman, Raymond
NAST, Elsa Ruth
  Werner, Elsa Jane
NATHAN, Daniel
  Dannay, Frederic
NAUTICUS
  Seaman, *Sir* Owen
NAYLOR, Eliot
  Frankau, Pamela
NEAL, Hilary
  Norton, Olive Marion
NEANISKOS
  Smithers, Leonard
NEBY, Al
  Johns, Walter T
NEIL, Frances
  Wilson, Christine
NELSON, Chris
  Huff, Darrell
NELSON, Gertrude
  Bobin, John W
NELSON, Lois
  Northam, Lois Edgell

NELSON, Marguerite
  Floren, Lee
NEMO
  Douglas, Archibald C
NEON
  Acworth, Marion W
NESBIT, E
  Bland, *Mrs* Edith (Nesbit)
NESBIT, Troy
  Folsom, Franklin Brewster
NESS, K T
  Grant, Donald *and*
  Wilson, William
NETTLETON, Arthur
  Gaunt, Arthur N
NEVILLE, C J
  Franklin, Cynthia
NEVILLE, Margot
  Goyder, Margot *and*
  Neville, Ann
NEVILLE, Mary
  Woodrich, Mary Neville
NEWCOMB, Norma
  Neubauer, William Arthur
NEWMAN, Ernest
  Roberts, E N
NEWMAN, Margaret
  Betteridge, Anne
NEWTON, David C
  Chance, John Newton
NEWTON, Francis
  Hobsbawm, E J
NEWTON, Macdonald
  Newton, William Simpson
NIALL, Ian
  McNeillie, John
NIALL, Michael
  Breslin, Howard

NICHOLAI, C L R
  Clair, Colin
NICHOLLS, Anthony
  Parsons, Anthony
NICHOLS, Fan
  Hanna, Frances
NICHOLS, Peter
  Youd, Samuel
NICHOLSON, John
  Parcell, Norman Howe
NICHOLSON, Kate
  Fay, Judith
NICKLEMANN, Henry
  Cather, Willa
NICODEMUS
  Pearce, Melville Chaning
NICOLAS, F R E
  Freeling, Nicholas
NIELSEN, Koef
  Koefed-Nielsen, Carl
NIELSON, Vernon
  Clarke, Percy A
NIELSON, Virginia
  McCall, Virginia
NIGHTINGALE, Charles
  Duddington, Charles Lionel
NILE, Dorothea
  Avallone, Michael Angelo Jr
NILSON, Bee
  Nilson, Annabel
NINA
  Nelson, Ethel
NITSUA, Benjamin
  Austin, Benjamin
NINESPOT
  Phillips, Hubert
NIXON, Kathleen
  Blundell, V R

NOBLE, Emily
  Gifford, James Noble
NOEL, John
  Bird, Dennis Leslie
NOEL, L
  Barker, Leonard Noël
NONG
  Lobley, Robert
NOON, T R
  Norton, Olive Marion
NOONE, Carl
  Chester, Charlie
NOONE, Edwina
  Avallone, Michael Angelo Jr
NORAH
  McDougall, Margaret
NORBURN, Martha
  Mead, Martha Norburn
NORDEN, Charles
  Durrell, Lawrence R
NORDICUS
  Snyder, Louis Leo
NORHAM, Gerald
  James, J W G
NORMAN, James
  Schmidt, James Norman
NORMAN, Louis
  Carman, Bliss
NORMYX
  Douglas, Norman *and*
    Fitzgibbon, Elsa
NORRIS, P E
  Cleary, C V H
NORTH, Andrew
  Norton, Alice Mary
NORTH, Colin
  Bingley, David Ernest

257

NORTH, Eric
  Cronin, Bernard
NORTH, Gil
  Horne, Geoffrey
NORTH, Howard
  Dudley-Smith, Trevor
NORTH, Mark
  Miller, Wright
NORTHE, Maggie
  Lee, Maureen
NORTHERNER
  Hughes, William
NORTHROP, *Capt* B A
  Hubbard, Lafayette Ronald
NORTHUMBRIAN GENTLEMAN
  Tegner, Henry
NORTON, André
  Norton, Alice Mary
NORTON, Bess
  Norton, Olive Marion
NORTON, Jed
  Lazenby, Norman
NORTON, S H
  Richardson, Mary Kathleen
NORTON, Victor
  Dalton, Gilbert
NORVELL, Anthony
  Trupo, Anthony
NORWAY, Kate
  Norton, Olive Marion
NORWOOD, Elliott
  Kensdale, W E N
NORWOOD, John
  Stark, Raymond
NOSTALGIA
  Bentley, James W B
NOTT, Barry
  Hurren, Bernard

NOVAK, Joseph
  Kosinski, Jerzy
NUDLEMAN, Nordyk
  Glassco, John
NUDNICK
  Nerney, Patrick W
NUNQUAM
  Blatchford, Robert
NURAINI
  Sim, Katharine Phyllis

§ §

*Cases of a man writing under a
woman's name are rare.*
*—Cassell's Encyclopaedia of
literature*

§ §

O P
  Eccleshare, Colin
O S
  Seaman, *Sir* Owen
OATES, Titus
  Bell, Martin
OBOLENSKY, Ilka
  List, Ilka Katherine
O'BRIAN, Frank
  Garfield, Brian
O'BRIEN, Bernadette
  Higgins, Margaret
O'BRIEN, Deirdre
  McNally, Mary Elizabeth
O'BRIEN, Flann
  O'Nolan, Brian
O'BRIEN, John
  Hartigan, Patrick Joseph

O'BRIEN, Richard C
  Conly, Robert Carroll
O'BYRNE, Dermot
  Bax, *Sir* Arnold
O'CATHASAIGH, P
  O'Casey, Sean
O'CONNELL, Robert Frank
  Gohm, Douglas Charles
O'CONNER, Clint
  Paine, Lauran Bosworth
O'CONNER, Elizabeth
  McNamara, Barbara Willard
O'CONNOR, Dermot
  Newman, Terence
O'CONNOR, Frank
  O'Donovan, Michael Francis
O'CONNOR, Patrick
  Wibberley, Leonard Patrick
    O'Connor
OCTAVIA
  Barltrop, Mabel
ODDIE, E M
  O'Donoghue, Elinor Mary
ODELL, Carol
  Foote, Carol
ODELL, Gill
  Foote, Carol *and* Gill, Travis
O'DONNELL, Donat
  O'Brien, Conor Cruise
O'DONNELL, K M
  Malzberg, Barry
O'DONNELL, Laurence
  Kuttner, Henry *and/or*
    Moore, C L
O'DONNEVAN, Finn
  Sheckley, Robert
O'FINN, Thaddeus
  McGloin, Joseph Thaddeus

OGDEN, Clint
  King, Albert
O'GRADA, Sean
  O'Grady, John
O'GRADY, Rohan
  Skinner, June O'Grady
O'GRADY, Tony
  Clemens, Brian
O'HARA, Kenneth
  Morris, Jean
O'HARA, Kevin
  Cumberland, Marten
O'HARA, Mary
  Sture-Vasa, Mary
O'HARRIS, Pixie
  Harris, Rona Olive
OKADA, Hideki
  Glassco, John
OKE, Richard
  Millett, Nigel
OKE, Simon
  Vann, Gerald
OLD COYOTE, Sally
  Old Coyote, Elnora A
OLDCASTLE, John
  Meynell, Wilfred
OLDFIELD, Peter
  Bartlett, Vernon
OLDHAM, Hugh R
  Whitford, Joan
OLGA
  Phillips, Olga
OLIVER, Frances
  Schneider, Monica Maria
OLIVER, Gail
  Scott, Marian Gallagher
OLIVER, Jane
  Rees, Helen

OLIVER, Laurence
  Brown, Laurence Oliver
OLIVER, Owen
  Flynn, *Sir* J A
OLIVER, Robert
  Carrier, Robert *and*
  Dick, Oliver Lawson
OLIVER, Roy
  Walker, Roy
OLIVIA
  Bussy, Dorothy
OLSEN, D B
  Hitchens, Dolores
OLSEN, Herb
  Olson, Herbert Vincent
OLYMPIC
  Hutton, Andrew Nielson
O'MALLEY, Frank
  O'Rourke, Frank
OMAN, Carola
  Lenanton, *Lady*
O'MARA, Jim
  Fluharty, Vernon
O'NAIR, Mairi
  Evans, Constance May
O'NEIL, Kerry
  MacIntyre, John Thomas
O'NEILL, Egan
  Linington, Elizabeth
ONIONS, Berta
  Oliver, Amy Roberta
ONIONS, Oliver
  Oliver, George
ONLOOKER
  Grant William
ONOTO WATANNA
  Reeve, Winifred Babcock

ONSLOW, Katherine
  Dennys, Elisabeth
OPHIEL
  Peach, Edward C
ORAGE, A R
  Orage, Alfred James
ORAM, John
  Thomas, John Oram
ORBISON, Keck
  Orbison, Roy *and*
  Keck, Maud
ORCHARD, Evelyn
  Swan, Annie S
ORDERLY SERGEANT, THE
  Murray, William Waldie
ORDON, A Lang
  Gordon, Alan Bacchus
ORIEL
  Sandes, John
O'RILEY, Warren
  Richardson, Gladwell
ORION
  Brooks, Ern
ORME, Alexandra
  Barcza, Alicja
ORME, Eve
  Williamson, Leila Isobel
ORMSBEE, David
  Longstreet, Stephen
ORR, Mary
  Caswell, Anne
ORTON, Joe
  Orton, John Kingsley
ORVIS, Kenneth
  Lemieux, Kenneth
ORWELL
  Smith, Walter Chalmers

ORWELL, George
  Blair, Eric
OSBORN, Reuben
  Osbert, Reuben
OSBORNE, David
  Silverberg, Robert
O'SHEA, Sean
  Tralins, S Robert
O'SULLIVAN, Seumas
  Starkey, James Sullivan
OSWALD, Sydney
  Lomer, Sydney Frederick
    McIllree
O'TOOLE, Rex
  Tralins, S Robert
OUIDA
  Ramé, Maria Louise
OUTLAW, THE
  L'Hotellier, Alf
OVERY, Claire May
  Bass, Clara May
OVERY, Martin
  Overy, Jillian P J
OWEN, Dean
  McGaughy, Dudley Dean
OWEN, Edmund
  Teller, Neville
OWEN, Hugh
  Faust, Frederick
OWEN, John Pickard
  Butler, Samuel
OWEN, Ray
  King, Albert
OWEN, Roderic
  Fenwick-Owen, Roderic
OWEN, Tom
  Watts, Peter Christopher

OXENHAM, Elsie Jeanette
  Dunkerley, Elsie Jeanette
OXENHAM, John
  Dunkerley, William Arthur
OYSTER, AN
  Boyes, W Watson
OYVED, Moysheh
  Good, Edward

P B
  Braybrooke, Patrick
P C
  Chalmers, Patrick
P C
  Jackson, Charles Philip Castle
    Kains
P O'D
  Donovan, Peter
PACKER, Vin
  Meaker, Marijane
PADESON, Mary
  Magraw, Beatrice
PADGETT, Lewis
  Kuttner, Henry *and/or*
    Moore, C L
PADMORE, George
  Nurse, Malcolm Ivan Meredith
PAGAN, Roberts
  Plomer, William
PAGE, Eileen
  Heal, Edith
PAGE, Eleanor
  Coerr, Eleanor Beatrice
PAGE, Lorna
  Rowland, Donald Sydney
PAGE, Marco
  Kurnitz, Harry

261

PAGE, Stanton
  Fuller, Henry B
PAGE, Vicki
  Avey, Ruby D
PAGET, John
  Aiken, John
PAIN, Barry
  Guthrie, P R
PALINURUS
  Connolly, Cyril
PALMER, Edgar A
  Posselt, Eric
PALMER, John
  Watts, Edgar John Palmer
PALMER, Lilli
  Peiser, Lilli
PAN
  Beresford, Leslie
PANBOURNE, Oliver
  Rockey, Howard
PANDORA
  Moore, Mary McLeod
PANLAKE, Richard
  Salmon, P R
PANTOPUCK
  Philpott, Alexis Robert
PARADISE, Mary
  Eden, Dorothy
PARIOS
  Lee, Henry David Cook
PARK, Jordan
  Kornbluth, Cyril M
PARKER, Leslie
  Thirkell, Angela
PARKER, Seth
  Lord, Phillips H

PARKES, Lucas
  Harris, John Wyndham Parkes
  Lucas Beynon
PARKES, Wyndham
  Harris, John Wyndham Parkes
  Lucas Beynon
PARKS, Ron
  Guariento, Ronald
PARR, *Dr* John Anthony
  Anthony, E
PARR, Robert
  Gardner, Erle Stanley
PARRISH, Jean J
  Church, Elsie
PARRISH, Mary
  Cousins, Margaret
PARSONS, Bridget
  Cox, Euphrasia Emeline
PARSONS, Paul
  Haslam, Nicky
PARTRIDGE, Anthony
  Oppenheim, E Phillips
PARTRIGE, Sydney
  Partridge, Kate Margaret
PASSMORE, Aileen E
  Griffiths, Aileen Esther
PASTOR FELIX
  Lockhart, Arthur John
PASTON, George
  Symonds, E M
PATER, Roger
  Hudleston, Gilbert Roger
PATIENT OBSERVER, The
  Strunsky, Simeon
PATRICK, Diana
  Wilson, Desemea
PATRICK, John
  Avallone, Michael Angelo *Jr*

PATRICK, John
 Goggan, John Patrick
PATRICK, Keats
 Karig, Walter
PATRICK, Q
 Wheeler, Hugh Callingham *and*
 Webb, Richard Wilson
PATROCLUS
 Lyall, James Robert
PATTEN, J
 Cobb, Clayton W
PATTERSON, Duke
 Leyland, Eric
PATTERSON, Harry
 Patterson, Henry
PATTERSON, Innis
 Patterson, Isabella Innis
PATTERSON, Olive
 Rowland, Donald Sydney
PATTERSON, Shott
 Renfrew, A
PAUL, Adrian
 McGeogh, Andrew
PAUL, Barbara
 Øvstedal, Barbara
PAUL, James
 Warburg, James Paul
PAUL, John
 Webb, Charles Henry
PAULSON, Jack
 Jackson, Caary Paul
PAVITRA
 Saint-Hilaire, P B
PAWNEE BILL
 Lillie, Gordon W
PAXTON, Lois
 Low, Lois

PAYE, Robert
 Campbell, Gabrielle Margaret
 Vere
PAYNE, Robert
 Payne, Pierre Stephen Robert
PEACE, Frank
 Cook, William Everett
PEACHUM, Thomas
 Oxman, Philip
PEARCE, A H
 Quibell, Agatha
PEARL, Irene
 Guyonvarch, Irene
PECKHAM, Richard
 Holden, Raymond
PEDRICK, Gale
 Pedrick-Harvey, Gale
PEEK, Bill
 Peed, William Bartlett
PEEL, Wallis
 Peel, Hazel
PEGDEN, Helen
 Macgregor, Miriam
PELHAM, Anthony
 Hope, Charles Evelyn
 Graham
PELHAM, Randolph
 Landells, Richard
PEMBROOKE, Kenneth
 Page, Gerald W
PENDER, Marilyn
 Jacobs, Thomas Curtis Hicks
PENDLETON, Conrad
 Kidd, Walter E
PENDLETON, Ford
 Cheshire, Gifford Paul
PENDOWER, Jacques
 Jacobs, Thomas Curtis Hicks

PENDRAGON, Eric
  Parry, Michel
PENGREEP, William
  Pearson, W T
PENMARE, William
  Nisot, Mavis Elizabeth
PENN, Ann
  Jacobs, Thomas Curtis Hicks
PENN, Arthur
  Matthews, James Brander
PENN, Christopher
  Lawlor, Patrick
PENN, Richard
  Sproat, Iain Macdonald
PENN, Ruth Bonn
  Rosenberg, Ethel
PENNAGE, E M
  Finkel, George
PENNY, Rupert
  Thornett, Ernest Basil
  Charles
PENT, Katherine
  Shann, Renée
PENTECOST, Hugh
  Philips, Judson Pentecost
PEPPER, Joan
  Alexander, Joan
PEPPERWOOD, Pip
  Stoddard, Charles Warren
PERCY, Edward
  Smith, Edward Percy
PERCY, Florence
  Akers, Elizabeth
PEREZ, Faustino
  Hoffenberg, Mason
PERKINS, Eli
  Landon, Melville de Lancy

PEROWNE, Barry
  Atkey, Philip
PERRY, Clay
  Perry, Clair Willard
PETERS, Alan
  Spooner, Peter Alan
PETERS, Bill
  McGivern, William Peter
PETERS, Bryan
  George, Peter
PETERS, Elizabeth
  Mertz, Barbara G
PETERS, Ellis
  Pargeter, Edith Mary
PETERS, Fritz
  Peters, Arthur A
PETERS, Geoffrey
  Palmer, Madelyn
PETERS, Geoffrey
  Trippe, Peter
PETERS, Jocelyn
  Oakeshott, Edna
PETERS, Lawrence
  Davies, Leslie Purnell
PETERS, Ludovic
  Brent, Peter Ludwig
PETERS, Maureen
  Black, Maureen
PETERS, Noel
  Harvey, Peter Noel
PETERS, Roy
  Nickson, Arthur
PETRIE, John
  Hewison, Robert John Petrie
PEYTON, K M
  Peyton, Kathleen Wendy *and*
  Peyton, Michael

PHEE, Hugh
  McPhee, Hugh
PHELIX
  Burnett, Hugh
PHILATICUS
  Finlay, Ian
PHILEBUS
  Barford, John Leslie
PHILIPPI, Mark
  Bender, Arnold
PHILIPS, Steve
  Whittington, Harry
PHILIPS, Thomas
  Davies, Leslie Purnell
PHILLIP, Alban M
  Allan, Philip Bertram Murray
PHILLIPS, John
  Marquand, John Phillips
PHILLIPS, King
  Perkins, Kenneth
PHILLIPS, Leon
  Gerson, Noël Bertram
PHILLIPS, Mark
  Garrett, Randall *and*
  Janifer, Laurence M
PHILLIPS, Michael
  Nutt, Charles
PHILMORE, R
  Howard, Herbert Edmund
PHIPPS, Margaret
  Tatham, Laura
PHIPSON, Joan
  Fitzhardinge, Joan Margaret
PHOENICE, J
  Hutchinson, Juliet Mary Fox
PICKARD, John Q
  Borg, Philip Anthony John

PICTON, Bernard
  Knight, Bernard
PIED PIPER, THE
  Mallalieu, J P W
PIERCE, Katherine
  St John, Wylly Folk
PIKE, Charles R
  Harknett, Terry
PIKE, Robert
  Fish, Robert Lloyd
PIKE, Robert L
  Fish, Robert Lloyd
PILGRIM
  Wright, Marjory Beatrice
PILGRIM, Adam
  Webster, Owen
PILGRIM, Anne
  Allan, Mabel Esther
PILGRIM, David
  Palmer, John Leslie *and*
  Saunders, Hilary Aidan
  St George
PILGRIM, Derral
  Coleman, John
PILIO, Gerone
  Whitfield, John
PINDELL, Jon
  Paine, Lauran Bosworth
PINDER, Chuck
  Donson, Cyril
PINE, M S
  Finn, *Sister* Mary Paulina
PINE, Theodore
  Petaja, Emil
PIPER, Evelyn
  Modell, Merriam
PIPER, Peter
  Langbehn, Theo

265

PIPER, Roger
  Fisher, John
PITCAIRN, Frank
  Cockburn, Claud
PITCHFORD, Harry Ronald
  Ebbs, Robert
PLAIDY, Jean
  Hibbert, Eleanor Alice Burford
PLAIN, Josephine
  Mitchell, Isabel
PLAUT, Martin
  Marttin, Paul
PLAYER, Robert
  Jordan, Robert Furneaux
PLEDGER, P J
  Tonkin, C B
PLOWMAN, Stephanie
  Dee, Stephanie
PLUMMER, Ben
  Bingley, David Ernest
POCRATES, *Dr* Hip
  Schoenfeld, Eugene L
POE, Bernard
  Hausman, Leon Augustus
POLLOCK, Mary
  Blyton, Enid
POLWARTH, G Marchant
  Polwarth, Gwendoline Mary
POMFRET, Joan
  Townsend, Joan
PONT
  Laidler, Graham
POOK, Peter
  Miller, J A
POOLE, Michael
  Poole, Reginald Heber
POOLE, Richard
  Wells, Lee Edwin

POOLE, Vivian
  Jaffe, Gabriel
POOTER
  Hamilton, Alex
POPULUS
  Cole, G(eorge) D(ouglas)
  H(oward)
PORLOCK, Martin
  MacDonald, Philip
PORTAL, Ellis
  Powe, Bruce
PORTER, Alvin
  Rowland, Donald Sydney
PORTOBELLO, Petronella
  Anderson, *Lady* Flavia
PORTRAB
  Bartrop, Edgar James
PORTSEA
  MacKenzie, *Sir* Edward
POTTER, Beatrix
  Heelis, Beatrix
POTTER, Margaret
  Betteridge, Anne
POWELL, Fern
  Samman, Fern
POWER, Cecil
  Allen, Grant
POWERS, Margaret
  Heal, Edith
POY
  Fearon, Percy
PRAIZE, Ann
  Blewitt, Dorothy
PREEDY, George
  Campbell, Gabrielle Margaret
  Vere

PREEDY, George R
   Campbell, Gabrielle Margaret
    Vere
PRENDER, Bart
   King, Albert
PRENTIS, Richard
   Agate, James
PRENTISS, Karl
   Purdy, Ken
PRESCOT, Julian
   Budd, John
PRESCOTT, Caleb
   Bingley, David Ernest
PRESCOTT, John
   Lucchetti, Anthony
PRESLAND, John
   Bendit, Gladys
PRESTON, Jack
   Buschlen, John Preston
PRESTON, James
   Unett, John
PRESTON, Jane
   Thomas, Reg
PRESTON, Richard
   Lindsay, Jack
PREVOST, Francis
   Prevost-Battersby, H F
PRICE, Evadne
   Smith, Helen Zenna
PRICE-BROWN
   Price-Brown, John
PRIESTLEY, Robert
   Wiggins, David
PRIESTLY, Mark
   Albert, Harold A
PRIMROSE, Jane
   Curry, Winifred J P

PRIVATE 19022
   Manning, Frederic
PROBERT, Lowri
   Jones, Robert Maynard
PROBYN, Elise
   McKibbon, John
PROCTER, Ida
   Harris, Ida Fraser
PROCTOR, Everitt
   Montgomery, Rutherford
    George
PROLE, Lozania
   Bloom, Ursula
PROUDFOOT, Walter
   Vahey, John George
    Haslette
PRUITT, Alan
   Rose, Alvin Emmanuel
PRUTKOV, Kozma
   Snodgrass, W D
PRYDE, Anthony
   Weekes, Agnes Russell
PULLING, Pierre
   Pulling, Albert Van Siclen
PULVERTAFT, Lalage
   Green, Lalage Isobel
PUNDIT, Ephraim
   Looker, Samuel Joseph
PURE, Simon
   Swinnerton, Frank
PUTNAM, Isra
   La Spina, Fanny Greye
    (Bragg)
PUTRA, Kerala
   Panikkar, Kavalam

Q
  Quiller-Couch, *Sir* Arthur
  Thomas
QUAD, M
  Lewis, Charles Bertrand
QUAESTOR
  Byford-Jones, Wilfred
QUARRY, Nick
  Albert, Marvin H
QUARTUS
  Hicks, E L *Bishop of*
  Lincoln
QUEEN, Ellery
  Dannay, Frederic *and*
  Lee, Manfred B
QUENTIN, Patrick
  Webb, Richard Wilson *and*
  Wheeler, Hugh Callingham
QUEX
  Nichols, *Captain* G H F
QUILIBET
  Fowler, Henry Watson
QUILL
  Puddepha, Derek
QUILLET
  Fowler, Henry Watson
QUIN, Dan
  Lewis, Alfred Henry
QUIN, Shirland
  Guest, Enid
QUINCE, Peter
  Day, George Harold
QUINCE, Peter
  Thompson, J W M
QUINLAN, William
  Lash, William Quinlan
QUIRK
  Squibbs, H W Q

QUIROULE, Pierre
  Sayer, Walter William
QUOD, John
  Irving, John Treat

§ §

No names, no pack-drill.
—British Army saying

§ §

R
  Colfer, Rebecca B
R D A
  Herbert, Robert Dudley
  Sidney Powys
R H C
  Orage, Alfred James
R H F
  Fairburn, R H
R H S
  Spring, Howard
R S
  Zinsser, Hans
R T L
  Vining, Charles A M
RACHEL
  Ferguson, Rachel
RACHEN, Kurt von
  Hubbard, Lafayette Ronald
RADIO PADRE
  Wright, Ronald Selby
RADYR, Tomos
  Stevenson, James Patrick
RAE, Doris
  Rae, Margaret Doris

RAE, Scott
  Hamilton, Cecily
RAESIDE, Jules
  Reside, W J
RAG MAN
  Burrows, Hermann
RAGGED STAFF
  Coley, Rex
RAILE, Arthur Lyon
  Warren, Edward Perry
RAIMOND, C E
  Robins, Elizabeth
RAINE, Richard
  Sawkins, Raymond Harold
RAKOSI, Carl
  Rawley, Callman
RALPH, Nathan
  Goldberg, Nathan Ralph
RALSTON, Jan
  Dunlop, Agnes M R
RAMAL, Walter
  De la Mare, Walter
RAME, David
  Divine, Arthur Durham
RAMEAUT, Maurice
  Marteau, F A
RAMPA, T Lobsang
  Hoskin, Cyril Henry
RAMSAY, Fay
  Eastwood, Helen
RAMSEY, Michael
  Green, T
RAN, Kip
  Randolph, Lowell King
RANA, J
  Bhatia, June

RAND, Brett
  Norwood, Victor George
  Charles
RAND, James S
  Attenborough, Bernard George
RAND, William
  Roos, William
RANDALL, Clay
  Adams, Clifton
RANDALL, Janet
  Young, Janet Randall
RANDALL, Robert
  Garrett, Randall and
  Silverberg, Robert
RANDALL, Rona
  Shambrook, Rona
RANDALL, William
  Gwinn, William R
RANDELL, Beverly
  Price, Beverly Joan
RANDOLPH, Ellen
  Ross, William Edward Daniel
RANDOLPH, Jane
  Ross, William Edward Daniel
RANDOM, Alan
  Kay, Ernest
RANDOM, Alex
  Rowland, Donald Sydney
RANGELY, E R
  Coleman, John
RANGELY, Olivia
  Coleman, John
RANGER, Ken
  Creasey, John
RANKINE, John
  Mason, Douglas Rankine
RANSOME, Barbara
  Ransome, L E

RANSOME, Stephen
  Davis, Frederick Clyde
RAPHAEL, Ellen
  Hartley, Ellen R
RASKIN, Ellen
  Flanagan, Ellen
RATH, E J
  Brainerd, Edith *and*
  Brainerd, J Chauncey
RATTRAY, Simon
  Dudley-Smith, Trevor
RAVENSCROFT, Rosanne
  Ravenscroft, John R
RAY, Nicholas
  Kienzle, Raymond N
RAYMOND, Mary
  Keegan, Mary Constance
RAYNER, Olive Pratt
  Allen, Grant
RAYNER, Richard
  McIlwain, David
RAYTER, Joe
  McChesney, Mary F
READ, Miss
  Saint, Dora Jessie
READE, Hamish
  Gray, Simon
READE, Rolf S
  Rose, Alfred
REDMAN, Joseph
  Pearce, Brian
REDMAYNE, Barbara
  Smithies, Muriel
REDWAY, Ralph
  Hamilton, Charles Harold
  St John

REDWOOD, Alec
  Milkomane, George Alexis
  Milkomanovich
REED, Cynthia
  Nolan, Cynthia
REED, Eliot
  Ambler, Eric *and*
  Rodda, Charles
REES, Dilwyn
  Daniel, Glyn Edmund
REES, J Larcombe
  Larcombe, Jennifer Geraldine
REEVE, Joel
  Cox, William Robert
REEVES, James
  Reeves, John Morris
REEVES, Joyce
  Gard, Joyce
REFUGITTA
  Harrison, Constance Cary
REGESTER, Seeley
  Victor, Metta Victoria Fuller
REID, Desmond
  Baker, William Howard
REID, Frank
  Vennard, Alexander Vindex
REID, Marshall
  McBride, Robert Medill
REID, Philip
  Ingrams, Richard *and*
  Osmond, Andrew
REID, Wallace Q
  Goodchild, George
REILLY, William K
  Creasey, John
REINER, Max
  Caldwell, Janet Taylor *and*
  Reback, Marcus

REJJE, E
  Hyde, Edmund Errol Claude
REMENHAM, John
  Vlasto, John Alexander
REMINGTON, Jemima
  Bevans, Florence Edith
REMINGTON, Mark
  Bingley, David Ernest
RENAR, Frank
  Fox, Frank
RENAULT, Mary
  Challans, Mary
RENIER, Elizabeth
  Baker, Betty
RENNIE, Jack
  Spooner, Peter Alan
RENO, Mark
  Keevill, Henry John
RENTON, Cam
  Armstrong, Richard
RENTON, Julia
  Cole, Margaret A
RENZELMAN, Marilyn
  Ferguson, Marilyn
REYNOLDS, Adrian
  Long, Amelia R
REYNOLDS, Dickson
  Reynolds, Helen Mary
    Greenwood Dickson
REYNOLDS, Jack
  Jones, Jack
REYNOLDS, John
  Fear, William H
REYNOLDS, Peter
  Long, Amelia R
RHODE, John
  Street, Cecil John Charles

RHOSCOMYL, Owen
  Vaughan, Owen
RICE, Craig
  Randolph, Georgiana Ann
RICH, Robert
  Trumbo, Dalton
RICHARDS, Clay
  Crossen, Kendell Foster
RICHARDS, Francis
  Lockridge, Frances Louise
    and Lockridge, Richard
RICHARDS, Frank
  Hamilton, Charles Harold
    St John
RICHARDS, Hilda
  Hamilton, Charles Harold
    St John
RICHARDS, Paul
  Buddee, Paul
RICHARDS, Peter
  Monger, Ifor
RICHARDS, Stella
  Starr, Richard
RICHARDSON, Henry Handel
  Richardson, Ethel Henrietta
RICHARDSON, Humphrey
  Gall, Michel
RICHES, Phyllis
  Sutton, Phyllis Mary
RICHMOND, Fiona
  Harrison, Julia
RICHMOND, Grace
  Marsh, John
RICHMOND, Mary
  Lindsay, Kathleen
RICKARD, Cole
  Barrett, Geoffrey John

271

RIDDELL, John
  Ford, Corey
RIDING, Laura
  Gottschalk, Laura Riding
RIFT, Valerie
  Bartlett, Marie
RIGHT CROSS
  Armstrong, Paul
RILEY, Tex
  Creasey, John
RIMMER, W J
  Rowland, Donald Sydney
RING, Adam
  Reed, Blair
RING, Basil
  Braun, Wilbur
RING, Douglas
  Prather, Richard S
RINGO, Johnny
  Keevill, Henry John
RINGOLD, Clay
  Hogan, Ray
RIORDAN, Dan
  Cooke, William Everett
RIPLEY, Alvin
  King, Albert
RIPLEY, Jack
  Wainwright, John
RIPOSTE, A
  Mordaunt, Evelyn May
RITA
  Humphreys, Eliza M J
RITCHIE, Claire
  Gibbs, Norah
RITSON, John
  Baber, Douglas
RIVERINA
  Winter, C H

RIVERS, Georgia
  Clark, Marjorie
RIVERS, Ronda
  Sveinsson, Solveig
RIVES, Amelia
  Troubetzkoi, *Princess*
RIX, Donna
  Rowland, Donald Sydney
RIXON, Annie
  Studdert, Annie
RIZA, Ali
  Orga, Irfan
ROADSTER
  Bays, J W
ROBB, John
  Robson, Norman
ROBBINS, Harold
  Rubins, Harold
ROBBINS, Tod
  Robbins, Clarence Aaron
ROBERTS, Dan
  Ross, William Edward
  Daniel
ROBERTS, David
  Cox, John
ROBERTS, Desmond
  Best, Rayleigh Breton Amis
ROBERTS, Ivor
  Roberts, Irene
ROBERTS, James Hall
  Duncan, Robert Lipscomb
ROBERTS, John
  Bingley, David Ernest
ROBERTS, Ken
  Lake, Kenneth Robert
ROBERTS, Lee
  Martin, Robert Lee

ROBERTS, Lionel
Fanthorpe, Robert Lionel
ROBERTS, McLean
Machlin, Milton
ROBERTSON, E Arnot
Robertson, Eileen Arbuthnot
ROBERTSON, Elspeth
Ellison, Joan
ROBERTSON, Helen
Edmiston, Helen J M
ROBERTSON, Muirhead
Johnson, H
ROBIN
Roberts, Eric
ROCHE, John
Le Roi, David de Roche
ROCK, Richard
Mainprize, Don
ROCKWELL, Matt
Rowland, Donald Sydney
ROCKWOOD, Harry
Young, Ernest A
RODD, Ralph
North, William
ROE, M S
Thomson, Daisy
ROE, Richard
Cowper, Francis
ROE, Tig
Roe, Eric
ROFFMAN, Jan
Summerton, Margaret
ROGERS, Anne
Seraillier, Anne
ROGERS, Floyd
Spence, William Duncan
ROGERS, Kerk
Knowlton, Edward Rogers

ROGERS, Phillips
Idell, Albert Edward
ROGERS, Rachel
Redmon, Lois
ROHMER, Sax
Ward, Arthur Sarsfield
ROLAND, John
Oliver, John Rathbone
ROLAND, Mary
Lewis, Mary Christianna
ROLAND, Nicholas
Walmsley, Arnold
ROLLS, Anthony
Vulliamy, Colwyn Edward
ROLPH, C H
Hewitt, Cecil Rolph
ROLYAT, Jane
McDougall, E Jean Taylor
ROMANY
Evens, George Bramwell
ROMLEY, Derek
Romley, Frederick J
ROMNEY, Brent
Larralde, Romulo
ROMNEY, Steve
Bingley, David Ernest
ROME, Anthony
Albert, Marvin H
ROME, Tony
Albert, Marvin H
RONALD, E B
Barker, Ronald Ernest
RONNS, Edward
Aarons, Edward Sidney
ROOKE, Dennis
Rotheray, Geoffrey Neville
ROOME, Holdar
Moore, Harold William

273

ROOS, Kelley
  Roos, William *and*
    Kelley, Audrey
ROOT, Henry
  Donaldson, William
ROSCOE, Charles
  Rowland, Donald Sydney
ROSCOE, Janet
  Prior, Mollie
ROSCOE, Mike
  Roscoe, John *and*
    Ruso, Michael
ROSE, Hilary
  Mackinnon, Charles Roy
ROSE, Phyllis
  Thompson, Phyllis
ROSE, Robert
  Rose, Ian
ROSENTHAL, Richard A
  Richards, Allen
ROSNA
  Rosman, Alice Grant
ROSS
  Martin, Violet Florence
ROSS, Adrian
  Ropes, Arthur
ROSS, Barnaby
  Dannay, Frederic *and*
    Lee, Manfred, B
ROSS, Clarissa
  Ross, William Edward Daniel
ROSS, Dan
  Ross, William Edward Daniel
ROSS, Dana
  Ross, William Edward Daniel
ROSS, Deborah
  Stoffer, Edith G

ROSS, Diana
  Denney, Diana
ROSS, Gene
  Newton, William
ROSS, George
  Ross, Isaac
ROSS, Ivan T
  Rossner, Robert
ROSS, J H
  Lawrence, T E
ROSS, Jean
  Hewson, Irene Dale
ROSS, John
  Winnington, Richard
ROSS, Jonathan
  Rossiter, John
ROSS, Katherine
  Walter, Dorothy Blake
ROSS, Leonard Q
  Rosten, Leo C
ROSS, Maggie
  Bermange, Maurine J L
ROSS, Marilyn
  Ross, William Edward Daniel
ROSS, Martin
  Martin, Violet Florence
ROSS, Michael D H
  Rosenthal, Michael D H
ROSS, Patricia
  Wood, Patricia E W
ROSS, Sutherland
  Callard, Thomas H
ROSS, W E D
  Ross, William Edward Daniel
ROSSITER, Jane
  Ross, William Edward Daniel
ROSTANT, Robert
  Hopkins, Robert Sydney

ROSTREVOR, George
  Hamilton, *Sir* George
  Rostrevor
ROSTRON, Primrose
  Hulbert, Joan
ROTHBERG, Winterset
  Roethke, Theodore
ROTHMAN, Judith
  Black, Maureen
ROTHWELL, Annie
  Christie, Annie Rothwell
ROUSSEAU, Victor
  Emanuel, Victor Rousseau
ROWANS, Virginia
  Tanner, Edward Everett
ROWE, Alice E
  Rowe, John Gabriel
ROWLAND, Iris
  Roberts, Irene
ROWLANDS, Effie Adelaide
  Albanesi, Effie Maria
ROWLANDS, Lesley
  Zuber, Mary E I
ROYAL, Dan
  Barrett, Geoffrey John
ROYCE, Kenneth
  Gandley, Kenneth Royce
RUBICON
  Lunn, *Sir* Arnold
RUCK, Berta
  Oliver, Amy Roberta
RUDD, Margaret
  Newlin, Margaret
RUDD, Steele
  Davis, Arthur Hoey
RUELL, Patrick
  Hill, Reginald

RUFFLES
  Tegner, Henry
RUNYON, Damon
  Runyan, Alfred Damon
RURIC, Peter
  Cain, Paul
RUSHTON, Charles
  Shortt, Charles Rushton
RUSSELL, Arthur
  Goode, Arthur Russell
RUSSELL, Erle
  Wilding, Philip
RUSSELL, Lindsay
  Stonehouse, Patricia Ethel
RUSSELL, Raymond
  Balfour, William
RUSSELL, Sarah
  Laski, Marghanita
RUSSELL, Shane
  Norwood, Victor George
  Charles
RUTHERFORD, Douglas
  McConnell, James Douglas
  Rutherford
RUTHERFORD, Mark
  White, William Hale
RUTLEDGE, Brett
  Paul, Elliot Harold
RYAN, J M
  McDermott, John Richard
RYBOT, Doris
  Pensonby, Doris Almon
RYDELL, Forbes
  Forbes, Deloris Stanton *and*
  Rydell, Helen
RYDER, James
  Pattinson, James

RYDER, Jonathan
   Ludlum, Robert
RYE, Anthony
   Youd, Samuel
RYLAND, Clive
   Priestley, Clive Ryland

§ §

I got an insurance card here.
Under the name of Jenkins.
See? Bernard Jenkins. Look.
It's got four stamps on it.
Four of them. But I can't
go along with these. That's
not my real name, they'd
find out, they'd have me
in the nick. I been going
around under an assumed
name.
—Harold Pinter. The caretaker

§ §

S, Elizabeth von
   Freeman, Gillian
S H S
   Spender, Stephen
S S
   Sassoon, Siegfried
S V F G
   Fitzgerald, Seymour Vesey
SABATTIS
   Gill, T M
SABBAH, Hassan i
   Butler, Bill
SABER, Robert O
   Ozaki, Milton K

276

SABIAD
   White, Stanhope
SABIN, Mark
   Fox, Norman Arnold
SABRE, Dirk
   Laffin, John
SABRETACHE
   Barrow, Albert Stewart
SACKERMAN, Henry
   Kahn, H S
SADBALLS, John
   Matusow, Harvey Marshall
SADDLER, K Allen
   Richards, Ronald C W
SAGITTARIUS
   Katzin, Olga
ST ANBECK, Roland
   Beck, Roland Stanley
ST CLAIR, Dester
   Winchell, Prentice
ST CLAIR, Everett
   Mansell, *Mrs* C B
ST CLAIR, Philip
   Howard, Munroe
ST CLAIRE, Yvonne
   Hall, Emma L
SAINT-EDEN, Dennis
   Foster, Donn
ST E A OF M AND S
   Crowley, Edward Alexander
ST EBBAR
   Rabbets, Thomas G
ST GEORGE, Arthur
   Paine, Lauran Bosworth
ST GEORGE, David
   Markov, Georgi *and*
    Phillips, David

ST GIRAUD
  Knott, William Cecil
ST JAMES, Andrew
  Stern, James
ST JOHN, Christopher
  Marshall, Christabel
ST JOHN, David
  Hunt, E Howard
ST JOHN, Philip
  Del Rey, Lester
SAINT-LUC, Jean de
  Glassco, John
ST MARS, F
  Atkins, Frank A
SAKI
  Munro, Hector Hugh
SALISBURY, John
  Caute, David
SALT, Jonathan
  Neville Derek
SALTAR THE MONGOL
  Williamson, Thames Ross
SALTEN, Felix
  Saltzmann, Sigmund
SALTER, Cedric
  Knight, Francis Edgar
SALTER, Mary D
  Ainsworth, Mary Dinsmore
SALTER AINSWORTH,
  Mary D
  Ainsworth, Mary Dinsmore
SAMPSON, Richard Henry
  Hull, Richard
SANBORN, B X
  Ballinger, William Sanborn
SANDERS, Brett
  Barrett, Geoffrey John

SANDERS, Bruce
  Gribble, Leonard Reginald
SANDERS, Daphne
  Randolph, Georgiana Ann
SANDERS, Dorothy Lucy
  Walker, Lucy
SANDERS, Jeanne
  Rundle, Anne
SANDERS, Winston P
  Anderson, Poul
SANDHURST, B G
  Green, Charles Henry
SANDS, Martin
  Burke, John Frederick
SANDYS, Oliver
  Evans, Marguerite Florence
SANTA MARIA
  Powell-Smith, Vincent
SANTEE, Walt
  King, Albert
SAPPER
  Fairlie, Gerard
SAPPER
  McNeile, H C
SARA
  Blake, Sally Mirliss
SARAC, Roger
  Caras, Roger
SARASIN, J G
  Salmon, Geraldine Gordon
SARBAN
  Wall, John W
SARGENT, Joan
  Jenkins, Sara Lucile
SARI
  Fleur, Anne Elizabeth
SARNE, Michael
  Plummer, Thomas Arthur

277

SARNIAN
  Falla, Frank
SASHUN, Sigma
  Sassoon, Sigfried
SAUER, Muriel S
  Stafford, Muriel
SAUNDERS, Abel
  Pound, Ezra
SAUNDERS, Anne
  Aldred, Margaret
SAUNDERS, Caleb
  Heinlein, Robert A
SAUNDERS, Carl McK
  Ketchum, Philip
SAUNDERS, Ione
  Cole, Margaret A
SAUNDERS, John
  Nickson, Arthur
SAUNDERS, Lawrence
  Davis, Burton *and*
  Davis, Clare Ogden
SAUNDERS, Marshall
  Saunders, Margaret Marshall
SAUNDERS, Wes
  Bounds, Sydney J
SAVA, George
  Milkomane, George Alexis
  Milkomanovich
SAVAGE, Leslie
  Duff, Douglas Valder
SAVAGE, Richard
  Roe, Ivan
SAVAGE, Steve
  Goodavage, Joseph F
SAWLEY, Petra
  Marsh, John
SAXON
  Matthews, Edith J

SAXON, John
  Gifford, James Noble
SAXON, John
  Rumbold-Gibbs, Henry
  St John C
SAXON, Peter
  Baker, William Howard
SAYRE, Gordon
  Woolfolk, Josiah Pitts
SCARLETT, Roger
  Blair, Dorothy *and*
  Page, Evelyn
SCARLETT, Susan
  Streatfeild, Noel
SCARLETT, Will
  Redman, William Xavier
SCHAW, Ruth
  Drummond, Alison
SCHWARTZ, Bruno
  Mann, George
SCIENCE INVESTIGATOR
  Speck, Gerald Eugene
SCIPIO
  Watson, Adam
SCOBEY, Marion
  Coombs, Joyce
SCOLLAN, E A
  O'Grady, Elizabeth Anne
SCOLOPAX
  Grant, Maurice Harold
SCORPIO
  Tucker, William Joseph
SCOT, Neil
  Grant, *Lady* Sybil
SCOTT, A
  Bloor, W A
SCOTT, Agnes Neill
  Muir, Wilhelmina Johnstone

SCOTT, Bradford
  Scott, Leslie
SCOTT, Bruce
  McCartney, R J
SCOTT, Casey
  Kubis, Patricia Lou
SCOTT, Catherine
  Ehrenberg, Golda
SCOTT, Dana
  Robertson, Constance Noyes
SCOTT, Denis
  Means, Mary *and*
    Saunders, Theodore
SCOTT, Douglas
  Thorpe, John
SCOTT, Elizabeth
  Capstick, Elizabeth
SCOTT, Grover
  King, Albert
SCOTT, Jack S
  Escott, Jack Leonard
SCOTT, Jane
  McElfresh, Adeline
SCOTT, John-Paul
  Farquhar, Jesse Carlton *Jr*
SCOTT, Norford
  Rowland, Donald Sydney
SCOTT, O R
  Gottliebsen, Ralph Joseph
SCOTT, Thurston
  Leite, George Thurston *and*
    Scott, Jody
SCOTT, Valerie
  Rowland, Donald Sydney
SCOTT, Warwick
  Dudley-Smith, Trevor
SCOTT, Will
  Scott, William Matthew

SCOTT-MORLEY, A
  Oakley, Eric Gilbert
SCROPE, Mason
  Mason, Arthur Charles
SCRUTATOR
  Sidebotham, Herbert
SEAFARER
  Barker, Clarence Hedley
SEAFORD, Caroline
  Cook, Marjorie Grant
SEAFORTH
  Foster, George Cecil
SEAFORTH
  Skues, George Edward
    Mackenzie
SEA-LION
  Bennett, Geoffrey Martin
SEAL, Basil
  Barnes, Julian
SEAMARK
  Small, Austin J
SEARCH-LIGHT
  Frank, Waldo David
SEARS, Deane
  Rywell, Martin
SEA-WRACK
  Crebbin, Edward Horace
SEBASTIAN, Lee
  Silverberg, Robert
SEC
  Manner, Marya
SECRIST, Kelliher
  Kelliher, Dan T *and*
    Secrist, W G
SEDGWICK, Modwena
  Glover, Modwena

SEEBLE
  Beresford, Claude R De La
  Poer
SEEKER, A
  Eagan, Frances W
SEFTON, Catherine
  Waddell, Martin
SEGUNDO, Bart
  Rowland, Donald Sydney
SEIFERT, Elizabeth
  Gasparotti, Elizabeth
SELDEN, George
  Thompson, George Selden
SELKIRK, Jane
  Chapman, Mary I *and*
  Chapman, John Stanton
SELL, Joseph
  Haley, W J
SELMARK, George
  Seldon Truss, Leslie
SENCOURT, Robert
  George, Robert Esmonde
  Gordon
SERAFIAN, Michael
  Martin, Malachi
SERANNE, Ann
  Smith, Margaret Ruth
SERANUS
  Harrison, Susie Frances
SERJEANT, Richard
  Van Essen, W
SERNICOLI, Davide
  Trent, Ann
SETH, Andrew
  Pattison, Andrew Seth P
SETON, Graham
  Hutchison, Graham Seton

SETOUN, Gabriel
  Hepburn, Thomas Nicoll
SEUFFERT, Muir
  Seuffert, Muriel
SEVERN, David
  Unwin, David Storr
SEVERN, Forepoint
  Bethell, Leonard Arthur
SEVERN, Richard
  Ebbs, Robert
SEWELL, Arthur
  Whitson, John Harvey
SEYMOUR, Henry
  Hartmann, Helmut Henry
SHALIMAR
  Hendry, Frank Coutts
SHALLOW, Robert
  Atkinson, Frank
SHAN
  McMordie, John Andrew
SHANE
  Richardson, Eileen
SHANE, John
  Durst, Paul
SHANE, Martin
  Johnston, George Henry
SHANE, Rhondo
  Norwood, Victor George Charles
SHANE, Susannah
  Ashbrook, Harriette Cora
SHANNON, Carl
  Hogue, Wilbur Owings
SHANNON, Dell
  Linington, Elizabeth
SHANNON, Monica
  Katchamakoff, Atanas
SHANWA
  Haarer, Alec Ernest

SHARMAN, Miriam
  Bolton, Miriam
SHARON, Rose
  Grossman, Judith
SHARP, Helen
  Paine, Lauran Bosworth
SHARP, Luke
  Barr, Robert
SHAUL, Frank
  Rowland, Donald Sydney
SHAW, Adelaide
  O'Shaughnessy, Marjorie
SHAW, Artie
  Arshavsky, Abraham Isaac
SHAW, Irene
  Roberts, Irene
SHAW, Jane
  Evans, Jean
SHAW, Jill A
  Keeling, Jill Annette
SHAW, Josephine
  Clarke, Dorothy Josephine
SHAW, T E
  Lawrence, T E
SHAYNE, Gordon
  Winter, Bevis
SHAYNE, Nina
  Gibbs, Norah
SHEARING, Joseph
  Campbell, Gabrielle Margaret
  Vere
SHELBY, Cole
  King, Albert
SHELDON, John
  Bloch, Robert
SHELDON, Raccoona
  Sheldon, Alice B

SHELLEY, Frances
  Wees, Frances Shelley
SHELLEY, Peter
  Dresser, Davis
SHELTON, Michael
  Stacey, P M de Cosqueville
SHEPARD, Fern
  Stonebraker, Florence
SHEPHERD, Joan
  Buchanan, B J
SHEPHERD, John
  Ballard, Willis Todhunter
SHEPHERD, Neal
  Morland, Nigel
SHERATON, Neil
  Smith, Norman Edward Mace
SHERMAN, George
  Moretti, Ugo
SHERRY, Gordon
  Sheridan, H B
SHIEL-MARTIN
  Old, Phyllis Muriel
  Elizabeth
SHIVAJI, Mahatma Guru Sri
  Paramahansa
  Crowley, Edward Alexander
SHONE, Patric
  Hanley, James
SHORE, Norman
  Smith, Norman Edward Mace
SHORE, Philippa
  Holbeche, Philippa
SHORT, Francis
  Harris, *Mrs* Herbert
SHORT, Luke
  Glidden, Frederick Dilley
SHOTT, Abel
  Ford, T W

SHROPSHIRE LAD
  Barber-Starkey, Roger
SHUTE, Nevil
  Norway, Nevil Shute
SHY, Timothy
  Wyndham Lewis, D B
SIBLEY, Lee
  Landells, Anne
SIDNEY, Margaret
  Lothrop, Harriet Mulford
SIDNEY, Neilma
  Gantner, Neilma B
SIGMA SASHUN
  Sassoon, Siegfried
SILLER, Van
  Van Siller, Hilda
SILURIENSIS, Leolinus
  Machen, Arthur
SILVER, Nicholas
  Faust, Frederick
SILVESTER, Frank
  Bingley, David Ernest
SIMA, Caris
  Mountcastle, Clara H
SIMMONDS, Mike
  Simmonds, Michael Charles
SIMMONS, Catherine
  Duncan, Kathleen
SIMMONS, Kim
  Duncan, Kathleen
SIMON
  Blakeston, Oswell *and*
  Burford, Roger d'Este
SIMON, Robert
  Musto, Barry
SIMON, S J
  Skidelsky, Simon Jasha

SIMONS, Peter
  Punnett, Margaret *and*
  Punnett, Ivor
SIMPLE, Peter
  Herbert, John; Hogg, Michael;
  Welch, Colin *and* Wharton,
  Michael
SIMPLEX, Simon
  Middleton, Henry Clement
SIMPSON, Warwick
  Ridge, William Pett
SIMS, John
  Hopson, William L
SIMS, *Lieut* A K
  Whitson, John Harvey
SINBAD
  Dingle, Aylward Edward
SINCLAIR, Jo
  Seid, Ruth
SINDERBY, Donald
  Stephens, Donald Ryder
SINGER, Bant
  Shaw, Charles
SINGER, Burns
  Singer, James Hyman
SINJOHN, John
  Galsworthy, John
SIOGVOLK, Paul
  Mathews, Albert
SION, Mari
  Jones, Robert Maynard
SIR TOPAZ
  Agate, James
SKEEVER, Jim
  Hill, John Alexander
SKOOKUM CHUCK
  Cumming, Robert Dalziel

SLADE, Gurney
  Bartlett, Stephen
SLAGG, Glenda
  Fantoni, Barry
SLATER, Patrick
  Mitchell, John
SLAUGHTER, Jim
  Paine, Lauran Bosworth
SLINGSBY, Rufus
  Siddle, Charles *and*
    Peel, Frederick
SLOANE, Sara
  Bloom, Ursula
SLOLUCK, J Milton
  Bierce, Ambrose
SLY, Christopher
  Neild, James Edward
SMALACOMBE, John
  MacKay, Louis Alexander
SMALL, Ernest
  Lent, Blair
SMEE, Wentworth
  Burgin, G B
SMEED
  Taylor, Deems
SMEED, Frances
  Lasky, Jesse L
SMITH, Adam
  Goodman, George Jerome W
SMITH, Caesar
  Dudley-Smith, Trevor
SMITH, Clyde
  Smith, George
SMITH, Cordwainer
  Linebarger, Paul
SMITH, Dodie
  Smith, Dorothy Gladys

SMITH, Elvet
  Marshall, Margaret
SMITH, Essex
  Hope, Essex
SMITH, Harriet
  Scott, Hilda R
SMITH, Jean
  Smith, Frances C
SMITH, Jessica
  Penwarden, Helen
SMITH, Naomi
  Vinter, Helen
SMITH, S S
  Williamson, Thames Ross
SMITH, Shelley
  Bodington, Hancy Hermione
SMITH, Spartacus
  Johnston, Alexander
SMITH, Stevie
  Smith, Florence Margaret
SMITH, Surrey
  Dinner, William *and*
    Morum, William
SMITH, Wade
  Snow, Charles Horace
SMITH, Z Z
  Westheimer, David
SMYTHE, James P
  McGarry, William Rutledge
SNAFFLES
  Payne, Charles J
SNOW, Lyndon
  Ansle, Dorothy Phoebe
SOMERS, J L
  Stickland, Louise Annie
    Beatrice
SOMERS, Paul
  Winterton, Paul

283

SOMERSET, Percy
  Hollis, Christopher
SOMERVILLE
  Somerville, Edith Oenone
SON OF THE SOIL
  Fletcher, J S
SOPHIE, May
  Clarke, Rebecca Sophie
SORACE, Richard
  Williamson, Lydia Buckland
SOSTHENES
  Coad, Frederick R
SOUTHCOTE, George
  Aston, *Sir* George
SOUTHERN CROSS
  Hill, *Mrs* E E
SOUTHWORTH, Louis
  Grealey, Tom
SOUTTER, Fred
  Lake, Kenneth Robert
SOUZA, Ernest
  Scott, Evelyn
SPADE, Mark
  Balchin, Nigel
SPAIN, John
  Adams, Cleve Franklin
SPALDING, Lucille
  Jay, Marion
SPARLIN, W
  Spratling, Walter Norman
SPENCE, Betty E
  Tettmar, Betty Eileen
SPENCE, Duncan
  Spence, William
SPENCER, Cornelia
  Yaukey, Grace
SPENCER, Edward
  Mott, Edward Spencer

SPENCER, John
  Vickers, Roy
SPENSER, James
  Guest, Francis Harold
SPERLING, Maria Sandra
  Floren, Lee
SPIEL, Hilde
  De Mendelssohn, Hilde
SPILLANE, Frank Morrison
  Spillane, Mickey
SPINELLI, Marcos
  Spinelli, Grace
SPOONHILL
  Reaney, James
SPRINGFIELD, David
  Lewis, J R
SPROSTON, John
  Scott, Peter Dale
SPROULE, Wesley
  Sproule, Howard
SPURR, Clinton
  Rowland, Donald Sydney
SQUARE, Charlotte
  Haldane, Robert Aylmer
SQUIRES, Phil
  Barker, S Omar
STACY, O'Connor
  Rollins, William
STAFFORD, Ann
  Pedlar, Ann
STAFFORD, Peter
  Tabori, Paul
STAGG, Delano
  Sabre, Mel R *and*
  Eiden, Paul
STAGGE, Jonathan
  Webb, Richard Wilson *and*
  Wheeler, Hugh Callingham

STAINES, Trevor
  Brunner, John
STAMPER, Alex
  Kent, Arthur
STAN, Roland
  Rowland, Donald Sydney
STAND, Marguerite
  Stickland, M E
STANDISH, Buck
  Paine, Lauran Bosworth
STANDISH, Burt L
  Patten, Gilbert
STANDISH, J O
  Horler, Sydney
STANDISH, Robert
  Gerahty, Digby George
STANGE, Nora K
  Stanley, Nora Kathleen
  Begbie
STANHOPE, Douglas
  Duff, Douglas Valder
STANHOPE, John
  Langdon-Davies, John
STANHOPE OF CHESTER
  Norman, C H
STANLEY, Arthur
  Megaw, Arthur Stanley
STANLEY, Bennett
  Hough, Stanley Bennett
STANLEY, Chuck
  Strong, Charles Stanley
STANLEY, Dave
  Dachs, David
STANLEY, F
  Crocchiola, Stanley Francis
  Louis
STANLEY, Margaret
  Mason, Sydney Charles

STANLEY, Marge
  Weinbaum, Stanley Grauman
STANLEY, Michael
  Hosie, Stanley William
STANLEY, Warwick
  Hilton, John Buxton
STANSBURY, Alec
  Higgs, Alec S
STANTON, Borden
  Wilding, Philip
STANTON, Coralie
  Hosken, Alice Cecil Seymour
STANTON, Marjorie
  Phillips, Horace
STANTON, Paul
  Beaty, David
STANTON, Schuyler
  Baum, Lyman Frank
STANTON, Vance
  Avallone, Michael Angelo Jr
STAR, Elison
  Comber, Rose
STARK, Joshua
  Olsen, Theodore Victor
STARK, Michael
  Lariar, Lawrence
STARK, Richard
  Westlake, Donald Edwin
STARR, Henry
  Bingley, David Ernest
STARR, Leonora
  Mackesy, Leonora Dorothy
  Rivers
STARRET, William
  McClintock, Marshall
STATTEN, Vargo
  Fearn, John Russell

STAVELEY, Robert
  Campbell, R O
STEEL, Byron
  Steegmuller, Francis
STEEL, Kurt
  Kagey, Rudolf
STEEL, Robert
  Whitson, John Harvey
STEELE, Addison
  Whitson, John Harvey
STEELE, Erskine
  Henderson, Archibald
STEELE, Tex
  Ross, William Edward Daniel
STEEN, Frank
  Felstein, Ivor
STEER, Charlotte
  Hunter, Christine
STEFFAN, Jack
  Steffan, Alice Jacqueline
STERLING, Helen
  Hoke, Helen L
STERLING, Maria Sandra
  Floren, Lee
STERLING, Peter
  Stern, David
STERLING, Stewart
  Winchell, Prentice
STERN, Elizabeth
  Uhr, Elizabeth
STERN, John
  Stearn, John Theodore
STERN, Paul F
  Ernst, Paul F
STEVENS, Christopher
  Tabori, Paul
STEVENS, Dan J
  Overholser, Wayne D

STEVENS, J D
  Rowland, Donald Sydney
STEVENS, Jill
  Mogridge, Stephen
STEVENS, Maurice
  Whitson, John Harvey
STEVENS, Robert Tyler
  Staples, Reginald Thomas
STEVENS, S P
  Palestrant, Simon
STEVENS, William Christopher
  Allen, Stephen Valentine
STEVENSON, Christine
  Kelly, Elizabeth
STEVENSON, Robert
  Naismith, Robert Stevenson
STEWART, C R
  Adam, C G M
STEWART, Eleanor
  Porter, Eleanor
STEWART, Jay
  Palmer, Stuart
STEWART, Jean
  Newman, Mona A J
STEWART, Kaye
  Howe, Doris Kathleen
STEWART, Logan
  Savage, Lee
STEWART, Logan
  Wilding, Philip
STEWART, Marjorie
  Huxtable, Marjorie
STEWART, Scott
  Zaffo, George J
STEWART, Will
  Williamson, Jack

STEWART-HARGREAVES,
  E H I
  White, Frank James
STEWER, Jan
  Coles, Albert John
STIRLING, Stella
  Ransome, L E
STIRLING, Veda
  Drummond, Edith Victoria
STITCH, Wilhelmina
  Collie, Ruth
STOCKBRIDGE, Grant
  Page, Norvell W
STODDARD, Charles
  Kuttner, Henry
STOKES, Cedric
  Beardmore, George
STONE, Eugene
  Speck, Gerald Eugene
STONE, Hampton
  Stein, Aaron Marc
STONE, Simon
  Barrington, Howard
STORM, Lesley
  Clark, Mabel Margaret
STORM, Virginia
  Swatridge, Irene M M
STORME, Peter
  Stern, Philip Van Doren
STORY, Josephine
  Loring, Emilie
STORY, Sydney A J
  Pike, Mary Hayden
STRAND, Paul E
  Palestrant, Simon
STRANG, Herbert
  L'Estrange, C James *and*
  Ely, George Herbert

STRANGE, John Stephen
  Tillett, Dorothy Stockbridge
STRANGEWAY, Mark
  Leyland, Eric
STRATEGICUS
  O'Neill, Herbert Charles
STRATHEARN-HAY
  Robertson, William
STRATTON, John
  Alldridge, John Stratten
STRATTON, Thomas
  Coulson, Robert Stratton *and*
  De Weese, T Eugene
STREET, Emmett
  Behan, Brendan
STRETTON, Hesba
  Smith, Sarah
STRIPPER
  Wilson, John
STRONG, Susan
  Rees, Joan
STRUTHER, Jan
  Maxtone-Graham, Joyce
STRYDOM, Len
  Rousseau, Leon
STRYFE, Paul
  Newman, James Roy
STUART, Alan
  Weightman, Archibald John
STUART, Alex
  Stuart, Vivian Alex
STUART, Anthony
  Hale, Julian Anthony Stuart
STUART, Brian
  Worthington-Stuart, Brian
  Arthur
STUART, Charles
  Mackinnon, Charles Roy

STUART, Clay
  Whittington, Harry
STUART, Don A
  Campbell, John Wood Jr
STUART, Florence
  Stonebraker, Florence
STUART, Frederick
  Tomlin, Eric
STUART, Gordon
  Wood, James
STUART, Ian
  Maclean, Alistair
STUART, John Roy
  McMillan, Donald
STUART, Logan
  Wilding, Philip
STUART, Margaret
  Paine, Lauran Bosworth
STUART, Matt
  Holmes, Llewellyn Perry
STUART, Sheila
  Baker, Mary Gladys Steel
STUART, Sidney
  Avallone, Michael Angelo Jr
STUART, V A
  Stuart, Vivian Alex
STUART, Vivian
  Stuart, Vivian Alex
STUDENT OF POLITICS, A
  Sidebotham, Herbert
STUDENT OF WAR, A
  Sidebotham, Herbert
STURGEON, Theodore
  Waldo, Edward Hamilton
STURGUS, J B
  Bastin, John
STUYVESANT, Polly
  Paul, Maury

STYLITES, Simeon
  Luccock, Halford Edward
SUAREZ LYNCH, B
  Borges, Jorge Luis *and*
  Bioy-Casares, Adolfo
SUBHADRA-NANDAN
  Prafulla, Das
SUBOND, Valerie
  Grayland, Valerie M
SUDORF, Fingal von
  Rosenquist, Fingal
SULLIVAN, Eric Harrison
  Hickey, Madelyn E
SUMMERS, D B
  Barrett, Geoffrey John
SUMMERS, Gordon
  Hornby, John Wilkinson
SUMMERSCALES, Rowland
  Gaines, Robert
SUNDOWNER
  Tichborne, Henry
SURFACEMAN
  Anderson, Alexander
SURREY, Kathryn
  Matthewman, Phyllis
SUTHERLAND, Joan
  Collings, Joan
SUTHERLAND, William
  Cooper, John Murray
SUTTLING, Mark
  Rowland, Donald Sydney
SUTTON, Henry
  Slavitt, David
SUTTON, John
  Tullett, Denis John
SUTTON, Penny
  Cartwright, Justin

SUTTON, Rachel B
　Sutton, Margaret
SVAREFF, *Count* Vladimir
　Crowley, Edward Alexander
SWAN, Annie S
　Burnett-Smith, Annie S
SWAYNE, Geoffrey
　Campion, Sidney
SWIFT, Anthony
　Farjeon, Joseph Jefferson
SWIFT, Benjamin
　Paterson, W R
SWIFT, Julian
　Applin, Arthur
SWIFT, Rachelle
　Lumsden, Jean
SWIFT, Stella
　Whish, Violet E
SYLVESTER, Philip
　Worner, Philip A I
SYLVIA
　Ashton-Warner, Sylvia
SYLVESTER, Anthony
　Laurencic, Karl
SYNGE, Don
　Edelstein, Hyman

T
　Thorp, Joseph
T J V
　Pound, Ezra
T P
　O'Connor, T P
T S
　Seccombe, Thomas
TAAFFE, Robert
　Maguire, Robert A J

TABARD, Peter
　Blake, Leslie James
TAFFRAIL
　Dorling, Henry Taprell
TAGGART, Dean
　King, Albert
TAINE, John
　Bell, Eric Temple
TALBOT, Hake
　Nelms, Henning
TALBOT, Henry
　Rothwell, Henry Talbot
TALBOT, Hugh
　Alington, Argentine Francis
TALBOT, Kathrine
　Barker, Ilse Eva L
TALBOT, Kay
　Rowland, Donald Sydney
TANIS
　Davis, Hilda A
TAPER
　Levin, Bernard
TARRANT, Elizabeth
　Leyland, Eric
TARRANT, John
　Egleton, Clive
TATE, Ellalice
　Hibbert, Eleanor Alice
　Burford
TATE, Richard
　Masters, Anthony
TATHAM, Campbell
　Elting, Mary
TAVEREL, John
　Howard, Robert E
TAYLOR, Ann
　Brodey, Jim

TAYLOR, Daniel
  Schneider, Daniel Edward
TAYLOR, H Baldwin
  Waugh, Hillary Baldwin
TAYLOR, John
  Magee, James
TAYLOR, Sam
  Goodyear, Stephen Frederick
TAYLOR, Toso
  Taylor, Thomas Hilhouse
TEARLE, Christian
  Jacques, Edward Tyrrell
TEG, Twm
  Vulliamy, Colwyn Edward
TELLAR, Mark
  Collins, Vere Henry
TELSTAR
  Goodwin, Geoffrey
TEMPEST, Jan
  Swatridge, Irene M M
TEMPLE, Ann
  Mortimer, Penelope
TEMPLE, Paul
  Durbridge, Francis *and*
    McConnell, James Douglas
    Rutherford
TEMPLE, Ralph
  Alexander, Robert William
TEMPLE, Robin
  Wood, Samuel Andrew
TEMPLE-ELLIS, N A
  Holdaway, Neville Aldridge
TEMPLETON, Jesse
  Goodchild, George
TENN, William
  Klass, Philip
TENNANT, Carrie
  Kelly, *Mrs* T

TENNANT, Catherine
  Eyles, Kathleen Muriel
TENNENBAUM, Irving
  Stone, Irving
TENNESHAW, S M
  Nutt, Charles
TERAHATA, Jun
  Kirkup, James
TERKEL, Studs
  Terkel, Louis
TERRY, C V
  Slaughter, Frank Gill
TEW, Mary
  Douglas, Mary
TEXAS RANGER
  Wallace, John
TEY, Josephine
  Mackintosh, Elizabeth
THANE, Elswyth
  Beebe, Elswyth Thane
THANET, Neil
  Fanthorpe, Robert Lionel
THANET, Octave
  French, Alice
THAYER, Jane
  Woolley, Catherine
THAYER, Lee
  Thayer, Emma Redington
THAYER, Peter
  Wyler, Rose
THEOPHANY
  Tofani, Louise E
THERION, The Master
  Crowley, Edward Alexander
THERSITES
  Whibley, Charles
THETA, Eric Mark
  Higginson, Henry Clive

THIRLMERE, Rowland
  Walker, John
THISTLETON, *Hon* Francis
  Fleet, William Henry
THOMAS, Caroline
  Dorr, Julia Caroline
THOMAS, Carolyn
  Duncan, Actea
THOMAS, Dorothy
  Thomashower, Dorothy
THOMAS, G K
  Davies, Leslie Purnell
THOMAS, Gerrard
  Kempinski, Tom
THOMAS, Gough
  Garwood, Godfrey Thomas
Thomas, H C
  Keating, Lawrence Alfred
THOMAS, J Bissell
  Stephen, Joyce Alice
THOMAS, Jim
  Reagan, Thomas B
THOMAS, Joan Gale
  Robinson, Joan Gale
THOMAS, Lately
  Steele, Robert V P
THOMAS, Lee
  Floren, Lee
THOMAS, Michael
  Benson, Michael
THOMAS, Murray
  Ragg, Thomas Murray
THOMAS, Tay
  Thomas, Mary
THOMPSON, Buck
  Paine, Lauran Bosworth
THOMPSON, China
  Lewis, Mary Christianna

THOMPSON, Eileen
  Panowski, Eileen Janet
THOMPSON, Madeleine
  Greig, Maysie
THOMPSON, Russ
  Paine, Lauran Bosworth
THOMSON, Audrey
  Gwynn, Audrey
THOMSON, Joan
  Charnock, Joan
THOMSON, Jon H
  Thomson, Daisy
THOMSON, Neil
  Johnson, Henry T
THORN, Barbara
  Paine, Lauran Bosworth
THORN, Whyte
  Whiteing, Richard
THORNTON, Maimee
  Jeffrey-Smith, May
THORNTON, W B
  Burgess, Thornton W
THORP, Ellen
  Robertson, Margery Ellen
THORP, Morwenna
  Robertson, Margery Ellen
THORPE, Sylvia
  Thimblethorpe, June
THORPE, Trebor
  Fanthorpe, Robert Lionel
THORSTEIN, Eric
  Grossman, Judith
THRIBB, E J
  Fantoni, Barry and
  Ingrams, Richard
THURLEY, Norgrove
  Stoneham, Charles Thurley

THURLOW, Robert
  Griffin, Jonathan
THURMAN, Steve
  Castle, Frank
TIBBER, Robert
  Friedman, Eve Rosemary
TIBBER, Rosemary
  Friedman, Eve Rosemary
TILBURY, Quenna
  Walker, Emily Kathleen
TILLEY, Gene
  Tilley, E D
TILLRAY, Les
  Gardner, Erle Stanley
TILTON, Alice
  Taylor, Phoebe Atwood
TIM
  Martin, Timothy
TIMON, John
  Mitchell, Donald Grant
TINA, Beatrice
  Haig, Emily Alice
TIPTREE, James *Jr*
  Sheldon, Alice B
TIVEYCHOC, A
  Lording, Rowland Edward
TODHUNTER, Philippa
  Bond, Grace
TOIL, Cunnin
  Lehmann, R C
TOKLAS, Alice B
  Stein, Gertrude
TOLER, Buck
  Kelly, Harold Ernest
TOLLER
  Lyburn, *Dr* Eric Frederic St John
TOMKINSON, Constance
  Weeks, *Lady* Constance Avard

TOMLINE, F Latour
  Gilbert, William Schwenck
TONKONGY, Gertrude
  Friedberg, Gertrude
TONSON, Jacob
  Bennett, Arnold
TOPICUS
  Goodwin, Geoffrey
TORQUEMADA
  Mathers, Edward Powys
TORR, Iain
  Mackinnon, Charles Roy
TORREY, Marjorie
  Hodd, Torrey
TORRIE, Malcolm
  Mitchell, Gladys
TORRO, Pel
  Fanthorpe, Robert Lionel
TORROLL, G D
  Lawson, Alfred
TOULMIN, David
  Reid, John
TOWERS, Tricia
  Ivison, Elizabeth
TOWNE, Stuart
  Rawson, Clayton
TOWNSEND, Timothy
  Robey, Timothy Lester
  Townsend
TOWRY, Peter
  Piper, David Towry
TRACEY, Grant
  Nuttall, Anthony
TRACEY, Hugh
  Evans, Kay *and*
  Evans, Stuart
TRACY, Catherine
  Story, Rosamond Mary

TRAFFORD, F G
  Riddell, *Mrs* J H
TRAFFORD, Jean
  Walker, Edith
TRAILL, Peter
  Morton, Guy Mainwaring
TRALINS, Bob
  Tralins, S Robert
TRALINS, Robert S
  Tralins, S Robert
TRAPROCK, Walter E
  Chappell, George S
TRASK, Merrill
  Braham, Hal
TRAUBE, Ruy
  Tralins, S Robert
TRAVEN, B
  Torsvan, Traven
TRAVEN, Robert
  Voelker, John Donaldson
TRAVERS, Hugh
  Mills, Hugh Travers
TRAVERS, Stephen
  Radcliffe, Garnett
TRAVERS, Will
  Rowland, Donald Sydney
TRAVIS, Gerry
  Trimble, Louis
TRAVIS, Gretchen
  Mockler, Gretchen
TRAWLE, Mary Elizabeth
  Elwart, Joan Frances
TREDGOLD, Nye
  Tranter, Nigel
TREE, Gregory
  Bardin, John Franklin
TREHEARNE, Elizabeth
  Maxwell, Patricia Anne

TREMAYNE, Sydney
  Taylor, Sybil
TRENT, Gregory
  Williamson, Thames Ross
TRENT, Lee
  Nuttall, Anthony
TRENT, Paul
  Platt, Edward
TRENT, Peter
  Nelson, Lawrence
TRESILIAN, Liz
  Green, Elizabeth Sara
TRESSALL, Robert
  Noonan, Robert
TRESSELL, Robert
  Noonan, Robert
TRESSIDY, Jim
  Norwood, Victor George
  Charles
TREVARTHEN, Hal P
  Heydon, J K
TREVENA, John
  Henham, E J
TREVES, Kathleen
  Walker, Emily Kathleen
TREVOR, Elleston
  Dudley-Smith, Trevor
TREVOR, Glen
  Hilton, James
TREVOR, Ralph
  Wilmot, James Reginald
TREVOR, William
  Cox, William Trevor
TREW, Cecil G
  Ehrenborg, *Mrs* C G
TRIFORMIS, D
  Haig, Emily Alice

293

TRING, A Stephen
  Meynell, Laurence Walter
TRIPP, Karen
  Gershon, Karen
TRITON, A N
  Barclay, Oliver Rainsford
TROOPER GERARDY
  Gerard, Edwin
TROTTER, Sallie
  Crawford, Sallie
TROTWOOD, John
  Moore, John
TROUT, Kilgore
  Farmer, Philip José
TROY, Alan
  Hoke, Helen L
TROY, Katherine
  Buxton, Anne
TROY, Simon
  Warriner, Thurman
TRUAX, Rhoda
  Aldrich, Rhoda Truax
TRUSCOT, Bruce
  Peers, Edgar Allison
TRY-DAVIS, J
  Hensley, Sophia Margaret
TSUYUKI SHIGERU
  Kirkup, James
TUCKER, Lael
  Wertenbaker, Lael Tucker
TUCKER, Link
  Bingley, David Ernest
TURNER, C John
  Whiteman, William Meredith
TURNER, Josie
  Crawford, Phyllis
TURNER, Len
  Floren, Lee

294

TURNER, Mary
  Lambot, Isobel Mary
TURVEY, Winsome
  Rusterholtz, Winsome Lucy
TUSTIN, Elizabeth
  White, Celia
TWAIN, Mark
  Clemens, Samuel Langhorne
TWEEDALE, J
  Bickle, Judith
TWIGGY
  Hornby, Lesley
TWO EAST LONDONERS
  Nash, Vaughan *and*
    Smith, Llewellyn
TYLER, Clarke
  Brookes, Ewart Stanley
TYLER, Ellis
  King, Albert
TYSON, Teilo
  McFarlane, David

§ §

I am become a name.
—Alfred, Lord Tennyson. Ulysses

§ §

UBIQUE
  Guggisberg, *Sir* F G
ULSTER IMPERIALIST
  Wilson, Alec
UNCLE GUS
  Rey, Hans Augusto
UNCLE HENRY
  Wallace, Henry

UNCLE MAC
  McCulloch, Derek
UNCLE MONTY
  Hamilton-Wilkes, Edwin
UNCLE REG
  Woodcock, E Page
UNCLE REMUS
  Harris, Joel Chandler
UNCUT CAVENDISH
  Meares, John Willoughby
UNDERCLIFFE, Errol
  Campbell, Ramsay
UNDERWOOD, Keith
  Spooner, Peter Alan
UNDERWOOD, Michael
  Evelyn, John Michael
UNDERWOOD, Miles
  Glassco, John
UNDINE, P F
  Paine, Lauran Bosworth
UNOFFICIAL OBSERVER
  Carter, John Franklin
URIEL, Henry
  Faust, Frederick
URQUHART, Guy
  McAlmon, Robert
URQUHART, Paul
  Black, Ladbroke Lionel Day
USHER, Margo Scegge
  McHargue, Georgess
UTTLEY, Alison
  Uttley, Alice Jane

V V V
  Lucas, E V
VACE, Geoffrey
  Cave, Hugh Barnett

VAGABOND
  Blake, George
VAIL, Amanda
  Miller, Warren
VAIL, Philip
  Gerson, Noel Bertram
VALE, Keith
  Clegg, Paul
VALENTINE
  Pechey, Archibald Thomas
VALENTINE, Jo
  Armstrong, Charlotte
VAN BUREN, Abigail
  Phillips, Pauline
VAN DINE, S S
  Wright, Willard Huntington
VAN DYKE, J
  Edwards, Frederick Anthony
VAN DYNE, Edith
  Baum, Lyman Frank
VAN HELLER, Marcus
  Coleman, John
VANCE, Ethel
  Stone, Grace Zaring
VANCE, Jack
  Vance, John Holbrook
VANDEGRIFT, Margaret
  Janvier, Margaret Thomson
VANE, Brett
  Kent, Arthur
VANE, Michael
  Humphries, Sydney
VANE, Phillipa
  Hambledon, Phyllis MacVean
VANSITTART, Jane
  Moorhouse, Hilda
VARANGE, Ulick
  Yockey, Francis Parker

VARDON, Roger
　Delafosse, Frederick Montague
VARDRE, Leslie
　Davies, Leslie Purnell
VAUGHAN, Carter A
　Gerson, Noel Bertram
VAUGHAN, Gary
　Boggis, David
VAUGHAN, Julian
　Almond, Brian
VAUGHAN, Richard
　Thomas, Ernest Lewys
VEDDER, John K
　Gruber, Frank
VEDETTE
　Fitchett, W H
VEDEY, Julien
　Robinson, Julien Louis
VEE, Roger
　Voss, Vivian
VEHEYNE, Cherry
　Williamson, Ethel
VEITCH, Tom
　Padgett, Ron
VENISON, Alfred
　Pound, Ezra
VENNING, Hugh
　Van Zeller, Claud H
VENNING, Michael
　Randolph, Georgiana Ann
VERA
　Bottomley, Kate Madeline
VERDAD, S
　Kennedy, John McFarland
VERNON, Claire
　Breton-Smith, Clare
VERNON, Kay
　Vernon, Kathleen Rose

VERNON, Marjorie
　Russell, Shirley
VERONIQUE
　Fisher, Veronica Suzanne
VERWER, Hans
　Verwer, Johanne
VESTAL, Stanley
　Campbell, Walter Stanley
VET, T V
　Straiton, Edward Cornock
VICARION, *Count* Palmiro
　Logue, Christopher
VICARY, Dorothy
　Rice, Dorothy
VICESIMUS
　Oakley, John, *Dean of*
　　Manchester
VICTOR, Charles B
　Puechner, Ray
VIDENS
　Mumford, A H
VIGILANS
　Partridge, Eric
VIGILANS
　Rice, Brian Keith
VIGILANTES
　Zilliacus, Konni
VILLIERS, Elizabeth
　Thorne, Isabel Mary
VINCENT, Heather
　Walker, Emily Kathleen
VINCENT, Honor
　Walker, Kathleen
VINCENT, Jim
　Foxall, P A
VINCENT, John
　Farrow, R

VINCENT, Mary Keith
St John, Wylly Folk
VINSON, Elaine
Rowland, Donald Sydney
VINSON, Kathryn
Williams, Kathryn
VINTON, V V
Dale, R J
VIOLA
Worthley, R G
VIPONT, Charles
Foulds, Elfrida Vipont
VIPONT, Elfrida
Foulds, Elfrida Vipont
VIRAKAM, Soror
Sturges, Mary d'Este
VISIAK, E H
Physick, Edward Harold
VIVA
Wilson, Viva
VIVIAN
Moynihan, Cornelius
VIVIAN, E Charles
Vivian, Evelyn Charles H
VIVIAN, Francis
Ashley, Arthur Ernest
VLOTO, Otto
Parkhill, Forbes
VON MUELLER, Karl
Miller, Charles Dean
VOX, Agnes Mary
Duffy, Agnes Mary
VOYLE, Mary
Manning, Rosemary
VUL' INDLELA
Becker, Peter

§ §

*Bingo had told him that I was
the author of a lot of mushy
novels by Rosie M Banks, you
know. Said that I had written
them, and that Rosie's name on
the title-page was my what d'you
call it.*
*–P G Wodehouse. Bingo and
the little woman*

§ §

W M
Jennings, Richard
WACE, W E
Nicoll, *Sir* William Robertson
WADE, Bill
Barrett, Geoffrey John
WADE, Henry
Aubrey-Fletcher, *Sir* Henry
Lancelot
WADE, Robert
McIlwain, David
WADE, Thomas
Looker, Samuel Joseph
WAGNER, Peggy
Wagner, Margaret Dale
WAINER, Cord
Dewey, Thomas Blanchard
WAKE, G B
Haynes, John Harold
WALDO, Dave
Clarke, David
WALDO, E Hunter
Waldo, Edward Hamilton
WALDRON, Simon
King, Albert

WALES, Hubert
  Piggott, William
WALES, Nym
  Snow, Helen Foster
WALFORD, Christian
  Dilcock, Noreen
WALKER, Barbara
  Middleton, Maud Barbara
WALKER, Harry
  Waugh, Hillary Baldwin
WALKER, Holly Beth
  Bond, Gladys Baker
WALKER, Ira
  Walker, Irma Ruth
WALKER, Jean Brown
  Walker, Edith
WALL, Max
  Lorimer, Maxwell
WALLACE, Agnes
  King, Albert
WALLACE, Betty
  Wallace, Elizabeth Virginia
WALLACE, Doreen
  Rash, Dora
WALLACE, John
  Davis, Will R
WALSER, Sam
  Howard, Robert E
WALTER, Katherine
  Walter, Dorothy Blake
WALTER, Kay
  Walter, Dorothy Blake
WALTERS, Hugh
  Hughes, Walter Llewellyn
WALTERS, Rick
  Rowland, Donald Sydney
WALTERS, T B
  Rowe, John Gabriel

WALTON, Francis
  Hodder, Alfred
WAND, Elizabeth
  Tattersall, Muriel Joyce
WANDERER
  Smith, Lily
WARD, Artemus
  Browne, Charles Farrar
WARD, Brad
  Peeples, Samuel Anthony
WARD, Herbert B S
  Molloy, Edward
WARD, Jonas
  Garfield, Brian
WARD, Kate
  Cust, Barbara Kate
WARD, Kirwan
  Kirwan-Ward, Bernard
WARD, Robert
  Howard, Robert E
WARDEN, Florence
  James, Florence Alice Price
WARE, Monica
  Marsh, John
WARNER, Frank
  Richardson, Gladwell
WARNER, Jack
  Waters, John
WARNER, Leigh
  Smith, Lillian M
WARREGO, Paul
  Wenz, Paul
WARREN, Andrew
  Tute, Warren
WARREN, Mary D
  Greig, Maysie
WARREN, Tony
  Simpson, Anthony McVay

WARREN, Wayne
  Braun, Wilbur
WARRINGTON, George
  Agate, James
WARSHOFSKY, Isaac
  Singer, Isaac Bashevis
WARWICK, Jarvis
  Garner, Hugh
WARWICK, Pauline
  Davies, Betty Evelyn
WASH, R
  Cowlishaw, Ranson
WATANNA, Onoto
  Reeve, Winifred Babcock
WATER, Silas
  Loomis, Noel Miller
WATSON, Andrew
  Watson, Albert Ernest
WATSON, C P
  Agelasto, Charlotte Priestley
WATSON, Frank
  Ames, Francis
WATSON, Will
  Floren, Lee
WATT, William
  Scott, William Matthew
WAVERLEY, John
  Scobie, Stephen Arthur Cross
WAY, Wayne
  Humphries, Adelaide
WAYFARER
  Cosens, Abner
WAYLAN, Mildred
  Harrell, Irene Burk
WAYLAND, Patrick
  O'Connor, Richard
WAYNE, Anderson
  Davis, Dresser

WAYNE, Heather
  Gibbs, Norah
WAYNE, Joseph
  Overholser, Wayne D
WAYNE, Marcia
  Best, Carol Anne
WAYSIDER
  Camm, Frederick James
WEALE, B Putnam
  Simpson, Bertram L
WEARY, Ogdred
  Gorey, Edward
WEAVER, Ward
  Mason, F Van Wyck
WEBB, Christopher
  Wibberley, Leonard Patrick
  O'Connor
WEBB, Neil
  Rowland, Donald Sydney
WEBSTER, Gary
  Garrison, Webb Black
WEBSTER, Jean
  Webster, Alice Jane Chandler
WEETWOOD, E M
  Tetley, Edith Madeline
WEI WU WEI
  Gray, Terence J S
WEINER, Henri
  Longstreet, Stephen
WEIR, Jonnet
  Nicholson, Joan
WEIR, Logan
  Perry, James Black
WELBURN, Vivienne C
  Furlong, Vivienne
WELCH, Ronald
  Felton, Ronald Oliver

WELCH, Rowland
  Davies, Leslie Purnell
WELCOME, John
  Brennan, John
WELLBROOK, Edna
  Orton, John Kingsley
WELLS, Hondo
  Whittington, Harry
WELLS, Jane Warren
  Picken, Mary
WELLS, John J
  Coulson, Juanita *and*
  Bradley, Marion Z
WELLS, Susan
  Siegel, Doris
WELLS, Tobias
  Forbes, Deloris Stanton
WELLS, Tracey
  Nuttall, Anthony
WENTWORTH, John
  Child, Philip A G
WENTWORTH, Patricia
  Turnbull, Dora Amy
WERNER, Jane
  Werner, Elsa Jane
WERNER, Peter
  Booth, Philip Arthur
WERRERSON, Talbot
  Robertson, Walter George
WESLEY, Elizabeth
  McElfresh, Adeline
WESLEY, James
  Rigoni, Orlando Joseph
WESSEX, Martyn
  Little, D F
WESSEX REDIVIVUS
  Dewar, Hubert Stephen Lowry

WEST, Anna
  Edward, Ann Elizabeth
WEST, Dorothy
  Wirt, Mildred
WEST, Douglas
  Tubb, E C
WEST, Keith
  Lane, Kenneth Westmacott
WEST, Laura M
  Hymers, Laura M
WEST, Mark
  Huff, Darrell
WEST, Michael
  Derleth, August W
WEST, Nathanael
  Weinstein, Nathan Wallenstein
WEST, Rebecca
  Fairfield, Cecily Isabel
WEST, Token
  Humphries, Adelaide
WEST, Tom
  Reach, James
WEST, Trudy
  West, Gertrude
WEST, Ward
  Borland, Harold Glen
WESTALL, Lorna
  Houseman, Lorna
WESTERHAM, S C
  Alington, Cyril Argentine
WESTERN, Barry
  Evans, Gwynfil Arthur
WESTERN-HOLT, J C
  Heming, Jack C W
WESTGATE, John
  Bloomfield, Anthony John
  Westgate

WESTLAND, Lynn
  Joscelyn, Archie Lynn
WESTLAW, Steven
  Pyke, John
WESTMACOTT, Mary
  Christie, *Dame* Agatha
WESTON, Allen
  Norton, Alice Mary *and*
  Hogarth, Grace Allen
WESTON, Patrick
  Hamilton, Gerald
WESTRIDGE, Harold
  Avery, Harold
WETZEL, Lewis
  King, Albert
WEYMOUTH, Anthony
  Cobb, Ivo Geikie
WHARTON, Anthony
  Macallister, Alister
WHEEZY
  Hounsfield, Joan
WHETTER, Laura
  Mannock, Laura
WHIM WHAM
  Curnow, Allen
WHITAKER, Ray
  Davies, John
WHITBY, Sharon
  Black, Maureen
WHITE, Dale
  Place, Marian Templeton
WHITE, Harry
  Whittington, Harry
WHITE, Heather
  Foster, Jess Mary Mardon
WHITE, James Dillon
  White, Stanley

WHITE, Jane
  Brady, Jane Frances
WHITE, Milky
  Emerson, Ernest
WHITEBAIT, William
  Stonier, George
WHITEFRIAR
  Hiscock, Eric
WHITEHAND, Satherley
  Satherley, David *and*
  Whitehand, James
WHITEHOUSE, Arch
  Whitehouse, Arthur George
  Joseph
WHITEHOUSE, Peggy
  Castle, Frances Mundy
WHITINGER, R D
  Place, Marian Templeton
WHITLEY, George
  Chandler, Arthur
WHITNEY, Hallam
  Whittington, Harry
WHITNEY, Spencer
  Burks, Arthur J
WHITTINGHAM, Sara
  Gibbs, Norah
WHITTLE, Tyler
  Tyler-Whittle, Michael Sidney
WHITTLEBOT, Hernia
  Coward, Noël
WHITTON, Barbara
  Chitty, Margaret Hazel
WHYE, Felix
  Dixon, Arthur
WICK, Stuart Mary
  Freeman, Kathleen
WICKHAM, Anna
  Hepburn, Edith Alice Mary

WICKLOE, Peter
  Duff, Douglas Valder
WIGAN, Christopher
  Bingley, David Ernest
WIGG, T I G
  McCutchan, Philip D
WIGGEN, Henry W
  Harris, Mark
WILDE, Hilary
  Breton-Smith, Clare
WILDE, Leslie
  Best, Rayleigh Breton Amis
WILDING, Eric
  Tubb, E C
WILEY, Gerald
  Barker, Ronnie
WILKINSON, Tim
  Wilkinson, Percy F H
WILL
  Lipkind, William
WILLEY, Robert
  Ley, Willy
WILLIAMS, Beryl
  Epstein, Beryl
WILLIAMS, F Harald
  Orde-Ward, F W
WILLIAMS, J R
  Creasey, Jeanne
WILLIAMS, Jeanne
  Creasey, Jeanne
WILLIAMS, Joel
  Jennings, John Edward
WILLIAMS, Michael
  St John, Wylly Folk
WILLIAMS, Patry
  Williams, D F *and* Patry, M
WILLIAMS, Rex
  Wei, Rex

WILLIAMS, Richard
  Francis, Stephen D
WILLIAMS, Rose
  Ross, William Edward Daniel
WILLIAMS, Roth
  Zilliacus, Konni
WILLIAMS, Russell
  Whitson, John Harvey
WILLIAMS, Tennessee
  Williams, Thomas Lanier
WILLIAMS, Violet M
  Boon, Violet Mary
WILLIAMS, Wetherby
  Williams, Margaret Wetherby
WILLIAMSON, Paul
  Butters, Paul
WILLOUGHBY, Hugh
  Harvey, Charles
WILLS, Chester
  Snow, Charles Horace
WILLS, Ronald
  Thomas, Ronald Wills
WILLS, Thomas
  Ard, William
WILMER, Dale
  Miller, William *and*
  Wade, Robert
WILSON, Ann
  Baily, Francis Evans
WILSON, Christine
  Geach, Christine
WILSON, D M
  Bentley, Frederick Horace
WILSON, Edwina H
  Brookman, Laura L
WILSON, Elizabeth
  Ivison, Elizabeth

WILSON, Holly
  Wilson, Helen
WILSON, John Burgess
  Wilson, John Anthony
    Burgess
WILSON, Lee
  Lemmon, Laura Lee
WILSON, Martha
  Morse, Martha
WILSON, Romer
  Wilson, Florence Roma Muir
WILSON, Snoo
  Wilson, Andrew James
WILSON, Yates
  Wilson, Albert
WINCH, John
  Campbell, Cabrielle Margaret
    Vere
WINCHESTER, Jack
  Freemantle, Brian
WINCHESTER, Kay
  Walker, Emily Kathleen
WINDER, Mavis
  Winder, Mavis Areta
WINDSOR, Rex
  Armstrong, Douglas
WINFIELD, Allen
  Stratemeyer, Edward
WINFIELD, Arthur M
  Stratemeyer, Edward
WING ADJUTANT
  Blake, Wilfred Theodore
WINGFIELD, Susan
  Reece, Alys
WINIKI, Ephraim
  Fearn, John Russell
WINN, Alison
  Wharmby, Margot

WINN, Patrick
  Padley, Arthur
WINSLOWE, John R
  Richardson, Gladwell
WINSTAN, Matt
  Nickson, Arthur
WINTER, John Strange
  Stannard, Eliza Vaughan
WINTERS, Bernice
  Winters, Bayla
WINTERS, Mary K
  Hart, Caroline Horowitz
WINTON, John
  Pratt, John
WINWAR, Francis
  Vinciguerra, Francesca
WITHERBY, Diana
  Cooke, Diana
WITHERS, E L
  Potter, George William
WODEN, George
  Slaney, George Wilson
WOLFENDEN, George
  Beardmore, George
WOOD, J Claverdon
  Carter, Thomas
WOOD, Mary
  Bamfield, Veronica
WOOD, Quality
  Wood, Violet
WOODCOTT, Keith
  Brunner, John
WOODFORD, Cecile
  Woodford, Irene-Cecile
WOODFORD, Jack
  Woolfolk, Josiah Pitts
WOODROOK, R A
  Cowlishaw, Ranson

303

WOODRUFF, Philip
  Mason, Philip
WOODS, Jonah
  Woods, Olwen
WOODS, Ross
  Story, Rosamond Mary
WOODS, Sara
  Bowen-Judd, Sara Hutton
WOODWARD, Lillian
  Marsh, John
WOOLLAND, Henry
  Williams, Guy Richard Owen
WOOLRICH, Cornell
  Hopley-Woolrich, Cornell
  George
WORTH, Martin
  Wigglesworth, Martin
WORTH, Maurice
  Bosworth, Willan George
WRAITH, John
  Devaney, Pauline *and*
  Apps, Edwin
WREFORD, James
  Watson, James Wreford
WREN, Jenny
  Cruttenden, Nellie
WRIGHT, Elnora A
  Old Coyote, Elnora A
WRIGHT, Francesca
  Robins, Denise
WRIGHT, Josephine
  Weaver, Harriet Shaw
WRIGHT, Rowland
  Wells, Carolyn
WRIGHT, Sally
  Old Coyote, Elnora A
WRIGHT, Ted
  Wright, George T

WRIGHT, Wade
  Wright, John
WU WU MENG
  Beiles, Sinclair
WYANDOTTE, Steve
  Thomas, Stanley A C
WYATT, Escott
  Leyland, Eric
WYCLIFFE, John
  Bedford-Jones, Henry
WYLCOTES, John
  Ransford, Oliver
WYNDER, Mavis Areta
  Winder, Mavis Areta
WYNDHAM, Esther
  Lutyens, Mary
WYNDHAM, John
  Harris, John Wyndham Parkes
  Lucas Beynon
WYNDHAM, Lee
  Hyndman, Jane Andrews
WYNDHAM, Robert
  Hyndman, Robert Utley
WYNGARD, Rhoda
  Truax, Rhoda
WYNMAN, Margaret
  Dixon, Ella Hepworth
WYNNE, Anthony
  Wilson, Robert McNair
WYNNE, Brian
  Garfield, Brian
WYNNE, Frank
  Garfield, Brian
WYNNE, May
  Knowles, Mabel Winifred
WYNNE, Pamela
  Scott, Winifred Mary

WYNYARD, John
  Harrison, J H

X
  Bloxam, John Francis
X Y Z
  Tilsley, Frank
XARIFFA
  Townsend, Mary Ashley

Y Y
  Lynd, Robert
YARBO, Steve
  King, Albert
YATES, Dornford
  Mercer, Cecil William
YERUSHALMI, Chaim
  Lipschitz, *Rabbi* Chaim
YES TOR
  Roche, Thomas
YLLA
  Koffler, Camilla
YORK, Andrew
  Nicole, Christopher
YORK, Jeremy
  Creasey, John
YORK, Peter
  Wallis, Peter
YORKE, Margaret
  Nicholson, Margaret Beda
YORKE, Roger
  Bingley, David Ernest
YORKE, Susan
  Telenga, Suzette
YOUNG, Agatha
  Young, Agnes
YOUNG, Edward
  Reinfeld, Fred

YOUNG, Filson
  Bell, Alexander
YOUNG, Jan
  Young, Janet Randall
YOUNG, Kendal
  Young, Phyllis Brett
YOUNG, Robert
  Payne, Pierre Stephen Robert
YOUNG, Rose
  Harris, Marion Rose
YOUNG, Thomas
  Yoseloff, Thomas
YUILL, P B
  Williams, Gordon Maclean *and*
  Venables, Terry
YUKON BILL
  Hayes, Catherine E Simpson
YULYA
  Whitney, Julie

ZACHARIA, Dan
  Novak, Cornelius Dan Zacharia
ZED
  Dienes, Zoltan
ZERO
  Ramsay, Allan
ZETA
  Cope, *Sir* Zachary
ZETFORD, Tully
  Bulmer, Kenneth
ZINKEN
  Hopp, Signe

§ §

*Wherefore is it that thou dost
ask after my name?*
—Bible. Genesis 32, 29

STANFORD UNIVERSITY LIBRARIES

WITHDRAWN